The Cortes of Castile-León
1188–1350

The Cortes
of Castile-León
1188–1350

JOSEPH F. O'CALLAGHAN

uɲɲ   *University of Pennsylvania Press* • *Philadelphia*

University of Pennsylvania Press
MIDDLE AGES SERIES
Edited by Edward Peters
Henry Charles Lea Professor
of Medieval History
University of Pennsylvania

A complete listing of the books in this series
appears at the back of this volume

Library of Congress Cataloging-in-Publication Data

O'Callaghan, Joseph F.
  The cortes of Castile-León, 1188–1350 / Joseph F. O'Callaghan.
    p.   cm. — (University of Pennsylvania Press Middle Ages series)
  Bibliography: p.
  Includes index.
  ISBN 0-8122-8125-X
    1. Castilla y León (Spain). Cortes—History.   2. Representative
government and representation—Spain—Castilla y León—History.
3. Castilla y León (Spain)—Politics and government.   I. Title.
II. Series.
JN8399.C245O27   1989
328.46'2'09—dc19   88-20555
                                                           CIP

To ANNE

. . . la mi mugier tan cumplida,
commo a la mie alma yo tanto vos queria.

Cantar de mío Cid, 278–279

Contents

viii   *Contents*

Preface

My interest in the cortes was first awakened while I was preparing *A History of Medieval Spain*. As I quickly discovered, Spanish historiography has only recently begun to give due attention to this topic, and in the English speaking world, only a handful of studies has been published in the last seventy years. An international congress, meeting in Burgos in October 1986, was the first concerted attempt by a body of scholars to explore the impact of the cortes of Castile and León on medieval and modern Spanish society.

My initial inquiries, meanwhile, led me to conclude that a full-scale history of the cortes of Castile-León from the late twelfth century to the middle of the fourteenth was in order. My expectation is that this will stimulate further inquiry into many of the issues discussed, and a more intensive search for pertinent documentation.

I am very much indebted to the many librarians, archivists, and others who responded to my queries and supplied me with microfilm or xerox copies of numerous texts. I must especially acknowledge the kindness of Professor Angus MacKay of the University of Edinburgh, who offered me a microfilm copy of texts in the Archives municipales of Nantes, France. I wish also to express my warm appreciation to Professor Teofilo Ruiz of Brooklyn College, who read my manuscript and gave me much needed counsel.

I am grateful to the Program for Cultural Cooperation Between Spain's Ministry of Culture and United States' Universities for aiding the publication of this book.

Introduction

The cortes of Castile-León, brought into being out of the unique conditions of life in the Iberian peninsula, exemplified a phenomenon characteristic of Western Europe in the High Middle Ages: the development of representative and parliamentary institutions. From the thirteenth century onward, parliamentary assemblies of one type or another came into existence in England, France, the Holy Roman Empire, Italy, Poland, Hungary, and Spain. Even before the close of the thirteenth century, the cortes had emerged in all the Christian states of Spain, namely Castile, León, Portugal, Aragón, Catalonia, Valencia, and Navarre. In this respect, Spain, as an integral part of Europe, shared a common European experience.[1]

Spain holds a special place in the history of medieval representative government because the appearance of urban representatives in the cortes antedated similar developments elsewhere. Townsmen were summoned to the royal council of León as early as 1188, and by the second half of the thirteenth century they were participating actively, along with bishops and nobles, in meetings of the cortes of Castile-León held nearly every two years. In the Crown of Aragón three separate parliamentary assemblies were convened for Catalonia, Aragón, and Valencia, as early as 1225, 1227, and 1283, respectively. The first cortes of Navarre may have taken place in 1253, while the earliest recorded cortes in Portugal was held in 1254. The English parliament, on the other hand, was still in its infancy. The initial admission of the commons to parliament is usually dated from Simon de Montfort's summons to the knights of the shire and the burgesses of the towns in 1265. All the estates of the realm took part in Edward I's so-called Model Parliament of 1295, but parliament did not achieve its characteristic organization until the early fourteenth century. Philip IV's convocation of the Estates in 1302 is traditionally cited as marking the beginning of French representative institutions, but they did not reach maturity until well into the fourteenth century.[2]

Representative assemblies had certain traits in common, but each one also had its distinctive characteristics. Thus, whereas the English parliament, consisting of two houses of lords and commons, was a single assembly for the entire realm, the prelates, nobles, and townsmen in the cortes of Castile-León remained separate entities. From time to time the monarch also convoked the cortes of Castile and León separately, or convened other limited assemblies of the three estates. In this respect, the parliamentary history of Castile-León bears a closer resemblance to that of France, where the king summoned the three estates to separate assemblies for Languedoil and Languedoc, and where provincial assemblies were also common.

On the other hand, assemblies of *hermandades*—associations of towns organized in response to the uncertainties of the times—were unique to Castile-León. Although not summoned by the king, they often had a powerful influence upon royal policy. Their close relationship with the cortes was such that the history of the cortes cannot be understood without taking them into account.[3]

In spite of the current surge of interest in the concept of representation and the growth of representative assemblies, the study of the medieval cortes as an early exemplar of these developments has not received the attention that it deserves. The triumph of monarchical absolutism under the Habsburgs and the Bourbons did not encourage serious inquiry into the medieval cortes, but the upheaval caused by the French Revolution, the convocation of the Cortes of Cádiz, and the adoption of the Constitution of 1812 sparked a debate on the nature and functions of parliamentary institutions.

Like the English politicians of the seventeenth century, Francisco Martínez Marina looked to the medieval past for precedents to justify his belief that the cortes, representing the three estates and jointly exercising legislative power with the king, was a manifestation of popular sovereignty and a necessary safeguard of liberty.[4] Manuel Colmeiro took issue with him, arguing that the cortes was essentially a consultative body always subordinate to the royal will.[5] Pointing to the failure of previous authors to demonstrate the chronological progression of the cortes, Wladimir Piskorski systematically treated its organization and competence but did not touch upon the problem of its origins. Although the merits of his study are indisputable, it is now dated.[6]

Twentieth-century Spanish historians, mirroring the crisis of the Civil War, tended to divide into two camps. Claudio Sánchez Albornoz saw the cortes as an expression of what he perceived to be the democratic character of the towns forged as a result of life on the frontier.[7] Others assumed a more conservative stance, stressing that the functions of the cortes were limited and that it was not a real restraint on royal authority.[8]

In a challenging essay treating the organization and functions of the cortes from the earliest period until well into modern times, José Manuel Pérez Prendes insisted that it was an instrument of the crown, that the king was always at liberty to summon it, to determine its business, and to act without it, if he chose to do so. Rejecting the idea that it was an assembly of the estates of the realm, he emphasized that the fundamental reason for summoning anyone to it was the general obligation of all subjects to give counsel to the king.[9] Evelyn Procter, in a most valuable contribution to the history of the cortes, focused on the transitional era from the late eleventh through the early thirteenth centuries. Describing the evolution of the cortes from the *curia regis*, she also discussed its composition and functions in the second half of the thirteenth century.[10]

These preparatory studies, provocative interpretations, and works of synthesis have greatly enlarged our understanding of the cortes. Nevertheless, these older histories reflect two principal deficiencies. First, they were based almost entirely on the documentary collection published in the nineteenth century by the Real Academia de la Historia. Second, by treating the subject in broad periods from the twelfth to the sixteenth centuries, or from the twelfth to the nineteenth, they were unable to illustrate variations due to specific historical circumstances. As a consequence, they tended to see the cortes as a static institution endowed with a peculiar permanency and immutability of character.

Historians, in addition, still have a tendency to use the term *cortes* in a rather casual manner. Aside from the loose and anachronistic reference in earlier centuries to a cortes as any assembly held by the Visigothic and Asturian kings, one still finds historians declaring uncritically that the cortes was held on such and such an occasion, for example, at Zamora in 1274, or at Carrión in 1317. An examination of the evidence in these and other cases leads to a contrary conclusion.

With the expectation of revealing the multifaceted character of the cortes and of the many other types of public assemblies held in Castile-León, I have undertaken a more comprehensive and systematic study, utilizing a wide range of narrative and documentary sources, both published and unpublished. By limiting the chronological scope to the period from Alfonso IX's summoning of representatives of the towns to his council in 1188, to the death of Alfonso XI in 1350, the transition from *curia regis* to cortes and the functioning of the cortes as a mature institution for a full century can be amply illustrated.

This study begins with a discussion of the formative period from the late twelfth century to the middle of the thirteenth, and then of the century from 1252 to 1350, when the cortes attained the fullness of its development. The beginning of the cortes can be traced to the reigns of Fernando II (1157–1188) and Alfonso IX (1188–1230) of León; Sancho III (1157–1158), Alfonso VIII (1158–1214), and Enrique I (1214–1217) of Castile; and Fernando III (1217–1252), king first of Castile and, after 1230, of both Castile and León. During these reigns representatives of the towns were summoned to join the bishops and nobles in the royal court. In the succeeding century when Alfonso X (1252–1284), Sancho IV (1284–1295), Fernando IV (1295–1312), and Alfonso XI (1312–1350) ruled both Castile and León, the cortes assumed a certain regularity as an assembly of prelates, nobles, and urban representatives convened by the king at fairly frequent intervals. By placing the cortes in the perspective of contemporary events, one can better understand the circumstances that brought it into existence and the vicissitudes it endured during successive reigns.

Next the details of the organization and functioning of the cortes must be examined. Among many questions to be considered are these:

What was the cortes? What were the different types of parliamentary assemblies? To what extent were the estates of the realm, or "all the men of the realm," believed to be present in the cortes? Could the cortes exist without the summons and presence of the king? Who were the prelates, nobles, and townsmen who attended? What were the methods of summons, the frequency of assembly, the preferred sites, the provision for lodging and security, and the procedures followed while the assembly was in session?

One must also ask what the cortes did. Did the king expect counsel and consent when he dealt with "the greater affairs of the realm"? Was the cortes always summoned to acknowledge a new king or the heir to the throne? What was its role in regulating regencies? Did it actively participate in foreign affairs? Was its consent necessary for legislation? Did ordinances enacted by the king in the cortes have the force of law? Was the consent of the cortes always required for extraordinary taxes? Did it attempt to place conditions on tax levies or to control collection and disbursement? What influence did it have on royal administration, especially on the chancery, the royal court, and territorial officials? How did it reflect relations among social classes, especially between Christians and Jews? Did it seek to pursue a consistent policy with respect to economic issues?

In carrying out this inquiry one must avoid the trap of reading back into earlier centuries ideas current in the modern age. This can only lead to a distorted perception of the cortes. Although there are limitations to the ability to see the cortes as its contemporaries did, this ought to be the goal. One must begin with the realization that the cortes was the king's court and, as such, subject to his control. Once in session, however, it often displayed a mind of its own and was not always willing to follow the king's lead. The cortes did not possess the great power and authority that Martínez Marina attributed to it, but neither was it always a docile and passive instrument of royal policy. If modern preconceptions can be kept at a distance, it ought to be possible to achieve a reasonably sound understanding of the nature of the medieval cortes. The first task is to appreciate the cortes for its own sake and to assess its impact upon government and society in the century of its mature growth. Once that has been accomplished, one will be able to judge the extent to which the cortes may have influenced modern ideas of representative government.

Every historical investigation must begin with an evaluation of the sources. In this instance, the sources shed abundant light upon many of the questions raised above, but they are scanty in number and do not permit many complete answers. They can be grouped as follows: ordinances; royal charters and private letters; narratives; and theoretical and literary treatises.

The most valuable documentary sources are the ordinances drawn up by the chancery, often on the basis of petitions presented in the assembly, and promulgated by the king at the conclusion of the cortes. The ordinances consisted usually of several sheets of parchment or paper bound together in booklets called *cuadernos*. Copies were given to the participants to carry home as a record of what was done. Copies retained by the chancery are regrettably no longer extant, due to the destruction of the royal archives. Scholars have been forced, therefore, to seek the originals in cathedral, monastic, noble, and municipal archives. After conducting an intensive search a century ago, the Real Academia de la Historia published a collection of *cuadernos*.[11] Since then additional *cuadernos* have been found, though at times they have been mistakenly identified as local privileges. A new edition of the *cuadernos*, collating all known manuscripts in conformity with modern standards, is desirable, but it must be a collaborative venture, necessitating a new and more extensive search of the archives.[12]

Other royal documents provide much supplementary information. Charters of the late twelfth century often bear a notation that the king was celebrating a *curia*, though the practice of noting such events was abandoned in the reign of Fernando III. Royal privileges also contain witness lists of bishops and nobles who most likely were summoned whenever the cortes met. Many charters also mention that the cortes was being held, or that specific actions were taken while it was in session, and some even record the names of municipal representatives. Private charters also occasionally mention the cortes.

The two major narrative sources for the formative era are the *De rebus Hispaniae* of Rodrigo Jiménez de Rada, Archbishop of Toledo (d. 1247), and the *Latin Chronicle of the Kings of Castile*, perhaps by Bishop Juan of Osma (d. 1246). Both are contemporary accounts providing useful data about various royal assemblies, but they end soon after the capture of Córdoba in 1236. The *Estoria de Espanna* reported the remaining years of Fernando III's reign, but with scant attention to extraordinary meetings of the royal court.[13]

A series of official chronicles presents the history of the late thirteenth and early fourteenth centuries. Fernán Sánchez de Valladolid, the chancellor of Alfonso XI, is the probable author of three chronicles of the reigns of Alfonso X, Sancho IV, and Fernando IV. The early chapters of the *Chronicle of Alfonso X* are a confusing chronological jumble, but the author is more confident in his discussion of the last fourteen years, when he seems to have had access to a contemporary account of events as well as to chancery documents. The chronicle seems biased against Alfonso X and favorable to his rebellious son, Sancho. The *Chronicle of Sancho IV* is a comparatively straightforward account, generally supportive of the king. Even more detailed is the *Chronicle of Fernando IV,* which is decidedly partial to Maria de Molina, who sought to preserve her son's rights to the throne. Fernán Sánchez also appears to have written a *Chronicle of Alfonso XI*, based on ample use of royal documentation but extending only to the fall of Algeciras in 1344. The *Poema de Alfonso XI*, fulsome in its praise of the king, is also useful for references to the cortes.[14]

The *Chronicle* of Jofre de Loaysa (d. 1307/1310), archdeacon of Toledo, briefly touches the last years of Fernando III but more thoroughly treats Alfonso X and Sancho IV; it concludes in 1305 in the middle of the reign of Fernando IV. Although comparatively short, it offers precise information about some meetings of the cortes.[15]

Several treatises contain interesting comments on royal policy and the king's relations with his subjects. The Franciscan Juan Gil de Zamora (d. after 1318), in his *Liber de preconiis Hispaniae,* (written for the instruction of Infante Sancho), made veiled criticisms of Alfonso X. Alfonso X's nephew, Juan Manuel (1282–1348), who played an active role in the reigns of Fernando IV and Alfonso XI, described contemporary society in his *Libro de los estados* but did not discuss the cortes. His letters are also a valuable source of information. Lastly, Álvaro Pelayo (d. 1353), a canon lawyer and bishop of Silves, dedicated his *Speculum regis* to Alfonso XI, though he occasionally castigated the king for his oppression of the people.[16]

Despite the paucity of sources and the inadequacies of those that do exist, the essential characteristics of the cortes, from the time it first emerged in the late twelfth century through the century of maturity, can be clearly delineated.

1

The Origins of the Cortes,
1188–1252[1]

The distinctive development of medieval Spain, much of which was occupied for centuries by the Muslims, not only sets it apart from the states of northern Europe but also explains the early appearance of the cortes in the public life of Castile-León. This is attributable in large measure to the reconquest, the continuing struggle against Islam, and to repopulation, the concomitant task of colonizing reconquered lands. A sketch of these developments, in conjunction with political, social, and legal considerations, will assist in understanding the circumstances that gave rise to the cortes.[1]

The greater part of the Iberian peninsula remained under Muslim domination from the invasion of 711 until the middle of the thirteenth century, when only the tiny Islamic kingdom of Granada survived in tributary dependence on Castile-León. Over the course of centuries, the existence of a continually expanding frontier, with lands beyond it to be conquered and colonized, contributed greatly to the strength of the Castilian-Leonese monarchy. The king's authority rested primarily upon his role as the principal military leader, charged with the task of expelling the Moors and reconstituting the Visigothic monarchy.[2]

If the survival of the kingdom depended on the king as its military champion, so too did the survival of the church. Under his direction the ecclesiastical organization disrupted by the Muslim invasion was reconstructed. From the middle of the eleventh century, the papacy began to exercise greater influence over the peninsular church, but the bishops, who were accustomed to doing the king's bidding, found it difficult to oppose him. They might grumble about royal intrusions on the liberties of the church, but unlike Thomas à Becket, the English archbishop of Canterbury, none of them ever had the courage to stand up to the king and suffer the consequences. Neither the bishops nor the pope had an adequate response to the king's claim that, as the chief defender of Christendom against Islam, he was entitled to control the resources of the church.

In the early stages of the reconquest, the monarchy also restrained members of the nobility, but as the kingdom expanded they steadily gained power. As feudal ideas permeated the peninsula in the twelfth century, the nobles were linked by vassalage to the king, and the greatest among them had vassals of their own. Unlike their contemporaries in northern Europe, who often held public offices and lands as benefices transmissible by hereditary right, the Castilian nobility was often rewarded for its services by grants of land in full ownership or by stipends (*soldadas*) paid from the tribute taken from the Moors. Public offices were held at the will of the crown and only occasionally passed from father to son. The nobility could now be divided into three groups: the magnates, known in the thirteenth century by the telling expression *ricos hombres* (rich men); the *infanzones*, men of notable birth but not as wealthy as the magnates; and the *caballeros*, or knights. As a distinct class, the nobles had a clearly defined juridical status entitling them to judgment by their peers in accordance with certain customs (*fueros*) and to exemption from tributes.[3]

Bishops and nobles were the king's natural counselors, but townsmen eventually came to share that responsibility. The growth of towns was a gradual process linked directly to repopulation. Colonization of the Duero valley, deserted since the eighth century, began in earnest in the late ninth and tenth centuries under the direction of the king, who claimed the right to dispose of all reconquered land. Once advanced positions had been secured, efforts were made to attract settlers, usually hardy adventurers and freemen, who owned their land and were independent of every lord save the king. These essentially agricultural and pastoral settlements were not towns, but their potential for growth was realized in the eleventh and twelfth centuries as the frontier was pushed steadily southward beyond the Duero to the Tagus and then to Andalusia.[4]

In the twelfth century the population increased in both the older, more settled areas north of the Duero and in Extremadura, and the municipal structure became more complex. Although still largely agricultural and pastoral, these places assumed vital importance as sources of large, mobile, military forces. Settlers grew wealthy from booty taken in war and raids on Muslim territory, and the towns along the Bay of Biscay began to take the first steps in developing maritime trade.

For administrative purposes, the region both north and south of the Duero was organized into municipalities, each consisting of an urban center and an extensive rural area dependent on it. Within the municipal district, besides the walled town, were many villages. The municipality was directly dependent on the crown and, as such, enjoyed administrative autonomy, with its own laws, institutions, and officials. The fundamental rights, privileges, and obligations of the inhabitants were embodied in charters or *fueros* granted by the king. The inhabitants were guaranteed possession of their property, the right to live under one law, and the right to elect their own officials. The payment of tributes, military duties, the administration of justice, and the imposition of fines were also regulated. In many towns the king was represented by a noble (*alcaide*) primarily responsible for guarding the rights of the crown and defending the citadel.[5]

The principal organ of municipal government was the council or *concejo*, an assembly of neighbors—or more precisely, the adult male property owners living in the municipal district who were admitted to citizenship. The council assembled at the sound of a bell or horn on Sunday following mass, to deal with questions of justice, taxes, military service, the market, and the election of magistrates and other functionaries. The political and judicial head was the *juez*, or judge, elected by the council, usually for one year. In the administration of justice, he was aided by several *alcaldes* chosen annually from the parishes into which the municipality was divided. Lesser officials regulated finances, inspected the market, and served as scribes, police officers, toll collectors, and guardians of woods and pastures.

In the very early stages of municipal growth, social distinctions were blurred, but they soon appeared more clearly. As certain men acquired horses, often as a result of raids upon the Moors, they became mounted warriors, or *caballeros villanos*, and thus were set apart from the footsoldiers, or *peones*. Men able to go to war on horseback, though not noble by birth, enjoyed a prestige due to their status and wealth and dominated the political life of the towns. Those living in the town proper tended to reserve public offices for themselves to the exclusion of the villagers.[6]

As a legally constituted entity of public law and administration, the municipality could buy and sell property and engage in litigation. By the early thirteenth century, municipalities were beginning to use seals, symbolic of their corporate character, to authenticate their acts.[7] In their dealings with other towns, bishops, monasteries, or military orders, municipalities were usually represented by their *alcaldes* or by *boni homines*, good men and true—that is, the most important men of the town, who often were *caballeros villanos*.

This municipal organization was also introduced into the former Muslim kingdoms of Toledo, Andalusia, and Murcia. Toledo, Córdoba, Seville, Murcia, and Cartagena were much more commercial and industrial than the smaller towns of León, Old Castile, and Extremadura, but their form of government was essentially the same and they also depended directly upon the crown. By contrast, the towns of northern Europe, with the exception of the communes of Flanders and the consular towns of Provence and Languedoc, had not progressed quite so rapidly toward autonomy.

In some measure, the towns of Castile-León came of age toward the end of the twelfth century and the beginning of the thirteenth, when the king summoned them to send representatives to his council, which came to be known thereafter as the cortes.

Older historians traced the origins of the cortes directly to the Visigothic Councils of Toledo. These were essentially ecclesiastical assemblies convened by the king, who often outlined the agenda and sanctioned the canons. In day-to-day affairs kings relied on a group of court officials (*officium palatinum*), magnates of the palace, and members of the royal *comitatus*, who together constituted the *aula regia*, the model for the king's court of the early Middle Ages. When significant matters were at issue, the king took counsel with all the great men, including bishops and governors of provinces.[8]

There is some evidence of the existence of the *officium palatinum* in the kingdom of Asturias, but there was no counterpart to the Councils of Toledo. In the tenth and eleventh centuries, numerous Leonese assemblies (often described as *concilia*) attended by the king, bishops, and magnates treated all manner of secular and ecclesiastical business. The Council held at León in 1017 by Alfonso V (999–1028) was a noteworthy example.[9]

In the second half of the eleventh century, as Christian Spain entered more fully into the mainstream of western Christendom, significant changes took place. The Council of Coyanza convoked by Fernando I (1035–1065) was in the tradition of the Councils of Toledo, but the reforms enacted heralded the beginning of the Gregorian Reform in Spain. A distinction between secular and ecclesiastical assemblies and affairs developed as papal legates convoked councils. Although kings often attended these councils, they clearly did not summon them, direct their proceedings, or promulgate their decrees.[10]

In imitation of French usage, the word *curia* (or *corte* in the thirteenth-century vernacular) came into use to refer both to the king's ordinary entourage and also to a large, extraordinary assembly. A more formal structure developed around the three principal officers: the *mayordomo*, the *alferez*, and the chancellor. The *mayordomo*, a distinguished noble, had general oversight of the court, while the *alferez*, also a noble of high rank, commanded the royal armies. As the title of chancellor was accorded to the archbishops of Compostela (León) and Toledo (Castile), subordinate clerics had responsibility for the day-to-day preparation of royal documents. As the same persons tended to serve for many years, experience was accumulated, continuity was given to the counsels of the king and to curial activities, and chancery documentation assumed a stereotypical form.

The court's principal function was to counsel the king on a variety of issues. Late twelfth-century charters often recorded the counsel and/or consent of the barons, nobles, princes, and counts—the chief men of the *curia* known as *ricos hombres* in the next century. Besides witnessing donations to churches, monasteries, and individuals (which the bulk of extant documentation records), the court also acted as a judicial tribunal. Towns were frequent suitors, usually in quarrels over boundaries. Property disputes between clerics and laymen were also heard there, and nobles might be tried on charges of treason or negligence in administration. The kings of León claimed jurisdiction over the crimes of rape, robbery, treachery, and destruction of highways. Under the influence of Roman law, appeals to the court were encouraged.[11]

When matters of the utmost importance had to be resolved, the king augmented his *curia* by summoning all the bishops, magnates, and territorial administrators. The lists of those who witnessed or confirmed royal privileges, though an uncertain guide to attendance at court (especially once uniformity was imposed on royal documents in the late twelfth century), probably indicate those who would have been summoned.[12]

Church councils were now recognizably distinct from royal assemblies, but occasionally the latter were described as *concilia*. The royal chronicle spoke of the Council of León in 1135 when Alfonso VII (1126–1157) was crowned as emperor of Spain, but the king himself referred to it as his *curia*. A few years later (30 March 1144), a royal charter issued "in curiis Vallisoletanis" employed the plural form of *curia* to emphasize that an extraordinary assembly was being held.[13] The use of the term *curia plena* on four occasions emphasized the plenary character of the assembly, but this did not become common terminology. Both royal charters and chronicles speak of the *curia* not so much as an institution but as an extraordinary event being celebrated.[14]

There were three principal reasons why the kings of León and Castile summoned representatives of the towns to the royal court. First, by virtue of their control of vast expanses of territory equivalent in size to the counties of France or the shires of England, the towns were major elements in the administrative structure. Second, the king had need of the urban militias for the conquest and defense of lands beyond the Tagus river in the twelfth century and beyond the Guadalquivir in the thirteenth. Once the frontier was stabilized, these contingents were still needed to guard against the threat of Granada and Morocco in the late thirteenth and fourteenth centuries. Third, as ordinary royal revenues no longer sufficed to meet the needs of both war and civil administration, the crown discovered that the growing wealth of the towns, derived in part from booty taken in war, was a valuable resource that could be tapped.

Roman law provided a theoretical justification for the convocation of the municipalities and the practical means to bring such a convocation about. The Reception of Roman law in the Iberian peninsula effected profound changes in the concepts of the state and justice, in the manner in which justice was administered, and in the very substance of the law. Roman law became a subject of study in the universities of Palencia and Salamanca, established respectively by Alfonso VIII of Castile and Alfonso IX of León. At first, Italian scholars familiarized peninsular students with the principles of Roman law, but later the Spaniards also made significant scholarly contributions.[15]

References in twelfth- and early thirteenth-century charters to the "status regni" or "utilitas regni" reflect the influence of Roman law on the development of the concept of the state as an abstract entity distinct from the king and the territory of the kingdom. In the late thirteenth and early fourteenth centuries, these terms appear as "estado de la tierra," "pro de la tierra," "buen paramiento de la tierra," and "fecho de la tierra." Ulpian's classic definition of justice as a "constant and perpetual desire to render to each man his due" (*Digest*, I.1.10) was cited in twelfth-century charters, while Roman legal procedures such as inquests and appeals became an integral part of the judicial system.[16]

The principle of Roman private law, *quod omnes tangit, ab omnibus debet approbari*, when applied to public law, encouraged the crown to take counsel with all those who might be affected by any major decision, but how to consult with the thousands living in the municipalities who might be so affected was a serious problem. The solution was the idea of a corporation, a body of individuals who by reason of their common interests could be treated as a single juridical entity. The corporation could act as a legal person in the marketplace, in courts of law, and in public assemblies. It did so through a duly appointed representative or procurator, who received letters of procuration conferring upon him *plena potestas*, or full power, whereby his constituents agreed in advance to be bound by the decisions that he might make.[17]

Cathedral chapters and monasteries were among the earliest institutions to be treated as corporations and to employ procurators to represent them. From at least the second quarter of the thirteenth century, the towns of Castile and León were represented in the royal court by procurators (often described as *personeros* or *omnes bonos*) with letters of procuration delineating their authority.[18]

Turning now to the participation of bishops, nobles, and townsmen in the extraordinary *curia* or cortes, we must establish at what point the townsmen were clearly present, which towns they represented, what powers they bore, and what business they transacted.

In three assemblies convened by Alfonso IX of León in 1188, 1202, and 1208, the presence of townsmen was explicitly recorded. Faced with the problem of establishing his authority on a firm basis and correcting his father's prodigality, he convoked a *curia* at León in April 1188. Together with the archbishop of Compostela and other bishops and magnates, the "elected citizens of each city" were in attendance. This is the earliest unequivocal attestation of the participation of townsmen in an extraordinary meeting of the royal court. Several years later, in March 1202, the king convened a *plena curia* at Benavente, attended by bishops, royal vassals, "and many men from each town of my kingdom." In February 1208, he summoned to an assembly at León bishops, barons, the chief men of the realm, and "a multitude of citizens from each city."[19] For the rest of his reign the evidence is uncertain, but it is possible that townsmen attended a *plena curia* held at Zamora in 1221 and the *curia* of Benavente in 1228.[20]

As for Castile, in the absence of explicit testimony one is left with conjecture. Alfonso VIII likely summoned the chief men (*maiores*) of fifty towns to a *curia* held at San Esteban de Gormaz in May 1187, and they may also have attended the *curia* celebrated at Carrión in June and July 1188.[21] In enacting an ordinance at Toledo in 1207, Alfonso VIII referred to the injury done to the "land, and to the archbishop and to the good men of my towns," but he did not plainly say that he had summoned the townsmen to his council.[22] We are on surer ground with the assembly of Valladolid in 1217 when "all who were present, both magnates and the people of the cities and towns," pledged homage to Fernando III as king of Castile. Two years later he celebrated a *curia* at Burgos with "a multitude of magnates, knights, and chief men of the cities."[23]

After inheriting the kingdom of León from his father, Alfonso IX, in 1230, Fernando III vigorously pressed the reconquest of Andalusia and Murcia. During those years he probably convened the bishops, nobles, and townsmen of Castile and León to consider the issues that that great military and economic effort entailed but the documentation remains imprecise. The king brought his reign and this formative stage in the history of the cortes to a close when he summoned townsmen to an assembly at Seville in November 1250.[24]

The question as to which towns were summoned to the extraordinary council is difficult to answer. Alfonso IX mentioned each city and each town, but generally the texts are not precise. The list of fifty towns whose chief men perhaps attended the *curia* of San Esteban de Gormaz in 1187 is the only document of its kind for this period. The question, ultimately, is one that cannot be answered with any degree of certainty.

The legal status of town representatives is also uncertain, because the terminology used—"chief men," "citizens," "good men," "men of the land"—is not exact. Regulations in the *fueros* concerning the dispatch of agents to judicial assemblies suggest, however, that the chief men or citizens mentioned in 1187, 1188, 1202, and 1208 were the *alcaldes* or other elected officers of town government. Other indications are that they were from the upper stratum of urban society, the *caballeros villanos*. From the second quarter of the thirteenth century, when towns began to send procurators to the royal court on judicial business, it is likely that they also sent procurators endowed with *plena potestas* to the cortes. Their function was essentially to accept a judgment pronounced by the king's court, or to assent to a policy proclaimed by the king after consultation with the principal political elements of the realm. The legists serving the crown recognized that it was in the royal interest to insist that urban representatives were fully empowered to commit their constituents to a judgment, a policy, or a course of action.[25]

Given the growing strength and influence of the municipalities, the king was probably anxious to have their participation in matters of exceptional importance, such as the recognition of an heir to the throne, a new king, or a newly wedded queen. The chief men of the Castilian towns may have been summoned to the *curia* of San Esteban de Gormaz in 1187 to take an oath guaranteeing the marriage contract between Berenguela, Alfonso VIII's heiress, and Conrad of Hohenstaufen. Witnessing their betrothal in the *curia* of Carrión in 1188, the chief men may also have acknowledged them as their future monarchs. Alfonso IX probably received an oath of allegiance from the bishops, nobles, and citizens of each city summoned to the *curia* of León in 1188, and perhaps asked the *curia* of Benavente in 1202 to recognize his son, Fernando, as heir to the throne. Townsmen played a large part in resolving the Castilian succession in favor of Fernando III at Valladolid in 1217. Two years later they joined the celebration of his marriage to Beatrice of Swabia in the *curia* of Burgos; they may also have witnessed his second marriage to Jeanne of Ponthieu in the *curia* of Burgos in 1237, but the sources are not explicit in this matter.[26]

Before enacting laws the king traditionally took counsel with the bishops and magnates, but townsmen were now also included. In the *curiae* held at León in 1188 and 1208, Alfonso IX, with the counsel and consent of those present, promulgated *decreta* and *constitutiones*. The decrees of 1188 benefited the townsmen insofar as the king promised to abide by the law of the land and to repress abuses of power, but it is unlikely that they had any significant role in drafting them. The constitutions of 1208, on the other hand, primarily concerned the prelates and nobility. Alfonso VIII's economic ordinance enacted at Toledo in 1207 was prompted by his concern for the well-being of the towns. He confirmed their charters at Burgos in 1212 and promised to reform the customs of the nobility, but the text of a royal enactment to that effect is not extant. Fernando III, after consulting the townsmen in the cortes of Seville in 1250 concerning the good estate of the realm, noted that they presented petitions to him. Convocation to the cortes thus gave the townsmen an opportunity to present their grievances to the king, but it is difficult to ascertain the extent of their influence on royal policy and legislation during this period.[27]

Sánchez Albornoz emphasized the financial needs of the crown as the chief reason for summoning townsmen to the cortes, but their role in financing the major campaigns of the reconquest is not easily determined. All the men of the realm in the *curia* of Benavente in 1202 granted Alfonso IX an extraordinary subsidy, known as *moneda forera*, in exchange for his pledge not to alter the coinage for seven years, but it has yet to be demonstrated that he convened the cortes every seven years thereafter to obtain consent to this levy. Nor is there evidence that any of the other assemblies of the first half of the thirteenth century granted the king an extraordinary tax. Fernando III obtained forced loans from the towns, collected *moneda*, and tapped the wealth of the clergy, but there is no detailed information concerning extraordinary taxation granted by the cortes until the second half of the century.[28]

The king also summoned the townsmen to secure their enthusiastic collaboration in projected military campaigns. The municipal militia forces, together with those of the nobility and the military orders, formed an integral part of the royal army. Alfonso IX's promise in the *curia* of León in 1188 that he would not make "war or peace or treaty except by the counsel of the bishops, nobles and good men by whose counsel I ought to be guided," likely meant only that he would not act without seeking the advice of his usual counselors, and not that he would consult the townsmen.[29] Although texts referring to other assemblies are insufficiently explicit, the convocation of the cortes to plan military strategy remains a matter of strong probability.

A substantial amount of judicial business was transacted while the cortes was in session. The resolution of a dispute at Benavente in 1202 between the king and the knights of the realm concerning landholding illustrates the judicial role of the *curia plena*. The summoning of bishops, nobles, and townsmen to the royal court facilitated the settlement of many lawsuits, as chancery documents issued during the cortes of Seville in 1250 reveal. These activities, however, usually involved only the litigants, rather than the cortes as a single entity.[30]

In the years between the *curia* of León in 1188 and the cortes of Seville in 1250, the royal court was transformed as representatives of the towns were summoned to join the bishops and nobles. The documentation is often exasperating in its brevity and imprecision, but it testifies to an ongoing process of growth and development. By the middle of the thirteenth century this period of tentative beginnings was over. The cortes had taken recognizable shape as an instrument that could serve the growing needs of the crown.

2

A Century of Maturity, 1252–1350

The vicissitudes of the century following the death of Fernando III prompted his successors to convene the cortes frequently, thereby further shaping its structure and defining its competence. Kings sought the counsel of the cortes on several great issues that persisted throughout this epoch. First among them was the continuing threat of Islam. Not only was there a substantial Muslim population still to be absorbed or replaced, but the loyalty of the king of Granada was never absolute, and the Marinid emirs of Morocco began a sustained effort in the late thirteenth century to seize control of the ports on the Straits of Gibraltar, which gave access to Spain.

The increasingly aggressive attitude of the nobility, emboldened by the riches of the reconquest, also posed a serious threat to royal authority. Charging that their customs were being violated, the nobles resisted royal efforts at legal innovation. Two royal minorities gave them extraordinary opportunities to utilize the agencies of government for their own profit, as did the continuing dispute over the succession. For

nearly thirty years, this dispute kept the kingdom in a state of civil disorder, enabling Castile's peninsular neighbors and the kingdom of France to intervene in the hope of securing advantages for themselves. In contending with these problems the monarchy employed the cortes as an instrument of moral, military, and financial support. As a consequence, the cortes played a vital and sometimes vigorous role in the political life of the kingdom.

Alfonso X: Years of Hope (1252–1272)

Repopulation of the newly conquered zones and the incorporation of the mudejars (the subject Muslim population) into the kingdom of Castile was the first task facing Alfonso X (1252–1284). He also had to contend with the enormous inflation that plagued the kingdom for many years. An ambitious ruler, Alfonso X planned to invade North Africa, and by reviving old Leonese imperial pretensions he hoped to lord it over his peninsular neighbors. Reaching farther afield, he claimed the Holy Roman Empire as a great-grandson of Emperor Frederick Barbarossa. All this required the outlay of substantial sums of money, resulting in the development of a system of extraordinary taxation and the repeated convocation of the cortes to consent to it.[1]

A charter of 2 March 1254, citing an assembly held according to custom at Toledo, is the first royal document to use the word *cortes*.[2] Referring to the same assembly on 5 May 1255, Alfonso X indicated what he understood by that term when he spoke of having celebrated a general court (*generalis curia*) with his brothers, the archbishops and bishops, the barons and chief men (*optimates*) of his court, and the procurators of cities and towns designated by their communities.[3]

In the first twenty years of Alfonso X's reign, the term *cortes* was used explicitly with reference to the assemblies of Toledo 1254, Burgos 1254, Toledo 1259,[4] Seville 1261,[5] and Burgos 1269.[6] In attendance at the first four cortes were the king's brothers, the archbishops, bishops, magnates, and good men of the towns (and in 1261 the masters of the military orders, abbots, and knights). These, then, were the people one would expect to find in the cortes. As their presence was also recorded at Seville in 1252–1253 and Valladolid in 1258, those convocations can also rightly be described as cortes.[7]

These assemblies between 1252 and 1269 were plenary or general cortes embracing all the realms, although the evidence is not explicit for Burgos 1254 or 1269, and there is the possibility that the cortes of Seville 1252–1253 was actually two successive regional cortes for Castile and León. The assembly of Jerez 1268 may have been a plenary cortes, inasmuch as merchants and good men from all the kingdoms were present, but the full participation of prelates and magnates is uncertain.[8] The nature of the assembly held at Palencia in May 1255 is unclear, but it may also have been a plenary cortes. Later in October of that year the king met the bishops at Valladolid.[9] Towns mainly from Extremadura were assembled at Segovia in 1256 and Seville in 1264.[10]

All told, Alfonso X convened twelve assemblies during the first twenty years of his reign. Seven of them were clearly plenary cortes (Seville 1252–1253, Toledo 1254, Burgos 1254, Valladolid 1258, Toledo 1259, Seville 1261, Burgos 1269); two others may have been (Palencia 1255, Jerez 1268); two were regional assemblies of towns (Segovia 1256, Seville 1264), and one was a meeting of bishops (Valladolid 1255). Other assemblies may have been summoned but certain evidence of their existence is not at hand.

In his first cortes at Seville in the fall of 1252, Alfonso X laid down the general lines of an economic policy aimed at alleviating inflation, conserving natural resources, and maintaining a favorable balance of trade. The repetition of these articles, with some variations, in the cortes of Valladolid in January 1258, of Seville in January 1261, and in the assembly of Jerez in January 1268, suggests that these were chronic problems not easily corrected. Nearly every group in society, moreover, felt aggrieved by Alfonso X's economic restraints.[11]

His alteration of the laws by which men lived provoked a similarly negative reaction. Intending to ameliorate the confusion created by a variety of laws, Alfonso X ordered the preparation of two new codes of law—the *Espéculo de las Leyes,* to be used in the royal court, and the *Fuero real,* for the towns of Castile and Extremadura. Both were probably promulgated in the cortes of Toledo in the spring of 1254.[12] At Segovia in 1256, Alfonso X reminded the Extremaduran towns that because they did not have an adequate municipal law he had given them the *Fuero real.* Soon after, work began on the *Siete Partidas,* but it does not seem to have been promulgated during Alfonso X's reign.[13] As a result of these innovations in the law, the king was accused of trampling on tradition, and later had to endure a major confrontation in the cortes.

Confusion over the succession to Alfonso X's throne also contributed to the uncertainty of his later years. His daughter, Berenguela, was duly acknowledged as his heir by the cortes of Toledo 1254, and together with her betrothed, Prince Louis of France, Berenguela received the homage and fealty of the assembled estates at Palencia in May 1255.[14] The cortes apparently was not convened to acknowledge the king's son, Fernando de la Cerda, born in October 1255, but his marriage to Blanche, the daughter of King Louis IX of France, was celebrated in the cortes of Burgos on 30 November 1269.[15] Fernando's tragic death in 1275 abruptly reopened the question of the succession, but that is best discussed later in this chapter.

The near completion of the peninsular reconquest allowed Alfonso X to plan an invasion of North Africa. He probably discussed it with his Moorish vassals in the cortes of Toledo 1254, and at that time also secured a promise of English aid (which ultimately proved valueless). The marriage of his sister Leonor to Prince Edward, heir to Henry III of England, in the cortes of Burgos on All Saints' Day in 1254, was intended to resolve a dispute over Gascony and to assure English collaboration in the African invasion.[16] After an assault on the Moroccan port of Salé, the cortes of Seville in January 1261 apparently counseled the king to attack Niebla, a Muslim vassal kingdom west of Seville, which surrendered in February 1262.[17]

To obtain effective military service for these campaigns, Alfonso X extended certain tax exemptions to the knights of the Extremaduran towns at Segovia in midsummer of 1256 and again at Seville in April 1264. Shortly thereafter, the king of Granada, who was fearful for his own independence, stirred up a revolt among the mudejars that forced Alfonso X to abandon his African ambitions.[18]

A decisive turning point in Alfonso X's career occurred in April 1257, when he was elected Holy Roman Emperor. He may have asked the cortes of Valladolid early in 1258 for a special tax to support the "affair of the empire." [19] The cortes of Toledo held at the end of 1259 also treated the "affair of the empire." [20] In spite of a lack of papal recognition, Alfonso X continued his pursuit of the imperial crown for the next fifteen years.

Alfonso X: Years of Crisis (1272–1284)

The years 1272 through 1284 were punctuated by a series of crises concerning the king's imperial quest, his alteration of the laws, the succession to the throne, and the Moroccan invasion. In most cases, these issues were drawn in the cortes. The royal chronicle described the meetings at Burgos 1272, Segovia 1278, and Seville 1281 as cortes. The king himself referred to the cortes held at Burgos in 1274. Jofre de Loaysa, though he did not use the word *cortes*, noted that prelates, nobles, and townsmen met at Burgos in 1276. The presence of bishops, magnates, knights, and townsmen at Burgos in 1277 permits one to identify that assembly as a cortes, but the evidence concerning a meeting at Burgos in February 1281 is insufficient to do so.[21] In a twelve-year span the king convened six plenary or general cortes (Burgos 1272, 1274, 1276, 1277; Segovia 1278; and Seville 1281), an average of one every two years.

In addition, Alfonso X convoked other assemblies of varied composition, which contemporaries evidently did not regard as cortes. Among them were meetings with the nobles at Almagro, with the townsmen of León and Extremadura at Ávila in 1273, and with the bishops at Peñafiel in 1275. Nobles, knights, and townsmen gathered at Alcalá at the end of the year, and the Castilian and Extremaduran towns met at Toledo in January 1276.[22] The towns of Castile, Extremadura, and the kingdom of Toledo were summoned to Toledo in the spring of 1279, and the Castilian towns may have met the king at Badajoz in 1280.[23]

In May 1282, the king's son, Sancho, summoned all the estates to an assembly (which he called a cortes) at Valladolid, even though Alfonso X had neither summoned nor authorized the meeting.[24] Whether he was aware of his father's objections or not, Sancho did not describe as a cortes the meeting of all the estates at Palencia in 1283. *Hermandades*, or brotherhoods of bishops and abbots and of the towns of Castile and León, were formed at Valladolid in 1282 to defend their rights and privileges.[25]

The chain of events that culminated in the downfall of Alfonso X began when he learned of the death of Richard of Cornwall, his rival for the imperial crown. Planning to leave the kingdom in stable condition while he journeyed to secure the prize that had so long eluded him, the king summoned the cortes of Burgos 1272. The nobles, followed by the bishops and townsmen, demanded certain tax reforms and the restoration of their *fueros*. Although he had to bow to these pressures, the king did gain enough financial aid to enable him to bring the affair of the empire to a conclusion.[26]

Many of the nobles who had gone into exile in Granada were persuaded to return when, at Almagro in March 1273, Alfonso X assured
them of fundamental tax reforms. Later he apparently discussed issues
that had arisen in the cortes of the previous year with the Leonese and
Extremaduran towns at Ávila.[27]

Free at last to undertake his "journey to the empire," the king appointed his son, Fernando de la Cerda, as regent in the cortes of Burgos
in March 1274, and obtained a tax to complete the "affair of the empire."[28] During his father's absence from the realm, Fernando attended
to the grievances of the bishops at Peñafiel in April 1275,[29] but his sudden death in November, while en route to defend the frontier against a
Moroccan invasion, brought disaster to the kingdom. The king's second
son, Sancho, halted the enemy advance but then asserted his claims as
heir to the throne even though Fernando's son, Alfonso de la Cerda,
was alive. The groundwork thus was laid for a dispute that would un-
settle the peace of the realm for more than thirty years.[30]

Returning home after failing to convince Pope Gregory X to acknowledge him as emperor, Alfonso X reviewed the military situation
at Alcalá in December and at Toledo in January 1276. He then convoked the cortes at Burgos in April to pledge homage and fealty to
Sancho as his heir.[31] In order to be able to direct his undivided attention
to the frontier, the king apparently entrusted Sancho with primary responsibility for the affairs of Castile and León in the cortes of Segovia
in May 1278.[32] Dissent within the royal family was revealed when Fernando de la Cerda's two sons were spirited to Aragón while their mother
went to France to beg the support of her brother, King Philip III.[33]

Alfonso X, meanwhile, hoping to deny the Marinids access to the
peninsula, prepared to besiege Algeciras. To provide for the defense of
the realm, the cortes of Burgos in the spring of 1277 had granted him a
tax levy for the remainder of his life.[34] Amid much grumbling, the Castilian and Extremaduran towns gathered at Toledo in the spring of
1279 responded to his plea for additional aid, but it was still insufficient
to allow him to terminate the siege successfully.[35] When he again emphasized his need for money during the cortes of Seville in the fall of
1281, the townsmen, though groaning under the burden of tributes,
nevertheless allowed him to do as he thought best.[36]

When the king declared that he wished to provide for Alfonso de la
Cerda by partitioning his dominions, Sancho left the cortes in anger
and summoned all the men of the realm to Valladolid in April 1282.

Recalling the accumulated frustrations and grievances of the past thirty years, they conferred the essential functions of government upon him but stopped short of deposing Alfonso X. The towns, as well as the bishops and abbots, organized their *hermandades* and intended to meet annually in defense of their rights.[37]

Alfonso X, refusing to yield his power, summoned his erstwhile enemy, the emir of Morocco, to wage war on his behalf, while Sancho vainly sought to secure control of the entire realm. Just before his death on 4 April 1284, Alfonso X disinherited Sancho and acknowledged Alfonso de la Cerda as his heir.[38]

The evidence suggests that Alfonso X played a major role in developing the cortes as an instrument of royal policy, using it to announce his economic policies, to promulgate new law codes, and to resolve, in some measure, the contentious question of the succession. The cortes, furthermore, financed his African interests, his imperial quest, and the wars with Morocco, but it proved to be more than a mere rubber stamp. The gathering together of so many men of diverse backgrounds and interests inevitably resulted in objections to this policy or that, and ultimately led to the challenge presented to him in 1282. The cortes could be seen as a two-edged sword that served the monarchy but which also might be turned against it.

Sancho IV (1284–1295)

When Sancho IV declared against his father in 1282, the people were ready to follow him as much because of their opposition to Alfonso X's heavy fiscal impositions and violations of their *fueros*, as because of their conviction that Sancho had the best right to the throne.[39] Once king, however, Sancho IV burdened his subjects more heavily with taxes than his father had.[40] The defense of the realm against Moroccan invasion was the chief drain on his resources, but he also had to expend money to fend off the rival claims of his nephew, Alfonso de la Cerda (alternately supported by France and Aragón); to persuade the pope to validate his marriage to his cousin, Maria de Molina; and to legitimate his children. Each of these efforts cost money, and in order to get it he resorted to policies similar to his father's.

The study of the cortes of Sancho IV is particularly frustrating because of the inadequacy of the documentation. *Cuadernos* exist for the cortes of Palencia 1286, Haro 1288, and Valladolid 1293,[41] and there are documentary references to the cortes of Valladolid 1284 and Burgos 1287.[42] Procter believed that he convened the cortes at Zamora in 1286, but this is uncertain.[43] During his eleven-year reign, Sancho IV convoked the cortes five times. This seems, at first glance, to be evidence of convocation at regular intervals, but four of those meetings were held in the first four years of the reign, and only one in the last seven. This pattern suggests his reluctance to convene the cortes once he felt securely established on the throne.

Besides the cortes, Sancho IV met with the magnates at Astorga in 1287 and the prelates at Medina del Campo in 1291. Other assemblies may have been held at Burgos in 1285, 1286, and Seville in 1285, but the documentation is inadequate to judge their nature. A general meeting of the *hermandad* took place at Medina del Campo in 1284, the first and only such meeting during Sancho IV's reign.[44]

Recognizing that royal authority had been weakened by his challenge to Alfonso X, the new king, in his first cortes held at Valladolid around Martinmas (11 November) 1284, revoked many of the charters that he had granted while still infante, and abolished the *hermandades*. Although they had supported him during the struggle with his father, Sancho IV now viewed them as potential challenges to his own authority.[45]

The birth of a son, Fernando, in December 1285, assured the king of an heir. Representatives of the towns were summoned to Zamora in January of the new year to swear allegiance, but it does not appear that the cortes was convened for that purpose.[46]

Giving high priority to the recovery of alienated royal rights, the cortes of Palencia in November 1286 urged the king to move in that direction.[47] In the following year, he enacted an ordinance in the cortes of Burgos that provided for the repossession of royal lands acquired by the church. But a contract concluded on 1 June with Abraham el Barchilón for the collection of revenues owed the crown since Alfonso X's later years was much less popular.[48]

The prime mover in this attempt to gather every penny due the crown was Lope Díaz de Haro, but he had a falling out with the king and was killed in June 1288.[49] After capturing Haro, Lope's chief stronghold, the king repudiated the fallen minister's fiscal policy. In the cortes held at Haro in 1288, a new ordinance concerning royal domains obtained by the church was enacted, while the contract with Abraham el Barchilón was abrogated in return for an annual tax for the next ten years. Thereby guaranteed a steady revenue, the king was also free of the need to summon the cortes regularly to gain consent to taxes. Consequently, five years elapsed before the cortes was convoked again.[50]

The renewed threat of Moroccan invasion nevertheless compelled the king to ask the prelates at Medina del Campo in the fall of 1291 for special taxes, and in the spring of the following year, without summoning the cortes, he collected others. With these funds he was able to capture Tarifa, one of the chief ports on the straits giving access to the peninsula.[51] In the aftermath of that victory, after listening to grievances concerning his financial expedients, the king assured the cortes of Valladolid in the spring of 1293 that he would seek consent before levying extraordinary taxes.[52]

Early in 1295, the king fell ill and appointed Queen Maria de Molina as regent for their son, the future Fernando IV. All the men of the realm pledged their allegiance, but there is no evidence that they were summoned to the cortes to do so. Sancho IV, believing the succession secure, died on 25 April 1295.[53]

Fernando IV: The Minority (1295–1301)

The kingdom of Castile was left in a critical state. The new king, Fernando IV (1295–1312), was a mere boy of nine whose rights to the throne were very much in doubt.[54] In defending them, Maria de Molina had to contend with several formidable opponents. Among them was Infante Enrique, a younger brother of Alfonso X, who had recently returned to Castile after long years of exile in Italy, and who now demanded the regency. Sancho IV's younger brother, Juan, claimed the throne by arguing that his nephew was illegitimate because his parents had never obtained a papal dispensation from the impediment of consanguinity. Alfonso de la Cerda maintained his rights with the backing of Aragón and Portugal, which both expected territorial advantages at Castilian expense.

The cortes, summoned nearly every year during the minority, was actively involved in this succession crisis. A general *cuaderno* and one given to the bishops reveal that the cortes of Valladolid 1295 was a plenary assembly attended by the men of Castile, León, Extremadura,

Galicia, Toledo, and Andalusia. The cortes of Valladolid 1298 was also plenary, although only the Castilians and Leonese were mentioned, and only a Castilian *cuaderno* survives. Castilians, Leonese, and Extremadurans participated in the cortes of Valladolid in 1299 and 1300, but whereas there are two *cuadernos* (one general and one Leonese) for 1299, there is only a Castilian one for 1300. Only Castilians were mentioned in the *cuaderno* for the cortes of Cuéllar 1297, but as Cuéllar was in the heart of Extremadura, it is likely that both Castilians and Extremadurans attended. Because of dissension between Infante Juan and other nobles, one regional cortes each was held in 1301 at Burgos and Zamora for the Castilians and Leonese, respectively; each received a separate *cuaderno*. Thus, during the seven years of the minority, the cortes met each year except 1296. Four assemblies were plenary (Valladolid 1295, 1298, 1299, 1300), two regional (Burgos and Zamora 1301), and one possibly plenary (Cuéllar 1297).[55]

The reconstitution of the *hermandades* of Castile, León and Galicia, Extremadura, Murcia, and Andalusia is equally notable. Determined to defend their rights against encroachments by the crown, but especially by the nobility, they wielded great clout in the cortes of Valladolid 1295 and functioned for several years afterward.[56] Aside from the general *hermandades*, others of more limited geographical extent were also established.[57]

The convocation of the cortes with such frequency was due to the need to win moral and financial support. The cortes of Valladolid in July 1295, after acknowledging Fernando IV as king, agreed that Maria de Molina should retain custody of her son while Infante Enrique assumed responsibility for the government of the realm.[58]

The *hermandades* of Castile and León were a strong presence in the cortes, decrying the breakdown of law and order and demanding that townsmen representing Castile, León, and Extremadura be given a voice in the royal council.[59] As set down in the cortes of Cuéllar in March 1297, the mandate claimed by these new members of the council touched all affairs concerning the estate of the realm.[60] By contrast, the prelates, objecting to the exceptional influence of the towns in the cortes of Valladolid 1295, insisted on the confirmation of ecclesiastical liberties.[61]

As civil disorder continued, Infante Juan vainly tried to persuade the Castilian *hermandad* at Palencia in January 1296 to support his bid for the throne. Although he was able to gain the allegiance of some Leonese towns,[62] those of Andalusia and Murcia and the seaports on the Bay of Biscay formed *hermandades* in defense of Fernando IV.[63]

The government, in the meantime, had to ask the cortes for financial aid to suppress civil war and repulse the king's external enemies. After an initial grant by the cortes of Valladolid in 1295, the amounts approved by the cortes of Cuéllar 1297 and Valladolid 1298, 1299, and 1300 rose steadily.[64] The cortes of Valladolid 1300 and Burgos and Zamora 1301 voted an additional levy to pay for papal bulls legitimating the king and dispensing him from the bonds of consanguinity with his intended bride, Constanza of Portugal.[65]

Fernando IV: The Domination of the Nobility (1302–1312)

Duly legitimated on 6 September 1301, Fernando IV married Constanza in January 1302 and assumed management of his own affairs. The stage was now set for the struggle between Infantes Enrique and Juan to gain ascendancy over the king.[66]

The divisions that plagued the realm were exhibited in the convocation of regional cortes for León, Extremadura, and the kingdom of Toledo at Medina del Campo in April 1302, and for Castile at Burgos in June. Separate *cuadernos* were given to the Leonese and Extremadurans at Medina del Campo. None are extant for the cortes of Burgos, but charters confirming the Castilian *fueros* were published, and an ordinance concerning the coinage (extant only in a copy of 1303) was enacted. The cortes of Medina del Campo 1302 asked that henceforth only the plenary cortes should be summoned. Consequently, the first plenary cortes of the king's mature years was held at Medina del Campo in April 1305, but regional differences were still so strong that three separate *cuadernos* were prepared for the Castilians, the Leonese, and the Extremadurans.

The cortes convened at Valladolid in June 1307 was also plenary, but the petitions of the towns and royal replies were presented in a common text. A royal ordinance is the principal evidence for the plenary cortes held at Burgos in June 1308. The king also held a plenary cortes at Madrid in February 1309 and confirmed the *cuadernos* of that cortes in 1312; but the text of the *cuadernos* has not yet been discovered.

The *cuaderno* of the last plenary cortes of the reign, assembled at Valladolid in March 1312, embodies both a royal ordinance and response to petitions. In the decade of the king's majority, five plenary cortes (Medina del Campo 1305, Valladolid 1307, Burgos 1308, Madrid 1309, Valladolid 1312) and two regional ones (Medina del Campo and Burgos 1302) were held.[67]

After the king's confirmation of the Castilian *hermandad* in 1302, there is no evidence of activity by the *hermandades*, but other assemblies did meet from time to time. Many nobles gathered at Valladolid in the fall of 1302 in support of Infante Enrique. Maria de Molina summoned the towns of the bishoprics of Ávila and Segovia to Coca in June 1303 to uphold her son's rights, and he met the Extremaduran towns at Olmedo in November. The assembly convoked by the king at Burgos in April 1304 had some of the characteristics of the cortes, but the charters issued to the Extremaduran and Castilian towns did not describe it as such, nor does it appear that the bishops attended. The nobles assembled again at Grijota, outside Palencia, in March 1308 to demand reforms and the convocation of the cortes of Burgos in June.[68] Two major assemblies met at Palencia in 1311, one in March with the bishops, some of whom had organized an *hermandad* in the previous year, and the second in October with the nobles.[69]

All those contending for power found the convocation of the cortes useful for their purposes. The king took control of his affairs in the cortes of Medina del Campo and Burgos in 1302, but Infante Juan used the occasion to undercut Maria de Molina's influence. The death of Infante Enrique in 1303 removed Juan's principal opponent, but factionalism continued to foment instability. By contrast, the controversy over the succession dating from the death of Fernando de la Cerda in 1275 was concluded in 1304 when Alfonso de la Cerda renounced his claims to the throne.[70] The convocation of a plenary cortes at Medina del Campo in 1305 was intended to celebrate the general reconciliation, but a dispute between Infante Juan and Diego López de Haro over the lordship of Vizcaya stirred further unrest until its resolution in the cortes of Valladolid two years later.[71]

The persistent theme of all the *cuadernos* of this period is the default of justice and the breakdown of law and order. Much of this was attributable to the disorders brought on by the civil war of the minority, but Fernando IV, buffeted as he was by the factions among the magnates, was slow to take matters in hand. The ordinance drawn up in the cortes of Valladolid 1312 represented a systematic attempt to organize the royal tribunal, to bring order into the chancery, to define the duties of territorial and local officials, and to assure the men of the realm of due process of law; but in view of the abrupt end of the reign, it is impossible to determine how effective this new regime might have been.[72]

The prelates were aggrieved by the king's failure to protect them against arbitrary impositions and other intrusions upon their liberties and they said as much in the Council of Peñafiel in 1302.[73] They confronted him again at Palencia in March 1311,[74] but the formation of an *hermandad* by the Leonese bishops in 1310–1311 was a sure sign of their lack of confidence in his ability to govern effectively.[75]

The magnates were divided by the controversies at first between Infantes Enrique and Juan and later between Juan and Diego López de Haro. Led by Infante Juan, they made a concerted effort at Grijota in 1308 to control appointment of the principal officers of the court. This was ratified in the cortes of Burgos in July of that year, but a proposal to decrease noble stipends was doomed to failure.[76] Meeting them at Palencia in October 1311, the king, intimidated once again, promised to pay their stipends and to allow Infante Juan to nominate his councilors.[77]

Given that he had to contend with the threat of Alfonso de la Cerda, buy the allegiance of the magnates, and provide for the defense of the frontier against Granada, Fernando IV's expenses (and revenues) were higher than those of his predecessors. The amount of the taxes approved by the cortes remained fairly constant, but additional levies imposed in 1305 and 1306 without the consent of the cortes prompted the cortes of Valladolid 1307 to demand that the king obtain such consent in the future, and that in the meantime he should attempt to live off his ordinary revenues. An accounting of the revenues was undertaken in the cortes of Burgos 1308 with an eye toward balancing the budget, but it did not succeed.[78]

The cortes of Madrid 1309, in support of the war with Granada, consented to a tax levy for several years which may have enabled the king to avoid convoking the cortes in 1310 and 1311. For that reason, the prelates insisted at Palencia in 1311 that they be summoned to the cortes before being asked to consent to taxation. The cortes of Valladolid 1312, after urging the king to balance the budget and try to live within his ordinary means, agreed to an extraordinary levy for the war against Granada. Despite the king's promises, the budget seems never to have been brought into balance, and the measures adopted for that purpose appear to have been ineffectual. It was unrealistic, however, for the cortes to imagine that the king could govern without extraordinary taxes.[79]

The war against Granada bore fruit when the king conquered Gibraltar in September 1309, but the withdrawal of Infante Juan and other discontented nobles forced him to abandon the siege of Algeciras in January 1310. Although he returned to the frontier after the cortes of Valladolid 1312, his death on 7 September cut short the campaign.[80]

Owing to the exceptional circumstances of Fernando IV's reign, the cortes regularly had the opportunity to participate in public affairs. The townsmen were persistent in demanding reforms in justice and finance, but their influence was outweighed by that of the magnates, whose interest lay in keeping the monarchy weak. Fernando IV was incapable of dealing firmly with them and more than once had to call on his mother to rescue him from disaster. How he would have dealt with the magnates, the prelates, and the cortes in his more mature years is unknown because he died suddenly at the early age of twenty-eight.

Alfonso XI: The Minority (1312–1325)

The accession of Alfonso XI (1312–1350), who was little more than a year old, brought about a recrudescence of violence and turmoil. During the thirteen years of his minority, several members of the royal family contended for custody of his person and control of the regency. Initially they included the Queen Mother Constanza; the Dowager Queen Maria de Molina; her son, Infante Pedro; and Infante Juan, the king's great uncle. The cortes was summoned relatively frequently to ratify the claims of one or another of the contenders, and the *hermandades*, so long quiescent, sprang to life again.[81]

The first plenary cortes of the reign was held at Palencia in April 1313 with representatives from Castile, León, Toledo, Extremadura, Galicia, Asturias, and Andalusia. Two *cuadernos* issued separately by the regents—Infante Juan on one side and Maria de Molina and Infante Pedro on the other—revealed the division of the government. In the next year, after meeting with their respective adherents, the three regents convened a unified assembly at Valladolid which can be included in the list of plenary cortes. The cortes that met at Burgos in June 1315 was also plenary. A *cuaderno* published in the name of all three regents survives, as well as a *cuaderno* given to the prelates.[82] The prelates also met the regents at Medina del Campo in April 1316.[83]

A plenary cortes was not convened again until 1321. Disagreements between the Castilians and the other men of the realm resulted in the convocation of a regional cortes at Valladolid (June 1318) for the Castilians and at Medina del Campo (August 1318) for the Leonese and Extremadurans. Only the *cuadernos* for the latter cortes are extant. As the struggle for the regency resumed, a plenary cortes was held at Valladolid in the spring of 1321, but no *cuadernos* have been discovered. A plenary cortes also assembled at Valladolid in May 1322, but a *cuaderno* published by Infante Felipe and several charters granted by other potential regents emphasize the divisiveness within the realm.[84] Thus, in the thirteen years of the minority there were five plenary cortes (Palencia 1313, Valladolid 1314, Burgos 1315, and Valladolid 1321 and 1322) and two regional ones (Valladolid and Medina del Campo 1318).

There were also numerous assemblies of the *hermandades* that had emerged again in every part of the kingdom. A *cuaderno* testifies to the meeting of the Leonese *hermandad* at Benavente in January 1313, and the Castilians met at Sahagún in February and the Extremadurans at Cuéllar. In September the combined Castilian and Leonese *hermandades* assembled at Sahagún.[85] Both the prelates and noble knights formed separate *hermandades* at Valladolid in June 1314.[86] The general *hermandad* of Castile, León, Extremadura, and Toledo convened during the cortes of Burgos in June 1315; the *cuaderno* indicates that the noble knights had joined with the towns. The Castilian *hermandad* met again at Burgos in 1316, and that of Extremadura and Toledo at Cuéllar.[87] A general assembly of the *hermandad* of noble knights and townsmen of Castile, León, Extremadura, and Toledo, often wrongly believed to be a meeting of the cortes, was held at Carrión in March 1317. In 1319 and 1320 there were also many meetings of regional *hermandades*.[88] The variety and frequency of these assemblies is a measure of the disorder that prevailed throughout the kingdom.

The principal reason for the convocation of the cortes during the minority of Alfonso XI was to regulate the regency. All the candidates recognized the necessity of convening the cortes in order to obtain a legal right to act as regents. One faction of prelates and urban procurators in the cortes of Palencia 1313 acknowledged Maria de Molina and Pedro, while another recognized Infante Juan. The death in November of Queen Constanza, who had supported Juan, weakened his cause significantly. While Maria and Pedro gathered their followers at Valladolid in June 1314, Juan met his at Carrión in July. After negotiation, an accommodation was achieved at Valladolid that provided for a joint regency.[89] The single *cuaderno* issued in the cortes of Burgos 1315 testified to the unification of the regency and spelled out the terms under which the three regents would govern the realm. Although suspicious of one another, the two infantes planned a joint expedition against Granada; it ended abruptly when both of them died suddenly in the summer of 1319.[90]

After their deaths, new claimants to a place in the regency appeared: Infante Felipe, a younger son of Maria de Molina; Infante Juan's son, Juan the one-eyed; and Juan Manuel, a nephew of Alfonso X. With the hope of averting the partition of the realm, Maria, who was ill, agreed to share the regency with the three princes in the cortes of Valladolid in the spring of 1321. Her death on 30 June, however, was followed by terrible anarchy—there was no longer anyone of sufficient prestige to dominate the rivals. Although the three surviving regents appeared at the cortes of Valladolid in May 1322, they quickly abandoned all pretext of unity. Effectively dividing the realm among themselves, the three princes exploited it for their personal benefit until Alfonso XI came of age in 1325.[91]

As they had in the minority of Fernando IV, the cortes insisted throughout Alfonso XI's minority that measures be taken to maintain law and order. The widespread activity of the *hermandades* during this time testified to the regents' failure to correct abuses and punish evildoers. In effect, the *hermandades* had to provide the protection that the government was unable to give; yet at the same time the very existence of the *hermandades* contributed to the general upset. The overall weakness of the regents is reflected in the fact that they confirmed the *hermandades* in the cortes of Palencia 1313, Burgos 1315, and Medina del Campo 1318, and allowed themselves to be intimidated by the *hermandad* assembled at Carrión in 1317.[92]

The regents assured the cortes of Palencia 1313 and Burgos 1315 that they would live within the budget of the crown's ordinary resources; but as this was a pledge that could not realistically be kept, the cortes of Burgos demanded an accounting of royal revenues before consenting to a tax levy. In the following year, the prelates assembled at Medina del Campo to approve a levy, as did the assembly of Carrión in 1317 after completing a second accounting. The cortes of Valladolid and Medina del Campo in 1318 authorized taxes for the war against Granada, but it is unknown whether the cortes of Valladolid 1321 and 1322 did so as well. Each of the regents, nevertheless, obtained funds from assemblies of their supporters in the years from 1320 to 1323.[93]

As the government steadily deteriorated toward a state approaching anarchy, the division of the cortes mirrored the divisions in Castile and León. Consequently, even though the cortes met fairly often, it was ineffective in maintaining the orderly processes of government.

Alfonso XI: Royal Ascendancy (1325–1350)

The long and terrible minority came to an end in the summer of 1325 when Alfonso XI, then fourteen years of age, declared his intention to assume personal power and to repair the damage done. He regarded the magnates who had parceled out the regency among themselves as enemies of the crown, and showed little enthusiasm for the cortes, perhaps seeing it as an instrument that had enabled them to bring about the ruination of his kingdom.

Nearly thirteen years passed before Alfonso XI could overcome the opposition among the nobility and be reasonably certain of their loyalty. The mutual mistrust initially limited the king's ability to concentrate on his primary interest, the war against Granada and Morocco for control of the Straits, but that enterprise occupied him almost continually during the last twelve years of his reign. He also effected significant changes in the institutions of government, especially the municipalities, the cortes, and taxation.

In his mature years Alfonso XI convoked only three plenary cortes, at Valladolid in the fall of 1325, Madrid in June 1329, and Alcalá de Henares in February 1348. Prelates, magnates, *infanzones*, knights, masters of the military orders, and procurators from the towns of Castile, León, Toledo, Extremadura, Andalusia, and Murcia attended these assemblies. Two *cuadernos* were issued to the townsmen and prelates at Valladolid in 1325. The *cuaderno* of Madrid 1329 recorded the petitions of the townsmen, but that of Alcalá 1348 contained petitions made on behalf of prelates, nobles, and townsmen. The convocation of only three plenary cortes in a quarter century surely is a sign of reluctance on the king's part to meet with the three estates simultaneously. This impression is strengthened when one considers that two of the cortes met in the first four years of his majority and that an interval of almost twenty years elapsed between the second and third cortes.[94]

By contrast, the king convened a variety of other assemblies, some of which were described as *ayuntamientos*, a word evidently meaning an assembly lacking the full participation of the three estates. The assembly of Medina del Campo in July 1326 was essentially a gathering of prelates,[95] whereas the procurators of the Castilian and Leonese towns met at Madrid in November 1339. The three *ayuntamientos* held in 1345 at Alcalá (March), Burgos (April), and León (June) were attended by the townsmen of Extremadura, Castile, and León, respectively. The towns also convened at Llerena in December 1340. One could probably describe the gathering of nobles at Burgos in April 1338 as an *ayuntamiento*, although the sources did not. In each of these instances, the king met primarily with only one of the three estates.[96]

The composition of several other assemblies was somewhat more varied. The prelates and nobles and some townsmen were summoned to Burgos in June 1332 to celebrate the king's coronation.[97] In March 1336 he met the nobles at Valladolid, in April the Castilian townsmen at Burgos, in May the Leonese townsmen at Zamora, and in February 1337 the clergy at Madrid. Then in 1342 he convened prelates and nobles at Burgos (January), León (February), and Zamora (March), consulting at the same time with the citizens of the host cities. Later he summoned the Extremaduran towns to a meeting at Ávila. There seems no reason not to call these *ayuntamientos*, even though the sources did not. Lastly, one should note the *junta* of Arriaga, an assembly of the people of Álava in April 1332 to acknowledge Alfonso XI as their lord.[98]

In the first cortes of his majority (Valladolid 1325), Alfonso XI announced his intention to restore the rule of law and forbade the organization of *hermandades*, repudiating agreements previously made with them.[99] Determined to end the intrigues of the former regents who were reluctant to give up power, Alfonso XI executed Juan the one-eyed in 1326; his uncle, Felipe, died the following year. Juan Manuel aspired to control the king through a marriage alliance but found himself thwarted when Alfonso XI married Maria of Portugal. As a consequence, Juan Manuel remained intermittently hostile for years thereafter. The king completed the process of taking personal control of the government when he reorganized his household in the cortes of Madrid 1329.[100]

To achieve his great ambition of completing the blockade of the Straits of Gibraltar, Alfonso XI sought funding from the cortes of Valladolid 1325 and Madrid 1329, as well as from the prelates at Medina del Campo 1326.[101] While conspiracies and rebellions diverted him from the reconquest, the emir of Morocco, with Granadan support, recaptured Gibraltar in 1333. In the hope of recovering it, the king resorted to loans and other fiscal devices and in 1336 persuaded the nobles at Valladolid to consent to the taxation of their vassals. The Castilian and Leonese towns, meeting at Burgos and Zamora, respectively, approved a similar levy in 1336, and at Madrid in the next year the clergy agreed to tax themselves.[102]

Intent on securing the most effective military service, Alfonso XI enacted an ordinance at Burgos in 1338 that regulated feuds among the nobility and specified their military obligations. In the next year at Madrid, he addressed the complaints of the townsmen so they would join wholeheartedly in his planned military campaign. When the emir of Morocco laid siege to Tarifa, Alfonso XI and his father-in-law, Afonso IV of Portugal, gained a decisive victory at the River Salado on 30 October 1340. Although no one realized it at the time, the threat from Morocco was finally over.

Flushed with victory and determined to begin the siege of Algeciras (opposite Gibraltar), the king asked the towns at Llerena for additional taxes in December.[103] He realized also the need for a new tax that would affect everyone alike, and after obtaining the consent of the prelates and nobles at Burgos, León, Zamora, and the Extremaduran towns at Ávila in 1342, he imposed the *alcabala*, a general sales tax. After Algeciras fell in 1344, the assemblies of Alcalá, Burgos, and León in 1345 agreed to a continuation of this tax for six years.[104]

In the final cortes of his reign (Alcalá 1348), Alfonso XI responded to the accumulated complaints of previous years and promulgated the Ordinance of Alcalá, which marked the culmination of his legal reforms. With the hope of closing the invasion route from North Africa for good, he then commenced the siege of Gibraltar. Unfortunately, Alfonso XI, like many of his troops, fell victim to the Black Death; he died on 27 March 1350. As a consequence, the siege was abandoned and the reconquest which he had pressed so vigorously was left in abeyance for nearly a century and a half.[105]

An assessment of the cortes during Alfonso XI's majority reveals that it was greatly weakened. The regularity of assembly was interrupted, with a consequent lessening of its importance and its potential as a forum in which the voices of all the people of the realm might be heard. Reflecting, no doubt, on the chaotic years of his minority, Alfonso XI preferred to act in accordance with the Roman proverb, "divide and conquer." By meeting separately with different groups and convoking the cortes only three times, he denied the estates the opportunity to challenge his authority effectively in a plenary assembly.

A European Perspective

Contemporary monarchs in the other peninsular states, as well as in France and England, faced comparable problems. The attempts of the kings of Portugal to recover alienated royal lands and manipulate the coinage provoked inevitable opposition and resulted in the deposition of Sancho II in 1245 and Afonso III's pledge in 1261 to seek the consent of the cortes before modifying the coinage. In Aragón and Valencia, the Union of nobles and towns resolved to preserve tradition and to control extraordinary taxation, confronting kings on these issues from 1283 to 1348. The Catalan corts, on the other hand, secured from Pedro III in 1283 constitutional guarantees concerning the enactment of laws and the imposition of taxes.[106]

In France, Philip the Fair's conflict with the papacy resulted in the convocation of the first meeting of the Estates of Languedoil in 1302. Needing extraordinary taxes to finance the Hundred Years War, Philip VI convened various general and provincial assemblies, but these lacked the structure and definition of the peninsular cortes or the English parliament.[107]

The struggle in England between the crown and the nobility—punctuated by the Magna Charta in 1215, the Provisions of Oxford in 1258, the Confirmation of the Charters in 1297, the Ordinances of 1311, and the Statute of York in 1322—helped to define the limitations of royal power. The near deposition of Henry III in 1264–1265 and the actual deposition of Edward II in 1327 also marked significant stages in this process. From its tentative beginnings under Edward I, the parliament gradually evolved and assumed its characteristic form during the reign of Edward III.[108]

We turn next to the organization and functions of the cortes and its influence on government, society, and economic growth, and present further comparison with representative institutions elsewhere in western Europe.

3

The King and the Estates of the Realm

The Estates of the Realm

The cortes of medieval Castile-León ordinarily consisted of prelates, nobles, and representatives of the towns, assembled upon the king's summons to treat with him the business that he set before them. Alfonso García Gallo defined the cortes as a "reunion of the king with the elements of the community that enjoyed political power." Contemporaries described those elements as estates or orders of men constituting society. The three estates, described in the *Siete Partidas* (II.21) and in Juan Manuel's *Libro de los estados*, were the nobles, who defended the realm, the clergy, who prayed for divine protection, and the workers, who cultivated the fields or labored in the towns.[1] The king was obliged to love, honor, and guard his people, "each one in his estate," just as they were bound to love, honor and obey him. The king and "all the men of the realm" formed a single body, of which he was the head and they were the members (*Espéculo*, II.1.1.4; *Partidas*, II.10.1.3, II.1.5).

Medieval sources do not speak of the summoning of estates, nor do they use the term *brazo* (literally, an arm, or a branch of the body politic), although modern authors often do. José Manuel Pérez Prendes rejected the idea that the prelates and nobles attended the cortes as *brazos* in representation of the clergy and nobility in general, but Julio Valdeón maintained that the nobles and clergy each belonged to a separate estate with a defined juridical status and that they were present in the cortes as such.[2] Conscious of their status and its attendant rights and privileges, the prelates and nobles virtually represented all the people in their respective estates and had the power to bind them to any decisions. The *cuadernos* issued in response to the petitions of prelates, nobles, or townsmen give evidence that each estate functioned as a unit in the cortes.

When the king stood before the cortes, he believed that "all the men of the realm," according to their distinctive functions and rights, were assembled before him and that their consent was tantamount to the consent of the entire kingdom.[3]

Plenary, Regional, and Particular Assemblies

Some royal assemblies were identified as cortes, others as *ayuntamientos*, and still others were given no specific designation. The word *cortes*, the plural of the vernacular *cort* (a translation of the Latin *curia*), was used in two thirteenth-century poems, the *Cantar de mío Cid* (lines 3129–3131) and the *Poema de Fernán González* (verses 564–568), to describe extraordinary assemblies, chiefly of nobles.[4] Referring to "my cortes" held at Toledo in 1254, Alfonso X also spoke of that assembly as a *curia generalis* attended by his brothers, the archbishops, bishops, barons, and nobles of his *curia*, and the procurators of cities and towns sent by their communities. This is the best evidence of what the king understood the cortes to be. For this reason, I believe that any assembly of prelates, nobles, and townsmen that was summoned by the king may be called a cortes, even though the texts do not always name them as such.[5]

From a geographic standpoint, the cortes were either plenary or regional. Participants in the former were prelates, nobles, and representatives of the towns of Castile, León, and Extremadura. References to the presence of "all the men of the realms," or "all the towns of all the realms," emphasize their plenary character. At times, Andalusia, Galicia, the kingdom of Toledo, and Murcia were also mentioned. In the broadest sense, Castile included not only Old Castile, the district around Burgos, but also all those areas subsequently conquered by the kings of Castile—the kingdom of Toledo, Extremadura (south of the Duero around Segovia and Ávila), Andalusia, and Murcia. Included in León were Galicia, Asturias, León proper, and Leonese Extremadura (around Salamanca and Zamora).[6] When the texts cite León and Extremadura, the latter usually indicated Castilian Extremadura; Leonese Extremadura was included in the kingdom of León. When only Castile and León are cited, I believe that a plenary cortes, including all the regions mentioned above, was convened.

Most of the cortes of Alfonso X and Sancho IV seem to have been plenary. So too were those of Fernando IV, but enmity between the Castilians and Leonese resulted in the occasional convocation of regional cortes. During the minority of Alfonso XI, the plenary cortes were often divided and regional assemblies were convened; once he came of age, he summoned only three plenary cortes.

Regional (or provincial) cortes included the prelates, nobles, and townsmen from one or two kingdoms, but not from all. No explicit reference to regional cortes in the reigns of Alfonso X and Sancho IV has been encountered, but the existence of separate *cuadernos* for Castile and León suggested to Antonio Ballesteros that Alfonso X held the Castilian cortes at Seville in October 1252 and the Leonese cortes in February 1253.[7] It seems more likely, however, that a plenary cortes was held in the fall, but that the preparation of the *cuadernos* extended into the new year. Foreign and domestic challenges to Fernando IV resulted in the convocation of the cortes of Castile (and probably Extremadura) at Cuéllar in 1297, and at Burgos in 1301 and 1302; the cortes of León met at Zamora in 1301, and in the next year the cortes of León, Extremadura, and the kingdom of Toledo assembled at Medina del Campo. After the Castilians protested at Burgos 1301 (art. 23), the king explained to the cortes of Medina del Campo 1302 (art. 6) that he held separate cortes because he wished to "avoid the conflicts and recriminations that could arise"; but he promised that "when I wish to assemble the cortes I shall do so with all the men of my kingdom together." These exchanges suggest that ordinarily the king convened the entire realm, rather than its separate parts. Due to rampant factionalism, a regional cortes for Castile was held at Valladolid in 1318 and another for León, Extremadura, and the kingdom of Toledo at Medina del Campo.

On attaining his majority, Alfonso XI preferred to convene assemblies of varied composition, some of which he called *ayuntamientos*. The distinction between cortes and *ayuntamiento* (a word that first appears in fourteenth century documents) apparently depended on the degree to which the estates of the realm were thought to be fully present. An *ayuntamiento* was limited either in personnel or in geographic representation; in other words, if only some prelates, nobles, and townsmen took part, or if only one of the estates were in attendance, or if the participants came from only one region, the meeting would probably be called an *ayuntamiento*. Thus Alfonso XI summoned some prelates, magnates, and procurators of some cities to the *ayuntamientos* at Alcalá, Burgos, and León in 1345. On the other hand, no specific name was given to the assemblies of some bishops, nobles, and townsmen at Burgos, León, Zamora, and Ávila in 1342.

When the king met individual estates, that gathering might be called an *ayuntamiento* or nothing at all. Meetings with the prelates took place at Valladolid in 1255, Peñafiel 1275, Medina del Campo 1291, Palencia 1311, Medina del Campo 1316 (*ayuntamiento*) and 1326, and Madrid 1337. The king and the nobles gathered at Almagro in 1273 (*ayuntamiento*), Palencia 1311, Valladolid 1336, and Burgos 1338. Royal assemblies of towns were more numerous: Segovia 1256 and Seville 1264 (Extremadura); Ávila 1273 (León and Extremadura); Alcalá 1275 (Castile and Extremadura); an *ayuntamiento* at Coca and Olmedo in 1303 (Extremadura); Burgos (Castile) 1336; Zamora (León) 1336; an *ayuntamiento* at Madrid in 1339 and another at Llerena in 1340.

Other assemblies not convened by the king, usually gatherings of the *hermandades* in time of crisis, often had a decisive impact, for instance the meetings at Valladolid in 1282 and 1295, Burgos in 1315, and the *ayuntamiento* of Carrión in 1317.

The Royal Family

As the king's court, the cortes came into being legally only when he or regents acting in his name summoned it. Infante Sancho's assembly at Valladolid in 1282, though called a cortes by various sources, was quite irregular. Juridically it was not a *cortes generales*, as Alfonso X pointed out, because he had not summoned it, nor had he authorized his son to do so. Nor were the assemblies at Benavente, Sahagún, and Cuéllar in January and February 1313 meetings of the cortes, but rather meetings of the *hermandades* of León, León and Castile, and Extremadura, respectively. Even if they had been summoned by Infantes Juan or Pedro, each of whom attended at least one meeting, neither prince had yet been recognized as regent, and so could not have issued a summons in the king's name. Nor did the king or the regents summon the assembly of Carrión in 1317.[8]

Although the royal summons was essential, the king did not have to be physically present at every session of the cortes; kings of adult age probably were, but when Alfonso XI resided at Ávila and then at Valladolid during his minority, he seems not to have attended the cortes of Palencia 1313, Burgos 1315, or Medina del Campo 1318. Stirred by the irregularity of this situation, the cortes of Medina del Campo 1318 (art. 1) demanded that future cortes meet wherever the king was. This was a protest not only against the king's absence, but also against the division of the cortes, whose power rested in its joint sessions. The cortes was held in 1321 and 1322 in Valladolid, where the king lived, but thereafter each of the regents convened assemblies of his respective adherents in different places without regard to the king's presence.

The king ordinarily determined when the cortes would meet and the nature of the business to be transacted, guided the proceedings, and brought them to a close; however, the regents performed these functions during the two minorities.

The queen may have attended the opening and closing ceremonies, but there is little evidence of her participation in the cortes; nor did the *cuadernos* refer to her as one whose counsel was sought. Two queens, however, did have exceptional influence. The Extremaduran towns at Seville in 1264 asked Queen Violante to intercede with Alfonso X, who later appointed her to look into the grievances of the prelates and townsmen (Burgos 1272). In 1273 she persuaded the nobles to come to terms at Almagro. A woman of considerable intelligence and diplomatic skill, Queen Violante became disenchanted with her husband in his later years and gave her support to Sancho at Valladolid in 1282 and at Burgos in 1283.

Maria de Molina, a woman of similar gifts, convinced her husband, Sancho IV, to grant the petitions of the towns in the cortes of Valladolid 1293. Named regent for Fernando IV, she induced the cortes to acknowledge him and to remain steadfast in its support. Constanza of Portugal, Fernando IV's wife, was present in the cortes only at Medina del Campo 1305; she could not compete with her mother-in-law for influence. Constanza's death in 1313 halted any influence in Alfonso XI's minority. Thereafter Maria de Molina had custody of the king until she died in 1321. Alone among the contenders for power, she seems to have been willing to rely on the good judgment of the cortes to rally behind the monarchy in time of crisis.

Alfonso XI never mentioned his wife, Maria of Portugal, or their children in any of his *cuadernos*. They record more frequently that the king took counsel with his uncles, brothers, or sons, though not all of them played outstanding roles.[9] Alfonso X's brother Manuel (d. 1283) was perhaps his closest counselor until Manuel decided to support Sancho at Valladolid in 1282. Another brother, Fadrique, served with Queen Violante as the king's emissary to the nobles in 1273, but for some unknown reason was executed in 1276. A third brother, Felipe, was the principal leader of the nobles opposing the king in the cortes of Burgos 1272. The king's first-born son, Fernando de la Cerda, was appointed regent in the cortes of Burgos 1274 with Fadrique's support. He settled the grievances of the clergy at Peñafiel in 1275, but died soon after. The king then relied heavily on his second son, Sancho, who was acknowledged as heir to the throne in the cortes of Burgos 1276 and given greater responsibilities at Segovia 1278, but their relationship collapsed at Valladolid in 1282. Alfonso X's younger sons, Jaime (d. 1284), Pedro (d. 1283), and Juan, after initially adhering to Sancho's rebellion, returned to their allegiance.

Returning from a long exile in Italy, Alfonso X's brother Enrique became regent for Fernando IV, but once the king came of age, his influence declined and he died in 1304.[10] Alfonso X's son Juan challenged Fernando IV's rights to the throne, but after submitting in 1300, he eventually gained ascendancy over him. Recognized as regent by the cortes of Palencia 1313, Juan shared power with Maria de Molina and her son Pedro until both Juan and Pedro died in 1319. Juan's son, Juan the one-eyed, and Pedro's brother, Felipe, were admitted to the regency at that point, and they participated in the cortes of Valladolid in 1321 and 1322. Juan Manuel, a nephew of Alfonso X, claimed the regency from 1322 to 1325 and continued to play a major role in affairs until his death in 1348.[11]

Royal Vassals

Besides members of the royal family, it is likely that some of those listed in royal privileges as the king's vassals also attended the cortes. When Ibn al-Aḥmar, king of Granada, became a vassal of Fernando III in 1246, he promised "to come to his cortes every year," but the silence of the documentation suggests that ordinarily he did not do so. Yet he renewed his vassalage in the cortes of Toledo 1254, when according to the *Anonymous of Sahagún*, Alfonso X was "much preoccupied with his vassals, the Moabite and Moorish kings"—probably a reference also to Ibn Maḥfūz, king of Niebla, and Ibn Hūd, king of Murcia. In 1259 Alfonso X remarked that he sought "the counsel of the king of Granada" concerning his imperial quest, but perhaps not in the cortes. The appearance of Muḥammad II's name among the witnesses confirming the *cuaderno* of the cortes of Medina del Campo 1305 is not necessarily proof of his presence, since these lists were stereotyped, but neither is there evidence, as Colmeiro suggested, that he was represented by a procurator.[12]

The Royal Council

The *cuadernos* do not record the participation of the king's council, nor do they cite any of the legists, but the *Castigos e documentos* attributed to Sancho IV noted that when the king convened his cortes "all his servants and intimates came with him."[13] Occasionally the king also mentioned "other good men who were with me." Some *cuadernos* (Medina del Campo 1302, 1305, Valladolid 1307, and Burgos 1315) referred to magnates and prelates who, by virtue of holding the chief offices of state, belonged to the royal council. Juan Núñez de Lara, the *mayordomo mayor* and *adelantado mayor*, and Diego López de Haro, the *alferez mayor*, were cited in several cortes of Fernando IV. Others included Pero Ponce, *mayordomo mayor*, Archbishop Gonzalo of Toledo, chancellor of Castile, and Bishop Alfonso of Astorga, notary for León. In Alfonso XI's cortes of Valladolid 1325, Álvaro Núñez de Osorio, *mayordomo mayor*, Garcilaso de la Vega, *justicia mayor*, and Yūsuf of Écija, *almojarife mayor*, were mentioned. Roy Pérez, Fernando IV's tutor and the master of Calatrava, appeared in the cortes of Valladolid 1295. At the end of each *cuaderno* the names of the royal notaries and scribes who prepared the document were recorded.

Whether mentioned specifically or not, the council surely influenced the king's decision to summon the cortes and helped to determine the agenda. The chancery staff and fiscal agents assured the smooth functioning of the cortes, including the preparation of documents and statements of the king's revenues.

The Prelates

Members of the ecclesiastical estate regularly attended the cortes. There are frequent references to prelates, a term that surely meant the archbishops and bishops, the king's chief spiritual counselors, but probably did not include the abbots or the masters of the military orders.[14]

By the middle of the thirteenth century there were twenty-eight episcopal sees in the kingdom of Castile-León. These included the three archbishoprics of Toledo (the primatial see), Santiago de Compostela, and Seville. Thirteen sees were situated in the kingdom of León: Santiago, Astorga, Badajoz, Ciudad Rodrigo, Coria, León, Lugo, Mondoñedo, Orense, Oviedo, Salamanca, Túy, and Zamora. In Old Castile there were four bishoprics: Burgos, Calahorra, Palencia, and Osma. Two sees, Ávila and Segovia, lay in Extremadura. In the kingdom of Toledo there were four: Toledo, Cuenca, Plasencia, and Sigüenza. Andalusia also had four: Seville, Cádiz, Córdoba, and Jaén. Murcia had only one: Cartagena. All twenty-eight archbishops and bishops could have attended any plenary session of the cortes, but the number was probably smaller when the cortes was limited to Castile, León, or Extremadura.

All archbishops and bishops were probably summoned to the cortes, and were expected to attend unless detained by illness or some other legitimate excuse.[15] Aside from general references to archbishops and bishops, individual bishops who held offices at court were cited either in the *cuadernos* or in royal charters issued during the cortes. Other evidence is insufficient to show that all the bishops eligible to attend were actually present in a given cortes.[16] Because of their moral influence and their status as royal vassals who often held important lordships or offices of state, the bishops' participation was essential.

The masters of the peninsular military orders of Calatrava, Santiago, and Alcántara often attended the cortes, as did the heads of the Orders of the Temple, the Hospital of St. John of Jerusalem, and the Holy Sepulchre, which had been established in the Holy Land. The Order of Santa Maria de Cartagena (created by Alfonso X, but soon absorbed by Santiago) also appeared briefly. The masters were summoned because they governed extensive lordships (mainly between the Tagus and the Guadalquivir Rivers), and their knights formed the vanguard of royal armies.[17]

The attendance of abbots of monasteries was less frequent. Cited for the first time in the cortes of Seville 1261, the greatest number of abbots seems to have assembled at Valladolid in 1282. Thirty-nine Benedictine, Cistercian, and Premonstratensian abbots concluded a pact of brotherhood, and twenty-seven pledged their support to Infante Sancho.[18] Abbots also took part in the cortes of Valladolid 1295 and Medina del Campo 1305. Alfonso XI replied to the petitions of Castilian abbots and abbesses in the cortes of Valladolid 1322, but it is not certain that they were actually there. Abbots, priors, and their procurators were last cited in the ordinances given to prelates in the cortes of Burgos 1315 and Valladolid 1325.

There is no satisfactory way of determining which abbots were summoned. Unlike the bishops and the masters, abbots did not figure as witnesses to royal privileges. Perhaps only a few houses were summoned, such as those with important lordships or those that received copies of the *cuadernos*, like Aguilar de Campóo (Valladolid 1293), Oña (Valladolid 1322, 1325), Sahagún, and Celanova (Valladolid 1325). At any rate, the participation of abbots seems to have been exceptional.

Representatives of the lower clergy, though not mentioned in the *cuadernos*, were occasionally summoned as well. Several secular clergy and Franciscan and Dominican friars were appointed to a commission in the cortes of Burgos 1272 to prepare a response to the demands of the nobles and the clergy. Clerics, acting as procurators for their respective cathedral chapters (and sometimes for their bishops), were also present at Burgos 1277 and Valladolid 1282 and 1295,[19] though it seems unlikely that these lower clergy were summoned very regularly.

The ecclesiastical estate often functioned as a unit in defense of the rights of the church. In return for the bishops' consent to a tax, Alfonso X made concessions to them at Valladolid in October 1255. They adopted an aggressive attitude in the cortes of Burgos 1272, presenting demands "such as other kings were not accustomed to grant." The king became so angry that he threatened to expel them from the realm, but he agreed to consider their grievances. The results were probably embodied in the accord reached at Peñafiel in April 1275 by Infante Fernando. Several bishops and numerous abbots joined Infante Sancho at Valladolid in 1282, but Bishops Fernando of Burgos and Juan of Palencia protested.[20]

Although it is unclear whether the prelates assembled at Medina del Campo in the fall of 1291 confronted Sancho IV, it is apparent that they did agree to a tax. Archbishop Gonzalo of Toledo protested that actions were taken in the cortes of Valladolid 1295 without his counsel and that privileges were issued wrongly indicating that the prelates had given consent. Despite this, Fernando IV enacted an ordinance in the cortes in response to the bishops' petitions. The bishops in the Council of Peñafiel 1302 threatened to use the ecclesiastical penalty of the interdict against the king if he violated their privileges.

Forming an *hermandad* in the Council of Salamanca in October 1310, Archbishop Rodrigo of Compostela and fourteen bishops agreed to meet each year to consider the well-being of the church. The bishops compelled Fernando IV to confirm their rights at Palencia in March 1311 and to promise not to tax them without first obtaining their consent in the cortes. At Zamora in July, Archbishops Rodrigo of Compostela and Aymón of Braga, with twelve bishops from León and Portugal, affirmed their *hermandad* in defense of the church.[21]

Archbishops Rodrigo of Compostela, Gutierre of Toledo, and Fernando of Seville, together with nine other bishops, formed an *hermandad* at Valladolid in April 1314 to demand that the regents for Alfonso XI confirm the liberties of the church, which they did in the cortes of Burgos 1315. The regents also agreed at Medina del Campo in April 1316 to postpone any attempt to recover royal lands acquired by the church until the king came of age. After enacting an ordinance concerning clerical grievances in the cortes of Valladolid 1325, Alfonso XI, in return for the bishops' consent to a tax at Medina del Campo 1326, renewed the agreement on royal lands made by the regents ten years before. The bishops do not appear to have challenged him thereafter.[22]

Despite opinions to the contrary, the bishops and other members of the clergy who attended these assemblies had a strong sense of belonging to an estate with distinctive rights and privileges.[23] In times of crisis, they demanded redress, protection, and acknowledgment of ecclesiastical liberties, but for the most part they remained submissive to royal authority.

The Nobility

From the earliest times the magnates were the king's chief collaborators.[24] In nearly every cortes until the middle of the fourteenth century, the presence of these *ricos hombres* was recorded. Alfonso X, who summoned the *barones et optimates nostrae curiae* to the cortes of Toledo 1254, emphasized that the king ought to love and honor them, "because they are the nobility and honor of his cortes and of his kingdoms" (*Partidas*, II.10.1).

Among members of the aristocracy, the magnates were the most prominent by birth, lineage, wealth, and power and, as royal vassals, owed counsel and military service in return for stipends (*soldadas*). From their numbers were selected the *alferez*, the *mayordomo mayor*, and the provincial governors. Their cohesiveness, based on common interests and intermarriage, and their tendency to entail their estates for the benefit of the oldest son—thereby concentrating wealth in a small number of families while providing for the younger sons in the military orders or the church—enabled them to become an ever more formidable challenge to the monarchy.

Pérez Prendes argues that the basis for the summons given to the magnates was the general duty of all subjects to counsel the king when required. While this is true, it is also true, as Sánchez Albornoz points out, that contemporaries emphasized their feudal obligation to give counsel as royal vassals.[25]

Whereas Gama Barros states that the magnates attended the cortes by reason of a personal right and effectively represented the nobility, Colmeiro and Pérez Prendes insist that no one had such a right and that the king was free to summon whomever he wished.[26] No claim to a personal right to be summoned has been found in the documents of this period, but the repeated appearance of the same people and families in the king's court and cortes suggests that attendance by the magnates tended to become, tacitly at least, hereditary right or privilege. Juan Manuel, an active politician in this epoch, declared that the king ran the risk of offending people by failing to summon those who thought they should be consulted in important matters, even though their advice might generally be known to be worthless.[27] Thus although there was a practical reason to summon all the magnates—to avoid stirring up jealousy or hostility—the implementation of many decisions taken in the cortes did require their positive collaboration.

Although the *cuadernos* usually refer to the magnates generally, citing only a few outstanding men by name, at times the chronicles also mention individuals. The twenty or twenty-five magnates who regularly witnessed royal privileges probably were those who were usually called to the cortes. Besides the Laras and the Haros, the list of distinguished families who were also recorded as attending includes Aguilar, Arana, Asturias, Cameros, Castañeda, Castro, Cisneros, Finojosa, Guzman, Manrique, Manzanedo, Mendoza, Meneses, Osórez, Ponce, Roa, Salcedo, Saldaña, Sarmiento, Villalobos, and Villamayor.

Members of the lower nobility, that is, the *infanzones* and the *caballeros fijosdalgo*, also participated in the cortes. The former group was a class of nobles in between the magnates and the knights.[28] Piskorski is probably correct in saying that only the *infanzones* and knights holding directly from the king were summoned. It is apparent, on the other hand, that the magnates were accompanied to the cortes of Burgos 1272 by *infanzones* and knights who were their vassals. There is no way of knowing their numbers, but 102 knights swore to abide by the terms of the *hermandad* at the cortes of Burgos 1315. Squires were present at the *hermandad* of Carrión in 1317 but were not mentioned again until the reign of Enrique II.[29]

In only a few instances did the magnates take concerted action to defend their interests in the assemblies of this period. Confronting Alfonso X in September 1272, they insisted that he confirm his agreements in the cortes of Burgos. While the principal leaders went into exile, Alfonso X made concessions to the more moderate among them at Almagro in February 1273; these were recorded at Toledo in March.[30]

With the support of Infantes Juan and Pedro, the magnates tried to resolve differences with Fernando IV at Palencia in October 1311. No doubt to enhance the authority of the compromise they worked out, the text was included in the *cuaderno* published at the cortes of Valladolid in the following year. Alfonso XI, in an assembly at Burgos in April 1338, tried to curb rivalries and antagonisms among the nobility by regulating their feuds, their military obligations, and the dress appropriate to their rank. Provisions of a similar nature were included in the Ordinance of Alcalá enacted in the cortes of 1348.[31]

Representatives of the Towns

As the chronicles, *cuadernos*, and royal charters testify, the largest element in the cortes was the municipal representatives. Principal cities such as Burgos, León, Valladolid, and Toledo, were surely summoned to all plenary cortes as well as to cortes and other assemblies for their respective regions. Towns in which royal assemblies were held were presumably represented: Alcalá de Henares, Ávila, Burgos, Cuéllar, Haro, Jerez, León, Madrid, Medina del Campo, Palencia, Segovia, Seville, Toledo, Valladolid, and Zamora. Yet it is unlikely that Llerena, a town held in lordship by the Order of Santiago, was represented in the assembly held there in 1340.

The number of towns summoned would depend on whether the cortes was plenary or regional. Royal statements that all the towns, or some of them, attended, are useful only in emphasizing the king's attempt to consult broadly or to curtail participation. Three lists of towns are helpful in this regard. First, the list of fifty Castilian towns that swore to uphold the marriage of Infanta Berenguela and Conrad of Hohenstaufen that had been arranged in the *curia* of San Esteban de Gormaz in 1187, may give some indication of the chancery's list of towns that were to be summoned to a royal assembly. Only nine of those towns do not appear in subsequent lists of towns attending the cortes. Fourteen of the twenty-eight towns assigned as Berenguela's dowry later participated in the cortes.[32]

Second, thirty-three Leonese and Galician towns, represented by sixty-three *personeros*, formed an *hermandad* in July 1295 during the cortes of Valladolid. At the same time twenty-three towns from Extremadura, represented by forty-seven *personeros*, concluded an *hermandad* with ten towns from the archbishopric of Toledo, represented by twenty-one *personeros*. Sixty-four Castilian towns, represented by 117 *personeros*, adhered to this pact. Thus a total of 130 towns represented by 248 *personeros* joined the *hermandad* and presumably took part in the cortes of 1295.[33]

Third, during the cortes of Burgos 1315 a similar *hermandad* was organized by one hundred towns from Castile, León, Extremadura, and the kingdom of Toledo, represented by 201 procurators. Forty-two Castilian towns sent seventy representatives; fifteen Extremaduran towns sent fifty-two representatives; twelve towns of the kingdom of Toledo sent twenty-four; and thirty-one Leonese towns sent fifty-six.[34]

Combining the lists of 1295 and 1315, and avoiding any duplication, we have a total of 170 towns (seventy-eight from Castile, twenty-nine from Extremadura, eighteen from Toledo, and forty-five from León). If we add ten Andalusian and Murcian towns known to have participated in the cortes, we have 180 towns attending the cortes on various occasions.

Some towns probably took part more frequently than others, for example, Burgos, Valladolid, León, Plasencia, Madrid, Segovia, Astorga, Palencia, Toledo, Medina del Campo, Cuéllar, Talavera, Carrión, Sepúlveda, Ávila, Zamora, Avilés, Arévalo, Alcalá de Henares, Belorado, Buitrago, Guadalajara, Haro, Logroño, Olmedo, Sahagún, Soria, Salamanca, Oviedo, Alba de Tormes, and Lugo. Many towns cited only once or twice may also have been summoned regularly, while every town that belonged to the *hermandad* may not have been summoned to every meeting.

The geographical distribution of towns represented in the cortes was very uneven. Few Galician towns attended. The Asturian towns taking part in the cortes were concentrated along the coast and in the vicinity of Oviedo. The towns of León and Leonese Extremadura can be plotted on a straight line from León to Salamanca, with Badajoz and Jerez de los Caballeros quite isolated farther south. Several Castilian towns belonging to the *hermandad de las marismas* along the Bay of Biscay participated in the cortes, as did many others stretching along the Ebro river, or located in the vicinity of Burgos, Palencia, and Valladolid. Towns from Castilian Extremadura and the kingdom of Toledo attending the cortes were spread generally throughout that area, but did not extend much south of Toledo itself. Given the number of towns in Andalusia and Murcia, it is surprising that only Seville, Córdoba, Écija, Niebla, Murcia, Mula, and Lorca took part in the cortes.

Few towns held in lordship seem to have attended the cortes. As the Galician bishops often had lordship of their cities, this probably explains the paucity of Galician representation. In the vast area from the Tagus to the Guadalquivir, held in large part by the archbishop of Toledo or by the military orders, only Cáceres, Trujillo, and Villarreal seem to have participated. Piskorski is no doubt correct in contending that all cities and towns were summoned or were eligible to be summoned, provided they were independent of every lord and possessed their own municipal organization in direct dependence upon the king, but there is also evidence of some exceptions.[35]

Several seigneurial towns were among the fifty swearing to maintain the accord reached at San Esteban de Gormaz in 1187. Alfonso X summoned Orense, whose bishop was its lord, to render homage to his daughter in 1256 and to Sancho in 1278. Seigneurial towns also participated in the *hermandades* of 1295 (Palencia, Sigüenza, Uceda, Talamanca, Lugo, Brihuega, Alcalá) and 1315 (Palencia, Buitrago, Lugo, Sahagún, Orense, Oña, Santo Domingo de Silos). The fact that some received *cuadernos* (Palencia 1295, 1301, 1302; Buitrago 1305; Illescas 1302) suggests that they may have been summoned to the cortes. Palencia (1283, 1286, 1313) and Alcalá (1345, 1348) were the sites of meetings of the cortes or other assemblies. In 1331 Alfonso XI required Sigüenza to attend his cortes whenever he convened it, and in 1347 summoned Santiago de Compostela to the cortes of Alcalá. In each case, the bishop was lord. Hilda Grassotti concludes that the exceptional circumstances of the royal minorities resulted in the convocation of some seigneurial towns, but the evidence is not limited to those years. As several towns were episcopal sees held in lordship (Santiago, Palencia, Sigüenza, Lugo, Orense), or seigneurial towns held by bishops (Buitrago, Alcalá, Talamanca, Uceda, Brihuega, Illescas) or by monasteries (Oña, Sahagún, Santo Domingo de Silos), one might argue that in summoning them, the king wished to make the point that the crown's authority was preeminent. If he wished to summon seigneurial towns, he could, and did, but the data are insufficient to prove that this was undertaken regularly.[36]

Recognizing that conclusions about the number of towns represented at any given cortes are tentative without a definitive list of those who were summoned, the following figures may be suggested. A plenary cortes including towns from Castile, León, Extremadura, Toledo, Andalusia, and Murcia may have had as many as 180 towns in attendance, perhaps even 200. In the two instances when the cortes for Old Castile was held separately from León, Extremadura, and Toledo (Burgos and Medina del Campo 1302, and Valladolid and Medina del Campo 1318), the Castilian cortes might have included as many as seventy-eight towns, and the other cortes ninety-two. These figures probably represent the maximum number of towns present in any assembly; more than likely, there were fewer.

The number and status of urban representatives must now be considered. Fernando III declared in the cortes of Seville 1250 that whenever a town sent representatives to his court, either in response to his summons or on its own initiative, it should send no more than three or four, unless he explicitly asked for more.[37] In the cortes of Valladolid 1258 (art. 8) and Seville 1261 (art. 13), Alfonso X limited the number of representatives to two. While these texts are primarily concerned with litigation in the royal court, the king probably intended to apply similar limitations in the cortes. The *hermandad* of 1284, for example, specified that whenever the king wished "to hold cortes," each town should send two good men, the same number that would be sent to meetings of the *hermandad*.[38] There are, however, occasional examples of three, four, or more representatives from a single town. Burgos, for instance, sent seven representatives to the cortes of Valladolid 1295 and four to the cortes of Burgos 1315. Most towns sent two in 1315, but Ávila had sixteen—an obvious exception. If two is taken as the usual number, there could have been as many as 360 representatives in a plenary cortes of 180 towns. For the Castilian cortes of Burgos 1302, the number could have been 156, and for the cortes of León, Toledo, and Extremadura held at Medina del Campo in the same year, 184. These figures, of course, are speculative, but they do suggest the size of the urban contingent in the cortes.

Who were these representatives and what was their status? In the third quarter of the thirteenth century the term used most often to designate them was good men (*omnes bonos*), that is, honest, God-fearing men who abided by the law. The term does not always mean townsmen, but might also be used to refer to nobles or officials of the king's court. Early in the fourteenth century *personero* (the legal equivalent of procurator)[39] was often used interchangeably with *procurador*, but by the reign of Alfonso XI the latter had become customary.[40]

Representatives came to the cortes with proctorial letters. Alfonso X instructed the towns to send to the cortes of Seville 1281 their "procurators with *personerías complidas* to grant all that should be decided before him." As yet no letter specifically appointing procurators to serve in the cortes has been found, but the *Partidas* (III.18.98) included a letter of the town council of Seville, appointing its *personero* "to demand and to respond" in litigation, and promising to accept "as firm and stable" whatever he did in its name. Several other letters exist in which towns named *personeros* to represent them in court or to act otherwise for them. Letters naming procurators for the cortes certainly must have been composed in the same form.[41]

In 1295, for example, Lorca appointed three "special and general procurators and legitimate *personeros*," giving them "all our power fully" to adhere to the Murcian *hermandad* and pledging to observe whatever they agreed to. Salamanca, in 1304, gave full power to "two sufficient and abundant procurators" to swear to uphold the peace between Castile and Aragón. Not only in these instances, but surely also in the cortes, procurators were expected to have full power (*plena potestas, poder cumplido*) to bind their constituents in advance by whatever actions they might take. The crown's insistence on full powers was a safeguard against the possibility that a town might attempt later to repudiate its representatives.[42]

The letters of procuration, other than stating that the representatives were appointed by the municipal council, do not indicate how these representatives were chosen and seldom mention their social rank or official capacity. In the cortes of Seville 1250, Fernando III ordered that representatives should be suitable knights chosen from the town council. The *hermandad* of Medina del Campo in 1284 provided that the two good men sent by each town to the cortes should be "the best, the most competent, men above suspicion, who fear God and love the well-being of the realm." The *hermandad* of Valladolid in 1295 also determined to send "the best men of the place."[43]

Besides the knights, men of lesser rank also attended the cortes. Alfonso X sought the counsel of merchants and other good men at Jerez in 1268. Four knights from the chief cities, together with six good men from their dependent villages and smaller towns, were summoned to the cortes of Seville 1281; two knights, two good men, and four taxpayers (*pecheros*) would be summoned from the smaller towns. Several towns were represented in the *hermandad* of Valladolid in 1295 by their *alcaldes*, while others sent their scribes to the cortes of Burgos 1315.[44] Most often, procurators seem to have been members of the knightly class, who represented the interests of the urban aristocracy rather than of the simple freemen.[45]

In the cortes of Seville 1250, Fernando III required the towns to compensate their representatives by paying them one half a *maravedí* a day for the journey as far as Toledo, and one *maravedí* if they had to continue as far as Seville. Each man was entitled to bring three animals, whose value would be determined prior to the journey so the owner could be compensated if any of them died en route. Alfonso X repeated these instructions in 1256 and again in the cortes of Seville 1261.[46]

Abundant evidence shows that the towns perceived themselves as a distinctive element in society with common interests that set them apart from the nobility and the clergy. In addition to forming *hermandades* in defense of their rights, the towns took advantage of the cortes to bring their concerns to the king's attention. Their petitions reveal a continuing opposition to encroachments on municipal liberties by royal officials, nobles, and clergy. They also became aware that the king would be more amenable to their demands for reform when he needed their consent to taxation.

A European Perspective

The concept of estates eventually gave rise to various types of parliamentary assemblies in other countries. The federative character of the Crown of Aragón resulted in the convocation of separate assemblies in the states of Aragón, Catalonia, and Valencia, but not Majorca. Occasionally, as at Monzon in 1289, a general cortes was convened for all the constituent states of the Crown of Aragón, but that did not become customary.

As in Castile, the cortes of Portugal and Catalonia consisted of the bishops, nobles, and representatives of the towns. In Aragón, however, the barons and knights were organized separately, thereby creating four estates. With the intention of weakening the nobility, unsuccessful attempts were made in Catalonia and Valencia to divide them into two groups. Given the much smaller size of the other kingdoms, the number of towns represented was less than in Castile. About a dozen towns in Aragón, Catalonia, and Portugal sent their procurators (usually two or three in number) to the cortes.

In England, in view of the greater unity of the realm and its more compact size, a single parliament came into existence. By the reign of Edward III the lower clergy had dropped out, and the knights of the shires assembled with the burgesses of the towns to form the House of Commons, while the bishops, abbots, and barons formed the House of Lords. The kings of France, on the other hand, were only beginning to extend their authority over the complex of diverse provinces constituting their realm. Thus instead of one assembly embracing the entire kingdom, provincial assemblies of prelates, nobles, and towns came into being. In the reign of Philip VI, the assemblies of the estates of the great circumscriptions of Languedoil and Languedoc (usually meeting in Paris and Toulouse, respectively) began to take shape.

Now, it is time to look again at the Castilian cortes from the time that the king summoned it into being until it was brought to a conclusion.

4

The Cortes in Session

The Convocation of the Cortes

No day-by-day account of the proceedings in the cortes has come down to us, but reports in the chronicles and information drawn from documentary sources make it possible to reach some understanding of this vital aspect of the history of the cortes.

The first step in bringing the cortes to life was the royal summons. The king or the regents determined who should be summoned, as well as the time and place, and the business to be treated. Nonetheless, external forces could compel him to summon the cortes when he did not necessarily wish to do so. The nobles, for example, after negotiating with Alfonso X, asked him to summon the cortes to Burgos in 1272, and his council meeting at Córdoba in August 1281 urged him to convene the cortes to Seville to deal with his finances.[1]

Infante Juan and Juan Núñez de Lara, hoping to consolidate their influence over Fernando IV, suggested that he summon the cortes to Medina del Campo in 1302. When Infante Juan and Diego López de

Haro reached agreement concerning Vizcaya, it was decided to publish it in the cortes of Valladolid 1307. The nobles at Grijota in 1308 insisted that the cortes be convened at Burgos for an accounting of royal revenues. Maria de Molina and Infante Pedro assured the cortes of Palencia 1313 (art. 11 M) that if they failed to summon the cortes every two years, the prelates and other royal councillors would do so. The three regents convoked the cortes of Burgos 1315 so they could announce the unification of the regency. Alfonso XI tells us that he took counsel with the "prelates, magnates, knights, and good men of the towns who were with me in my court," concerning the convocation of the cortes of Madrid in 1329.[2] These instances show that there were times when the king called the cortes because others thought it would serve the interests of the crown (his council) or because it would be to their advantage (the nobles).

The nature of the summons is known not only from the preambles to some of the *cuadernos*, but also from several surviving letters of summons and occasional descriptions in the chronicles.[3] As Alfonso X indicated in *Cantiga* 386, the summons might be oral or written.[4] Individual letters of summons were most likely sent to the archbishops, bishops, magnates, masters of the military orders, and abbots of selected monasteries, but if they were resident in the royal court, they were perhaps summoned orally.

It is not at all clear how the *infanzones* and knights were summoned, but perhaps it was similar to the English practice described by King John (Magna Charta, art. 14) who promised to summon the lesser barons generally through his sheriffs and bailiffs. Perhaps the lesser nobility received a collective summons from royal *porteros* sent to different regions of the kingdom. Just as no one seems to have been overly troubled if the lesser English barons failed to appear, so it is likely that the absence of individual *infanzones* and knights was also overlooked. Letters of summons were also sent to cathedral chapters and to towns requiring them to send a specified number of representatives.

The cortes of Palencia 1313 (art. 11 M) made the point that those summoned had to attend, but they might offer a valid excuse of illness, imprisonment, conditions of travel (floods, snow), or other appropriate difficulties. Archbishop Juan of Toledo excused himself from attending the cortes of Valladolid 1321 because of the discomfort that he suffered in excessive heat. Infante Fadrique, master of Santiago, asked Pedro the

Cruel's permission not to attend the cortes of Valladolid in 1351. If one were unable to attend, one might send a representative, as Gonzalo Pérez Pereira, commander of the Hospital in Spain, did when he appointed Juan Núñez, commander of Consuegra, to attend the cortes of Burgos 1269 in representation of the Priory of Castile and León.[5] Defiance of the summons was bound to provoke the *ira regis* and its attendant penalties. According to the *Espéculo* (III.1.1), a magnate who failed to respond would lose whatever he held from the king, while others of lesser rank would be fined 500 *maravedís*. The fine for greater towns was set at 1,000 *maravedís*, but for smaller ones it would be determined according to their means. In *Cantiga* 386 (line 18) Alfonso X stressed that everyone came to the cortes of Seville 1281 so as not to incur his anger.[6]

Yet when Fernando IV summoned the first cortes of his majority to Medina del Campo in April 1302, most of the towns questioned the influence of Infante Juan and Juan Núñez de Lara and inquired of Maria de Molina whether they should attend. She ordered them to do so, lest their refusal cause her son to lose his kingdom. The citizens of Medina del Campo were also reluctant to open their gates to the king and the cortes, but Maria, realizing that any disobedience would diminish his sovereignty, insisted that they do so.[7]

Some examples of letters of summons will illustrate the process of convoking an assembly. Alfonso X, on 14 December 1255, required Orense to send three good men to "wherever I may be," with a letter sealed with the seal of the municipal council and authorizing them to swear allegiance to his daughter, Berenguela. Required to appear on the first Sunday after receipt of the summons before the feast of Candlemas (2 February), they came to Vitoria early in the new year, though the bishop and chapter of Orense protested on the grounds that the bishop held the town in lordship (31 January 1256). Sánchez Albornoz declared that this was "the first known letter of summons to the cortes in Castile," but there is no indication that the king intended to hold the cortes. The fact that the archbishop and chapter of Santiago pledged homage at San Esteban de Gormaz on 10 February gives added emphasis to this point. Twenty years later (30 April 1276) the king ordered Salamanca to send two good men to Burgos to recognize Sancho as heir to the throne; although this text is no longer extant, it would seem to be the first known letter of summons to a cortes.[8]

Infante Sancho issued several summonses on his father's behalf in

1279. Although the Castilian towns had been ordered to send their good men to Valladolid on the feast of St. Luke (18 October) concerning matters the papal legate had brought to the king's attention, few townsmen appeared. Those that did so insisted that they could give no reply "at least until the other good men of the towns of Castile were present." Thereupon, on 17 November, Sancho ordered Burgos to send two good men with a *carta de personería* saying that "you will grant and hold firmly all that they will do with me" at Salamanca on 1 December next, concerning "the very great service of God and the king and myself and the well-being of the land." On 28 November he postponed the meeting until 10 December. As the king had decided to meet the towns at Badajoz, Sancho commanded Burgos to provide its good men with expenses for the journey from Salamanca to Badajoz, and with a *carta de personería* saying that "you will hold firmly all that they will do with the king and with me, and you will send a blank letter sealed with your pendant seal to affirm all the things that will be done there, and in this you will make no excuse." Later, after the rupture with his father, Sancho ordered the cathedral chapter of León "to choose among yourselves good, sensible men who shall be with me at Palencia . . . with a *carta de personería* sealed with your seal, so that whatever they do and accord with us in this matter you will hold firmly." [9]

Fernando IV stated that he had commanded the men of Avilés to send two good men with a *carta de personería* to the cortes of Medina del Campo 1305, to discuss "many things that are to the service of God and myself, and to the benefit of all the realm." Alfonso XI told Murcia on 15 August 1325 to send its procurators with credentials and full power (*poder complido*) to Valladolid without delay "to agree and to ordain and to do with me all those things that will be to my service, the safeguarding of my sovereignty and the well-being of my kingdom." A similar letter was sent to Murcia on 15 August 1328, convoking the cortes to Burgos on 30 September, but it did not meet. Finally, on 25 October 1347 the king summoned the city of Santiago to send two good men with full powers to Alcalá de Henares where he planned to hold the cortes in mid-December, "to do and to grant all those things that we will determine there for our service and advantage and for the protection of the realm." [10]

Technically only the last three documents of Alfonso XI were letters of summons to the cortes, but there is no reason to doubt that the form was essentially the same, whether the meeting was a cortes or another type of assembly. The differences between Infante Sancho's summonses and those of Alfonso XI are not substantial. The summons ordered the designation of representatives to be present at the place of meeting at an appointed time, bearing a letter of procuration giving them full power to act and to bind their constituents. The business to be transacted was usually described only in very general terms, such as the service of God, the king, and the kingdom. That did not allow the towns, unless they had information from unofficial sources, to plan their response in advance. In effect, they had to depend upon the good judgment of their representatives.

These few examples do not permit a definitive judgment as to the notice given to the towns prior to the opening of the cortes. When Infante Sancho summoned Burgos on 17 November to be at Salamanca on 1 December, the advance notice was about two weeks. His summons to the chapter of León on 12 October 1283 to appear at Palencia on 1 November also allowed two weeks. Burgos and León were close to the central part of the kingdom where assemblies were normally held, and two weeks was evidently deemed adequate for the selection of representatives and the journey to Salamanca or Palencia. Alfonso XI, on the other hand, gave Murcia about a month and a half's advance notice from his summons of 15 August 1328 to 30 September when the cortes was to begin. His summons to Santiago on 26 October 1347 also allowed about a month and a half for the city to choose its representatives and send them to Alcalá by mid-December. Both Murcia and Santiago were at the extremes of the kingdom and would need a longer preparation time.

Once the participants assembled in the cortes, it is probable that they had to present their letters of summons and procurations to the chancery officials for verification. The only documentary indication of this is a stipulation of the cortes of Valladolid 1312 (art. 8) forbidding royal scribes to exact any fees for "recording *personerías*."

Frequency, Location, and Duration

The cortes was convened with a high degree of frequency, a sign of its importance in the public life of the realm. While meetings were often held at critical times, some kings felt strong enough to ignore the cortes. Fernando III's cortes of Seville 1250 was intended to resolve many issues left in abeyance during the siege of Seville. Alfonso X, in a reign of thirty-two years, summoned the plenary cortes at least thirteen times, while Sancho IV convened five plenary cortes in eleven years, four of which were held in the first four years of his reign. In the seventeen-year reign of Fernando IV, the cortes met in plenary session nine times and five times in regional cortes. The cortes met almost every year during his reign, the longest interval between meetings occurring from 1309 to 1312. In the cortes of Palencia 1313 (art. 11, 16 M) Maria de Molina and Infante Pedro pledged to summon the cortes every two years to report on their conduct as regents. For the thirty-eight years of Alfonso XI's reign, eight plenary and two regional cortes were convened, though nineteen years elapsed between the cortes of Madrid 1329 and Alcalá 1348. Thus in the century from the cortes of Seville 1250 to the death of Alfonso XI, the cortes was convoked in plenary or regional sessions forty-two times, or on the average of one every 2.8 years.

Sessions were held at sites easily accessible to the great towns. Indeed, Maria de Molina and Infante Pedro promised at Palencia 1313 (art. 11 M) to hold the cortes in "a convenient place." The cortes of Medina del Campo 1318 (art. 1) stipulated that it should be wherever the king was. Most assemblies were held in the towns of Old Castile and Extremadura, but Seville, especially in the reign of Alfonso X, was occasionally host to the cortes. No assemblies were convoked for Asturias, Galicia, or other remote regions. The customary sites were Valladolid (14 times), Burgos (11), Seville (3), Medina del Campo (3), Toledo (2), Palencia (2), Madrid (2), and once each in Segovia, Haro, Cuéllar, Zamora, and Alcalá de Henares. Besides the cortes, other assemblies were held in many of these towns, as well as in Jerez, Peñafiel, Ávila, Almagro, León, and Llerena.

The royal palace, cathedral, or monastic cloister usually served as the place of assembly. In 1272, for example, Alfonso X agreed to the demand of the nobility that the cortes meet in the Hospital of Burgos, adjacent to the monastery of Las Huelgas just outside the city walls. Bishops Fernando of Burgos and Juan of Palencia testified that the deposition of Alfonso X took place in the royal palace of Valladolid in 1282. In the cortes of Palencia 1313 the supporters of Infante Juan gathered in the monastery of San Pablo, while those favoring Maria de Molina and Infante Pedro met in the monastery of San Francisco.[11]

It is difficult to determine the length of the sessions of the cortes.

The usual dates for convocation were probably on or about the principal festivals of the year—Michaelmas (29 September), Martinmas (11 November), Christmas, the Circumcision (1 January), Epiphany (6 January), Candlemas (2 February), Easter, Pentecost, St. John's Day (24 June), and the Assumption (15 August). In only a few instances is there mention of a specific date of convocation. The *cuadernos*, though they were not necessarily dated on the final day of the assembly, give some indication when the essential business of the cortes was concluded.

The date of the earliest *cuaderno* of the cortes of Seville 1252 is 6 October; thus it is possible that it was convoked at Michaelmas. The January dates of the *cuadernos* of the cortes of Valladolid 1258 and Seville 1261 suggest convocation at Christmas, the Circumcision, or the Epiphany. The cortes of Burgos 1272 was convened at Michaelmas and perhaps concluded its business at Martinmas. The cortes of Seville 1281 was to meet at Martinmas; Infante Sancho's appearance at Córdoba on 27 December indicates that the meeting was over by that time.[12]

The *hermandad* meeting at Medina del Campo in September 1284 expected Sancho IV to call the cortes to Valladolid at Martinmas; a royal charter issued on 5 December during the cortes suggests that he did so.[13] The 2 December date of the *cuaderno* of Palencia 1286 implies that the cortes was also convened at Martinmas. The cortes of Haro 1288, held while the king was besieging Haro from 20 June to 2 August, may have been summoned for St. John's Day; the *cuaderno* was dated 13 August.

The convocation of the cortes of Valladolid 1295 was set for St. John's Day and the *cuaderno* was dated 7 August. The regents and Fernando IV, when he came of age, seem to have favored spring convocation around Easter and Pentecost. According to the royal chronicle, the cortes of Valladolid 1299 and 1300, Burgos 1301, Medina del Campo 1302, and Valladolid 1307 and 1312 were all summoned in April.[14]

Although Maria de Molina and Infante Pedro promised to convene the cortes every two years between Michaelmas and All Saints' (Palencia 1313, art. 11 M), the cortes held during the minority of Alfonso XI seem to have been summoned around Easter or St. John's Day.[15] When he reached his majority, he complained on 15 August 1325 that "a very great time" had passed since the date when the cortes of Valladolid was supposed to begin. His summons may have been misinterpreted because Juan Manuel expected to give up the regency at Michaelmas. That date may mark the beginning of the cortes of Valladolid, as the *cuadernos* were dated 12 December. The king summoned the cortes of Alcalá 1348 for mid-December 1347, but his presence there is documented only from late January. The Ordinance is dated 28 February and the *cuadernos* 8 March.[16]

These dates suggest that the cortes lasted for only a few days (e.g., from 29 September to 6 October 1252), or for several weeks (29 September to 11 November 1272), or for several months (29 September to 12 December 1325, or 25 January to 8 March 1348), depending on the extent of the business to be transacted.

At best, one can only estimate the duration of any given cortes and suggest the season when it was likely to have been summoned to meet in plenary session. The most popular period for convocation was the Easter season, from the beginning of Lent until Pentecost, when the cortes met nineteen times.[17] Next were St. John's Day (six times), Circumcision/Epiphany (five times), Martinmas (four times),[18] twice each at Pentecost, Michaelmas, and Candlemas, and once each at the Assumption and Christmas.[19]

Plenary sessions attended by prelates, magnates, and townsmen probably lasted several days, during which the petitions and responses were prepared and taxes were voted. That done, this phase of the cortes was finished, and most of the townsmen departed for home, except for those who wished to present petitions on behalf of individual towns or respond to litigation. Towns were not likely to subsidize their procurators to remain at the cortes for months at a time, nor would the procurators, who had personal affairs to attend to, wish to absent themselves from home for extended periods. In sum, the principal business of the cortes was probably settled in several days or a week, while other related matters were resolved in the weeks following dissolution of the assembly.

Lodging and Security

The difficulty of providing suitable lodgings for the comparatively large numbers of people attending the cortes was serious and probably aroused the ill will of the citizens of the town where the meeting was held. The royal lodging master apparently requisitioned rooms from canons, monks, and townspeople, who often did not welcome the intrusion.

Alfonso X declared that the prelates, abbots, magnates, knights, and townsmen attending the cortes of Toledo 1259 should have good lodgings and commanded the knights and good men of the city to provide the best that they had. Once the cortes was over, he assured the citizenry on 6 February 1260 that in the future nothing would be done contrary to their *fueros*, which stated that they did not have to lodge anyone without their consent. He had already given such guarantees to the canons of Toledo on 29 December 1259. Following the cortes of Seville (1261, 1281), Jerez (1268), and Burgos (1272), similar pledges were made to the people of Seville (24 March 1261), the canons of Córdoba (30 May 1261), the people of Jerez (28 June 1268) and Burgos (27 September 1273), and the canons of Seville (22 August 1284). Lodgers were expected to pay rent and were forbidden to steal clothing or other goods from householders.[20]

In every instance, the promise was given after the fact, so that it would seem that the people of the city where the cortes was held had to make room and endure the inevitable inconveniences. Fernando IV pledged in the cortes of Medina del Campo 1302 (art. 7 E, 9 L) to provide good lodgings, and at Valladolid 1312 (art. 37) he assured townsmen coming to his court that they would be suitably housed.

The principle that all those who came to the king's court should enjoy his protection was stated in the *Espéculo* (II.14.2−3), the *Fuero real* (II.3.8), and the *Siete Partidas* (II.16.1−4). This guarantee extended to the journey to and from the royal court. That the principle also applied to those attending the cortes is self-evident. When Alfonso X convoked the cortes of Burgos 1272, the nobles, expressing fear for their safety, refused to enter the city unless he granted them a truce and allowed them to bear arms. He declared that this was "quite contrary to reason, since all men were secure in his court and had no need for a truce nor to bear arms"; but as they persisted, he and "all the men of the realm" went to meet the magnates at the Hospital of Burgos outside the walls.[21]

The *hermandad* of 1295 (art. 16 L, 14 E) guaranteed the security of those attending its meetings, including the three weeks before and after. Fernando IV confirmed this principle, which was repeated by the *hermandad* of Carrión 1317 (art. 56). Because the security of those coming to the cortes had been threatened during the recent civil wars, the king assured the cortes of Valladolid 1300 (art. 22) and Medina del Campo 1302 (art. 7 E, 9 L) that he would uphold it. The cortes of Medina del Campo 1305 (art. 2 E, 5 C, 6 L) asked him to impose the penalties of death, confiscation, and disinheritance on anyone who killed another person attending the cortes.[22]

When Infantes Juan and Pedro came to the cortes of Palencia 1313, each brought a large body of troops to intimidate his opposition. In order to allow the prelates and procurators of the towns the freedom to choose a regent, Maria de Molina proposed that all the contenders should withdraw to the surrounding suburbs. The memory of such disorders prompted Alfonso XI, when he came of age, to enact an ordinance at Medina del Campo (October 1328) guaranteeing the security of every man "while the cortes that the king now commands to assemble, is assembling, and is concluded"; anyone found guilty of murder, robbery, or theft would suffer the death penalty. This was repeated in the cortes of Madrid 1329 (art. 10).[23]

The Speech from the Throne

Once the participants were assembled, the king met with them in a plenary session to discuss the reasons for convocation. In *Cantiga* 386, Alfonso X related that after convening the cortes of Seville 1281, he "told them why he had caused them to come by word and by writ." As the royal chronicle elaborated, he requested funds for the war with the Moors, pointing to his treasury depleted by the conquest of Murcia, the Moroccan invasion, and the debasement of the coinage. Justifying her son's rights to the throne, Maria de Molina reminded the cortes of Valladolid 1295 that he bore the name of his great-grandfather, Fernando III, whom all knew to have been a good king. Similarly, Alfonso XI announced to the cortes of Valladolid 1325 that, having terminated his minority and dismissed his regents, he was now assuming responsibility for directing his own affairs.[24]

In the speech from the throne the king or regent discussed "the estate of the realm," "the improvement of the estate of the realm," or the necessity to do those things that would redound to the service of God, the king, and the well-being of the realm. In the preamble to the *cuadernos* of Valladolid 1295, Fernando IV, no doubt echoing remarks made by his mother to the entire cortes, expressed the desire to show favor to

his people because "we know that it is to the service of God and our-
selves and to the very great benefit of all our kingdoms and to the improvement of the estate of all our realms." Similar sentiments were
voiced on many other occasions.[25]

In more specific terms the king might refer to projects that were
especially dear to him, for example, "the affair of the empire" (Toledo
1259, Burgos 1272, 1274), "the affair of Africa" (Seville 1261), the administration and defense of the frontier (Burgos 1269, 1277), or preparations for war against the Moors (Burgos 1276, Seville 1281, Madrid
1309, Valladolid 1312).[26] In other instances, the theme was the duty to
render homage to the heir to the throne (Toledo 1254, Burgos 1276,
Segovia 1278) or the shortage of goods and the high cost of living
(Jerez 1268).[27] Most often the king acknowledged the need to correct
abuses. In the cortes of Seville 1252, Alfonso X admitted that certain
agreements made by his predecessors had not been observed due to the
pressure of war, and he declared that he was now prepared to confirm
them. Sancho IV similarly informed the cortes of Valladolid 1293 of his
desire to reward his people for previous services and asked to hear their
grievances. In the cortes of Madrid 1329, Alfonso XI announced that he
wished to do justice to all, to improve the estate of his household and of
his realms, and to correct the many abuses that had occurred since the
death of his father.[28]

The Response of the Estates

Whether each of the estates made an immediate response to
the royal discourse is uncertain, though it seems highly probable. As
primate of Spain, the archbishop of Toledo was the logical spokesman
for the clergy. Archbishop Gonzalo's protest in the cortes of Valladolid
1295 that he had not been called to council to discuss "the affairs of the
realm" indicates that he had expected to play that role. In the cortes of
Medina del Campo 1302, the archbishop protested any attempt to tax
ecclesiastical vassals.[29]

The lord of Lara came to be acknowledged as the respondent for
the nobility. When Alfonso X requested advice concerning the disposition of the Algarbe, Nuño González de Lara was the first member of his
council to reply. Juan Núñez de Lara had a preeminent position among
the nobility during the reigns of Sancho IV and Fernando IV, but there

is no evidence from this period that affirms positively that the house of Lara had the prerogative of responding to the king on behalf of the nobles. In 1373, however, Maria de Lara, sister of Juan Núñez, lord of Vizcaya, reminded Enrique II of the family's traditional right, stating that "the lord of Lara always speaks in the cortes for the nobles of Castile." The precedent for that right was apparently of long standing.[30]

Evidence that a speaker was designated to respond in the name of the towns comes from a dispute between Burgos and Toledo in the cortes of Alcalá de Henares 1348. Pedro López de Ayala related that a similar controversy arose in the cortes of Valladolid 1351, and that King Pedro the Cruel, on taking counsel, discovered that the issue had been debated three years before. At that time Juan Núñez de Lara upheld the right of the procurators of Burgos to speak first because "it is the head of Castile." Juan Manuel, on the contrary, supported Toledo's claims as "the head of Spain." The division among the magnates brought the business of the cortes to a halt until Alfonso XI resolved the argument by declaring that "the men of Toledo will do all that I command them, and so I speak for them; therefore, let Burgos speak." This was probably a traditional prerogative of Burgos, but Toledo, mindful of its ancient status as the seat of the Visigothic monarchy, apparently decided to make a bid for supremacy. It is unknown who spoke for the Leonese and Extremadurans when they met, but it is likely that León claimed that right in a Leonese cortes. Alfonso XI, in reply to the demands of the assembly of León 1345 (art. 5, 32), promised to give León precedence over Toledo in the royal intitulation in charters addressed to León.[31]

The speakers probably thanked the king, promising to weigh his remarks carefully and to return with a more specific reply to his proposals. When Alfonso X requested counsel concerning the projected African crusade, the cortes of Seville 1261 responded well and loyally, like true vassals. So, too, the cortes of Valladolid 1325 expressed its pleasure that Alfonso XI had come of age and intended to do justice and defend his realm against the Moors.[32]

While there is no specific evidence of any curtailment of freedom of speech in the cortes, both the *Espéculo* (II.1.10, II.2.1–6) and the *Partidas* (II.13.17–18) prescribed the decorum that ought to prevail in the royal court. No one should contradict the king, but if he was in error he should be informed discreetly so that he could make the necessary correction. When the prelates in the cortes of Burgos 1272 made demands "such as were not accustomed to be granted by other kings," Alfonso X became so angry that he threatened to expel them from the realm. In *Cantiga* 386 he remarked that after he had finished speaking to the cortes of Seville 1281, all present strongly approved and cursed anyone who went contrary to his command. He then granted the petitions that were rightfully presented, noting that "it is a strange thing for one to demand something wrongfully from his lord." The royal chronicle related, however, that the cortes was intimidated and responded to his proposals "more out of fear than love," telling him that he should do what he thought best. Not daring to speak their minds, the townsmen then appealed to Infante Sancho to intercede for them.[33]

The Presentation of Petitions

Once the opening formalities were concluded, the cortes got down to the business at hand. Brief comments in the preambles to the *cuadernos* and in the chronicles encapsulate the course of the proceedings but do not describe them in detail. Without being bound to a rigid procedure, the cortes accomplished its work in several ways, depending on the issues at hand. In some instances, debate seems to have taken place in a general session. In the cortes of Burgos 1276, called to resolve the dispute over the succession, Juan Núñez de Lara and his brother Nuño upheld the claims of Alfonso de la Cerda, while Infante Fadrique and Lope Díaz de Haro defended Sancho's rights. Some of the prelates and townsmen may also have expressed their views.[34]

Most often each estate assembled separately to consider matters that directly affected its interests. The *cuadernos* for the reign of Alfonso X do not distinguish the role of individual estates in this respect. The agreement embodied in the *cuaderno* of the cortes of Seville 1252 was likely prepared by his council, but it is not clear whether the estates were consulted individually or in a general session. The king acknowledged the initiative of the estates in the cortes of Valladolid 1258, when he approved "what they set down." In a like manner, the cortes of Seville 1261 "reached agreement" concerning the need for redress. The detailed list of wages and prices enacted at Jerez 1268 could only have been drawn up by a committee, perhaps consisting of merchants and members of the council who then presented their work to the entire assembly.[35]

Sancho IV stated that he asked the townsmen to tell him their grievances, but the presentation of petitions asking for redress presupposes that they first consulted among themselves. Thus in the cortes of Palencia 1286 they "took counsel and showed me those things about which they agreed to ask my favor." At Valladolid 1293 "they all came to agreement among themselves" and presented their grievances. In at least one instance, the townsmen received unexpected assistance in the preparation of their petitions. Maria de Molina, fearing that the towns in the cortes of Valladolid 1307 might undermine her son's already weak position, offered to help them draft petitions that would further "the service of God, the king, and the well-being of the entire realm." Recognizing "that she was the one who sought the good of the whole realm," they acquiesced.[36]

The repetition of articles found in earlier *cuadernos*, often in precisely the same words, demonstrates that the townsmen consulted the records of previous cortes in preparing their petitions. In those instances when separate *cuadernos* were drawn up for the different realms (Valladolid 1293 and Medina del Campo 1305), it is apparent that representatives from each kingdom met separately to draft their proposals; but the similarities of their respective texts reveal that they also communicated with one another. There is little evidence, on the other hand, of consultation with the nobility or the prelates.[37]

Once drafted, the petitions were presented to the king, who sought advice before responding. Thus Alfonso X consulted with the archbishop of Seville, the bishops, magnates, masters, and other men of the orders who were with him at Seville in 1264. Four years later at Jerez he took counsel with infantes, prelates, magnates, merchants, and other good men. In the cortes of Burgos 1272, however, he appointed a committee consisting of Queen Violante, Infante Fadrique, six magnates, four knights, four bishops, four clerics, five Franciscans and Dominicans, and seventeen townsmen to attend to the petitions of the nobles and prelates (and perhaps of the towns as well).[38]

Maria de Molina's exclusion of Archbishop Gonzalo of Toledo and the magnates from consideration of the petitions presented by the towns in Valladolid 1295 drew forth a strong protest from the primate, and Juan Núñez de Lara left the cortes in anger. Maria personally heard the petitions of the towns from morning until mid-afternoon, eliciting praise for her diligence. She was equally assiduous in the cortes of Cuéllar 1297. Together with Infante Juan and other good men appointed by Fernando IV in the cortes of Valladolid 1307, she attended to petitions for several days in the chapel in the houses of the Magdalena.[39]

The ordinary procedure probably required the submission of petitions to those designated to receive them. A committee such as those headed by Queen Violante in 1272 and by Maria de Molina in 1307 likely was given the responsibility of preparing an appropriate response on the king's behalf. The cortes of Valladolid 1295 determined that general affairs should be considered first and granted to all in common, and then the petitions of individual towns would be considered. General and special petitions were also treated separately by the cortes of Medina del Campo 1305. Whether this procedure was always followed is unknown, but it emphasizes that the townsmen, besides presenting general petitions for the good of the whole, also took advantage of their attendance at the cortes to transact business primarily of benefit to their own towns. They might seek confirmation of privileges or represent their towns in litigation before the royal court. Much of this business was probably resolved after the plenary sessions were concluded and most of the participants had departed.[40]

At times the nobles and prelates also presented petitions. Whether the demands put forward by the nobility in the cortes of Burgos 1272 were in written or oral form is uncertain, but the king chose to respond orally. He conducted himself so well in his point-by-point discussion that "all those present realized that he was in the right and in accord with law" and that the nobles were "making an uproar without reason." The committee headed by Queen Violante delivered a report (the text in the royal chronicle beginning "estas son las cosas") concerning these demands after the cortes had been dissolved. Although Alfonso X accepted the committee's recommendations, the nobles were dissatisfied and gave a written statement to Infante Manuel to present to the king. Alfonso X was loath to accept it, but on the urging of his council he eventually did. After a meeting with the magnates at Almagro, a final resolution of the dispute was recorded at Toledo on 28 March 1273. In this instance the initial demands were made in the cortes, but the subsequent debate and presentation of additional demands took place after the dissolution of the cortes.[41]

The nobles also challenged Fernando IV in a meeting at Palencia in 1311, making "very strong demands upon him." The agreement reached on 28 October was later incorporated into the ordinance promulgated in the cortes of Valladolid 1312. The king's council no doubt consulted the nobles assembled at Burgos before preparing the ordinance that Alfonso XI enacted in May 1338, and later included in the Ordinance of Alcalá 1348 (XXIX – XXXI).[42]

Queen Violante and her committee were also charged with the duty of replying to the demands made by the prelates in the cortes of Burgos 1272, but a definitive response was not forthcoming until Infante Fernando's assembly at Peñafiel in 1275. The prelates also presented petitions in the cortes of Valladolid 1295, 1307, 1325, and Burgos 1315. In the cortes of Burgos 1315 (art. 1 P), Alfonso XI confirmed the pact concluded by the bishops and Fernando IV at Palencia in March 1311. Alfonso XI also responded to ecclesiastical petitions at Valladolid 1325 and met the bishops again at Medina del Campo in July 1326 to resolve unfinished business.[43]

Thus it would seem that while the petitions of the towns were usually considered in the cortes, those of the nobles and prelates might be presented in the cortes, but settled later, or a resolution might be reached outside the cortes, and then confirmed during the next cortes.

The Voting of Taxes

The townsmen (and sometimes the prelates) also had to determine their reply to the king's request for taxes. Although Roger Merriman states that the towns never made the voting of taxes dependent on redress of grievances, there is good reason to doubt that this was true.[44] Both the townsmen and the prelates had ample opportunity to discover that they could demand a *quid pro quo* from the king. When Alfonso X pressed the cortes of Seville 1261 for the means to carry out his proposed expedition to Africa, he was asked to correct abuses. The cortes may have consented to a tax levy, but the evidence is not explicit. Moreover, the concession of a tax in the cortes of Burgos 1272 to enable Alfonso to make his journey to the empire probably was given in return for his confirmation of the traditional *fueros*. In the cortes of Seville 1281 he apparently agreed to abandon the practice of conducting inquests into taxes past due, in return for consent to his proposal concerning the coinage.[45] Given Maria de Molina's favorable response to their petitions, the towns in the cortes of Valladolid 1295 agreed to a *moneda forera,* even though a full seven years had not elapsed since the previous grant. In a like manner, once the petitions had been heard, the cortes of Cuéllar 1297 consented to a tax. The order of business described by the royal chronicle also implies that the cortes of Valladolid 1307 agreed to a subsidy after the king responded to petitions.[46] This may not always have been the case, but considering that a recurrent theme in the *cuadernos* of the royal minorities was the need to restore justice and prosperity to an impoverished kingdom, it would seem that the cortes insisted often enough that reforms and consent to a subsidy were mutually dependent. Unless the king or the regents promised to govern rightly, they could not expect the cortes to agree blindly to a levy of taxes.

The Conclusion of the Cortes

Consent to taxes probably was given in a plenary session when ordinances were also promulgated. Appearing in the royal palace before the cortes of Valladolid 1307, Fernando IV, with the "counsel of the queen his mother, the infantes, prelates, magnates, masters, *infanzones,* and knights," announced his reply to the petitions. The text of the *cuaderno* embodying the petitions and responses was read to the assembly.[47] Copies of the *cuadernos,* dated when each one was finished, rather than on the day of the final session, were prepared by chancery clerks for distribution to towns, monasteries, bishops, and nobles. The king usually agreed that the *cuadernos* should be issued without payment of a chancery fee.[48]

In *Cantiga* 386, Alfonso X tells us that while charters were being drawn up during the cortes of Seville 1281, he invited the entire assembly to a banquet. Seeing the multitudes who were there, the royal stewards worried that there would not be enough fish to feed them all. Undaunted, the king told them to place their hopes in the Virgin Mary, and to go to the royal canals, where they found four ships loaded with fish. Consequently all were fed in abundance to the great joy of the king, who praised the Virgin who had again shown her favor to him.[49]

Alfonso X's successors perhaps did not imitate this extravagance, but they surely convened final plenary sessions not only for official purposes, but also to thank the assembly for its labors. That done, permission was granted for all to withdraw; without it, no one was free to

leave. While many then set out on the homeward journey, others probably remained to take care of private business.

A European Perspective

Evidence from France and England as well as other peninsular
realms reveals certain similarities in the processes of convening parliamentary assemblies. Edward I of England, for example, required the
sheriffs to cause the election of two knights from each shire and two
citizens from each city to come, with "full and sufficient" authority, to
the parliament of 1295, "to do whatever in the aforesaid matters may be
ordained by common counsel." Jaime II summoned Huesca in 1301 to
send "your syndics and procurators . . . with full authority and free
power" to the cortes of Zaragoza, "to treat, consent, do, and confirm
each and every thing that will be ordained in the said cortes." [50]

The idea of frequent convocation was also emphasized. Pedro III,
meeting with the estates in Aragón, Valencia, and Catalonia in 1283,
promised to convene the cortes annually. Four years later Alfonso III
reiterated this pledge in the Aragonese cortes of Zaragoza. Finding it
difficult to observe these promises, Jaime II informed the corts of Barcelona (and Valencia) in 1301 that he would hold the assembly every
three years. In 1307 he told the Aragonese cortes of Alagón that he
would convoke them every two years where it was convenient, rather
than in Zaragoza, as his predecessors had promised. In the course of his
reign of twenty-seven years he held the Catalan corts eleven times and
the Aragonese nearly as often. Pedro IV convened the Catalans thirty
times in fifty-one years. [51]

The Portuguese cortes, on the other hand, met rather infrequently.
In the century from 1248 to 1357 Afonso III held only three cortes,
Dinis, five or six, and Afonso IV only four. Not until 1385 did the Portuguese request an annual cortes. The French estates were not organized strongly enough to ask for an annual convocation, but in England
the demand was put forward in the Ordinances of 1311 and in the parliament of 1330. Perhaps due to his continual need for money, Edward
III summoned forty-eight parliaments in fifty years.

5

The Cortes and the Kingly Office

The Legal Foundations

Juan Manuel remarked that kings often displayed their magnificence by assembling the cortes, and the *Partidas* (II.5.5) noted that on great feast days "when they held their cortes," kings wore golden crowns encrusted with precious stones.[1] No occasion was more solemn than when the transfer of royal power was celebrated. Updating the Visigothic Code, the *Partidas* (II.13.19) declared that upon the death of a king, "the prelates, other magnates, masters of the orders, and good men of the cities and great towns" should come to bury him and to recognize his successor. If he had no adult heirs and had not appointed a regent, "all the great men of the realm" should choose a guardian, "because the affair of the king touches all and all have a part there." The new king, as well as the "prelates, magnates, noble knights, and good men of the cities and towns" should pledge to defend the unity of the realm, because it was the ancient custom that it should never be divided or alienated. If all could not assemble to pledge homage, they could do so in each town. The king, in turn, would swear to uphold all the laws and customs of the realm.[2]

Succession to the Throne

These principles more than likely reflected thirteenth- and early fourteenth-century practice. Enrique I, for example, was recognized in the *curia* of Burgos 1214 by prelates, nobles, and "people of the cities." Upon his death in 1217, the Castilian nobility and "the chief men of Extremadura" offered the crown to his sister Berenguela at Valladolid, but she yielded her rights to her son, Fernando III. "All who were present, both the magnates and the people of the cities and other towns," pledged homage to him, and he swore to uphold the laws of the land.[3]

Fernando III succeeded his father, Alfonso IX of León, in 1230, settling the claims of his half-sisters on 11 December in an assembly at Benavente attended by the archbishops of Toledo and Compostela as well as many barons and townsmen. Whether the Castilian towns participated is uncertain, so it is best described as a Leonese *curia*, rather than as the first *curia plena* of a reunited Castile and León.[4]

Alfonso X probably received a pledge of allegiance from the cortes of Seville 1252, and perhaps crowned himself in the cortes of Toledo two years later. The poet Gil Pérez Conde alluded to this when he recorded an instance "in Toledo when you took the crown there."[5] Sancho IV was also crowned in Toledo (in 1284), but it does not seem that he summoned the cortes to witness the ceremony. Mindful of Toledo's role as the seat of the royal and imperial traditions, and perhaps recalling his father's example, Sancho IV commanded that all his successors be crowned there. His first cortes held at Valladolid at Martinmas 1284 probably swore allegiance to him.[6]

Fernando IV was acclaimed in the cathedral of Toledo in 1295 and swore to uphold the laws, but there is no mention of his coronation. As the validity of Sancho IV's marriage to Maria and the consequent legitimacy of their children were in question, the king's uncle, Juan, revived his claims to the throne, and Alfonso de la Cerda continued to maintain his. Intent on securing the throne for her son, Maria de Molina summoned the cortes to meet at Valladolid on St. John's Day, 24 June 1295.[7]

Fearful of disorder, the towns began to form *hermandades* in support of Fernando IV, and in defense of their liberties. The Castilian towns gathered at Burgos on 6 July; the Leonese and Galicians followed suit at Valladolid on 12 July, as did the towns of Castilian Extremadura and the archbishopric of Toledo on 3 August. The Castilian, Leonese, and Galician towns also subscribed to this last pact. The three texts are quite similar, though there are some significant differences. Recalling many injustices suffered under Alfonso X and Sancho IV, the towns declared their intention to defend their *fueros*, even if it meant opposing the king when he failed to amend abuses. The three associations planned to meet annually on Trinity Sunday—the Castilians at Burgos, the Leonese at León, and the Extremadurans at Alcalá de Henares.[8]

When the cortes opened (probably in early July), Maria de Molina urged the towns to acknowledge her son, pointedly recalling that he was named for his great-grandfather Fernando III, a just and honest king. Although Aparicio Martínez of León tried to persuade them to recognize Infante Juan, the towns declared that they would accept Fernando IV and no other.[9]

Even though the cortes and the Andalusian and Murcian *hermandades* gave their allegiance to Fernando IV,[10] Infante Juan and Alfonso de la Cerda, backed by Portugal and Aragón, continued to challenge him. They proposed that "all the men of the realm should be assembled" to determine who had the best right to the kingdom, but before that assembly took place Juan was proclaimed king of León and Alfonso, king of Castile. Simultaneously, the kings of Aragón, Portugal, and Granada threatened the frontiers. Yet the realm, for the most part, remained loyal to the king. Reiterating its fidelity to Fernando IV, the Castilian *hermandad*, meeting at Palencia in January 1296, repudiated Infante Juan.[11] The towns of the Bay of Biscay and those of Álava also organized new *hermandades* to defend themselves.[12]

The coalition against Fernando IV suffered a blow when King Dinis of Portugal made peace in 1297 and arranged the marriage of his daughter Constanza to the Castilian monarch. With the consent of the cortes of Valladolid early in 1298, Maria and the *hermandad* of León appealed to Dinis for help, but his response—a proposal to partition the realm—was unacceptable. Rejecting it, the Extremaduran and Leonese towns affirmed their loyalty to the king.[13]

The submission of Infante Juan in June 1300 further weakened the opposition to Fernando IV, but the price of his allegiance was money that had been earmarked by the cortes of Valladolid 1300 to pay for papal bulls legitimating the king. Yet after the cortes of Burgos and Zamora in 1301 consented to additional taxes, Boniface VIII legitimated Fernando IV on 6 September. Reaching his majority two months later, he married Constanza of Portugal in January 1302.[14]

Hopes were high that Alfonso de la Cerda, now Fernando IV's sole challenger, would soon come to terms. During the cortes of Medina del Campo 1302 Archbishop Gonzalo of Toledo and Bishop Simón of Sigüenza, acting on behalf of the pope, urged the king to seek peace with Alfonso. Although he promised to consult the cortes about this, it is unknown whether he did so. Be that as it may, Alfonso and his brother, Fernando, renounced their claims to the Castilian throne on 8 August 1304, bringing this era of uncertainty to a close. The presence of Fernando de la Cerda in the cortes of Medina del Campo in April 1305 demonstrated the end of the rivalry.[15]

As the dispute over the succession dating from the death of Fernando de la Cerda in 1275 was now resolved, there was no one to challenge Fernando IV's thirteen-month-old son Alfonso XI, who was proclaimed at once after his father died in 1312. Some years after reaching his majority, in 1332, he crowned himself at Las Huelgas de Burgos, after being anointed by the archbishop of Compostela. No source describes this essentially festive gathering as a cortes, nor is it certain that municipal procurators were summoned to attend.[16]

In summary, because the monarchy was hereditary, the cortes did not elect the king. In two instances, however, the cortes influenced the determination of the succession. The assembly of Valladolid 1217 acknowledged Berenguela's rights to the throne, but encouraged her to cede them to her son Fernando III, as she wished to do. The cortes of Valladolid 1295 could have opted in favor of Infante Juan or another candidate but preferred to extend recognition to Fernando IV. In general, the cortes seldom did more than accept a king who was already proclaimed and who had been the acknowledged heir to the throne. His moral authority, nevertheless, was greatly strengthened by the support of the cortes, as this was tantamount to acceptance by the entire realm.

Royal Weddings

At times the cortes was convened to celebrate a royal marriage. Fernando III, for example, convoked a *curia* at Burgos in 1219 and again in 1237 on the occasion of his marriages, and in 1224 when his daughter Berenguela married John of Brienne. During the cortes of Burgos in 1254, Alfonso X's sister Leonor married Prince Edward of England, who was knighted at that time. The wedding of the king's heir, Fernando de la Cerda, to Blanche of France, was also solemnized during the cortes of Burgos in November 1269. These would seem to be exceptional instances, however, as no other marriages, either of the king or the heir to the throne, appear to have taken place during the cortes.[17]

Recognition of the Heir to the Throne

From time to time the cortes was also called on to pledge allegiance to the heir to the throne. Alfonso VIII, for example, celebrated a *curia* in May 1187 at San Esteban de Gormaz to acknowledge his daughter Berenguela, who was to be married to Conrad of Hohenstaufen. The marriage contract signed at Seligenstadt in April 1188 listed fifty towns whose *maiores* (probably their elected magistrates) swore to guarantee observance of the pact. Though dated in Germany, the contract was prepared at San Esteban in 1187, so it is likely that the chief men of the fifty towns were summoned to the *curia* to take the oath. In July 1188 Conrad attended the *curia* of Carrión where he was knighted by Alfonso VIII and betrothed to Berenguela. "The entire realm"—a phrase that probably should be understood to include representatives of the towns—pledged homage to him.[18] Berenguela subsequently married Alfonso IX of León and gave birth to Fernando III in August 1201. "The whole Leonese kingdom" swore allegiance to him, perhaps at the *curia* of Benavente in March 1202. He, in turn, summoned the chief men of Castile to Burgos on 21 March 1222 to render homage to his first-born son Alfonso.[19]

In accordance with "royal sanctions and the custom of Spain," Alfonso X convened the cortes of Toledo in March 1254 to pledge homage to his infant daughter Berenguela.[20] Fernando de la Cerda, born on 23 October 1255, supplanted her as heir to the throne, but there is no evidence that the king convened the cortes at Vitoria in 1256 to acknowledge him. He did, however, insist on receiving a further pledge of homage to Berenguela when her marriage to Prince Louis of France was arranged in 1256. Orense's representatives, summoned on 14 December 1255 "to wherever I may be," seem to have pledged homage at Vitoria, but the procurators of the archbishop and chapter of Compostela did so on 10 February 1256 at San Esteban de Gormaz. Thus, it is likely that homages were given individually rather than in cortes.[21]

When Fernando was designated as regent, the cortes of Burgos 1274 pledged to receive him as king, if Alfonso X should die during his absence from the realm. Perhaps at that time the king also "caused all the towns and castles of the kingdoms of Castile and León to do homage to his grandson, Alfonso de la Cerda . . . as . . . he had arranged with the king of France." On the basis of this text, the *Crónica general de 1344*, Jerry Craddock suggests that Alfonso X and Philip III made a pact after the birth of Alfonso de la Cerda in 1270, giving him preference over his uncles in the matter of succession. It is not inconceivable that Alfonso X would have asked the cortes of Burgos to accept Fernando as his heir, and to recognize the rights of Fernando's first-born son.[22]

Fernando's sudden death in November 1275 opened the question of the succession and created a crisis that would plague the Castilian monarchy for more than a quarter century. As he lay dying, he expressed the hope that his son, Alfonso de la Cerda, would eventually gain the throne, and entrusted him to Juan Núñez de Lara. The king's second son Sancho, however, demanded recognition as heir apparent. Lope Díaz de Haro urged the king "to summon all the councils of all the cities and towns of the kingdom to send their procurators with certain powers" to pay homage to Sancho.[23]

Alfonso X convoked the cortes of Burgos (rather than Segovia as the royal chronicle has it) in the spring of 1276 to advise him concerning the respective rights of the two claimants. Juan Núñez de Lara and his brother Nuño pleaded on behalf of Alfonso, while the king's brother Fadrique, Lope Díaz de Haro, and many other nobles, prelates, and townsmen favored Sancho. Ballesteros argues that Alfonso X vacillated and did not designate Sancho as his heir until April 1278.[24] Yet Alfonso X was under great pressure to resolve this issue. The fact that Alfonso de la Cerda was under age and that Sancho had recently distinguished himself against the Moors and had the support of a substantial body of people required the king to commit himself. Sancho's designation as *fijo mayor et heredero* as early as 10 June 1276, and the testimonies of Jofre de Loaysa and Bernat Desclot, invalidate Ballesteros's argument. The rejection of Alfonso de la Cerda's claims appears to be confirmed by the decision of his principal supporter, Juan Núñez de Lara, to withdraw to France, where he pledged homage and fealty to Philip III (the uncle of the infantes de la Cerda) in September 1276.[25] Urged by Philip III, Alfonso X promised to celebrate a *curia* with his prelates and barons before Christmas 1277 to adjudicate the dispute, but he never did.[26]

Two years later in the cortes of Segovia, Alfonso X reaffirmed his designation of Sancho, but also entrusted him with even greater responsibilities. Fray Juan Gil de Zamora, Sancho's tutor, remarked that he began to reign together with his father in 1278. He did not receive the royal title but, as Alfonso X stated in his will of 8 November 1283, he had given Sancho "greater power than any king's son had in his father's lifetime." Perhaps this decision was taken because he turned twenty years old in May, thereby reaching his majority according to the *Partidas* (II.15.3), and if his father had died, he could.have reigned without out a regency. Alfonso X required Santo Domingo de Silos "and all the others of my realm" to send two good men to pay homage to Sancho "my oldest son and heir" wherever he might be.[27]

Soon after the cortes of Segovia, Fernando de la Cerda's widow, Blanche, fled to Aragón with her mother-in-law Queen Violante and her two sons. There the boys were left in the care of Violante's brother, King Pedro III, while Blanche continued to France to enlist the support of her brother, Philip III. During the cortes of Seville 1281, Alfonso X, under continued pressure from France and the papacy, revealed his desire to allow his grandsons a share in his dominions and exchanged harsh words with Sancho.[28]

Protesting that the unity of all the realms should be preserved, Sancho summoned the men of the realm to Valladolid in April 1282. Alarmed at this, Alfonso X proposed celebrating a *curia* at Villarreal to resolve the issue, but Sancho rebuffed him. The assembly at Valladolid was a plenary one, including Queen Violante, the king's brother Manuel, Sancho's brothers, the bishops, abbots, masters of the military orders, procurators of cathedral chapters, magnates, knights, and townsmen. In all outward appearances it resembled the cortes, and Sancho described it as such, but as it had not been convoked by the king, Alfonso X scoffed at this celebration of "*cortes generales*, if indeed one can give it that name."[29]

The main business of the assembly was Alfonso X's future as king. The magnates and other men of the realm agreed that Sancho should be made king and given full power to rule, but he was unwilling to assume the royal title during his father's lifetime. Ballesteros believes that exactly the reverse was true, that is, that Sancho wanted the title but the assembly was not ready to give it to him. Infante Manuel proposed that Alfonso X should continue to be acknowledged as king, but that authority over justice, taxes, and castles should be entrusted to Sancho. In effect, he would become a sort of regent or guardian of the realm until his father's death. Alfonso X later complained bitterly that "without being cited, nor warned, nor without having given a confession, nor having been convicted," sentence was rendered against him, "not by any judge, but by our enemies and rebels."[30]

The degradation of the king was not achieved without dissent. Bishops Fernando of Burgos and Juan of Palencia alleged on 21 April that Infantes Pedro and Juan, with other barons and knights, suddenly entered their lodgings and demanded that they come at once to the palace where Sancho was meeting with the barons, knights, and citizens. They argued that to deprive the king of his authority was a weighty matter requiring careful examination and deliberation, but, bullied and threatened, they went to the palace, where they found Sancho with various prelates, barons, and knights behind closed doors. The judgment against the king was read out, the doors were opened, and the bishops left. Once free, they drew up a protest, declaring their refusal to ratify the judgment to which they had given neither counsel nor consent.[31]

Sancho, meanwhile, confirmed the privileges of towns, monasteries and bishoprics, and granted away royal revenues to his supporters without taking care to provide adequately for his own needs.[32]

The extent of his support and the size of the assembly of Valladolid is indicated by the *hermandades* organized at that time. Denouncing the arbitrary actions of Alfonso X, the *hermandades* were principally concerned with defending their own rights. Aside from a reference to their convocation by Sancho, there were few political overtones to the pact concluded on 2 May by forty Benedictine, Cistercian, and Premonstratensian abbots, who promised to pray for one another.[33] Less spiritually minded were the Leonese bishops of Astorga, Zamora, Mondoñedo, Túy, Badajoz, and Coria, who on the next day formed an *hermandad* with twenty-five Benedictine, Cistercian, and Premonstratensian abbots of the kingdom of León and the prior of the Order of the Holy Sepulchre in Spain. Pledging to defend their liberties, they called for daily prayers for "the good estate of the realm," and prayed that Sancho would rule "for the service of God and the utility of the realm." They planned to meet every two years on Jubilate Sunday (9 May) and set the meeting for the next year at Benavente. In a post-datum, they stipulated that the bishops, abbots, priors, and procurators of cathedral chapters and monastic communities should come every year on 27 April to the place where "the *hermandad* of the kingdoms of León and Galicia will be celebrated."[34]

While the Leonese and Galicians were forming this *hermandad*, seven Andalusian towns organized a similar association at Andújar on 10 May,[35] and thirty Castilian towns did so at Burgos on 27 May.[36] Accusing Alfonso X of many injustices, the Leonese and Castilians concluded a joint pact on 8 July at Valladolid and called on Sancho to preserve their *fueros*. The text incorporated the substance of the Leonese *hermandad*, including a pledge to uphold Sancho's rights to justice and taxes, and to defend their own *fueros* against encroachments by anyone, including Sancho or a future king. The Leonese agreed to meet every year on 1 May at a convenient place. The substance of this pact was repeated on 23 September 1282. Several more limited agreements were also reached at this time.[37]

The formation of the Leonese and Castilian *hermandades* marked the beginning of the development of those general associations that were to play such an important role in other times of crisis. As the driving force behind the movement, the towns proposed to hold annual meetings as a means of guarding their privileges. Whereas the cortes depended for its existence on the king's willingness to summon it, the yearly assemblies of the *hermandades* were intended to be fixed and regular. The *hermandad* was an autonomous association organized to defend municipal rights. If Sancho violated the law, the *hermandad* was prepared to admonish him and would take whatever steps were necessary to compel him to amend his ways. In other words, the right of resistance was expressly affirmed and Sancho acknowledged it, as in those circumstances he could hardly do otherwise.

To sum up, the assembly of Valladolid transferred the essential powers of government from Alfonso X to his son. Abandoned by his family and so many of his subjects, the king retained the loyalty only of

Seville and Murcia, who formed an *hermandad* on 8 January 1283. He denounced Sancho's treason in scathing language, disinherited him, and willed his realms to the infantes de la Cerda. Hard pressed for cash, he borrowed money from his erstwhile enemy the emir of Morocco, who also sent troops to plunder the peninsula, ostensibly on the king's behalf.[38]

Reiterating their support for Sancho, the *hermandad* of León and Galicia, and the Leonese bishop, abbots, and procurators of churches gathered at Benavente in May 1283 in a call for peace and reform. The Leonese and Galician *hermandad* also met at Toro in July 1283.[39] Sancho assured the assembly of Palencia (in effect a cortes without the legality of royal convocation) that he would seek an accord with the king (All Saints' Day 1283). Nevertheless, as Pope Martin IV had excommunicated him and imposed an interdict on the land until the people returned to their allegiance, the assembly declared that anyone exhibiting a copy of the papal bull should be executed, and the interdict should not be observed. Indeed, Sancho appealed to the next pope, or to a future council, or to God, against the injury that Martin IV had done to the kingdom.[40]

Proposals for a reconciliation between father and son remained inconclusive, however, and in January 1284 in his last will, Alfonso X reasserted his repudiation of Sancho's claims to the throne. When the king died at Seville on 4 April 1284, this time of turmoil and uncertainty came to an end.[41]

The designation of the heir to the throne was the initial reason for this prolonged conflict, but the end result was the near deposition of the king. Resentful of royal policies, the estates of the realm assembled at Valladolid in 1282, judged Alfonso X unfit to rule, and transferred his powers to Sancho, who received a status equivalent to that of a regent. Alfonso X pointed out that the assembly was not officially a cortes, but the realities of practical politics enabled Sancho to present himself as a champion of the law of the land and the rights of the people, rather than a willful son acting out of mere personal ambition. The *hermandad*'s strong condemnation of the excesses of Alfonso X's government, and its admonition to Sancho and other monarchs to abide by the law, demonstrate that the assembly of Valladolid was not merely a passive instrument of the infante's will.

The designation of the heir to the throne was far less dramatic in later years. Sancho IV may have asked the cortes to recognize his daughter Isabel as his heir at the time of his accession, but this is uncertain. Procter believes that he convened the cortes at Zamora in January 1286 to acknowledge his new-born son Fernando, but this is doubtful as the king was there for only two days. It is more likely that members of the court rendered homage at once, while other prelates, nobles, and townsmen were summoned to do so as soon as they could reach Zamora. He ordered the municipal council of Zamora to appoint twelve knights and twelve good men to receive, in his name, the homage of the men of León, Castile, and Andalusia. The *personeros* of the city of León pledged homage on 24 February 1286, by which time the king was long gone. Nor does it appear that he summoned the cortes in 1295 when he designated Maria de Molina as regent and "caused all the men of the realm" to swear allegiance to Fernando.[42]

When Fernando IV demanded that the nobles render homage to his son Alfonso (born on 13 August 1311), they were on the verge of rebellion and refused, but they probably did give homage when they came to terms with him at Palencia in October 1311.[43] Alfonso XI apparently did not convoke the cortes to do homage to his son, Fernando, but in November 1332 he did instruct the towns to send to Valladolid two knights and two good men with full powers to do so. As they arrived randomly through mid-February 1333, it is evident that a cortes had not been convened.[44] After Fernando died, Alfonso XI required the towns to send their representatives with full powers to Burgos to pledge homage to his second son Pedro, but again there is no sign that the cortes was convoked.[45]

Although it was generally accepted that the heir to the throne should be solemnly acknowledged by all the men of the realm, the cortes was summoned only occasionally for that purpose. Alfonso X convened the cortes of Toledo 1254 on this account, and the cortes of Burgos 1276, Segovia 1278, and Seville 1281 were concerned with this issue, but later monarchs allowed the process of pledging allegiance to extend over several months.

The evidence contradicts Martínez Marina and Piskorski, who hold that the heir to the throne had to be recognized by the cortes in order to have a legitimate right to the crown. Pérez Prendes correctly insists that the heir derived his right from birth. Recognition by the men of the realm, whether in the cortes or not, strengthened the heir's position during his father's lifetime and gave him some assurance that he would not be opposed when the time came for him to assume the crown, but it did not give the heir a right to rule, which was his by reason of parentage.[46]

Regencies

The cortes was most actively involved in affairs touching the kingship when a regency had to be established. The *Partidas* (II.15.3) provided that the great men of the realm should assemble to choose a regent if the king had not already. Before Alfonso X traveled to southern France to plead for papal recognition as Holy Roman Emperor, he summoned the cortes to Burgos in March 1274 and named his oldest son, Fernando de la Cerda, as regent during his absence. Giving him the royal seals and authority to appoint all officials, he admonished him to do justice to everyone. As already discussed, Fernando's sudden death in the next year opened a great controversy, which culminated at Valladolid in 1282 when Sancho assumed royal authority. He had had the effective status of regent for Alfonso X, who was considered incapacitated.[47]

Just before he died in 1295, Sancho IV named Maria de Molina as regent for their nine-year-old son, Fernando IV, and she summoned the cortes to Valladolid to guarantee the succession. Before the cortes began, her husband's uncle, Infante Enrique, tried to manipulate the towns into promising him custody of the king and the kingdom. Thus, he assured the towns of the bishoprics of Osma and Sigüenza at Berlanga that he would uphold their *fueros;* in return, they urged the Extremaduran towns to aid him, but apparently without success. Like Burgos, they preferred to await the judgment of all the men of the realm in the cortes. The towns of the archbishopric of Toledo and of the bishoprics of Cuenca, Segovia, and Ávila threatened to leave the cortes rather than accept Enrique, but Maria persuaded them to stay. In her anxiety to secure Fernando IV's rights to the throne, she decided to compromise by retaining custody of her son while allowing Enrique to act as guardian of the realm. The cortes not only recognized Fernando IV as king, but also accepted this accord. The townsmen demanded, however, a place in the royal household and chancery, as well as a role in the collection of taxes and the custody of royal castles. The regents also assured the prelates that their rights would be upheld. Thereafter, Maria and Enrique shared the regency without further dispute until the king reached his majority in December 1301.[48]

Far more complex was the contention over the regency during the years from Alfonso XI's accession in 1312 (when he was little more than a year old), until his coming of age in 1325. When Fernando IV died suddenly on the frontier, Maria de Molina urged the bishop and citizens of Ávila, to whom custody of the child had been entrusted, not to give him up to anyone "until all the men of the realm were assembled in cortes." Infante Juan, the younger brother of Sancho IV and a great-uncle of the new king, appealed to the Leonese *hermandad* at Benavente on 15 January 1313 to support his bid to control the regency. The *hermandad* supported him, with the stipulations that the nurture and custody of the king should be entrusted to good men of the towns, that illegal tributes should not be imposed, and that royal castles and towns should not be alienated. If the regent violated their *fueros*, and redress was not forthcoming, they would choose another regent.[49]

Juan had achieved an apparent coup, but Infante Pedro, a younger brother of the deceased monarch, minimized the importance of the assembly by pointing out that only three towns (León, Zamora, and Benavente) had supported his rival. Both princes also attempted to manipulate the Castilian and Leonese towns at Sahagún in February 1313 and the Extremaduran *hermandad* at Cuéllar. Lest there be any doubt about it, the assemblies of Benavente, Sahagún, and Cuéllar were not meetings of the cortes, as some historians have alleged, but rather of the *hermandades* of León, León and Castile, and Extremadura. Meanwhile, the Andalusian towns formed their own *hermandad* on 8 May.[50]

After months of political maneuvering, the infantes, each attended by a large body of troops, met in the cortes of Palencia in April 1313. Maria de Molina suggested that they leave the city so a regent could be freely chosen, but when they had done so the prelates and procurators split immediately into two parties. One, assembled in the monastery of San Francisco, elected Maria and Pedro, while the other, in the monastery of San Pablo, chose Juan.[51]

The towns, fully conscious of their power, laid down conditions that had to be accepted, but the *cuadernos* issued by Juan (5 June) and Maria and Pedro (15 June) to their respective supporters reveal differing attitudes toward the regency.[52] Infante Juan's term of office was unlimited, and he was not bound by any council. The twenty knights and townsmen whom he appointed, with the consent of the towns, were only guardians of the king's person (art. 1–2 J). Maria and Pedro, on the other hand, were restricted to two years (art. 48 M) and could do nothing without their council of twenty prelates, knights, and townsmen nominated by the cortes (art. 4–6 M). The cortes had no specific role in Juan's regency, but he could be ousted if he violated his own conditions (art. 45 J). In contrast, Maria and Pedro had to convoke the cortes every two years to review their activities. If they failed to do so, their council could summon the cortes to amend the terms of the regency or to choose new regents (art. 11, 16 M). On the whole, the *cuaderno* promulgated by Maria and Pedro provided greater safeguards for the preservation of peace, harmony, and good government.

The failure of the cortes of Palencia became apparent almost immediately. Infante Juan met the Castilian and Leonese *hermandades* at Sahagún in September, but the death of Queen Constanza (his chief supporter) in November weakened his position and induced him to seek a unified regency.[53] The basic terms of an accord were hammered out in the monastery of Palazuelos outside Valladolid at Easter 1314. Maria and Pedro then assembled their adherents at Valladolid, while Juan met his at Carrión. Legal niceties fail to give any guidance here, but the meetings at Valladolid and Carrión may be considered as separate sessions of a cortes that was soon to be unified. The pact signed at Palazuelos on 1 August provided for a joint regency, with the king entrusted to Maria de Molina. If she died before he reached his majority, the men of the realm would determine who would be given custody. If the regents violated the pact, the men of the realm would choose whomever they wished as regent.[54]

On the same day, Archbishops Gutierre of Toledo, Rodrigo of Compostela, and Fernando of Seville, who had formed an *hermandad* with nine other bishops at Valladolid, obtained the regents' pledge to defend the liberties of the church.[55]

To resolve difficulties arising from the implementation of their pact, the regents convened the cortes at Burgos in the late spring of 1315. At that time they confirmed a new *hermandad* between the towns and the lesser nobility (who had formed their own *hermandad* at Valladolid, probably in the previous summer). More numerous, better organized, and more conscious of its own strength than before, the *her-*

mandad was resolved to influence the regency counsels. To accomplish their aims, the Castilians, Leonese, and men of Extremadura and Toledo would hold separate assemblies each year. The regents, meanwhile, reaffirmed their desire to maintain unity.[56]

As intense rivalry between Juan and Pedro continued, the Castilian *hermandad* meeting at Burgos (Martinmas 1316) demanded that the regents give hostages as security against arbitrary actions, as well as a detailed accounting of royal revenues. When the *hermandad* of Castile, León, Extremadura, and Toledo assembled again at Carrión in March 1317, it was in an ugly mood. Some members were intent on ousting Pedro (who was on the frontier), but a review of royal accounts showed nothing to indicate any wrongdoing on his part. Infante Juan proposed that the regents renounce their office so the assembly could choose a single regent, in the expectation that the new election would be in his favor. At this point Maria came to Carrión to oppose him and, while acknowledging the *hermandad*'s legitimate concern for reform (art. 71), she served notice that the regents would not be intimidated.[57]

In order to divide the *hermandad* the regents summoned the Castilians to the cortes at Valladolid in June 1318, and the Leonese and Extremadurans to Medina del Campo some months later. Both assemblies granted taxes to enable the infantes to carry out a joint campaign against the Moors.[58]

When both Juan and Pedro died suddenly in 1319, the renewal of conflict over the regency was inevitable. In accordance with the decision of the cortes of Burgos 1315, Maria de Molina was the sole regent, but Juan Manuel, a grandnephew of Alfonso X, was recognized by the *hermandad* of Toledo and Extremadura at Cuéllar in October 1319. Moreover, Felipe, Maria's youngest son, and Juan the one-eyed, son of Infante Juan, also claimed a place in the regency. On Juan's urging, the Castilian *hermandad* meeting at Burgos in May 1320 asked Maria not to accept either of his rivals; upon her refusal to come to Burgos to settle the issue, the *hermandad* withdrew its recognition of her.[59]

Encouraged by the papal legate Cardinal William of Santa Sabina, Maria convened the cortes to meet at Palencia on 8 April 1321. Although it apparently met instead at Valladolid, it accepted Maria, Felipe, Juan, and Juan Manuel as regents. Maria was ill, however, and after entrusting the king to the care of the townsmen of Valladolid, she died on 30 June 1321.[60]

As there was now no one with sufficient prestige to command the respect of all, terrible disorder followed. The citizens of Valladolid urged the regents to summon the cortes, but nothing was settled when the assembly met there in the spring of 1322. The threefold division of the realm was perpetuated as Juan gained recognition in Castile, Juan Manuel in Extremadura and Toledo, and Felipe in León. Convening their respective supporters from time to time, the regents exploited the kingdom for their personal benefit, until Alfonso XI, upon reaching the age of fourteen (13 August 1325), brought the regency to an end. Summoning the cortes to Valladolid, he asked the regents to surrender their authority, which they did prior to 5 September.[61]

One may conclude that the convocation of the cortes was necessary to confirm anyone's right to act as regent. Although Sancho IV intended that Maria de Molina should be regent for their son, Infante Enrique insisted on sharing power, and the cortes of Valladolid 1295 acquiesced. This precedent encouraged Infante Juan to challenge Fernando IV's designation of his brother Pedro, with the resulting division of allegiance in the cortes of Palencia 1313, and the increased strength of the *hermandades*. Impelled by similar ambition, Juan, Juan Manuel, and Felipe compelled the cortes of Valladolid 1321 to accept them. The regents apparently believed that recognition by the cortes, even though it might not be unanimous, gave them the right to claim that the entire realm approved of what they were doing. Mirroring the dissension that was rampant throughout the kingdom, the cortes was unable to preserve the necessary unity of government.

A European Perspective

Other European parliamentary assemblies participated in diverse ways in the resolution of similar issues relating to the royal office. The people's obligation to swear allegiance was emphasized, for example, by Afonso IV of Portugal, who received the homage of the cortes of Évora in 1325. In the Crown of Aragón the king customarily pledged to uphold the laws in successive cortes in each of his realms, as Pedro IV did in 1336 at Zaragoza, Lérida, and Valencia.[62]

None of the peninsular kings was deposed through parliamentary action, though the Union of Aragón threatened to transfer its allegiance if Alfonso III did not grant the Privileges of the Union in the cortes of Zaragoza in 1287. In England, on the other hand, Edward II was deposed by a parliament summoned in his name in 1327, and a regency was established for his minor son Edward III. The parliament then invited him to abdicate, which he did, although he was murdered some months later.[63]

The right of women to succeed to the throne, admitted in Navarre, was disputed in both France and Aragón. The Navarrese *cort general* at Olite in 1274 appointed a governor of the realm during the minority of Jeanne I. As the male line of Capetian kings petered out, the rights of female heirs were rejected by assemblies of notables in 1317 and 1328. In Aragón Pedro IV, after declaring his daughter Constance as his heir, promised not to arrange her marriage without consulting the cortes, but the protest of the Aragonese Union in the cortes of Zaragoza in 1347 forced him to revoke his decree.[64]

6

The Cortes and Foreign Affairs

Historians have rendered varying judgments on the importance of the cortes in foreign affairs. Martínez Marina, after commenting on the disasters attendant upon wars unleashed by kings without the consent of their subjects, argues that the Castilian cortes "always had the right to intervene in military deliberations, in matters of war and peace, and in the conclusion of treaties of alliance, confederations and truces, and nothing was done without its consent and counsel." Colmeiro, on the contrary, holds that the kings sought the consent of the cortes to make war and to provide the money necessary to do so. Piskorski puts it somewhat more strongly when he insists that the right to consent to declarations of war, the conclusion of peace, or the signature of treaties was one of the most important rights of the cortes. In more recent times, Pérez Prendes qualifies Piskorski's judgment as optimistic, and enters a cautionary note when he insists that in such matters "the mission of the cortes is consultative, but the king is not bound to follow its counsel, but only to give it knowledge of the enterprises being undertaken." [1]

Piskorski based his judgment on article 3 of the *decreta* enacted by Alfonso IX in the *curia* of León in 1188. The king established a fundamental principle concerning foreign affairs when he declared that he would not make "war or peace or treaty except by the counsel of the bishops, nobles, and good men by whose counsel I ought to be guided." In emphasizing what had been and would continue to be the practice of medieval rulers, the king was acknowledging that without the collaboration of the chief men of the realm he could not realistically carry on war, or expect peace to prevail or an alliance to be effective. Contrary to those who argued that the king was also promising to include representatives of the towns among those whose counsel he would seek, Procter pointed out that the good men mentioned here were probably members of his council.[2] Indeed, it is unlikely that the king was binding himself at that time to consult with the towns, but once the cortes developed with regular participation by the townsmen, one may say that they, together with the prelates and nobles, had a role in foreign affairs. War and peace and treaties were matters that touched all the men of the realm, and as such necessitated consultation and oftentimes consent. The extent and nature of counsel and consent varied, however, according to circumstances.

Relations with Christian Powers

Relations with other Christian powers were sometimes treated in the cortes. Representatives of fifty towns, along with several bishops, princes, and nobles, swore to uphold the marriage contract between Berenguela and Conrad of Hohenstaufen, drawn up in the *curia* of San Esteban de Gormaz in 1187. The betrothal was celebrated in the *curia* of Carrión in 1188, and Conrad received the accolade of knighthood from Alfonso VIII.[3] Because of Conrad's early death, the alliance with the Holy Roman Empire projected by this marriage never came to fruition.

Alfonso IX, the new king of León, also was knighted by Alfonso VIII during the *curia* of Carrión in 1188, and he kissed Alfonso VIII's hand in sign of vassalage. The subordination which that implied never sat well with Alfonso IX and for many years he maintained a hostile attitude toward Castile. Perhaps for this reason when he returned to his own kingdom he promised the *curia* of León in 1188 that henceforth he would not make treaties or go to war without seeking proper counsel.[4]

Alfonso X convened the cortes of Toledo 1254 in part to witness the resolution of his pretensions to Gascony, derived from his great-grandmother, Eleanor, the daughter of Henry II of England. In a treaty signed at Toledo on 31 March 1254, he yielded his rights to his sister Leonor and her betrothed, Prince Edward, the son and heir of King Henry III. Their marriage was solemnized in the cortes of Burgos in November. Alfonso X's objective in all this was not Gascony, but rather Africa. In exchange for surrendering his claims, for whatever they were worth, he persuaded Henry III to promise assistance for a projected invasion of North Africa. Henry III, it seems, never seriously considered fulfilling this pledge.[5] Although there is no sign that the king asked the cortes to approve or reject the treaty of Toledo, he certainly needed support for his African policy and probably informed the cortes of the substance of the treaty.

Whether Alfonso X's claims to supremacy over Navarre were also aired in the cortes is uncertain. Ever since the time of Alfonso VII (1126–1157), the kings of Castile had planned to annex Navarre or to partition it with Aragón. With the intention of imposing his suzerainty, Alfonso X was present at Vitoria on the Navarrese frontier from 2 December 1255 to 24 January 1256. Pedro Marín, the prior of Santo Domingo de Silos at that time, reported that "King Thibault of Navarre came to his cortes and became his vassal." Although Alfonso X was accompanied by his usual entourage of some nobles, some prelates, and some towns summoned to provide military support, it is unlikely that he had called the cortes to such an eccentric location as Vitoria. Thibault I, moreover, was not recorded in any charter as Alfonso X's vassal for Navarre, though on 1 January 1256 he did receive the towns of San Sebastián and Fuenterrabia for life, and probably did homage for them at Vitoria.[6]

One of the issues most persistently presented to the cortes were the claims of the infantes de la Cerda, which, in varying degrees, concerned France, Aragón, and Portugal. As this topic has already been discussed at length in Chapter 5, a summary will be sufficient here. The problem had its origin in the marriage of Fernando de la Cerda to Blanche of France in the cortes of Burgos 1269, and Alfonso X's subsequent recognition of Infante Sancho instead of Alfonso de la Cerda as heir to the throne.[7] The cortes of Valladolid 1295 recognized Fernando IV's rights against Alfonso and also encouraged his marriage to a Portuguese princess in the hope of gaining the support of King Dinis. With the consent of the towns in the cortes of Valladolid 1298, Maria de Molina appealed to Dinis to help her son retain his crown. The cortes of Valladolid 1300 and Burgos and Zamora 1301 responded positively to the proposed marriage and voted funds to obtain a papal dispensation and legitimation. When the king was urged, during the cortes of Medina del Campo 1302, to make peace with Alfonso de la Cerda, he replied that he would take counsel with the cortes, though we know nothing further of this. In these several instances the cortes, and particularly the townsmen, were actively involved in the determination of policy. Not only did the cortes stand fast in its allegiance to the king, rejecting counterclaims and proposals to partition the realm, but it also vigorously promoted an alliance with Portugal.[8]

Alfonso X and the Holy Roman Empire

Alfonso X presented his quest for the crown of the Holy Roman Empire to the cortes on several occasions. In order to win the votes of the electors in April 1257 and to counteract his rival Richard of Cornwall, Alfonso X had to expend great sums of money. Jofre de Loaysa remarked that the king incurred almost unbelievable expenses on this account and had "to ask the men of his kingdom for *servicios* and to impose unaccustomed levies upon them." The royal chronicle also commented that his quest for empire "brought great poverty to the kingdoms of León and Castile."[9]

The empire may have been discussed during the cortes of Valladolid 1258, a few months after Alfonso X accepted election. The solemnity of the occasion was enhanced by the arrival on 3 January of Princess Kristin of Norway, who was to marry one of Alfonso X's brothers. A Castilian-Norwegian alliance was intended to further the king's imperial ambitions and his projected crusade in North Africa. The king and his future sister-in-law were met at the gates of the city by a "numberless force of knights, barons, archbishops, bishops, and both Christian and infidel envoys." This last reference suggests that possibly representatives of the Moorish kings of Granada, Murcia, and Niebla attended the cortes. Kristin's wedding to the king's brother Felipe was solemnized on 31 March, probably after the conclusion of the cortes.[10]

As Alfonso X had already begun to issue privileges and pensions to his German supporters, his financial needs may have prompted him to ask the cortes for a subsidy. When he confirmed the exemption of the knights of Toledo from *moneda forera* on 6 February 1260, he stated that in the previous year they owed him two *monedas*, one "which they had to give us by right" because the seven-year period was up, and the other for "the affair of the empire." [11] The second *moneda* was an extraordinary levy intended to assist him in pursuing his imperial ambitions, and as such was probably approved by the cortes of Valladolid 1258.

The quest for the imperial crown was the reason for the convocation of the cortes of Toledo 1259. There are no extant *cuadernos*, but on 6 February 1260 Alfonso X declared, "we thought it well to hold our cortes in the noble city of Toledo concerning the affair of the empire." In a letter to the bishop of Cuenca, dated 20 June 1264, he stated that he had held "our cortes in Toledo concerning the affair of the empire." [12] The business at hand, in the king's words, was "the affair of the empire," but what was precisely determined is a matter of conjecture. Richard of Cornwall had gone to Germany to be crowned, and Alfonso X seems to have hoped to go to Rome to be crowned by the pope, though he would have first needed to set domestic affairs in order and assure peace with his neighbors. While continuing his diplomacy abroad, he may also have wished to exhibit the magnificence appropriate to his imperial rank, not only to his own subjects but also to the many foreign lords who were now his vassals, some of whom may have come to the cortes. [13] Perhaps at this time, with the intention of displaying a grandeur worthy of an emperor, he gave money to Marie de Brienne—wife of Baldwin II, the Latin emperor of Constantinople—to enable her to redeem her son, Philip of Courtenay, who had been mortgaged to the Venetians. This action might have served Alfonso X's imperial aims, but it caused another great drain on his treasury. [14]

In addition, Alfonso X may have chosen this occasion to proclaim his hegemony over the entire Iberian peninsula, thereby resurrecting the imperial claims of the kings of León, who claimed to be heirs of the Visigoths who had ruled all of Spain. Fernando III had wished to revive the Hispanic empire but had not done so because the time was not propitious; however, his son may have concluded that he could now link Leonese aspirations to imperial rule in Spain with his own claims to the Holy Roman Empire. Alfonso X would first need to obtain the recognition of his fellow peninsular monarchs, which may have been a principal reason for summoning the kings of Granada, Murcia, and Niebla to the cortes. That his peninsular claims were not mere fantasy is indicated by the decision of his father-in-law, Jaime I of Aragón, to appoint a procurator to oppose any assertion that Alfonso X "should be emperor of the Spains and that we and our kingdoms and lands should be in any subjection to him by reason of empire" (27 September 1259).[15]

News of the death of his archrival, Richard of Cornwall, in April 1272, encouraged Alfonso X to believe that the Germans and the newly elected pope, Gregory X, would unite in accepting him as emperor. His current objective was to set his kingdom in order so that he could journey abroad to secure recognition of his rights. With this in mind he summoned the cortes to Burgos in the fall of 1272, "concerning the business of sending knights to the empire."[16]

The confrontation with the magnates in the cortes of Burgos 1272 forced him to postpone his departure, but the cortes apparently granted him a subsidy to make his journey possible. The royal chronicle (whose account of these events is jumbled) recorded the following:

> He took counsel with his people as to how he should go to the empire. And to facilitate this he asked the men of the realm to give him every year, until the affair of the empire was concluded, two *servicios* besides the tributes and rents that they owed him. And all the magnates, *infanzones*, knights and men of the cities and towns of his kingdoms granted it to him.[17]

The amount of the tax, two *servicios*, is incorrect. In another chapter, the chronicle reported that the cortes of Burgos "granted him a *servicio* each year for a certain time in the entire realm," so he could undertake the journey to the empire. Royal charters issued two years later indicate that this grant was made for as long as the king thought necessary.[18]

Alfonso X apparently intended to send a contingent of men to Italy while he personally tried to persuade the pope to acknowledge him as emperor. At the end of the following year the rebellious nobles returned to their allegiance, and the king of Granada also renewed his vassalage, promising payment of 300,000 *maravedís* annually in tribute and making a special contribution of 250,000 *maravedís* for the journey to the empire.[19]

In preparation for the most important journey of his career, Alfonso X summoned the cortes to Burgos in early March 1274. A royal charter of 13 April, given in the year "when we held the cortes in Burgos concerning the matter of sending knights to the empire of Rome," is the only direct reference to it. A description in the royal chronicle of a meeting held in March to prepare for this journey also seems to refer to the cortes of Burgos, although the chronicle places the event in Toledo, probably confusing it with the cortes held there in 1259.[20]

The business of the cortes was three-fold: to establish Fernando de la Cerda as regent during his father's absence; to arrange for a retinue of knights who would accompany the king on his journey; and to obtain the necessary financial aid. The king reminded the cortes that the Lombards had often entreated him to come to them, but it was only now that he could do so, as the realm was at peace with the Moors and the rebellious magnates had returned to their former loyalty. Fernando was duly designated as regent, arrangements were made for the defense of the frontier, and the cortes consented to a subsidy for two years so the king could complete "the affair of the empire."[21]

Alfonso X's plea before Gregory X at Beaucaire in May 1275 was a futile one because the pope had already acknowledged Rudolf of Habsburg, whom the German princes had elected as emperor in 1273.[22] Although the overwhelming weight of reality indicated that his pretensions would never be fulfilled, Alfonso X probably never abandoned them. His decision to give a large sum of money to the marquess of Monferrat, whose daughter married Infante Juan at Burgos in 1281, and to send troops to Lombardy to uphold the Ghibelline cause angered Sancho and others, not only because of the diversion of men and money from the war against the Moors but also because it was apparent that Alfonso X had not surrendered his imperial illusions.[23]

The Wars Against the Moors

As the most significant aspect of Castilian foreign relations, the reconquest could not have taken place without the collaboration both of the nobility, who served personally with their vassals, and of the towns, who were obliged to provide troops and consent to essential tax levies. Not surprisingly, then, the king consulted with the cortes about future campaigns.

Alfonso VIII, for example, after taking counsel with the prelates and nobles in September 1211, probably at Toledo, ordered all the men of the realm to prepare for war. Perhaps at that time, the clergy pledged half their yearly income to finance the campaign. Fernando III celebrated a *curia* at Carrión in July 1224 concerning his first campaign against the Moors, but the documentation is inadequate to determine to what extent he planned his later campaigns in the cortes.[24]

Alfonso X seems to have often discussed relations with the Moorish kings of Spain and Morocco in the cortes and other assemblies. The *Estoria de Espanna* reported that Ibn al-Aḥmar, the king of Granada, pledged homage and fealty to Fernando III in 1246, promising to attend his cortes and to pay an annual tribute. Ibn Maḥfūz, king of Niebla, and Ibn Hūd, king of Murcia, probably made similar commitments. To affirm his supremacy over Muslim Spain, Alfonso X summoned all of his Moorish vassals to the cortes of Toledo in March 1254; the *Anonymous of Sahagún* testified that Alfonso X was "then much preoccupied with the Moabite and Moorish kings, his vassals." Ibn al-Aḥmar was received with great honor and lodged outside the city, and he confirmed his previous agreements with Alfonso X.[25]

The African Crusade

During this period of apparent tranquility, Alfonso X discussed his plans for an invasion of North Africa in several cortes held early in the reign. The belief that Morocco had once been part of the Visigothic realm provided the ideological justification, but in practical terms the king wished to close the Straits of Gibraltar to any further Moroccan incursions. Preparations for an African expedition may well have been presented to the cortes of Toledo 1254; further evidence includes the attendance of the Moorish kings, the first appearance of the admiral of the fleet being readied for this venture, and Henry III of England's commitment to participate in it.[26]

Various sources reveal a continuing preoccupation with the African affair. With the hope of securing the most effective military service, Alfonso X (at Segovia in 1256) granted certain fiscal exemptions to the knights of the Castilian and Extremaduran towns, provided that they maintained horses and arms suitable for war.[27] During the cortes of Valladolid in 1258, he urged the towns of Galicia and Asturias to make certain that their sailing ships were ready for the projected crusade against Cádiz in May.[28]

Developments following the cortes of Toledo 1259 suggest that the African affair was also considered at that time. Not only did Alfonso X seek the counsel of the king of Granada and persuade Jaime I to allow his subjects to take part in the enterprise, but, filled with a great desire "to carry forward the affair of the crusade beyond the sea," he appointed Juan García de Villamayor as *adelantado mayor de la mar.* Then in September 1260, a Castilian fleet assaulted the port of Salé on the Atlantic coast of Morocco.[29]

Elated, even though no permanent occupation was effected, the king sought the counsel of the cortes of Seville 1261 concerning "the affair of Africa that we have begun." Responding as loyal vassals, they pointed out that there were certain matters injurious to the well-being of the realm that required reform.[30] The cortes probably also stressed the importance of securing the coastal regions against a possible Moroccan invasion, because soon afterward the king laid siege to Niebla, the seat of the Moorish kingdom west of Seville. Inasmuch as the king many years later ordered an accounting of taxes in arrears since the campaign of Niebla, it is possible that the cortes consented to a tax levy to finance the expedition. Niebla surrendered in February 1262 after a siege of ten months.[31]

Although the king was determined to press on, the Extremaduran towns, which had been summoned to serve on the frontier, voiced their complaints about high taxes at Seville in April 1264 and asked Queen Violante to intercede. After taking counsel the king confirmed the tax exemptions given to the knights in 1256 and extended them to their dependents, with the intention of making their position more attractive and thus maintaining his military strength.[32]

Soon afterward, Ibn al-Aḥmar, the king of Granada, incited a general revolt among the mudejars of Andalusia and Murcia. He considered his own situation to have become more precarious by Alfonso X's conquest of Niebla and his demand for the cession of Gibraltar and Tarifa (ports giving access to the peninsula). For the next several years Alfonso X, aided by his father-in-law Jaime I, was occupied with the suppression of the uprising and the pacification of the frontier.[33] Several Andalusian towns, threatened by the rebellion, formed an *hermandad* at Andújar on 26 April 1265 to defend the realm against the Moors; each town promised to send two knights to the annual assembly of the *hermandad* to be held at Andújar two weeks after Easter.[34]

Once Ibn al-Aḥmar returned to his allegiance, Alfonso X convened an assembly at Jerez (January 1268) with the hope of restoring peace and prosperity to the realm. The expulsion of the Moors of Jerez who had taken part in the rebellion, and the introduction of Christian settlers, gave cause for celebration; most important, however, a number of economic measures were taken, such as the regulation of prices and wages, in an attempt to repair the economic distress caused by the war.[35]

An uneasy peace prevailed between the two kingdoms for the remainder of Ibn al-Aḥmar's reign. After the cortes of Burgos 1272, the rebellious nobles, led by the king's brother Felipe, repudiated their allegiance and went into exile to Granada, where they assisted Muḥammad II (1273–1302) in securing the throne. Once Violante had negotiated peace, Alfonso X sealed the agreements at Seville in December 1273 and conferred knighthood upon Muḥammad II, who became his vassal and resumed payment of annual tributes.[36]

The Struggle for the Straits of Gibraltar

In the last decade of his reign, Alfonso X convened the cortes and other assemblies to defend the realm against the Benimerines of Morocco, who invaded the peninsula for the first time in the spring of 1275. The king's son and heir, Fernando de la Cerda, died suddenly on his way to meet them, but Infante Sancho temporarily stemmed their advance. Consulting Sancho and the nobles and townsmen who were on the frontier at Alcalá de Henares in late December, and again at Toledo in January 1276, Alfonso X convinced the towns to grant his request for a subsidy in view of the gravity of the situation.[37] In the cortes of Burgos in the spring of 1276, the king updated the privileges granted to the towns twenty years before, exempting knights and their dependents from tributes, provided they were suitably equipped for war. The prelates also consented to a tax levy.[38]

With an eye to a likely invasion by the Benimerines, the king gained the consent of the cortes of Burgos 1277 to an annual tribute payable for the rest of his life. In order to deal with "the affair of the frontier," he also sought agreement concerning the modification of the coinage.[39] Quite possibly the cortes of Segovia 1278 granted him a tax levy for the siege of Algeciras, whose capture would help shut off the invasion route from North Africa. Only the demonstrated vulnerability of the peninsula to repeated invasion from Morocco would have persuaded the cortes to make such an exceptional concession.[40]

Problems relating to the siege of Algeciras were the principal reason for the convocation of "the knights and good men of the towns of Castile, Extremadura and beyond the mountains" at Toledo in the spring of 1279. Complaining about several matters, they agreed to an additional tax to support the siege.[41] The destruction of the Castilian fleet, however, compelled Alfonso X to lift the siege in July and to conclude a truce with Morocco. Continuing to press the war against Granada, he informed the cortes of Seville 1281 of his intention to devalue the coinage rather than impose a new tax.[42] Ironically, after being dispossessed at Valladolid in 1282, Alfonso X had to borrow from the emir of Morocco, who now ravaged the peninsula apparently as his ally.[43]

The situation along the frontier remained quite critical during the reign of Sancho IV. In view of arrangements made in the spring of 1285 to collect arrears of taxes going back to 1275, it seems likely that Sancho IV discussed the Moroccan threat in the cortes of Valladolid in the fall of 1284.[44] After successfully defending Jerez against a Moroccan siege in the summer of 1285, he concluded a truce which allowed him a respite of several years. Upon the expiration of the truce, he obtained a tax levy from the prelates at Medina del Campo in 1291 that enabled him to equip a fleet to close the Straits to access from Morocco. Following the capture of Tarifa in October 1292, he summoned the cortes to Valladolid in the spring of 1293 to celebrate his triumph and reward his people for their help. A Moroccan attempt to recover Tarifa was repulsed in the following year.[45]

Despite the strategic importance of that port, Infante Enrique (who shared the regency for Fernando IV with Maria de Molina) proposed the sale of Tarifa to Muḥammad II of Granada, reasoning that this would end hostilities and would raise enough money to forestall the imposition of new taxes. Aware of Maria's opposition, he did not dare to act without first consulting the cortes. As expected, when he informed the cortes of Cuéllar 1297 of his plan, Maria expressed her strong dissent, pointing out that the money raised would scarcely resolve the crown's financial problems. She argued further that to yield the city that Sancho IV had captured after the expenditure of so much energy would be a grave blow to Christendom and would raise the danger of a new Moroccan invasion, and a possible conquest of Spain as in the time of the Visigoths. In the cortes of Valladolid 1298 Enrique again urged the sale of Tarifa, but the queen opposed him once more. As in so many instances, she carried the day, and Enrique found himself thwarted and the plan abandoned. If he had attempted unilaterally to sell Tarifa, the cortes, urged by Maria de Molina, might have ousted him as regent.[46]

The cortes of Medina del Campo 1302 (art. 11 E, 13 L), the first of Fernando IV's majority, urged him to take counsel so that people on the frontier could be protected against attacks launched by Muḥammad III, the new king of Granada. When Fernando IV asked for a tax levy for this purpose, the towns willingly granted the money in their concern for the security of the frontier. The Castilian towns assembled in the cortes of Burgos 1302 also gave consent, similarly mindful of the Muslim threat.[47]

With the expectation of carrying out a joint campaign against the Moors, Fernando IV and Jaime II of Aragón concluded an alliance at Alcalá de Henares on 18 December 1308. Fernando IV then announced his intentions to the cortes of Madrid in February 1309, explaining that he wished to serve God as his predecessors had, and asked for a subsidy so that he could do so. The towns hesitated at first, stressing their poverty, but when the king explained his plans, they consented to the tax. Perhaps some objection to the proposed cession of a portion of the kingdom of Granada to Aragón was also raised.[48]

The military campaign had mixed results. After taking Gibraltar in September, Fernando IV had to abandon the siege of Algeciras, and Jaime II had to give up the siege of Almería. The two kings renewed their alliance in 1311, and Fernando IV persuaded "all the men of his realms" to consent to new taxes in support of the war in the cortes of Valladolid 1312. The campaign was aborted, however, as he fell ill shortly after the surrender of Alcaudete and died on 7 September 1312.[49]

After the unification of the regency for Alfonso XI, Infantes Pedro and Juan persuaded the Castilians meeting in the cortes of Valladolid in June 1318, and the Extremadurans and Leonese in the cortes of Medina del Campo in September, to finance their planned expedition against Granada. Disaster struck, however, when both Infantes died suddenly in June 1319 while campaigning in the plain of Granada.[50]

Alfonso XI, on reaching his majority, asked the cortes of Valladolid 1325 for sufficient funds to fortify the castles on the frontier. Four years later, in the cortes of Madrid, he declared his intention to "conquer the land that the Moors, the enemies of the faith, kept from him by force," and requested funds so that he could pay the stipends of the nobility and arm a fleet. Pleased by his determination to prosecute the war against Granada, the cortes acceded to his request. Continued internal disorder thwarted his efforts to mount a sustained campaign, however, and resulted in the loss of Gibraltar to the Moroccans in 1333. Looking to the future, he enacted an ordinance concerning the military obligations of the nobility in the assembly of Burgos in April 1338. This ordinance carefully spelled out the duties of royal vassals, the number of troops they were required to bring to the host, and the horses, arms, and armor with which they were to be equipped (art. 14–32).[51]

The establishment of these military requirements came at an appropriate moment, as the Moors resumed hostilities all along the frontier in 1339. In the fall, the assembly of Madrid consented to a levy of taxes which was put to good use, but even greater sums were required after the Castilian fleet was routed by the Moroccans and the combined Moroccan and Granadan forces besieged Tarifa in September 1340. The pope granted crusade indulgences and authorized Alfonso XI to utilize ecclesiastical resources for the war. Upon the approach of the Castilians, now joined by Afonso IV of Portugal and other foreign contingents, the Moors shifted their forces to the river Salado, where Alfonso XI won a decisive victory on 30 October 1340.[52]

Flushed with victory, he informed "the procurators of the cities, towns, and places of his realms" assembled at Llerena (about ninety kilometers north of Seville) in early December, that as the Moors would surely attack again, he needed additional funds. Despite the burden of previous tax levies, they promised to assist him "for the protection and defense of the realm."[53]

Concentrating his energy on the capture of Algeciras, the chief port of access between Morocco and the peninsula, Alfonso XI obtained the consent of assemblies at Burgos, León, Zamora, and Ávila in 1342 to the imposition of the *alcabala*—a tax on all commercial transactions. As a consequence, Algeciras was taken on 25 March 1344. The assemblies held at Alcalá, Burgos, and León in the following year extended the grant of the *alcabala* so that Algeciras could be adequately defended. The king began his final effort against the Moors when he laid siege to Gibraltar in 1349, but he fell victim to the plague early in the following year and died.[54]

Counsel and Consent

The foregoing pages should make clear that it would be a mistake to state categorically that the king was always bound to seek the counsel and/or consent of the cortes in foreign affairs. The evidence reveals that the king concluded treaties, arranged truces, and carried on military campaigns without the prior consultation of the cortes. Yet the influence of the cortes on relations with other kingdoms was considerable. As the treaty with Henry III of England (concluded at Toledo in 1254 while the cortes was in session) touched on matters of great importance to both the king and the kingdom, it seems improbable that Alfonso X would not have informed the cortes of its impact on his interests in Gascony and Africa.

Although there is no evidence that he asked the cortes of Toledo 1254 to ratify the treaty, testimony that his imperial ambitions were discussed in the cortes of Toledo 1259, Burgos 1272, and Burgos 1274 is unambiguous. There is also good reason to believe that this issue was brought to the attention of the cortes of Valladolid 1258. Surely the king did not ask the cortes whether he should accept the imperial crown, but to attain his goal he required both the moral and financial support of the cortes.

The counsel and consent of the cortes was similarly needed during the continuing intervention of Aragón, France, and Portugal in the dispute over the rights of the infantes de la Cerda. The cortes of Valladolid 1295 decisively affirmed the rights of Fernando IV, and Maria de Molina consulted the cortes in subsequent years about the best means of thwarting her son's domestic and foreign enemies.

In considering the reconquest as the foreign policy issue most frequently brought before the cortes, three points must be taken into account: first, the objective to be attained; second, the strategy and tactics to be employed; and third, the military forces and the finances necessary to achieve it. The military objective might be a crusade to North Africa, an attack on the frontier of the kingdom of Granada, or the siege of Algeciras, Tarifa, or Gibraltar. Ordinarily the king and his military strategists determined the specific objective as well as the strategy and tactics to be employed, as was the case in 1340 when Alfonso XI proposed to his military council the relief of Tarifa, then besieged by the Benimerines.

Once the objective and tactics were clear, the king would inform the cortes of his plans. The sources say little about this stage, but it is possible that the representatives of the towns, whose militia forces were experienced in war, would endeavor to present their views, if only to concur in the choice of objectives and strategies. The cortes of Seville 1261, for example, responding to Alfonso X's request for counsel concerning the African crusade, may have advised him to concentrate his efforts on the capture of Niebla, rather than attempt any further overseas operations. In a similar manner, the negative reaction of the cortes of Cuéllar 1297 and Valladolid 1298 to Infante Enrique's plan to sell Tarifa to the enemy forced him to withdraw it.

At times the cortes may have taken the initiative in foreign affairs, as when the cortes of Medina del Campo 1302 urged Fernando IV to take the necessary steps to protect the people on the frontier from Moorish assaults. In most cases, however, the king brought these issues to the attention of the cortes. Alfonso XI's announcement of his plans to attack the Moors, for example, drew the applause of the cortes of Valladolid 1325 and Madrid 1329.

The king's responsibility was to demonstrate to the cortes that he had given due consideration to all the possibilities and that the expedition he proposed had a reasonable chance of success. He did not require the consent of the cortes to act, but he did have to seek its counsel. When he requested counsel, he may not have considered himself bound by it, though in some instances he would have been foolish to act contrary to it. As he was dependent on the nobility and the urban militia forces for a significant part of his army, he had to present a reasonable case to win their enthusiastic support. Although they were bound to respond to his call to military service, there was little wisdom in summoning them if a proposed expedition seemed ill-planned or foolhardy. Fernando IV, for example, probably did not think it necessary to ask the cortes of Madrid 1309 to ratify his alliance with Jaime II, but in explaining his strategy for the war against Granada, it would have been to his advantage to point out that the king of Aragón was going to collaborate with him.

The means of carrying out a military strategy included the organization of the army and taxation. Any modification of the military obligations of the towns or the nobles required consent as well as counsel. The changes in the service of the urban militia enacted at Segovia in 1256 and again at Seville in 1264, and of the nobility enacted at Burgos in 1338, could be implemented only with the consent of those affected—the townsmen and the nobles.

Consent was also necessary when the question of financing an expedition arose. Procter is certainly correct in saying that "it was the need of money, rather than the need of advice on, or consent to," foreign policy that prompted the king to summon the cortes,[55] but it is equally correct to say that without the consent of the cortes he could not execute his plans. To gain consent, the king had to present a clear and effective rationale to justify his foreign policy. Although the chronicles mention little of the discussion leading to the granting of taxes, it is obvious that it did not occur in a vacuum. The cortes did not give consent blindly, but complied only after questions of foreign policy were fully discussed. As Jaime II reported, the cortes of Madrid 1309 responded to Fernando IV's request for taxes only after he "told them why."[56] Taxation, therefore, cannot be separated from the issues of foreign policy.

One may say, in conclusion, that the king recognized the wisdom of consulting the cortes in times of crisis—when he wished, for example, to mount a major campaign against the Moors, or when the kingdom was threatened by its Christian neighbors. In matters of military strategy he took counsel with the magnates, and in questions of marriages and alliances he normally acted with the advice of the bishops, magnates, and professional civil servants who formed his council. When his plans had been drawn they were presented to the cortes in plenary session. In this manner, the cortes was informed and its counsel requested, but it is not likely that any extensive debate was expected except in critical situations such as those just cited. The cortes could give its counsel and consent by declaring that what the king proposed would redound to the benefit of the entire realm. In practical terms, the townsmen, and occasionally the prelates, consented by providing the necessary means for him to execute his plans.

A European Perspective

Elsewhere in Europe, kings similarly consulted their advisors concerning marriage alliances, treaties, war and peace, and the like, but usually did not ask the consent of the estates of the realm. No parliamentary assembly gained the right to ratify treaties or to declare war. Yet kings could not make war without the support of the estates, and that required an explanation of why the war was being undertaken. Thus Pedro IV of Aragón asked the Catalan corts of Perpignan in 1350 for funds to support his efforts to subdue Sardinia. Again at Perpignan in 1356 he needed help against the Genoese, and two years later he asked the corts of Barcelona to assist him in defending his realm against the assaults of Pedro the Cruel of Castile. In like manner, King John of France summoned the Estates of Languedoil in 1355 to counsel him how best to resist his enemies. Edward III also frequently asked the English parliament to grant subsidies for his French wars, but what is particularly interesting is the decision of the commons in the parliament of 1348 to excuse themselves, on account of their "ignorance and simplicity," from giving advice on foreign affairs. Like the commons, municipal representatives in other parliamentary assemblies surely came to realize that giving counsel entailed taking responsibility for the consequences, both good and bad; perhaps they were not always willing to accept it.[57]

7

The Cortes and the Making of Laws

Discussion of the legislative role of the cortes has evoked a considerable diversity of opinion. Martínez Marina, stressing the separation of powers, assigns the executive authority to the king and the legislative power to the cortes. Colmeiro argues that the cortes was merely a consultative body which could petition the king for redress of grievances, but that only he could legislate and for that matter could do so independently of the cortes. Piskorski, however, holds that at least until the end of the fourteenth century, the cortes collaborated with the king in making law. Legislation, according to Procter, "was certainly one of the functions of the cortes during the second half of the thirteenth century, although not all legislation was promulgated in the cortes."[1]

The issue has been confused by the application of modern ideas to a medieval problem. Rather than adopt an a priori stance conditioned by modern conceptions of how laws are made, we have to look at the way law was made in the Middle Ages and then ask what roles the king and the cortes had in this process.

The Royal Right of Legislation

The Visigothic Code (I.1.1–9) recognized the king's right to make new laws, but the right was exercised infrequently before the twelfth century. Alfonso IX, for example, "with the consent and common deliberation of all," enacted *decreta* or *constitutiones* in the *curiae* of León in 1188, 1194, and 1208. The bishops and magnates surely were among those who deliberated with him, but it is not clear that the townsmen were also involved.[2]

The law codes compiled by Alfonso X—the *Espéculo* (I.1.3), *Fuero real* (prologue, I.6.1–5), and *Siete Partidas* (I.1.11–12)—stated emphatically that only the king could make new laws. He could do so "because we have no one greater above us in temporal affairs" and because Roman law, canon law, and the "laws of Spain made by the Goths" affirmed that emperors and kings "have the power to make laws, to add to them, to diminish them and to change them whenever necessary" (*Espéculo*, I.1.3, 13).[3]

The point of these texts was to establish the principle that the king could make laws, a matter of no small importance if one recalls that for much of the early Middle Ages law was thought of as customary and unenacted, having existed substantially unchanged for as long as the mind of man could remember. The new conception, derived from Roman law, treated law as something dynamic and attributed to the king the chief responsibility for seeing that law corresponded to reality.

In certain versions of the *Partidas* (I.1.17–19), the king's sole right to make the laws was limited. His obligation to seek the counsel of knowledgeable, intelligent good men and experts in law, before amending, undoing, or adding to the law, was emphasized, because law is "so much better and stronger the more it is agreed upon and the more it is understood."[4]

None of the texts speaks explicitly of the cortes in this respect, but the statement that the king, before amending the law, ought to consult as broad a group of good men as possible and from as many lands (*tierras*) as possible—presumably from all the kingdoms subject to his rule—indicates that more than a small coterie of royal counselors or professional lawyers was intended. This new conception of legislation implied that whereas the king was ultimately the authority promulgating the law, all the men of the realm had a share in the work of making, altering, or undoing the law. How they would participate in that task was not spelled out, but evidence from the period suggests that they utilized the cortes.

The Alfonsine Codes

There is a good reason to believe that Alfonso X promulgated the *Espéculo* and the *Fuero real* in the cortes. By means of these codes, he hoped to implement his father's determination to ameliorate the consequences of the diversity of laws prevailing in his dominions. As the traditional laws by which all men were governed would be altered, the Roman legal principle, *quod omnes tangit, ab omnibus debet approbari*, required that the king obtain consent. The *Partidas* (I.2.9) affirmed this, stating that a *fuero* ought to be made "with the counsel of good men, knowledgeable men, and with the will of the lord and the consent of those upon whom it is imposed." [5]

Alfonso X declared in the prologue to the *Espéculo* that it was "a mirror of law, whereby all the men of our realms and our dominions may be judged." So that all men would be able to know the law,

> we give a book, sealed with our leaden seal, to each town, and we kept this written text in our court, from which all the others that we gave to the towns are taken. Wherefore, if a doubt should arise concerning the understanding of the laws, and appeal should be made to us, the doubt might be resolved in our court by this book that we made with the counsel and consent of the archbishops, bishops of God, magnates, and the most honored experts in the law that we could have and find, and also of others who were in our court and our kingdom.

The passage quoted refers first of all to the *Fuero real* and then to the *Espéculo*. The book "sealed with our leaden seal" was the *Fuero real*, a code of municipal law given by the king to each town to supplement the older *fueros*. Copies of the *Fuero real* were taken from "this written text" kept in the royal court, that is, the *Espéculo*. The *Espéculo* would be applied in the royal court and would also be used to adjudicate appeals brought from the municipal courts where the *Fuero real* was employed. It was precisely to minimize the divergence between local law and the law of the royal court that the *Espéculo* was used as a basis for the structure of the *Fuero real* and as a source of some of its contents. The *Espéculo* was a mirror of law, in which all other laws, including the *Fuero real*, were reflected. [6]

Historians have generally assumed that the *Espéculo*, incomplete (only five of its seven books are extant) and undated, was never promulgated. From the passage cited we know that the king "made" or "enacted" (*feziemos*) it with the counsel and consent of the prelates, nobles, jurists, and other men of his court and kingdom. If the other men of his kingdom included representatives of the towns, then it would seem that the king was describing a meeting of the cortes.

Robert MacDonald suggests that Alfonso X, in his concern to assure the succession of his daughter, Berenguela (born on 6 December 1253), may have promulgated the *Espéculo* in the cortes of Toledo in March 1254. All those present pledged homage and fealty to her, admitting her right to rule if there were no male heirs. Louis of France, Berenguela's husband-to-be, was informed of this fact on 5 May 1255 at Palencia. Pointing out the similarities between the contract drawn up for the projected marriage and the law in the *Espéculo* (II.16.1) concerning the inheritance of the throne by the oldest son, or, in default of male heirs, by the oldest daughter, Craddock proposes that the law was composed with an awareness that she was the king's only heir at that time.[7]

The *Ordinance* enacted at Zamora in 1274, on the other hand, lends support to the view that promulgation occurred at Palencia in the spring of 1255. In article 4, Alfonso X stated that fees for charters sealed in the royal chancery should be no greater than those set down "in his book which was made *por corte* in Palencia, in the year that Edward married." This passage refers to a section of the *Espéculo* (IV.13.4), where a schedule of fees for sealing charters was set down, and to the marriage of Edward of England to the king's sister at Burgos in November 1254. The promulgation of the *Espéculo*, therefore, could be dated at Palencia in the spring of 1255.[8]

MacDonald proposes three possible explanations: (1) that the *Espéculo* and *Fuero real* were proclaimed in their actual form in the cortes of Toledo 1254 and promulgated in finished form, *por corte*, in Palencia 1255; (2) that both were promulgated in their normal form in the cortes of Toledo and proclaimed in finished form by the court at Palencia; or (3) that the *Espéculo*, redacted before December 1253, was promulgated de jure in the cortes of Toledo 1254 and was put in force de facto by the court at Palencia in 1255. Given the fulfillment of some of the dispositions of the *Espéculo* before May 1255, MacDonald favors the third alternative.[9] Insofar as Alfonso X was conscious of the significance of Toledo, his birthplace, as the ancient seat of the Visigoths and of the emperors of Spain, I am inclined to believe that he seized the occasion of his first cortes there in 1254 to promulgate both the *Espéculo* and the *Fuero real*.

In the prologue to the *Fuero real*, Alfonso X tells us that because many cities and towns lacked a *fuero* and asked him to give them one, he did so, after taking "counsel with our court and with experts in the law." The request for a *fuero* may have been made in the cortes of Seville 1252 or (at the latest) Toledo 1254. The book was finished by the beginning of 1255 when he gave it as a supplementary law ("in a book sealed with our leaden seal") to Aguilar de Campóo and Sahagún.[10] Some of the extant codices were addressed to "many cities and towns of our realms," while others were directed specifically to Burgos, Valladolid, Santo Domingo de la Calzada, Carrión, and Arévalo. To accommodate all the towns, anywhere from fifty to one hundred copies of the text were probably needed, making the task of duplication truly formidable. The copies were dated variously at Valladolid on the day each one was completed (not the day of promulgation), that is, 14 June, 18 July, 25 August, and 30 August 1255.[11]

Other sources testify to the variety of names by which the *Fuero real* was known: the "book sealed with our leaden seal," the *Fuero de las Leyes*, the *Fuero castellano*, the *Libro del Fuero*, and the *Fuero del Libro*. The royal chronicle, alluding perhaps to the derivation of the *Fuero real* from the *Espéculo*, noted that the king ordered the composition of the "*Fuero de las leyes*, in which he summarized very briefly many laws and he gave it as a *fuero* to Burgos and to the other cities and towns of the kingdom of Castile." The Ordinance of Zamora was published nineteen years after the king gave the *Fuero castellano* to Burgos on 15 August 1255 at Valladolid. In 1313 Infanta Blanca, granddaughter of Alfonso X, gave Briviesca the *Libro del Fuero* that the king had given to Burgos and to the "whole realm." The text was finished at Valladolid on 18 July 1255. The prologue to the *Fuero viejo*, written around the middle of the fourteenth century, relates that the king gave the *Fuero del Libro* to the towns of Castile in 1255.[12]

We also know that the *Fuero del Libro* was given to the towns of Extremadura. In an assembly of the Castilian and Extremaduran towns held at Segovia in July 1256, Alfonso X issued at least ten charters, giving individual towns "that *fuero* that I made with the counsel of my court, written in a book, and sealed with my leaden seal." In subsequent years, similar charters, with some variations, were given to other towns. In 1264 the king confirmed the privileges of all the towns of Extremadura, including "the *Libro del Fuero* that we gave them." [13]

The charters of 1256 are proof that the book "sealed with our leaden seal" mentioned in the prologue to the *Espéculo* and given to each town was the *Fuero real*, rather than the *Espéculo* itself as García Gallo erroneously insists. These charters, nevertheless, do not mark the initial cession of the *Fuero real* to specific Castilian and Extremaduran towns. On the contrary, the main purpose of these charters was not to grant the *Fuero real* but to render military service more attractive to the urban knights by giving them tax exemptions. In addition to those new benefits, the king recalled that the *Fuero real* was a favor already granted. [14]

Thus, the *Fuero real* was the book "sealed with our leaden seal" given to each town, as recorded in the prologue to the *Espéculo;* it was the same as the *"fuero* that I made with the counsel of my court, written in a book and sealed with my leaden seal" mentioned in the charters of 1256. Prepared by jurists in the king's service, partly in response to a petition presented by the towns (perhaps in the cortes of Seville 1252) for a new and better *fuero,* the *Fuero real* was promulgated together with the *Espéculo,* probably in the cortes of Toledo 1254. The cortes evidently had no role in the task of drafting either the *Espéculo* or the *Fuero real,* but served as an appropriate forum in which they could be promulgated.

A year had hardly elapsed when Alfonso X, inspired by the hope of gaining the crown of the Holy Roman Empire, ordered work to commence on the great law code known as the *Siete Partidas.* The *Partidas,* elaborated on the foundation of the *Espéculo,* was completed in 1265, but apparently it was not promulgated during Alfonso X's reign. When Alfonso XI gave the *Partidas* the full force of law in the cortes of Alcalá 1348 (XXVIII.1), he declared that it had never before been promulgated. [15]

Reaction Against the Alfonsine Codes

During the cortes of Burgos 1272, the use of the *Espéculo* and the *Fuero real* was challenged, forcing the king to confirm the traditional *fueros* of the nobility and of the Castilian and Extremaduran towns. Discontented with innovations in law and taxation, the nobles confronted the king at Burgos early in September, protesting that they and their vassals were judged by the *fueros* of the municipalities where they resided. The application of the *Fuero real* in the towns of Castile and Extremadura and of the *Espéculo* in the royal tribunal apparently prompted this objection. They also decried the lack of Castilian judges (*alcaldes de Castilla*) or noble judges (*alcaldes fijosdalgo*) to adjudicate their suits in the royal court—an assertion of the principle of trial by peers and an implied objection to the presence of Roman legists there. Declaring that the nobles should enjoy their customs as in the past and should not be judged according to the municipal *fueros* unless they wished, Alfonso X also promised to name Castilian judges in his court. If any noble had a quarrel with him, judgment would be given by the nobles themselves in accordance with the "ancient *fuero*." The nobles, professing to be satisfied, asked only that he confirm what he had said in the presence of the cortes.[16]

The cortes of Burgos 1272 was, without question, the most important of Alfonso X's reign. The appointed time for the assembly was Michaelmas (September 29), and business continued to be transacted throughout the month of October and as late as Martinmas (11 November). Participants included "infantes, prelates, magnates, knights, nobles, and procurators of the towns." Once the cortes assembled, the disgruntled nobles, expressing fear for their safety, refused to enter the city unless the king granted them a truce and allowed them to bear arms. Stating that every man was secure in his court, Alfonso X nevertheless agreed to speak with the magnates and "all the men of the realm" at the Hospital of Burgos, not too far from the monastery of Las Huelgas, just outside the city walls. There he affirmed the pledges already made, but the magnates now escalated their demands to include matters relating to the administration of the realm and the taxation of their vassals. As before, they insisted on trial by their peers, demanding the appointment of two noble judges for this purpose. Perhaps they were influenced by Jaime I's promise in 1265 to name a justiciar from the ranks of the Aragonese nobility to adjudicate their suits. Although Alfonso X objected to the claim that none of his predecessors had ever appointed noble judges, he now promised to do so. A commission of knights, good men of the towns, clerics, and friars was also designated to hear the complaints of both the king and the magnates. According to the *fuero* of Castile, the king was entitled first to receive amends, but he declared that he wished rather to correct any wrong that he might have done before seeking redress for wrongs done to him. He also promised to issue charters under the royal seal pledging to uphold their *fueros* and to observe the promises that he had made in the cortes.[17]

By confirming the traditional customs of the nobility and the *fueros* of the towns, Alfonso X significantly modified his plan to establish a single royal law applicable throughout his realms. The *Fuero viejo* (codified in its present form in the reign of King Pedro the Cruel), after stating that Alfonso X issued the *Fuero del Libro* to the towns of Castile in 1255, added that "they judged according to this book until St. Martin's day in November" 1272. On the urging of the magnates, the king then restored the *fueros* that had been in use in the time of his predecessors, and also "ordered the men of Burgos to judge according to the old *fuero* as they used to before." [18]

Thus, Alfonso X assured both the nobility and Burgos (and probably the other Castilian and Extremaduran towns to whom he had given the *Fuero real*) that they would be judged by their old *fueros* once again. This would seem to imply that in disputes with townsmen the nobles would not be subject to the municipal *fueros*, and if they appeared in the royal court they would not be judged in accordance with the norms of the *Espéculo*. Henceforth, presumably, their suits would be adjudicated by noble judges appointed by the king.[19]

As the recalcitrant nobles repudiated their homage and fealty and prepared to go into exile in Granada, Alfonso X upbraided them, pointing out that "if they demanded *fueros*, he gave them to them, and granted them by his word in court and also by his privilege." The privilege in question probably was drawn up during the cortes of Burgos and may well be the text included in the chronicle, beginning "Estas son las cosas." In this and in subsequent negotiations with the nobility, Alfonso X promised to confirm their *fueros*, usages, and customs.[20]

Several charters confirm that Alfonso X also restored the old *fueros* to the Castilian and Extremaduran towns at this time. From 27 to 31 October 1272 at Burgos, he issued identical charters to Madrid, Soria, Béjar, Cuenca, and Sepúlveda, confirming their *fueros* and privileges. Similar charters were probably issued to all the Castilian and Extremaduran towns in return for the grant of an annual tribute to enable him to carry out his projected journey to the empire.[21]

Although these charters, together with other evidence cited above, provide convincing evidence of the restoration of the municipal *fueros*, it is nevertheless apparent that the *Fuero real* continued in use. García Gallo, who believed that the *Libro del Fuero* was identical with the *Espéculo*, concluded that its application in the towns was now abrogated, and that its usage in the royal court was restricted to the so-called *casos de corte*, whose nature and extent were specified in the Ordinance of Zamora of 1274.[22]

The decisions taken in the cortes of Burgos 1272 to modify his juridical program prompted Alfonso X to consult with prelates, religious magnates, and judges of Castile and León (probably judges of the royal court) at Zamora in June to July 1274. Most historians have assumed that this was a meeting of the cortes, but I doubt that that was the case. Neither the text of the Ordinance nor that of the *Leyes del Estilo* citing the Ordinance (ley 91) refer to the cortes. The king had just concluded the cortes of Burgos in March 1274, and it seems improbable that he would convene another cortes so soon thereafter. After consulting his council concerning the functions of the royal tribunal, he promulgated the Ordinance of Zamora, specifying the cases pertaining exclusively to royal jurisdiction and regulating the roles of lawyers, judges, scribes, and the king himself in the administration of justice. While the Ordinance was not the work of the cortes, nor promulgated in the cortes, it did correspond to problems that had been elicited in previous meetings of the cortes and reflected the changed judicial situation after the confrontation at the cortes of Burgos in 1272.[23]

Ordinances Enacted in the Cortes

The law of the land also included royal charters, privileges, and ordinances, sometimes enacted in the cortes, sometimes not. The term *ordenamiento*, or ordinance (derived from *ordenamos* or *ordene*), was used commonly, as in France, to describe laws formally enacted. Ordinances drafted by the royal council usually employed such language as "mandamos" or "tenemoslo por bien," indicating that the initiative came from the king. The Ordinance of Zamora 1274 and the Ordinance of the Mesta 1278 are examples of ordinances enacted outside the cortes. Another was Sancho IV's ordinance on chancery revenues, which is no longer extant.[24] Alfonso XI's Ordinances of Medina del Campo 1328,

Villarreal 1346, and Segovia 1347 were not enacted in the cortes, contrary to common opinion. Even so, the Ordinance of Medina del Campo was incorporated into the *cuadernos* of the cortes of Madrid 1329 and the Ordinances of Villarreal and Segovia into the Ordinance of Alcalá 1348.[25]

Many ordinances, however, were enacted by the king in the cortes. In a few instances, the text was prepared by the royal council and then promulgated in the cortes. The technical nature of Fernando IV's ordinance on the coinage promulgated in the cortes of Burgos 1302 necessitated its preparation by his council rather than by the cortes. An ordinance regulating his court and household, carefully crafted by his council, was promulgated in the cortes of Valladolid 1312 (art. 1–78). The royal initiative in the preparation of both ordinances is suggested by the words *mando, otrossi mando,* or *otrossi tengo por bien,* with which each article begins.[26]

Alfonso XI, "with the counsel of the prelates, magnates, knights and good men who were with us in this cortes . . . and with the judges of our court," promulgated the *Libro de las Leyes,* better known as the *Ordenamiento de Alcalá,* in the cortes of Alcalá de Henares 1348. The technical treatment of a variety of legal and judicial matters reveals that this ordinance was prepared by the king and his council, or more precisely by the jurists of his court, and then promulgated in the cortes.[27]

Most of the ordinances enacted by the king in the cortes were in response to statements of grievances or petitions submitted to him and his council by one or another of the estates. No detailed information concerning the preparation of these texts exists, but it is apparent that the townsmen especially used the records of previous cortes—many issues were restated time and time again in nearly the same language. The towns of Castile, León, Extremadura, Andalusia, and Murcia presented separate statements (as for example in the cortes of Valladolid 1293), but evidently consulted one another during their preparation, as the similarity of their proposals makes clear. The royal council or committee appointed to review the texts often drew up an ordinance in the king's name, summarizing the proposals made and the action taken; perhaps in doing so the original statement was revised to suit the interests of the king.

The ordinances of Alfonso X usually stated what had been determined, but it was clear that he was acting in reply to detailed complaints of failure to observe prior agreements, or deficiencies in government or in the economy. In the cortes of Seville 1252 he commanded the observance of the *posturas* made by Alfonso VIII, Alfonso IX, and Fernando III "for their own benefit, that of the people, and of the entire realm," and of the *posturas* that he now made with the counsel and consent of the infantes, bishops, magnates, knights, men of the orders, and good men of the towns. *Posturas* evidently meant a contractual agreement between the king and his people. Alfonso X declared that the laws in the *Espéculo* (I.1.1) were "*posturas*, establishments and *fueros*," and he referred to the *Espéculo* itself as a *Libro de posturas*. *Posturas* then were laws, and in 1252 they were enacted by the king with the counsel and consent of the cortes.[28]

Six years later in the cortes of Valladolid he again ordered observance of the *posturas* enacted with the counsel and consent of infantes, prelates, nobles, and good men of the towns, who had first reached agreement among themselves. In the cortes of Seville 1261, when he asked for counsel, the assembly "reached their accord" concerning matters injurious to the realm and requiring correction. He set them down in a *cuaderno*, in fact repeating many of the articles enacted at Valladolid in 1258.[29] The *cuadernos* of the cortes of Seville 1252, Valladolid 1258, and Seville 1261 seem to have been based on texts previously approved by the king, updated as circumstances required, and presented to him again for confirmation.

In their cortes, Alfonso X's successors often referred to his ordinances, at times quoting the texts verbatim. Touching on a variety of themes (such as excommunication, exports, usury, and pawnbroking), some of these ordinances may have been included in books of the *Espéculo* that are no longer extant; others may have been enacted in the cortes, though they are not identical with texts in the existing *cuadernos*.[30]

Sancho IV's ordinances enacted in the cortes of Palencia 1286, Haro 1288, and Valladolid 1293 attended to the grievances of his people. After the townsmen had taken counsel among themselves at Palencia 1286, he accepted their statement of grievances. When he exempted the people from many taxes at Haro 1288, he was apparently responding to general complaints about the burden of taxation, rather than to specific grievances. The towns of Castile, León, Extremadura, Andalusia, and Murcia at Valladolid 1293, after reaching agreement among themselves, presented him with five separate statements of grievances.

The last four *cuadernos* are essentially the same, but they also reveal similarities to the Castilian text. At that time the practice of recording the text of the petition and then the royal response (usually, *otrossi a lo que nos pidieron . . . tenemos por bien . . .*) was used for the first time, but it would be a mistake to say that this was the first instance when the cortes took the initiative in presenting its grievances to the king. The response occasionally was a simple consent (*tenemoslo por bien e otorgamos gelo*) but it might be a more extensive modification of the original petition.[31] Later cortes also referred to various ordinances enacted by Sancho IV.[32]

During the minority of Fernando IV, the regents promulgated several ordinances in his name. In the cortes of Valladolid 1295, after expressing concern to improve the estate of the realm and taking counsel with his regents and members of his court, the king declared, "we ordain and give and confirm and grant these things forever." Although the articles that followed were not set down in the form of petitions and responses, it is obvious that they were directed to specific demands for reform aired in the cortes. The prelates also "showed" the king "many grievances that they had received," to which he replied, with the consent of the regents and his court. The format of the ordinances enacted in the cortes of Cuéllar 1297, Valladolid 1298 and 1299, and Burgos 1301 was basically the same as that of the general *cuaderno* of Valladolid 1295. In the Leonese *cuaderno* of 1299 and that of Zamora 1301 he responded to specific petitions (*otrossi me pidieron . . . a esto uos digo*).[33]

After the king came of age, he continued to record the petitions and then his replies in the cortes of Medina del Campo 1302 and 1305, and Valladolid 1307. At times his response was a simple assent (*tengo por bien et mando*), but more often than not it was highly nuanced. The first part of the *cuaderno* published in the cortes of Valladolid 1312, in which most articles begin *otrossi tengo por bien*, is in the form of an ordinance drawn up by the king and his court, but articles 79 to 105 contain his replies to petitions.[34]

The ordinances enacted by Infante Juan, Maria de Molina, and Infante Pedro in the cortes of Palencia 1313 stated the conditions on which they were accepted as regents for Alfonso XI by their respective constituents. The first nineteen articles of the ordinance enacted by Maria and Pedro were prepared by the assembly and accepted by the regents (*otrossi ordenaron . . . tenemoslo por bien e otorgamos gelo*). The remaining thirty-one articles were petitions (*otrossi nos pidieron* . . .). The *cuaderno* of the cortes of Burgos 1315 is largely an amalgam taken from the texts of Palencia 1313. In addition to confirming the *hermandad*, whose text was incorporated into the *cuaderno*, the regents also replied to the petitions of the prelates. Two years later at Carrión, Infante Juan and Maria de Molina responded to the demands of the *hermandad*, employing the familiar formula (*otrossi alo que nos pidieron . . . a esto rrespondemos* . . .). The *cuaderno* of the cortes of Medina del Campo 1318 was prepared in essentially the same manner. The *cuaderno* of the cortes of Valladolid 1322, recognizing Infante Felipe as regent (and whose substance was drawn from those of Palencia 1313, Burgos 1315, and Carrión 1317), began: "These are the conditions on which we accept a regent." In the same cortes, Juan the one-eyed answered petitions presented by the abbots and abbesses of Castile.[35]

By the time of Alfonso XI's majority, it was routine to record the text of each petition and then the king's answer, a practice that may have served the interests of both the crown and the cortes. As the text of the petitions tended to grow longer, the king and his court probably found it easier to reply article by article, giving a simple consent, qualifying the petition, or rejecting it altogether. The petitioners may also have preferred it that way, because they would then have a record of the petition as it was submitted originally, and could see at once to what extent the king had accepted, modified, or refused it. In the cortes of Valladolid 1325, Alfonso XI granted the petitions of the towns and swore to observe them. The same format was used in the ordinances enacted for the clergy at Valladolid 1325 and Medina del Campo 1326. In all three cases the king did not hesitate to alter or deny petitions. He asked the cortes of Madrid 1329 to inform him of matters needing amendment so he could correct them with its consent; then "what I agreed to and ordained and they advised me" was recorded in the *cuaderno*. His response—often a short statement of approval—followed each petition, though at times it changed or refused it. The formula employed in the assembly of Madrid 1339 varied somewhat but returned to a more customary pattern in the assemblies of Alcalá, Burgos, and León 1345, and in the cortes of Alcalá 1348 (*a lo que nos pedieron . . . a esto rrespondemos*). The *cuaderno* of Alcalá 1348 contained the petitions and responses as well as several additional ordinances (art. 54–131) enacted by the king on his own authority concerning, among others, usury, military stipends, and clothing.[36]

Several other ordinances were enacted by the king in assemblies with one or another of the estates. Alfonso X, for example, on the request of Queen Violante and with the counsel of his court, rectified the grievances of the Extremaduran towns in the assembly of Seville in 1264, though no consistent formula was used to record each petition and reply. The *posturas* regulating prices and wages that were enacted in the assembly of Jerez 1268 were the outcome of consultation by the king with the infantes, prelates, and magnates who were present, as well as with merchants and other good men from the towns. The text, partially based on earlier attempts to regulate prices and wages, also included much that was new. With the counsel of his court, Fernando de la Cerda recorded each complaint of the prelates at Peñafiel in 1275, and then gave his reply (*otrossi querellaron . . . tengo por bien . . .*). Although the wording of the ordinance published at Palencia 1311 indicates that Fernando IV was acting on his own in conceding the liberties of the church (*otrossi tenemos por bien . . .*), it is known that he was responding to the challenge of the prelates. In the fall of that year, also at Palencia, he promised to observe articles presented to him by the nobility. Alfonso XI, endeavoring to encourage peace and friendship among the nobility, enacted an ordinance at Burgos in 1338 with the consent of the magnates, *infanzones*, and knights.[37]

One of the common elements in most of the ordinances enacted in the cortes was the royal confirmation of *fueros*, charters, and privileges granted by previous monarchs. The confirmations by Alfonso IX in the *curia* of León 1188 and Alfonso VIII at Burgos 1212 were typical in this regard.[38] Sometimes the king also confirmed specific acts of previous monarchs or of himself. In the cortes of Medina del Campo 1302 (art. 3), for example, Fernando IV ratified the actions taken by the regents during his minority, and at Valladolid 1312 (art. 43) he confirmed the pact he had made with the nobles at Palencia in the previous year. Similarly, Alfonso XI, in the cortes of Valladolid 1325, confirmed an ordinance on excommunication made by his predecessors (art. 9) and validated the decisions of his regents, save for any acknowledgment of the rights of the *hermandad* (art. 40).

The ordinances usually concluded with the king's confirmation of the text, his pledge to observe it, and his command that all the men of the realm heed it. In the cortes of Seville 1261, Alfonso X ordered "that all the aforesaid matters shall be kept and observed in every way and we forbid anyone to dare to act contrary to them in anything."[39] Sometimes public officials were specifically directed to obey the ordinance or to execute certain of its articles. The royal confirmation was followed by a sanction, a penalty on those who violated the laws thus established. Fines, confiscation of property, exile, or placing the violator's body and goods at the disposal of the crown were frequently cited. Alfonso X asked the bishops to excommunicate anyone who acted contrary to the dispositions of the cortes of Valladolid 1258.[40]

Copies of these texts, usually addressed to the entire realm (*sepan quantos esta carta vieren . . .*) but at times to a particular town,[41] were given to all the participants. The distribution of these documents, described variously as ordinances, charters, privileges, or *cuadernos*,[42] was intended to give the widest publicity to the decisions reached by the cortes.

Observance of the Law

As a general principle, the king was expected to obey all the laws, including the ordinances enacted in the cortes. Both the *Espéculo* (I.1.9) and the *Partidas* (I.1.9) in its earliest redaction emphasized—in words reminiscent of the imperial law, *Digna vox* (*Codex Iustinianus*, I.14.4)—that all men, but especially kings, ought to obey the laws. The kings themselves "are honored and protected by the laws," and "it is right that since they make [the laws] they should be the first to obey them." Otherwise both the king and his laws might be held in contempt. It is obvious, however, that the laws were not always enforced.

Several rulers did admit to transgressions of the laws. In the cortes of Seville 1252, Alfonso X acknowledged that, due to the pressures of war, the agreements made with the people by Alfonso VIII, Alfonso IX, and Fernando III had not been duly observed. In the cortes of Valladolid 1293, Sancho IV indicated that he was prepared to make amends for his previous negligence in observing the laws. Fernando IV complained to the cortes of Valladolid 1307 that there were so many articles in the *cuaderno* that it was difficult to keep track of them; even though he promised to keep a copy of the text in his chamber, he asked to be informed if he violated any of the articles (art. 36). Alfonso XI emphasized the paramount validity of the ordinance enacted in the cortes of Valladolid 1325 when he declared that no charters would be issued contrary to it (art. 42). In practice the king could and did neglect to observe the enactments of the cortes, as he was often reminded by that body, but as a matter of principle both he and the cortes believed that he was bound by its acts.

If a king did act contrary to the ordinances enacted in the cortes, his mistake was usually attributed to negligence and inefficiency in government, rather than to royal imperiousness or a blatant disregard for the law. In the prologue to the *Espéculo*, Alfonso X declared that if anything in that book required amendment, he would amend it "with the counsel of his court." The *Partidas* (I.1.18) stated clearly that the laws ought not to be revoked "except with the great counsel of all the good men of the realm, the best and most honored and most knowledgeable." Thus although Sancho IV revoked many charters and abolished the *hermandades*, he did so in the cortes (Valladolid 1284).[43] Fernando IV assured the cortes of Medina del Campo 1305 that he would not revoke or violate any of the articles contained in the *cuaderno* without first summoning another cortes (art. 14 L).

The Cortes and the Law of the Land

Reflecting on the preceding discussion, several conclusions may be drawn. First, the cortes participated with the king in the legislative process, but it did not have exclusive control over it. Alfonso X claimed the initiative in making laws for the well-being of the people and the right to amend them if necessary. He exercised these rights when he drew up the *Espéculo*, a code of laws to be used in the royal court, and the *Fuero real*, a code of municipal law, but he apparently promulgated both codes in the cortes of Toledo 1254. That served not only to publicize them, but also to confer on them the sanction of the assembled estates of the realm. When these innovations in the law were subsequently challenged, the king had to confirm the traditional *fueros* of the nobility and of the towns in the cortes of Burgos 1272. The process of developing a uniform royal law for the entire realm was not abandoned, nor did the king yield his right to enact ordinances on his own authority. The most important of these later ordinances, the Ordinance of Alcalá, drawn up with the counsel of the royal court, was promulgated in the cortes of Alcalá 1348. During the same cortes, Alfonso XI gave the force of law to the *Siete Partidas*. The cortes thus provided the king with a convenient forum for the promulgation of law codes and ordinances prepared by jurists in the king's service.

A second conclusion is that the estates assembled in the cortes took the legislative initiative when they submitted their petitions and requested redress of grievances. Once the king promulgated an ordinance accepting or rejecting their petitions, that ordinance was recognized as the law of the land. Fernando IV even admitted that he would not revoke ordinances enacted in the cortes, except in the cortes.

Third, a principal weakness of the cortes was the failure of the estates to join together in presenting common proposals to the king. Each estate acted on its own and did not recognize that its interests might be linked to those of the other estates.

Nor did the cortes develop any effective mechanism to monitor the enforcement of the laws. Existing only when the king chose to summon it, the cortes had no permanent delegation to oversee observance of the laws or to demand that the king rectify negligence or transgressions. In times of grave crisis the *hermandades* approximated this function, but they were fundamentally private associations rather than instruments of government, and they received legal sanction only when recognized by the king or his regents.

A European Perspective

A comparable struggle over the legislative role of parliamentary assemblies took place in other western European countries. The general purpose of such assemblies, as Afonso III of Portugal announced to the cortes of Leiria in 1254, was to consider "the estate of the realm and matters to be corrected and improved." In language more precise than that used in any other kingdom, Pedro III of Aragón expressed the legislative role of the Catalan corts of Barcelona in 1283 when he declared that he would only make a general constitution or statute "with the approval and consent of the prelates, barons, knights, and citizens of Catalonia, or the greater and wiser part of those summoned." The thrust of the Statute of York enacted by Edward II of England in 1322 was similar, in that matters touching the estate of the king and the estate of the realm would be determined in parliament.[44]

As in Castile, the king might utilize the cortes to promulgate a law code or the assembled estates might take the opportunity to present their petitions to him. Jaime I of Aragón, for example, published the Code of Huesca in the cortes of Huesca in 1247. The Aragonese nobility and townsmen rather forcefully petitioned Pedro III and Alfonso

III in the cortes of Zaragoza in 1283 and 1287 to issue the Privileges of the Union.[45]

Whether a king could ignore parliamentary enactments was much debated. In Portugal and France the king seems to have been able to do so without significant objection, but Alfonso III, in the general cortes for the Crown of Aragón held at Monzón in 1289, assured the Catalans that he would not enact a law contrary to the acts of the corts. Jaime II promised the corts of Barcelona in 1299 that he would submit to it any law requiring clarification. By contrast, in 1342 Edward III of England nullified a statute enacted in the parliament of the previous year that was not to his liking; the parliament repealed the offending statute the following year.[46]

Obviously, not every realm was advanced in its constitutional development, but even in states like Catalonia where the corts exhibited an acute consciousness of its role in legislative matters, the mere enunciation of a constitutional principle or a royal pledge to abide by the laws did not guarantee automatic observance thereafter.

8

The Cortes and Taxation

Historians agree that the voting of taxes was one of the principal functions of the cortes. As royal responsibilities became more complex and more ambitious, and as the standard of living rose, the king's customary revenues proved insufficient to meet his needs. He often had to obtain additional funds by levying extraordinary taxes.[1]

Contemporary moralists cautioned kings not to burden their subjects unjustly. Fray Juan Gil de Zamora, tutor to Infante Sancho, warned that royal avarice and unaccustomed exactions could result in the impoverishment of the kingdom. Early in the fourteenth century, Álvaro Pelayo complained that kings "afflict the people of God unduly with tallages and exactions and oppress them in bodies and goods."[2]

The Principle of Consent

The king could not arbitrarily impose taxes. The principle that he ought not to deprive any man of his property without just cause, and the Roman principle, *quod omnes tangit, ab omnibus debet approbari*, emphasized that consent was necessary. The *Partidas* (II.1.8) affirmed that "at those times when there is such great need for the common good of the land, that it cannot be excused," the king was entitled to levy taxes. He should presumably ask the cortes for consent, but whenever that was impossible or particularly difficult, he could have recourse to what was his without doing so. In some cases, he seems to have done just that, while in others, he obtained the consent of individuals or small groups.

The principle of consent was recognized explicitly on several occasions. Assuring the bishops at Valladolid in 1255 that neither he nor his successors would demand a *servicio* as a matter of law or take it by force, Alfonso X declared that the clergy should pay it only "when you wish to give it according to your pleasure and good will." He also told the cortes of Burgos in 1277 that none of his successors would be entitled "as a matter of right or custom" to the tax then granted. Infante Sancho made a similar pledge on 28 December 1282,[3] and later promised the cortes of Valladolid 1293 (art. 9 C) that he would ask the cortes for money "whenever we have need." The *hermandad* of 1295 complained of royal attempts to take forced loans and other illegal tributes, refusing to grant them "at least until it has been agreed upon by the entire *hermandad*." By arbitrarily levying several *servicios* in 1306, Fernando IV stirred such a protest that he told the cortes of Valladolid 1307 (art. 6) that "if it should happen that I have need of any tributes, I have to ask for them, and otherwise I will not impose any tributes upon the kingdom." At Palencia in 1311 he also pledged that before taxing the clergy he would summon the prelates and ask their consent; nor would he tax their vassals "without summoning all the prelates personally to our cortes or *ayuntamiento*, whenever we hold it, to ask their consent."[4] In the cortes of Madrid 1329 (art. 68), Alfonso XI expressly stated that he would not "levy any extraordinary tribute, special or general, in the entire realm, without first summoning the cortes." In fact he did not abide by that promise.

In order to gain consent, the king had to justify his need. Alfonso X announced that he required funds for "the affair of the empire" (Valladolid 1258), "the journey to the empire" (Burgos 1274), "the affair of Africa" (Seville 1261), "the affair of the frontier" (Burgos 1269), and the war against Granada and Morocco (Burgos 1277, Seville 1281).[5] The siege and defense of Tarifa was Sancho IV's principal obligation (Haro 1288, Medina del Campo 1291).[6] Money was needed to defend

Fernando IV's rights to the throne (Valladolid 1300, Burgos and Zamora 1301), but once he came of age, his main expenditures concerned the capture of Gibraltar and the siege of Algeciras (Madrid 1309, Valladolid 1312).[7] The defense of the frontier continued to be the priority during the minority of Alfonso XI (Valladolid and Medina del Campo 1318); when he came of age, he complained of the sorry state of his finances and declared his need for money to restore law and order (Valladolid 1325) and to finance the wars against the Moors (Madrid 1329).[8]

The need to obtain consent would seem to imply the right to refuse it, but there was no specific instance during this period when a request for taxes was rejected. At Alcalá in 1275, the representatives of Burgos hesitated to consent to a tax granted by the other towns of Castile and Extremadura without first informing their town council. This seems to be an isolated example of reluctance, though not of outright refusal to consent.[9]

Emphasizing the judicial character of consent, Gaines Post points out that just as the king had the primary responsibility to preserve the well-being of the *status regni* (*estado de la tierra*), so too the people, when informed that the necessity or utility of the state required a tax, had to respond positively.[10] The question was not whether they would consent, but whether they would agree to the amount requested. They might grumble that they were being reduced to poverty, and they might insist that the king live within his means, but ultimately they would give consent.

Taxation of the Estates

Each of the estates was called on at times to consent to extraordinary taxation. Confirming the exemption of the clergy at Nájera in 1180, Alfonso VIII promised not to take anything from them by force, "but only with their love and good will." Yet when he needed money for the coming campaign of Las Navas de Tolosa, he did not hesitate to ask them, at Toledo in September 1211, to pledge half their yearly income.[11] Pope Gregory IX in 1236 instructed the bishops to contribute to Fernando III's campaigns, and a decade later Innocent IV authorized the king to take the *tercias reales* (the third of the tithe destined for the upkeep of churches) for three years for the siege of Seville.[12]

Hoping to dissuade the king from collecting the *tercias* beyond the designated period, the bishops gained Alfonso X's promise in the cortes of Seville 1252 that he would deal with the issue as soon as he visited Castile and León. At Valladolid in October 1255, he declared that the tithe not only served the needs of the church but also might be used for "the service of kings, for their benefit and that of their realm when necessary." All men were obliged to pay it, but before any disposition of the harvest was made royal officials would take what pertained to the crown, thereby filling the royal coffers.[13] In 1265 Clement IV granted Alfonso X a tenth of ecclesiastical income for three years, provided that he abandon the *tercias*, but Nicholas III's remonstrance of 1279 indicates that he did not.[14] Alfonso XI was able to persuade the papacy to grant him the *tercias* and a tenth of ecclesiastical income in 1329 and 1340 for his wars against the Moors.[15]

Kings also obtained the consent of the prelates to extraordinary levies in cortes or assemblies held at Valladolid 1255, Burgos 1276, Medina del Campo 1291, 1316, 1326, and Madrid 1337. The prelates insisted at Peñafiel 1275, Valladolid 1295, Medina del Campo 1302, Palencia 1311, and in their *hermandad* at Valladolid 1314 that their consent was necessary before any tax could be levied on them or their vassals.[16]

The nobility, though exempt from direct taxation, consented in the cortes of Burgos 1269 to a special levy on their vassals. Three years later, again in the cortes of Burgos, they protested this levy, forcing the king to modify the amount at Almagro 1273. Thereafter their consent is recorded only at Carrión 1317 and Valladolid 1336.[17]

Most often the burden of taxation fell on the townsmen. At least from the early thirteenth century, the crown demanded forced loans (*emprestítos*) from certain towns. Fernando III, for example, asked the Galician towns in 1248 to lend him money according to a scale based on individual income. In response to protests, Alfonso X declared at Valladolid 1255 and Segovia 1256 that he would not make similar requests. The *hermandad* of 1295 insisted that the king seek consent. The practice seems to have been intermittent thereafter, but Alfonso XI demanded forced loans in 1333 and 1337.[18]

Moneda Forera

The principal extraordinary taxes were known as *moneda forera*, *ayuda*, and *servicio*. *Moneda forera*, levied every seven years in return for the king's assurance that he would maintain a stable coinage, can be traced at least to the *curia* of Benavente 1202 when Alfonso IX sold his coinage in return for a *maravedí* payable by each non-noble freeman. Alfonso X granted exemptions from *moneda forera* to cathedral canons at Valladolid 1255 and to the knights of Toledo, Seville, and Córdoba on other occasions.[19]

From time to time the cortes granted this tax. Alfonso X's exemption of the canons of Toledo in February 1253 indicates that it was being collected and that the cortes of Seville 1252 may have given consent to it. The cortes of Valladolid 1258 authorized a double *moneda* for "the affair of the empire"—one due later that year, the other an exceptional levy. The nobles demanded at Toledo 1273 that *moneda* be collected only every seven years, an implied charge that it had been exacted on other occasions. Infante Sancho pledged to maintain his grandfather's sound coinage in the assembly of Valladolid 1282 and received a *moneda* even though it was not then due.[20]

Sancho IV also obtained a *moneda* at his accession, and a second one in 1288, but he agreed not to request another for the next ten years, and not more than one every seven years after that. However, there is no sign that he asked the consent of the cortes in either 1284 or 1288. Nevertheless, in the cortes of Palencia 1286 (art. 3) and Haro 1288 (art. 19), he pledged to preserve the coinage intact without reference to *moneda*.[21]

The cortes of Valladolid 1295 granted Fernando IV a *moneda* although seven years had not elapsed, and he obtained another from the cortes of Valladolid 1312. Alfonso XI received *moneda* from the cortes of Valladolid in 1318 and 1325, according to the seven-year schedule. The concession by the cortes of Madrid 1329 was exceptional in that it fell within the seven-year period, but thereafter authorization was given regularly by the assemblies of Burgos, Zamora, and León in 1336, and by the townsmen gathered for the siege of Algeciras in 1343. In the last case, the grant was made in return for his pledge to maintain the coinage. In the summer of 1344 an exceptional *moneda* was approved.[22]

On the basis of the documentation one cannot determine whether the king summoned an assembly every seven years to obtain consent. Probably *moneda* became a customary tax that could be collected every seven years without formal consent. It appears to have been recorded when it was an exceptional grant made outside the usual time frame. *Moneda* was also conceded to a new monarch at the beginning of his reign (for example, when the cortes of Valladolid 1295 granted it to

Fernando IV), and a new seven-year period would be calculated from then on. *Moneda forera* was considered a sign of royal sovereignty that could not be alienated, and exemptions were granted only rarely.[23]

Servicios

Servicio was the term most commonly used to refer to taxes voted by the cortes. When stated as equivalent to *moneda forera*, it was a capitation tax, but otherwise it was a tax on movable property. Occasionally a certain number of *servicios* (or *monedas*) were described as an aid (*ayuda*).

The word *servicio* in the sense of a money grant appeared for the first time when the prelates at Valladolid in 1255 gave it to Alfonso X, who acknowledged that it was a matter of grace, rather than fulfillment of a legal obligation.[24] In the cortes of Burgos 1269 the nobles agreed that six *servicios*, each equivalent to a *moneda*, could be levied on their vassals. Two years later they consented to an additional *servicio* for that year. The king's letter to Burgos on 27 December 1271 suggests that the towns had also granted a *servicio*, perhaps in the cortes of Burgos 1269, on the condition that he lift restrictions on wages and prices and improve the coinage. In the cortes of Burgos 1272 the nobles demanded that the king cease collecting the six *servicios* and give written guarantees that they were not due as a matter of right; but at Almagro 1273 he agreed to cancel only two of the six.[25]

The towns and monasteries in the cortes of Burgos 1272, apparently in exchange for the restoration of their *fueros*, consented to an annual *servicio* (the equivalent of a *moneda*) for as long as Alfonso X thought necessary. Encouraged by his compromise with the nobility, the towns in the cortes of Burgos 1274 persuaded him to collect two *servicios* in the current year to finance his journey to the empire and to relinquish his right to an annual *servicio* thereafter.[26]

After visiting the pope, Alfonso X asked the towns of Castile and Extremadura for an aid (*ayuda*) amounting to a *moneda* each year for three years, to defend the frontier (December 1275). In the cortes of Burgos 1276, the prelates agreed to a levy of three aids (*ayudas*) payable by their vassals, again with the king's pledge not to demand a *servicio* without their consent.[27] As his financial needs continued to mount, he contracted with Jewish tax farmers in October 1276 to recover taxes owed at least since 1261.[28] When this evoked protest, Alfonso X exempted the townsmen in the cortes of Burgos 1277 from arrears, in return for a *servicio* equal to a *moneda forera* of 5⅓ *maravedís* payable each year for the rest of his life. None of his successors would be entitled to this tax as a matter of right or custom.[29] The towns, arguing that they would be able to pay their taxes more easily, also asked him to issue a cheaper coinage, but Alfonso X would not until the pope released him from his pledge (perhaps given at Jerez 1268) to maintain the coinage without alteration. The cortes then sent a petition to Rome; its outcome, however, is unknown.[30] The cortes of Segovia 1278 apparently agreed to an additional *servicio* for the blockade of Algeciras, but continued fiscal deficiencies compelled Alfonso X to lift the siege in July 1279.[31]

Objections to the rising tide of taxation were reflected in the failure of towns to keep up their payments, as Alfonso X's and Sancho's letters to Burgos in 1279 reveal.[32] The general feeling was expressed clearly in the cortes of Seville 1281 when the townsmen complained that they were "very poor and the tributes great." But when Alfonso X proposed debasing the coinage rather than imposing a new tax, they responded, "more out of fear than love," that he should do what he thought best.[33]

Reacting against this, Sancho, in return for *moneda*, promised the assembly of Valladolid 1282 that he would maintain sound money.[34] Later that year the towns gave him an *ayuda*, equal to a *moneda*, but this was not to be taken as matter of right or custom. Both the *hermandad* of León and Galicia at Toro (July 1283) and the assembly at Palencia in November granted him a *servicio*.[35]

Bound by the same financial constraints as his father, Sancho IV resorted to similar measures to overcome them, causing Jofre de Loaysa to remark that he imposed greater tributes than his father ever had. After Sancho IV's coronation, he sent to towns and monasteries asking for an *ayuda* for his journey to the frontier.[36] Determined to collect every penny owed the crown, he concluded a contract in March 1285 with Abraham el Barchilón, authorizing him to collect all revenues and past debts dating back to 1273.[37] The royal accounts for 1285 indicate that the king was promised *servicios* at Burgos and two *servicios* at Seville for the relief of Jerez, but it is not known whether the cortes gave consent.[38] The fact that the rate of taxation was set in the cortes of Palencia 1286 (art. 10) seems to imply that a tax was also granted, but there is no direct evidence to support this idea.

An outcry against the royal financial policies and their architect, Lope Díaz de Haro, resulted in his downfall in June 1288. Reclaiming his authority, Sancho IV cancelled all arrears of taxes in the cortes at Haro in return for an annual *servicio* for the next ten years (art. 1–3), and he promised not to alter the new coinage he had minted in 1286 (art. 19). Thus assured of a regular income for the next decade, and seemingly free of the necessity of summoning the cortes to consent to new taxes, he could feel reasonably satisfied that he had discovered a solution to the age-old problem of making ends meet.[39]

The renewal of warfare with Morocco, however, made it clear that he would require much more. In 1291 he asked the prelates at Medina del Campo (who probably had not voted to tax themselves at Haro) to consent to a *servicio* and an *ayuda* of 1,400,000 *maravedís* for the siege of Algeciras. In the next spring, apparently without convening the cortes, he sent to the men of the realm asking for three *servicios* to maintain the siege. The royal chronicle's assertion that the townspeople paid easily seems astonishing, because these new levies seem to have been in addition to the tax granted at Haro. The Moroccan threat, however, was very real, so it would have been difficult to raise strenuous objections. The king's demand was justified, at any rate, by the conquest of Tarifa in October 1292.[40]

Still, the irregularity of the proceedings was noted in the cortes of Valladolid 1293. Reminding the Castilians that they had guaranteed that he would "have our taxes fully," Sancho IV promised "whenever we have need of them," he would ask for their help (art. 9 C). He also indicated that he would continue collecting the sixth of the *servicios* granted at Haro and the three *servicios* granted for the siege of Tarifa (art. 14 M, 15 LE, 24 A).[41]

While allaying complaints about his previous fiscal activities, Sancho IV evidently enacted an ordinance in the cortes of Valladolid 1293 concerning a novel tax. Known as the *sisa*, it was a levy of one percent on all sales transactions except those of the clergy, knights, and their families, who were exempt. While it was being collected, the king promised not to ask for any other *servicios* (save those currently due), *moneda forera*, or *fonsadera*.[42] Yet when the Moroccans besieged Tarifa in 1294, he demanded aid from the clergy, apparently without convening the prelates to obtain consent.[43]

The *sisa*, meantime, had become an irritant. After Sancho IV's death the Leonese *hermandad* of 1295 charged that he had imposed the *sisa* and other taxes "without reason and without law." All the *hermandades* denounced forced loans, declaring that no tribute should be levied without consent. Aware of the unpopularity of the *sisa*, Maria de Molina announced its abolition. The cortes of Valladolid 1295 granted Fernando IV *moneda forera* as a sign of sovereignty, but it is unlikely that it also consented to a *servicio*. The prelates, moreover, were assured that the king would not demand any tribute from them in the future that was contrary to the liberties of the church.[44]

Thereafter *servicios* were granted regularly and in increasing amounts, chiefly for the suppression of the rebels. The cortes of Cuéllar 1297 granted one *servicio*, Valladolid 1298 agreed to two, and Valladolid 1299 to three. The cortes of Valladolid 1300 authorized four, adding a fifth to pay for papal bulls legitimating the king; but as the fifth was turned over instead to Infante Juan who renounced his claims to the throne, the intention of the cortes was thwarted. The cortes of Burgos (Castile) and Zamora (León-Extremadura) 1301 (art. 15) complained about this diversion of funds, but Maria de Molina argued that, as the king would soon come of age, it was imperative that he be legitimated and that a dispensation for his marriage be obtained. Thus four *servicios* were approved to pay the stipends of the nobles and a fifth for the papal bulls, which were granted in September 1301.[45]

Jofre de Loaysa's comment that Fernando IV burdened the kingdom with greater taxes than either his father or his grandfather should not be understood to mean that he was more extravagant; rather, the cost of living and the expenses of warfare and administration were constantly rising. During Fernando IV's majority, he often asked for funds for the war against the Moors. Both the cortes of Medina del Campo and Burgos 1302 acceded to his request for five *servicios*, one for his needs and the other four to pay the stipends of the nobility.[46]

After the Council of Peñafiel publicized Boniface VIII's bull, *Clericis laicos*, forbidding taxation of the clergy, Archbishop Gonzalo of Toledo protested in the cortes of Medina del Campo any attempt to tax ecclesiastical vassals. The king, pointing to the need to defend archiepiscopal lands exposed to Muslim attack, overcame the archbishop's opposition by offering him half the *servicios* collected from his vassals. Other bishops were similarly placated.[47]

Returning from the frontier in 1303, the king received five *servicios* from the Extremaduran towns at Olmedo. In the next year Castilian and Extremaduran towns at Burgos granted an *ayuda* (amounting to a *moneda forera* of eight *maravedís* payable by each taxpayer) in exchange for his promise not to demand an accounting of past tributes, except for those owed since the cortes of Medina del Campo 1302.[48]

The cortes of Medina del Campo 1305 authorized five *servicios*— four for noble stipends and the fifth for the king, but as that was insufficient Fernando IV collected another later in the year. In April 1306 he levied four *servicios*, and in June he collected a fifth.[49] This imposition of taxes without consent provoked the cortes of Valladolid 1307 to demand that the king live within the limits of his ordinary revenues so he would not have to levy *servicios*. Not only did he agree, but he also pledged to ask consent for further taxes if he needed them (art. 6). He also assured the bishops that, without first asking their consent, he would not impose any tributes on their vassals. Perhaps taking into account the six *servicios* levied without consent since the cortes of Medina del Campo 1305, the cortes of Valladolid now approved only three.[50]

Fernando IV's ordinance enacted in the cortes of Valladolid 1307, in Colmeiro's view, set down as a matter of written law the principle that the king had to obtain consent to extraordinary taxes. From that day on, Colmeiro concludes, "the cortes was a necessary institution for the monarchy." González Mínguez attempts to distinguish between ordinary *servicios* that the cortes regularly approved, and extraordinary ones that the king often imposed without consulting the cortes, but the distinction is invalid. *Servicios* by their very nature were extraordinary taxes requiring the consent of the taxpayers. The imposition of *servicios* (or taxes not spelled out in the *fueros*) without consent was the reason the cortes of Valladolid 1307 insisted that the king live off his customary revenues and that he promise not to levy extraordinary taxes unless approved by the cortes.[51]

The value of these promises was soon to be tested. The king's collection without consent of five *servicios* in the fall of 1307, for the purpose of paying noble stipends for three months, resulted in a demand for an accounting of revenues and expenses in the cortes of Burgos 1308. To no one's surprise, a deficit was revealed. Hoping to avoid a confrontation with the cortes, Infante Juan proposed collecting all overdue taxes, but Maria de Molina, recalling the controversies that had arisen when Alfonso X and Sancho IV had attempted to do the same,

urged that a *servicio* would be less objectionable. Fernando IV acknowledged the wisdom of Maria's views, but bowed to Infante Juan's insistence. The ordinance enacted at this time indicates, however, that only
a limited effort was made to recover outstanding tributes.[52]

The reluctance of the cortes to consent to new taxes was noted by
Jaime II of Aragón, who heard that the cortes of Madrid 1309, alleging
the poverty of the realm, "did not wish to give him [Fernando IV] anything until he told them why." Even so, the cortes authorized five *servicios* for that year and three for each of the next three years, so that
Fernando IV could take the offensive against Granada.[53] Lulled by his
promise to pay noble stipends from his ordinary revenues (art. 83), and
persuaded by the fall of Gibraltar that the money voted three years before was well spent, the cortes of Valladolid 1312 approved five *servicios*
and a *moneda*. Finding that insufficient, the king asked the towns of the
archbishopric of Toledo for another *servicio* for a fleet to defend Tarifa
and Gibraltar.[54]

As his needs escalated and extraordinary grants proved inadequate,
tensions heightened, producing a negative reaction during the minority
of Alfonso XI. Protesting the excessive tributes imposed "without reason and without law" since Alfonso X's time, the Leonese *hermandad* at
Benavente in 1313 insisted that anyone aspiring to act as regent should
pledge not to levy any illegal tributes. In the cortes of Palencia 1313
Infante Juan, Maria de Molina, and Infante Pedro declared that they
would govern within the limits of the ordinary revenues of the crown
(art. 4 J, 10 M). There is no indication that any *servicios* were authorized; given the mood of the cortes, it would seem unlikely. Nor is there
any mention of *moneda forera*, though the king could have claimed it as
a sign of sovereignty.[55]

The *hermandad* of bishops at Valladolid in 1314 reaffirmed the principle of consent, declaring that they would not agree to any tax until,
after consulting their chapters, they met to consider the needs of the
kingdom and the rights of the church. Nevertheless, at Dueñas Infante
Juan received four *servicios* from the prelates, nobles, and military
orders. In the cortes of Valladolid 1314 Maria de Molina and Infante
Pedro obtained five *servicios*—four to pay stipends and the fifth for the
crown.[56]

The regents assured the cortes of Burgos 1315 that they would live
within a budget, expending royal revenues in such a manner that no ex-

traordinary tribute would be imposed (art. 4). However, the cortes, concerned that the resources of the crown be carefully husbanded, demanded a financial report. When the report was announced, it became apparent that the treasury was much depleted. Thus, the cortes authorized customs duties as well as two *servicios* and three *ayudas* (each of which amounted to a *moneda*) for the defense of the frontier.[57]

Hoping to improve the fiscal situation, the regents, much to the irritation of the prelates, proposed to recover royal lands acquired by the church since the cortes of Haro 1288 (art. 54). To avert that, the prelates at Medina del Campo in 1316 consented to a *servicio* and an *ayuda*, on condition that no action be taken until the king came of age. That summer the frontier towns granted Infante Pedro a *servicio* of a million *maravedís* for the war against Granada.[58]

When the government tried to collect arrears of taxes going back to the cortes of Madrid 1309, the *hermandad* of Carrión 1317 objected, arguing that Fernando IV had exempted the people from any inquiry into taxes past due in return for *servicios*. Even though some towns had not paid their taxes and so could not claim exemption, the regents agreed to abandon the attempt (art. 10). When a new accounting revealed a huge deficit, a grant of five *servicios* payable by the working class (*los labradores*) was approved. When the nobles engaged in an unseemly quarrel over the apportionment of these funds, Maria de Molina left the assembly. In the next year the cortes of Valladolid and Medina del Campo granted four *servicios* and a *moneda* (which fell due at that time) for the sustenance of the king and his household, and for the payment of stipends to the nobles participating in the war against Granada.[59]

As the regency broke down, each of the contenders for power levied taxes on his or her constituents. The *hermandad* of Burgos 1320 gave Juan the one-eyed seven *servicios*, while Maria de Molina collected six from the vassals of the nobility and the church. Juan Manuel obtained seven and a half from his supporters at Madrid in 1321. In the cortes of Valladolid 1322, Infante Felipe pledged to expend the ordinary revenues of the crown so that no *servicios* or illegal tributes would be imposed (art. 16). Juan the one-eyed's adherents granted him five *servicios* at Burgos in 1323, and Juan Manuel, boldly explaining that he would not be able to collect these taxes once the king came of age, asked for a like amount from his followers at Madrid in 1324. Thus the regents exploited the kingdom for their personal benefit, levying extraordinary taxes even though after 1319 there was no war with the Moors or with the king's other enemies.[60]

After he came of age, Alfonso XI effected significant changes in extraordinary taxation. He failed to summon the cortes regularly, thereby diminishing its role in voting taxes, and he changed the types of taxes so as to yield greater revenue without provoking as much protest. As his finances were in disorder, the cortes of Valladolid 1325 approved a grant of five *servicios* and a *moneda*.[61] The prelates at Medina del Campo in 1326 also gave him a *servicio*, in return for his renunciation of claims to royal lands acquired by the church. The cortes of Madrid 1329, pleased by his resolve to launch an offensive against the Moors and by his promise not to impose any extraordinary tribute without consent (art. 68), authorized four *ayudas* and a *moneda*.[62]

Thereafter, Alfonso XI avoided summoning the cortes and sought to raise money in other ways. The magnates, knights, and masters of the military orders at Valladolid in 1336 granted five *servicios* and a *moneda* payable by their vassals, but also urged him to summon the towns to get their consent. Only the more important Castilian towns were summoned to Burgos, and the Leonese to Zamora, but their consent was taken as the consent of all. Rather than convene the cortes, the king preferred to meet separately with three different bodies—the nobles, the townsmen of Castile, and the townsmen of León. Because "the men of the realm were in such great poverty on account of the many tributes," he asked the prelates at Madrid in 1337, and the towns two years later, for unspecified sums. Following his victory at Salado in October 1340, the towns at Llerena approved a small quantity of *servicios* and *monedas* in expectation of a renewed enemy assault.[63] In succeeding years, Alfonso XI looked for other, more productive sources of revenue. Before we consider them, however, several questions concerning *servicios* need to be addressed.

Receipts and Rates of Taxation

The disappearance of fiscal records makes it difficult to determine how much the king realized from any extraordinary tax. Utilizing surviving royal accounts for 1288, 1292, and 1294, Ladero Quesada estimates that Sancho IV received more than 1,500,000 *maravedís* from each *servicio*. This would accord with the grant of 1,400,000 by the prelates in 1291, but the *servicio* granted to Infante Pedro in 1316 amounted only to 1,000,000. If five *servicios* were intended to meet the deficit of 8,000,000 *maravedís* revealed at Carrión 1317, then each *servicio* would have amounted to 1,600,000—but it is apparent that the sum collected was insufficient. Unless more detailed records come to light, the amount garnered by the imposition of *servicios* will remain uncertain.[64]

The rate of taxation is similarly difficult to estimate. On occasion the *servicio* or *ayuda* was a capitation tax payable at the same rate as *moneda*, but at other times it was a tax of variable amount on movables. When the *curia* of Benavente 1202 gave *moneda* to Alfonso IX, each taxpayer was to pay one *maravedí*. The *servicios* authorized by the cortes of Burgos 1269 and 1272 evidently amounted to a *moneda* each, or one *maravedí* payable by each taxpayer. In the cortes of Burgos 1277, however, the *moneda* amounted to five and a third *maravedís* per person, and at Burgos 1304 it was eight *maravedís*. Yet at Madrid 1339 each *moneda* and each *servicio* amounted to half a *maravedí* (art. 2).[65]

At other times the tax rate varied. When Fernando III asked for an *emprestíto* in 1248 the rate was 5%. The three aids granted to Alfonso X in 1275 and at Burgos 1276 were payable at the rate of 10 *sueldos* for every 10 *maravedís*, or 20%. Burgos contracted in 1279 to pay *servicios* at the same level, which seems inordinately high; in fact, the men of the realm could justifiably complain that they were being reduced to poverty. In the cortes of Palencia 1286 (art. 10, 13), Sancho IV, stipulating that *servicios* would be payable in the same manner as *moneda*, fixed the rate at 10%. Personal clothing was excluded from estimated wealth, and anyone worth less than five *maravedís* would pay nothing. He declared in the cortes of Haro 1288 (art. 20) that *servicios* should be paid at the same rate as *moneda*, but not *per capita*; thus new assessments (*padrones*) should be prepared each year. When Juan Manuel levied *servicios* in Extremadura in 1321 the rate was 6%. On the basis of this scanty information, no judgment can be made as to the usual rate of taxation, or even whether there was one.[66]

Servicio de los Ganados *and Customs Duties*

Aside from direct taxes on income, the cortes also authorized or regulated exceptional taxes on migratory sheep and on exports and imports. As sheepraising became more profitable and herds traveled long distances to take advantage of southern pastures, the crown sought to tap that resource. Alfonso X seems to have first levied the *servicio de los ganados* in 1269 for the marriage of his oldest son, but whether he asked the cortes of Burgos to consent to it is unknown. The nobles at Toledo in 1273 demanded that he abandon this *servicio*, but he evidently refused. It may have become a customary tax levied without the consent of the cortes.[67] The cortes of Valladolid 1293 (art. 8 LEM), and later cortes as well, insisted that the tax not be levied on livestock within municipal districts or on animals taken to market.[68]

Alfonso X designated certain frontier towns where customs duties would be collected (Jerez 1268, art. 21–23). Pressed by the magnates in the cortes of Burgos 1272 to give up the duties, he offered at Almagro 1273 to do so after six years. The demand of the Leonese *hermandad* of 1282 (art. 7) that duties be levied as in the time of Alfonso IX and Fernando III reveals not only that they continued to be a regular source of income but also that the amounts had steadily increased. The cortes of Palencia 1313 tried to persuade Infante Juan to levy them at the rate prevailing under Fernando III (art. 4 J), and the assembly of Carrión 1317 (art. 22) demanded that collection be restricted to Fernando IV's customs posts. The cortes of Valladolid 1325 granted customs duties for three years to Alfonso XI, but he continued to take them beyond that term, despite the protest of the cortes of Madrid 1329 (art. 86).[69]

The Alcabala

Alfonso XI recognized the inadequacy of income taxes and turned to the *alcabala*, a tax on all sales, as a primary means of getting the funds he wanted. Alfonso X had authorized Burgos to levy this tax for the upkeep of its walls, but when the nobles protested in the cortes of Burgos 1272, he exempted them, even though they had consented to it. Sancho IV's similar device, the *sisa*, was condemned by the *hermandad* of 1295 and promptly abolished.[70]

The *alcabala*, an indirect tax falling on nobles, clergy, and the people of the realm generally, seemed less likely to elicit an outcry than the *servicios*. Recalling that the Moors had just recovered Gibraltar in 1333, Alfonso XI appealed to Seville, Córdoba, and Murcia, hoping that once they consented the smaller towns would follow suit. Thus the *alcabala*, a tax on sales of bread, wine, fish, and clothing, was introduced in a limited way and was probably renewed when it expired three years later.[71]

Intent on besieging Algeciras, but realizing that "the workers and those who could do little were especially burdened, while the magnates paid only small amounts," the king decided to extend the *alcabala* to all commercial transactions. As this was an extraordinary tax not previously collected, he convened four separate assemblies of varied composition at Burgos, León, Zamora, and Ávila in 1342 to obtain consent. Burgos expressed its reluctance, but by emphasizing that the siege was essential to the well-being of his kingdom and Christendom, the king persuaded Burgos and the prelates and nobles assembled there to give consent for the duration of the war. In the assemblies of León, Zamora, and Ávila there was no significant opposition.[72]

Three years later, after the fall of Algeciras, the assemblies of Alcalá (art. 8, 12, 15), Burgos (art. 8, 11–12), and León (art. 26–29) authorized the *alcabala* for six years. During that time no other tributes were to be levied, except *moneda forera* when it fell due every seven years, and *fonsadera* when necessary. In the future, the *alcabala* would not be taken as a matter of custom. Sales of horses and arms—important for military defense—were exempted, but the plea of the Castilian merchants to be exempted from customs duties so long as they paid the *alcabala* was refused (Burgos 1345, art. 2).[73]

The cortes of Alcalá 1348 complained that men were unable to pay the *alcabala* and *tercias* due to harsh weather and a poor harvest in the preceding fall, but the king promised relief only if it were proved that they were truly in need (art. 35). In spite of this bluster, the cortes apparently consented to the continuance of the *alcabala* for the defense of Algeciras, Tarifa, and the frontier. In later years, the *alcabala* became one of the most important sources of royal revenue.[74]

Control of Taxation

As extraordinary taxation became an inescapable fact of political and economic life, the cortes began to seek some control over the frequency of such levies, the uses to which the money was put, and the process of collection. At a time when extraordinary taxation was still a novelty, both Alfonso X and Sancho IV were able to persuade the cortes to accede to long-term levies. The cortes of Burgos 1272 gave Alfonso X an annual *servicio* for as long as he thought necessary, and the cortes of Burgos 1277 granted another for life. That would seem to have limited the need to convoke the cortes regularly, but that was not the case. The cortes of Haro 1288 (art. 1–3), on the other hand, enabled Sancho IV to avoid convening the cortes for at least five years by granting him an annual tribute for ten years. In fulfilling the distasteful but necessary duty of voting taxes, the townsmen may have hoped that the king would never bother them again, but they soon discovered that that was not true.[75]

Not surprisingly, the levies approved by the cortes in the minority of Fernando IV (Cuéllar 1297, Valladolid 1298, 1299, 1300, Burgos and Zamora 1301) were for one year only. This practice continued through Fernando IV's mature years (Medina del Campo and Burgos 1302, Medina del Campo 1305, and Valladolid 1307, 1312), though the cortes of Madrid 1309 did approve one three-year grant (according to the royal chronicle, it was for an indeterminate period).[76]

The cortes of Valladolid 1307 (art. 6) seems to have been the first to suggest that if the king lived off his customary revenues he would not have to ask for extraordinary taxes. This idea was taken up again during the minority of Alfonso XI by the cortes of Palencia 1313 (art. 4 J, 10 M), Burgos 1315 (art. 4), and Valladolid 1322 (art. 16). As that suggestion proved unrealistic, new levies were made, probably for a year at a time (Valladolid 1314, Burgos 1315, Carrión 1317, Valladolid and Medina del Campo 1318, Valladolid 1325, and Madrid 1329). Alfonso XI's haphazard convocation of the cortes and other assemblies thereafter made it impossible to control him.[77] The assemblies of Alcalá (art. 8, 12, 15), Burgos (art. 8, 11–12), and León 1345 (art. 26–29), which authorized the *alcabala* for six years, were keenly aware that it might become a customary tribute collected without consent.

At times, especially in the minorities, the cortes tried to control the use of taxes. The Castilians at Cuéllar 1297 (art. 1) demanded that twelve townsmen be admitted to a regular place in the royal household to give advice concerning the disposition of royal revenues. For the first time in its history, the cortes of Valladolid 1300 (art. 3) explicitly limited the expenditure of taxes to a particular end, to the exclusion of all others, insisting that money given to the king (specifically to suppress his enemies and to obtain a papal dispensation) should be used "for no other purpose." Nonetheless, much of it was diverted to other ends.

Accounting of Royal Revenues

Attempts were also made to obtain an accounting of the king's finances. The cortes of Valladolid 1307 (art. 6) asked him to determine how much he received from his customary revenues. To implement this proposal, Maria de Molina suggested an accounting to the magnates at Grijota 1308; they agreed but insisted that the townsmen be convened for this event. Thus the matter of balancing the budget was the main business of the cortes of Burgos 1308. When the audit was completed, a deficit of 4,500,000 *maravedís*, caused by the constant rise in noble stipends, was revealed. The king decided to decrease the stipends (art. 3), but one cannot imagine that the magnates willingly accepted a significant reduction of their income. To increase revenues, charters conceding tributes to individuals or towns (art. 4, 9) and special tax exemptions were revoked (art. 10–11), but these measures were offset by the king's confirmation of an ordinance made at Burgos 1304, remitting arrears of taxes (art. 18). Thus, financial reforms were not consistently enforced and fell far short of what was necessary. The king's pledge in the cortes of Valladolid 1312 (art. 83) to balance the budget, so that stipends and other expenses could be covered by his ordinary income without further impoverishing the people, is evidence of the continuance of this problem.[78]

The cortes of Palencia 1313 (art. 4 J, 10 M) urged Alfonso XI's regents to be limited by customary revenues, but when the cortes of Burgos 1315 demanded an audit, it became apparent that the treasury was greatly depleted and that extraordinary taxes were essential. The Castilian *hermandad* at Burgos in 1316 also insisted on a detailed accounting, a process that took four months. The results, presented at Carrión 1317, showed that royal revenues amounted to 1,600,000 *maravedís* levied on the entire realm except the frontier, while expenses (the maintenance of the king and his court, custody of castles, and noble stipends) amounted to 9,600,000, leaving a deficit of 8,000,000.[79]

Alfonso XI, in the cortes of Valladolid 1325 (art. 1), bound himself to carry out an accounting, but it is uncertain whether he did. When he asked the cortes of Madrid 1329 to tell him what matters he should correct "with their consent," they asked him to account for his revenues, retaining a sufficient amount for himself and apportioning the remainder among the nobility (art. 24). However, there is no evidence that he acceded to this request. In neither instance does the petition to Alfonso XI appear to have been made with great urgency.

Tax Collectors

The cortes also tried to control the collection of taxes, which was under the general supervision of the *almojarife mayor*, usually a Jew. Infante Juan promised the cortes of Palencia 1313 (art. 31 J) that no Jew would be appointed; however, Alfonso XI named Yūsuf of Écija to the post, until the complaints of the cortes of Madrid 1329 resulted in Yūsuf's dismissal and the king's pledge to appoint only Christians, with the title of *tesorero*. This, too, proved to be only a temporary change.[80]

Jews were also employed as tax farmers. In 1276 and 1277 Alfonso X concluded five contracts with Zag de la Maleha (Isaac ibn Zadok—then the *almojarife mayor*) and several others, authorizing them to collect arrears, including *servicios*, from the campaign of Niebla in 1261 to the current year. In return, they would pay 1,670,000 *maravedís*. This intensive scrutiny of accounts dating back fifteen years exacerbated relations between the king and his subjects but was resolved when he cancelled the contracts in the cortes of Burgos 1277, in exchange for an annual *servicio* for life.[81] Sancho IV made a similar contract with Abraham el Barchilón in 1287, but opposition soon forced him to abrogate the contract in the cortes of Haro 1288 (art. 1–18, 26–27) in return for a *servicio* for ten years.[82]

From the cortes of Palencia 1286 (art. 10) onward, the constant reiteration of demands that taxes be collected by knights and good men of the towns, to the exclusion of Jews, nobles, clerics, and other officials, suggests that the king continued to farm his taxes and to entrust their collection to those who were not townsmen.[83]

In some places a capitation or poll tax (*por cabeza*) was payable in a fixed amount, but usually a list (*padrón*) of taxpayers was prepared with an estimate of their wealth determined by an inquest among their neighbors, so that each man paid proportionate to his worth. In the cortes of Haro 1288 (art. 20), Sancho IV required new *padrones* to be drawn up each year so that levies would not be made by head, but the cortes of Medina del Campo 1318 (art. 10) acknowledged that payment might be either by head or by assessment. Charges were made at Madrid 1339 (art. 2) that in the preparation of taxrolls, wealth was often deliberately concealed or underestimated.[84]

According to the cortes of Burgos 1315 (art. 6), no man was liable for more than he was assessed, nor could he be forced to pay another's capitation tax (Madrid 1329, art. 32). If he had no property that could be taken for taxes, he could not be seized for nonpayment (Burgos 1301, art. 2; Zamora 1301, art. 20), for as the cortes of Valladolid 1312 (art. 10) declared, this was "contrary to God and to law." If he had other chattels, his oxen, his wheat, or his clothing or that of his family could not be seized.[85]

Tax collectors were authorized to seize the goods of taxpayers only where they resided; movable property had to be sold to pay the king's taxes within nine days and real estate in thirty. If taxpayers attempted to defraud the king by refusing to purchase property thus offered for sale, five or six of the richest men of the community could be compelled to buy it (Valladolid 1293, art. 11 C).[86] Local magistrates were empowered to resolve any disputes.[87]

Tax collectors were expected to render accounts to their superiors. Ordinary collectors did so in the seat of the bishopric where they resided (Palencia 1313, art. 39 J), but principal collectors appeared in the king's household (Burgos 1315, art. 6) before two knights or good men from Castile, León, Extremadura, and Andalusia (Valladolid 1322, art. 21).[88] In no case could a town be held responsible for malfeasance by one of the tax collectors.[89]

Extraordinary Taxation

The development of extraordinary taxation is the principal characteristic of this period. As fiscal requirements mounted, new sources of revenue had to be found. Although the king at times acted arbitrarily in levying taxes, he often acknowledged his duty to seek consent and convoked the cortes for that purpose. Yet he could not expect the passive consent of an inert and unthinking body of men. He had to justify his request, and the cortes, admitting the validity of his argument, had to assist him. Taxation thus was a collaborative activity involving both the king and the cortes.

The king first tried to meet his newly developing needs by altering the coinage, and then promised not to tamper with it further in return for *moneda*—a fixed payment of one *maravedí*; but as this was insufficient, *servicios* payable in either fixed or variable amounts became the preferred tax. The burden was not distributed equitably, and tax exemptions vitiated the entire process. The nobles and clergy were ordinarily exempt, although the clergy and the vassals of the nobility were taxed from time to time. Monastic communities, more often than not, were exempted. It is one of the ironies of the age that the knights of the towns who usually represented the municipalities, together with their families, were often exempted, at the request of the cortes.[90] Thus, taxation fell most heavily on merchants, artisans, and peasants. By contrast, the *alcabala* had the virtue of affecting all classes.

As time passed, the cortes recognized the dangers inherent in the concession of *servicios* for life or for long terms and opted to limit them, usually to one year. In at least one instance, the cortes strictly defined the purpose of the grant (Valladolid 1300). While occasionally asking to see the king's books, or urging him to adhere to a budget, the cortes did not establish a permanent, effective, and independent system of budgetary review.

Ideally, the cortes preferred the king to live frugally on his ordinary revenues and not to trouble the people for exceptional taxes. He was expected, unrealistically, to defend the realm, administer justice, and maintain internal order on the basis of an inadequate revenue structure. Whenever the cortes did recognize the legitimacy of his needs, it also objected to any attempt to recover arrears of taxes, declaring that the people were being reduced to poverty.[91] In sum, the attitude of the cortes toward taxation was confusing and contradictory.

A European Perspective

The experience of other western European monarchies was similar. In Portugal, Afonso III obtained a *monetágio* from the cortes of Leiria in 1254 by pledging to maintain the coinage for seven years. He also had to admit, in the cortes of Coimbra in 1261, that he could not devalue the coinage without the consent of the cortes. The general reluctance to accept extraordinary taxes was reflected in Pedro III's guarantee to the Catalan corts of Barcelona in 1283 that he would not introduce any new taxes without consent. Concern about the use of tax monies led the Catalan corts of Monzón in 1289 to appoint a commission to supervise collection. Eventually this resulted in the development of the *Generalitat*, a body representing the corts when it was not in session.[92]

Philip VI of France tacitly accepted the principle of consent when, in return for a sales tax, he assured the Estates of Languedoil in 1343 that he would maintain a sound money. During the crisis of 1355–1356, the Estates also tried to control collection and disbursement.[93] Edward III, declaring that a wool tax granted by the English parliament in 1340 should not be taken as a precedent, pledged to seek consent for future taxes. The parliament in 1341 asked to examine royal accounts, but this did not become a standard practice for many years.[94] Although several precedents were established at this time, their full implementation did not come until much later.

9
The Cortes and the Government of the Realm

Documentation pertaining to the cortes touches on a myriad of issues reflecting contemporary concerns and attitudes. This chapter will consider actions taken in the cortes to improve the government of the realm. No attempt will be made to delineate fully any one governmental body or function, but only to point out problems and the solutions then proposed and adopted. The critique of the cortes ranged widely, touching on the royal household, chancery and tribunal, the activities of territorial administrators, difficulties encountered by municipalities, the steady diminution of the royal domain, and the breakdown of law and order. By its insistence on good government, the cortes was able to set its stamp on many contemporary institutions.

The Casa del Rey

The cortes seldom criticized the king directly, but it did not hesitate to express its views about his entourage of private servants and public officials. This body was usually described as the *casa del rey*, a phrase that replaced the Latin *curia regis*. At times *corte del rey* was used to designate the royal court functioning as a judicial tribunal, but the terms were often used interchangeably.

Both the *Espéculo* (II.12) and the *Partidas* (II.9.1–2, 27–28) described the personnel of the royal household and court. While many of those who accompanied the king were domestic servants, others performing services of a public character formed his council (*consejo del rey*). They included the chancellor, *mayordomo mayor*, *alferez*, and various nobles, clerics, and legists (sometimes referred to as *omnes bonos de mi corte*).[1] On occasion the king might include the great men of the realm, but ordinarily it was a small group that advised him on day-to-day business.

From time to time, the cortes stressed the need to reorganize the royal court or to correct abuses (Burgos 1308, art. 2). Two major restructuring ordinances were enacted by Fernando IV and Infante Felipe at Valladolid 1312 and 1322, respectively. The cortes was also concerned about the types and qualities of persons serving the king. All royal officials were required to serve in person and to give an account of their activities. They had to take an oath to protect the kingdom against injury and to see that justice was done so that men might live in peace (Valladolid 1312, art. 50, 73). Only natives of the realm who would observe the *fueros* should be appointed (this excluded Jews and Moors, as well those who bought their offices), and no one was permitted to hold more than one office (Madrid 1329, art. 32, 34–37). During the two minorities the cortes demanded the ouster of officials who had served previous monarchs. In other instances, protests made in the cortes eventually resulted in the downfall of unpopular officials.[2]

The cortes argued during the minorities that townsmen should be included in the royal council. Fernando IV promised the cortes of Valladolid 1295 (art. 4) that he would include townsmen but not Jews. Two years later, in the cortes of Cuéllar (art. 1), he agreed that twelve good men from the Castilian towns should advise him in matters of justice and finance. Later the cortes of Medina del Campo 1302 (art. 4) persuaded him to ask townsmen from Castile, León, Toledo, and Extremadura to serve in the council.

As regents for Alfonso XI, Infante Juan, Maria de Molina, and Infante Pedro assured the cortes of Palencia 1313 (art. 1–2, 20 J, 4–5 M) that they would designate a council of four prelates and sixteen townsmen. The *hermandad* at Burgos 1315 (art. 14) emphasized the role of townsmen in the council, and at Carrión two years later it severely criticized the regents for attempting to downgrade them (art. 1, 42). Infante Felipe agreed that the council should include twenty-four knights and good men of the towns (Valladolid 1322, art. 3–4, 14). Alfonso XI, on coming of age, also guaranteed them a place (Valladolid 1325, art. 4).

Extravagance in the household and court often roused the indignation of the cortes, which sought to curb expenditures and the number of those living off the king's bounty. Regulations in the cortes of Valladolid 1258 (art. 1–6) and Seville 1261 (art. 1) concerned the food and dress of the king and members of the household and curtailed the number of minstrels and serving women, who were probably seen as a source of scandal. Gambling in the household was also forbidden (Valladolid 1312, art. 32). As outsiders were both a strain on the budget and a cause of unseemly conduct, vagabonds were to be ejected and access to the household limited to those who had business there. Magnates, restricting the size of their retinues, were to come only when summoned and had to pay their own expenses.[3] The size of the royal entourage and crimes committed by its members as they traveled about the realm also gave rise to complaints.[4]

The king was customarily entitled to hospitality (*yantar*) from certain towns during his personal visits. Sancho IV stipulated that he would ask for 600 *maravedís* for himself and 200 for the queen (Palencia 1286, art. 4), but he later added that his son would receive 300 *maravedís* when he exercised authority in his father's name. Sancho IV also claimed *yantar* even when detained by a military campaign, a meeting of the cortes, or the confinement of the queen due to pregnancy or childbirth (Valladolid 1293, art. 5 C).

These were apparently new conditions that the towns found difficult to accept. Abuses of *yantar* seem to have been common, given the frequency with which the subject was mentioned. Fernando IV was asked not to levy it until he had determined how much Fernando III had received, but he announced that he would observe his father's ordinance.[5] In the cortes of Valladolid 1307 (art. 10), because of the difference between his father's coinage and his own, Fernando IV increased the amount due upon his personal visitation to 1000 *maravedís* for the next six years. As the term came to an end, the amount was reduced to 600.[6] During the minority of Alfonso XI, attempts were made to restrict payment to personal visits only,[7] but once he came of age, Alfonso XI reiterated his right to collect *yantar* when on campaign or engaged in a siege.[8]

Objections to the burdens of hospitality and provisions (*conducho*) are attributable in part to the growth of the royal household. Complaints were made that royal officials abused the right to draw on local communities for provisions by breaking into houses and seizing food and drink and other supplies without payment (Valladolid 1293, art. 8 C, 12 M, 13 LE). Announcing that payment would be made, Fernando IV even agreed to make restitution for whatever had been taken unlawfully in his father's time.[9] The king's men were also accused of taking pack animals without payment and never returning them; houses were disrupted, gardens and vineyards uprooted, bread, wine, meat and straw taken by force, and livestock destroyed. The principle that these had to be paid for was stated again and again.[10] Restrictions were also imposed on royal demands for the service of guides.[11]

The business of securing suitable lodgings for the household was also a source of controversy. Sancho IV assigned this responsibility to the royal lodging master, who acted in conjunction with local officials. Magnates and knights, who often disrupted a town, would be lodged instead in surrounding villages (Valladolid 1293, art. 7 C). A separate quarter near the king would be provided for the principal officers of the court, as would appropriate lodgings for visitors.[12]

The security of those attending the court was guaranteed not only by the law codes but also by ordinances enacted in the cortes. Townsmen who wished to speak with the king were assured that royal porters would take care of them and that they would be secure both during their visit to court and on the journey to and from their homes.[13] Anyone drawing a weapon in the court would be executed; if anyone killed, wounded, or dishonored another in the court or within five leagues of it, he would suffer the penalties of death and confiscation. Fernando IV was asked to amend this ruling so that the guilty party would not be protected by the church or by any infante or magnate.[14]

The cortes clearly took an obvious interest in the organization of the royal court. Not only did it protest what it believed to be excessive or unnecessary expenses and the hardships imposed on communities visited by the court, but it also sought to gain direct access to the seat of power by demanding that townsmen have a place in the council and household.

The Chancery

One of the most important organisms of the household, the chancery was responsible for drawing up royal documents and maintaining the archives. A description of its officers and their functions is found in the *Espéculo* (II.12.2–3, 6; IV.12.1–6) and the *Partidas* (II.9.4, 7–8; III.18–20). The cortes frequently referred to the chancery with exasperation, usually to complain that it was in a state of disarray. Criticisms focused principally on personnel, the issuance of charters, and chancery fees.

Disorder in the chancery and calls for its improvement developed mainly during the two minorities. Fernando IV pledged to reorganize the chancery in accordance with the ordinances of Alfonso X and Sancho IV, but nothing much was done until he published his own ordinance in the cortes of Valladolid 1312.[15] It does not seem to have been implemented, however, probably because contention over the regency for Alfonso XI resulted in a divided chancery. Even though the regents agreed in the cortes of Burgos 1315 (art. 9) that the chancery would be reunited, continued anarchy there elicited an expression of disgust from the assembly of Carrión 1317 (art. 2). Acknowledging the need for reform, Infante Felipe ordered the chancery to remain with the king and repeated the substance of Fernando IV's ordinance of 1312 (Valladolid 1322, art. 5–8). Even so, the continuing struggle over the regency and the difficulties of Alfonso XI's first years of personal rule hampered the establishment of an efficient chancery office (Madrid 1329, art. 26).

As the post of chancellor was essentially an honorific one held by the archbishops of Toledo and Compostela, the ordinary chancery functionaries were the *notarios mayores* of Castile, León, Toledo, and Andalusia, and the scribes.[16] Extremadura requested its own notary but was rejected because it had never had one (Valladolid 1307, art. 17). The cortes often demanded that these offices be given to laymen.[17] The assembly of Carrión 1317 (art. 2, 4) was most insistent on the ouster of clerics and the appointment of laymen belonging to the *hermandad*, because if a layman committed an offense, the king could punish him in body and goods, which would be impossible in the case of a cleric. Infante Felipe confirmed that only laymen would be appointed, to the exclusion of prelates, clerics, and Jews (Valladolid 1322, art. 6). When Alfonso XI came of age, he reserved freedom to appoint whomever he wished, declaring only that the chancellor and notaries should be suitable for their positions (Madrid 1329, art. 26–27).

Because the responsibility for drafting and publishing royal documents rested with the four notaries, they were expected to guard against the dispatch of charters that might diminish the king's rights. On his orders, they made notes for the document to be prepared and reviewed the text written by the scribes. The document was then recorded in registers and a seal of wax or lead was affixed to the original.[18] If the notaries were unable personally to supervise the preparation of charters, they were required to appoint laymen not susceptible to bribery to take their places (Valladolid 1300, art. 5).

Fearing the issuance of charters of an objectionable nature, the cortes emphasized the need for proper review by the notaries before sealing; they were also entrusted with the register and the seals.[19] In the reigns of Alfonso X and Sancho IV only the notaries of Castile and León were permitted to have keys to the boxes in which the seals were kept, but this practice seems to have broken down during the minority of Alfonso XI.[20] The assembly of Carrión 1317 (art. 2–3) demanded that only the regents and the *mayordomo mayor* should have keys and that no charter should be sealed without prior review. Infante Felipe announced that the seals would remain with the king in the care of townsmen who were natives of the realm, and he identified the officials who would review charters before sealing them (Valladolid 1322, art. 5–8). When he assumed personal control, Alfonso XI reestablished the custom whereby only the notaries of Castile and León had keys to the seals as well as the responsibility for review and maintenance of the registers (Madrid 1329, art. 26–29).

In his ordinance of 1312, Fernando IV assigned a certain number of scribes to himself, the queen mother, and the notaries and judges of the royal court, requiring them to take an oath to execute their duties faithfully.[21]

Aside from personnel, the most frequent complaints of the cortes concerned the dispatch of charters and the apparent chaos in the archives. Charters issued under the privy seal and use of the writ known as *albalá* drew fire because ordinary chancery controls were bypassed.[22] The emission of charters contrary to the municipal *fueros* or contradicting rights or privileges already granted was often condemned.[23] Especially pernicious were blank charters, which could be filled in at whim to order the arrest or execution of individuals without due process of law. Widely used during the two minorities, they were often repudiated.[24] Fernando IV provided the death penalty for those falsifying charters or the royal seal (Valladolid 1312, art. 22).

Chancery fees were also a subject of debate. Alfonso X specified fees for a variety of royal documents in the *Espéculo* (IV.12.54–59). Sancho IV confirmed his father's ordinance and apparently enacted one of his own, which Fernando IV, Infante Felipe, and Alfonso XI confirmed at the request of the cortes.[25]

The continuing criticism of the chancery indicates that there were chronic problems with its organization and functioning, complicated by the fact that more and more people besieged the king for favors. The issuance of contradictory charters or others in violation of the *fueros* illustrates the inadequacy of the chancery's control of its registers. The multiplication of seals and the use of blank charters compounded the problem. The peripatetic character of the court made it difficult to establish a convenient and relatively permanent repository for the royal archives. The persistent picture of the chancery, consequently, is one of confusion and disorder.

The Royal Tribunal

The royal tribunal played a significant role in shaping the law and dispensing justice. The cortes, therefore, was especially attentive to its activities. The functions and composition of the tribunal were defined in the *Espéculo* (IV.2), *Partidas* (III.4), the Ordinances of Zamora 1274, Valladolid 1312, Alcalá 1348, and the *cuadernos*. One of the essential tasks of the king was to see that justice was done and that every man received his due.[26] Thus the royal court had jurisdiction over specific types of cases involving the magnates, as well as disputes among nobles, towns, and monastic communities concerning land and boundaries; it also received petitions and heard appeals from judgments rendered elsewhere.[27] At times royal officials who had personal litigation with townsmen summoned them to the court, but the townsmen objected that they should be heard first in their own communities according to the local *fuero;* only then could the case be appealed to the king's court.[28]

As this was the king's court, the cortes often asked him to take a personal role in judgment. Litigation could become a major drain on his time, and as the law became more complex not every king could claim to be master of it. Even so, Alfonso X promised to hear suits on Mondays, Wednesdays, and Fridays.[29] Fernando IV agreed to hearings every Friday, and Alfonso XI said he would hear petitions and civil disputes on Mondays and criminal cases on Fridays.[30]

The cortes and the law books spelled out the qualifications for the judges, who handled the bulk of the business brought before the king's court. They were expected to be men who feared God and the king, who knew the law and would observe it, and who would apply it so as to guard every man's right and avoid partisanship.[31] They should be knights and good men of the towns, rather than clerics, members of religious orders, or foreigners; above all they ought not to be criminals, or supporters of such—a particular concern during Fernando IV's minority.[32] Paid good salaries,[33] they would be able to carry out their duties effectively and would not be tempted easily by bribes. If found guilty of accepting gifts, loans, or bribes for themselves or their relatives, or associating with lawyers and litigants, the judges would be expelled from court, declared infamous, and penalized for perjury.[34]

The Ordinance of Zamora 1274 (art. 17) specified that there should be nine judges from Castile, six from Extremadura, and eight from León, who would alternate their service during the year. One of the Leonese judges was expected to be a knight expert in the *Fuero Juzgo* and the customs of that realm. The cortes several times asked that a sufficient number of justices and scribes be appointed.[35] Fernando IV established a group of twelve judges, all laymen—four each from Castile, León, and Extremadura (Valladolid 1312, art. 2)—who would adjudicate cases originating in their respective kingdom.[36]

Besides the ordinary judges of the royal court, there were others with exceptional responsibilities. Prompted by their concern to be judged by their peers in accordance with the traditional *fueros,* the Castilian nobility in the cortes of Burgos 1272 demanded that Alfonso X appoint two noble judges, knowledgeable in the old law, to hear their pleas. Although the king consented, he pointed out that none of his predecessors had done so.[37] The nobles participating in the *hermandad* of Carrión 1317 (art. 33) repeated this request, and some years later Alfonso XI promised to include noble justices in his court (Madrid 1329, art. 2).

Alfonso X guaranteed the right of appeal to his court (Seville 1252, art. 35). The Ordinance of Zamora 1274 (art. 19–20) provided for three judges to hear appeals from the entire realm, except for Castile, where appeals would be carried from the ordinary royal judges to the *adelantado mayor* of Castile and ultimately to the king.[38] Leonese appeals would be resolved according to the *Fuero Juzgo*.[39] At times, contradictory judgments were issued when litigants in appeals mistakenly appeared separately before the king or one of the regents (Carrión 1317, art. 38).

Royal judges were encouraged to administer justice impartially, without delay, and to make it accessible to everyone.[40] Scribes (who were laymen), assigned to record the proceedings, were warned not to issue documents without judicial authorization, and the judges were forbidden to order the illegal imprisonment or execution of anyone.[41] Failure to answer a summons to the royal court was punishable by heavy fines.[42] The cortes also defined the obligations of lawyers to their clients and their conduct in court. Although lawyers were not permitted to argue Castilian pleas, they could be used elsewhere as long as they were laymen—clerics were allowed to argue only their own cases or those of the church.[43]

The responsibilities of the *justicia mayor de la casa del rey*, or *alguacil*, the officer charged with effecting arrests on the king's command and maintaining order in the royal court, were set down in the cortes of Valladolid 1312. Forbidden to arrest anyone "without reason and law," he had to bring the accused before the king's justices at once to be charged; without their authorization he could not release anyone, or subject anyone to torture, imprisonment, or other punishment.[44]

The criticisms directed at the royal tribunal seem, on the whole, moderate. The desire of the cortes that the king preside in court was perhaps due to a suspicion of the judges as professionals. Because the king could not possibly hear all the suits brought before him, the cortes requested the appointment of more judges so that judicial business could be expedited, though constant travel probably hindered their work. By insisting that litigation be heard only by judges from the kingdom where the suit originated, the cortes impeded royal efforts to achieve legal uniformity. The exclusion of the clergy as judges and law-yers reflects the antipathy of the cortes to Roman and canon law, as well as a general anticlericalism among the townsmen. Lawyers, whether clerics or laymen, seem to have been viewed with scepticism.

Adelantados *and* Merinos Mayores

The cortes carefully scrutinized those officials responsible for governing the kingdoms or provinces constituting the crown of Castile. They were the *adelantado mayor de la frontera* (Andalusia), the *adelantado mayor* of Murcia, and the *merinos mayores* (sometimes called *adelantados mayores*) of Castile, León, and Galicia (and, occasionally, Álava and Guipúzcoa). Their qualifications, responsibilities, limitations, and ac-countability were spelled out in the *cuadernos*.[45] Expected to be men who loved justice, they had to be natives of the provinces they governed and reside there when not summoned to court. According to the cortes of Valladolid 1295 (art. 13), magnates were supposed to be excluded from the post of *merino mayor* in the northern regions, though men of this rank usually served as *adelantados* in Andalusia and Murcia, where the military responsibility was paramount. On appointment they were required to name sureties in case they committed serious crimes or in-juries while holding office. At the end of their service they had to re-main in the province for a month to respond to possible complaints. If convicted of negligence or crime, they could be dismissed and severely punished.[46]

Admonished not to intrude on one another's authority (Burgos 1308, art. 17), the *adelantados* and *merinos* were also forbidden to enter the immunities of bishops, monasteries and military orders, except in the four cases specified by Alfonso IX: homicide, rape, pursuit of known criminals, and highway robbery.[47] They were also forbidden to enter royal cities and to appoint notaries or scribes there, though they were often blamed for injuring townsmen.[48] For their services, *merinos* were entitled to an annual *yantar* of 150 *maravedís*, where customary.[49] They were expected to appoint upright men and natives of the region as sub-ordinate *merinos* (or *porteros*), who would help them carry out their du-ties. Only good men who were not evildoers would be given custody of royal castles.[50]

The maintenance of law and order was one of the principal duties of the *adelantados* and *merinos*. Sancho IV castigated them for not visiting justice on highwaymen who robbed and assaulted merchants and others traveling to fairs, markets, and seaports. Demanding a list of accused criminals, the king pledged to seize anyone of power and influence whom royal officials did not dare to arrest (Valladolid 1293, art. 4 C). Without the authorization of a judge, the *adelantados* and *merinos* were forbidden to summon, arrest, fine, or execute anyone, or to confiscate his property.[51]

During the two minorities, the cortes often demanded that the *merinos* and *adelantados* bring criminals to justice[52] and compel rebels to surrender and make restitution for injuries. If rebels refused to submit, their houses and property would be destroyed, and anyone giving them aid and comfort would suffer the same penalties.[53] Armed gatherings of nobles and other troublemakers were prohibited,[54] and fortresses used as a refuge by criminals were destroyed.[55]

Unfortunately, *adelantados* and *merinos* were charged with many of the same crimes as those branded as *malfechores*. Instead of protecting the people and seeing that justice was done, they and their subordinates killed, plundered, and destroyed houses and crops.[56] They were faulted not only for not serving personally but also for allowing their subordinates to behave like tyrants. The reputation of the *adelantados* and *merinos* was generally negative.

The Municipalities

While the oppressive conduct of the *adelantados* and *merinos* drew fire from the cortes, no issue was as important to the townsmen as the integrity and autonomy of the municipality itself. Besides asking for the confirmation of their *fueros*, the representatives of the towns in the cortes often complained of assaults on the integrity of the municipal district. The king often alienated villages lying within the district to nobles, clergy, and others. Both the municipality and the crown consequently suffered a loss of revenue and jurisdiction. The townsmen, therefore, called for the restoration to the municipalities of villages, castles, lands, and tributes formerly belonging to them.[57] They also demanded the right to collect taxes in all villages within the district and to prevent nobles and others from appointing scribes or judges or establishing markets there.[58]

The acquisition of property within a municipality by the nobility or clergy was also viewed with alarm. Two problems were involved—the claim by nobles to be exempt from municipal jurisdiction, and from any kind of municipal taxation. Anxious to exclude the nobles altogether, the towns demanded that they be prohibited from acquiring property in the municipalities by purchase or by gift.[59] If a noble did gain entrance into a town, he would be subject to the municipal *fuero* and answerable in the local court,[60] but he was not permitted to hold any municipal office or to serve as a tax collector or tax farmer.[61] Nobles were regarded as troublesome neighbors at best, and their demands for *yantar* and *conducho* evoked frequent protests.[62]

The question of urban autonomy was raised in connection with the appointment of the principal officers (judges and scribes) of municipal administration. Although the king promised to do justice whenever he visited a town (Valladolid 1312, art. 41), the *alcaldes* ordinarily had this responsibility. The king, however, often intervened to appoint justices, superseding those chosen on the local level. Municipal autonomy was breached, and as the king gained direct control, a trend toward uniformity in the law was encouraged. From time to time he promised to withdraw the judges whom he had appointed, entrusting the administration of justice to the good men of the town. Only if the municipal council or a majority thereof asked him would he appoint a judge, and the one chosen would be a native of the kingdom. These *jueces de salario* or *jueces de fuera*, as they were called, were required to remain in the towns they served for thirty days to answer possible accusations, though criminal charges were reserved for the king's determination.[63]

Alfonso XI greatly expanded the practice of sending royal officials into the towns. Although he promised the assembly of León 1345 (art. 8) that he would only appoint *jueces de salario* when the town council requested it, he had already sent *alcaldes veedores* (*emendadores* in Castile) to many Castilian, Extremaduran, and Leonese towns to do justice and especially to punish criminals. He refused the plea of the assemblies of Alcalá 1345 (art. 2), Burgos (art. 4), and León (art. 13–15) to remove them, but he did agree to pay their salaries. Described as *corregidores* in the cortes of Alcalá 1348 (art. 47), they became the principal agents of royal authority in the towns. The king had also begun to appoint groups of *regidores* who assumed the functions of the older municipal council, but he refused to pay their salaries, insisting that this should be done in accordance with custom (Alcalá 1348, art. 41). In any case, the autonomy of the towns, despite the protests of the cortes, was greatly compromised by the king's actions.[64]

Until these momentous changes, justice was ordinarily administered in the towns by magistrates chosen by the townsmen (*alcaldes de fuero*). If they were negligent, appeal could be made to the king.[65] The right of townsmen to be tried before their own judges according to the municipal *fueros* was often abused. Royal officials who had private suits against townsmen often cited them to the royal court, but Sancho IV permitted this only if the official was in his household or service. Fernando IV stipulated that this could be done only if the contract in dispute had been concluded in his court.[66] Occasionally *merinos* imprisoned townsmen instead of bringing them before the local judge for trial, and nobles often seized their property.[67] Towns were accused of appropriating the goods of other towns, rather than seeking justice in the local court (Valladolid 1293, art. 15 C). Sometimes pledges taken in this manner were moved from place to place, making it difficult for the defendant to have a hearing in court, but he was allowed to go before any local judge, who was obliged to render justice without malicious delay (Madrid 1329, art. 85). Lawyers could be used in litigation where customary (Madrid 1329, art. 73). Municipal courts were also authorized to hear appeals, where customary, from ecclesiastical lands (Valladolid 1325, art. 19).

The cortes expressed concern for the qualifications of municipal notaries and scribes, and fear of royal encroachments on urban autonomy in this respect. The responsibility of notaries (León) and scribes (Castile, Extremadura, Murcia, and Andalusia) who drew up public documents such as contracts was a grave one, and their fees were an important source of income. Whether chosen by the towns according to their *fueros* or appointed by the king, they were expected to be natives of the towns they served.[68] Fernando IV and Alfonso XI, however, reserved the right to appoint those whom they thought best suited, and stipulated that when the appointee was needed in the royal household he could name a substitute.[69] Alfonso X's ordinance fixing scribal fees was to be observed by all.[70] No one was to hold more than one notariate, and it could not be leased to anyone.[71] By the reign of Alfonso XI, leasing in fact had become such a common practice that the assembly of Madrid 1339 (art. 11) asked only that lessees should be Christians of good repute and that scribes should be townsmen. Fernando IV planned to use municipal scribes to record extensive information about activities in the towns, but this was objected to as contrary to usage, because scribes ought to testify only to matters that transpired before them and to litigation that they had recorded in court (Valladolid 1312, art. 49, 96). The cortes wished to prevent ecclesiastics from functioning as public scribes and Jews from having their own scribes, but Fernando IV demurred; later the regents for Alfonso XI allowed clerical notaries to record pleas involving clerics, but no one else.[72]

In the reign of Alfonso XI royal interference with the municipal notariate greatly increased. Not only was the office leased and its functions entrusted to persons of bad reputation, but the king also began to retain the revenues permanently. Although he confirmed the *fueros* authorizing the towns to have notaries or scribes, he would not pledge to accept the candidates presented to him, but only to follow the custom of his predecessors; nor would he commit himself to appoint only natives and residents who would serve personally (Madrid 1329, art. 40–43). When the assemblies of Alcalá (art. 3), Burgos (art. 3), and León 1345 (art. 24) asked for the restoration of scribal fees, Alfonso XI refused, explaining that he needed the money to build a shipyard for his fleet. In the cortes of Alcalá 1348 (art. 34) he confirmed the ordinance he had made concerning the notariate in the cortes of Madrid 1329.

Municipal militias became a major factor in royal armies during the reconquest, but as the threat of Islam receded and the towns were farther removed from the frontier, the need for military preparedness no longer seemed so pressing. The towns tried to curtail their military obligation, but Alfonso X reaffirmed the duty of every man to be prepared with horse and arms as the local *fueros* demanded (Seville 1252, art. 44). To make service more attractive, he exempted the knights of the Extremaduran towns from tribute if they maintained horse and arms (Segovia 1256).[73] This exemption was confirmed and amplified in the assembly of Seville in 1264.[74]

Later enactments indicate that the towns hoped to elude or minimize their military obligations and to limit the imposition of *fonsadera*, a tribute related to military service. Thus, Sancho IV assured the towns that he would summon them to the royal host only when necessary (Palencia 1286, art. 5), but he also emphasized the duty of rural inhabitants of municipalities to serve along with towndwellers (Valladolid

1293, art. 16 C). Rejecting the pleas of the Castilian towns at Burgos in 1345 (art. 16), Alfonso XI declared that no one was exempt, and that every native of the kingdom had a duty to serve; nor would he agree that he was bound by exemptions granted by previous kings, though he did acknowledge his own.

Although some towns were obliged to pay *fonsadera* if the king himself went to war, they tried to evade it by arguing that they should not have to pay it if they sent their contingents to the royal host.[75] Some towns had the right to retain the money, sharing it among the troops going to war.[76] Others were exempt altogether but complained that their privileges were not observed, especially during the royal minorities.[77] When the seaport towns of the Bay of Biscay protested to Alfonso XI that they should not have to pay *servicios* when they had to supply ships for his fleet, he promised only to consider the matter (Madrid 1329, art. 50–51).

The determination of the municipalities to maintain control over their internal life is also reflected in another area. The cortes often asked the king to give custody of castles and *alcazares* within municipal districts to townsmen, rather than outsiders, who sometimes used them as bases for criminal activity and rebellion.[78]

The municipalities saw clearly the twin dangers facing them. There was the threat, on one hand, of the steady erosion of their territory due to alienations by the crown to reward faithful servants or buy the allegiance of recalcitrant vassals. On the other hand, the loss of autonomy also loomed as the crown intruded more frequently into the appointment of municipal officials. The hints of danger perceived by the municipalities at this time would be realized in the later fourteenth and fifteenth centuries.

The Royal Domain

As the municipalities endeavored to protect their own lands and rights, they also demanded that the crown exhibit greater care in recovering royal domain lands (*realengo*) acquired by the church or the nobility. The monarchs themselves tried occasionally to curb alienations or to repossess those already made. Thus, Fernando II, noted for his liberality, decided to review his donations in the *curia* of Benavente 1181. After Alfonso IX ascended the throne he undertook, on "the judgment and sentence" of the *curia* of León 1188, to revoke his father's charters alienating royal granaries and other rights. Looking to the future, Alfonso VIII of Castile, in the *curia* of Nájera 1184, enacted an ordinance prohibiting the alienation of royal lands to the church or to the nobility. In the *curia* of Benavente 1228, Alfonso IX similarly forbade ecclesiastics to acquire royal lands without prior consent.[79] The confirmation of these acts in the later cortes is indicative of their importance. The principle of inalienability was also established in the law codes, although kings often felt at liberty to ignore it.[80]

On the insistence of the cortes, the principles of nonalienation and recovery were affirmed on numerous occasions. Sancho IV promised the cortes of Palencia 1286 (art. 1, 11) that he would recover royal lands alienated from the time of his uprising to the present. He evidently enacted a similar ordinance in the cortes of Burgos 1287, but at Haro 1288, he abandoned any attempt to recover royal lands already in the hands of others (art. 1–3) in return for a guaranteed tax for ten years.[81] The regents for Fernando IV pledged not to alienate any royal town and to recover alienations made since the cortes of Haro. The difficulties involved in trying to dispossess those in occupation were emphasized when the cortes insisted on the observance of the ordinance of Haro and on the obligation of nobles, clergy, Jews, and Moors who purchased royal lands to pay taxes on them.[82] The cortes of Valladolid 1307 (art. 23) proposed a radical change of policy when it called for the recovery of all royal lands alienated since the *curia* of Nájera in 1184. Fernando IV countered by arguing that his father had granted the clergy royal lands now in their possession, but he promised to take up the issue at the following Martinmas. There is no evidence that he did, though he later asserted that he would recover all alienations and forbade future acquisitions by the nobility or clergy (Valladolid 1312, art. 87). The regents for Alfonso XI made a similar pledge[83] but also agreed to allow the clergy to retain royal lands until the king came of age (Medina del Campo 1316). Ten years later, again at Medina, Alfonso XI confirmed that agreement, but he later ordered the recovery of lands acquired by the church since 1326.[84] He also promised not to alienate any royal towns.[85]

In spite of ordinances prohibiting alienation, and in spite of royal pledges to recover what had already been alienated, one is left with the impression that the royal domain suffered from a continual hemorrhage. With the consequent depletion of revenues, the crown was forced to seek compensation by increasing demands for higher taxes, which evoked the insistent protest of the taxpayers. The pace of alienation, unfortunately, quickened measurably in the later fourteenth and fifteenth centuries.

The Administration of Justice

The interest of the cortes in the administration of justice is suggested not only by enactments concerning the role of the king and other public officials in this respect, but also in its insistence on due process of law, adherence to proper procedure, and the maintenance of law and order. The principle of due process, asserted by Alfonso IX in the *curia* of León 1188, was affirmed repeatedly by later cortes to the effect that no one should be imprisoned, injured, condemned, or executed, or have his goods confiscated, until he had first been heard and judged according to law.[86] In the implementation of this principle the cortes demanded that two common procedures—the inquest and the taking of pledges—be used in accordance with appropriate legal norms.

The sworn inquest (*pesquisa*) was a governmental device employed to gather information concerning taxes due, alienations of royal lands, or exports of prohibited goods, and also to identify criminals.[87] The use of a closed, general inquest was condemned in the cortes of Palencia 1286 (art. 7) and many times thereafter; if the inquest were closed, the results would not be made known at once to those named therein, who thus would have no way of preparing their defense. An an ordinary rule, therefore, there would be no closed inquests; a general inquest could be carried out only on the order of the king and at the request of the people in certain cases. When completed, the text would be given to the affected parties who would then be heard and judged according to law.[88]

Pledges usually were taken to guarantee the appearance of a defendant in court, but the cortes prohibited anyone from taking a pledge without a judge's authorization. Animals used for ploughing could not be taken if the defendant had other property; nor were pledges to be carried from one town to another. Before the goods thus attached were returned, the rights of a successful plaintiff had to be satisfied.[89]

The preservation of the peace was a matter of serious concern not only to the king but also to the cortes. In the *curia* of León 1188, Alfonso IX promulgated a constitution for the suppression of crime and criminals. Sancho IV warned the towns and the military orders to be on their guard against thieves and other wicked men, such as *golfines*, who preyed upon flocks of sheep.[90] During the royal minorities, armed gatherings of nobles and outright rebellion contributed greatly to criminal activity. Bands of criminals used fortresses as bases of operations. The prevalence of crime prompted the cortes to demand that the *adelantados* and *merinos* take all necessary measures to restore order.[91] The assembly of Carrión 1317 (art. 6) also pointedly reminded the regents of their responsibility to punish criminals. Alfonso XI, when he came of age, promised especially to do justice to those charged with crime (Madrid 1329, art. 22).

The inquest was commonly employed to identify criminals. *Pesquisidores* were appointed in each *merindad* to carry out inquests in criminal matters, and the *adelantados* were authorized to do so in cases of unexplained deaths and other crimes. Fernando IV asked municipal officials to send him a report on crimes, so the criminals thus identified could be tried by local authorities or brought to justice anywhere in the kingdom.[92]

The security of persons and their property and the inviolability of the household were guaranteed in the *curia* of León 1188 (art. 4, 11).[93] Ordinances enacted in the cortes severely punished those who threatened or injured people giving evidence or royal judges and other officials. Insults, blinding, slashing, robbery, killing, and similar crimes were punishable by fines, exile, confiscation, and execution, as were seizing another's animals or goods, or destroying trees, vineyards, or houses.[94] Vagabondage was prohibited as well as gambling, but laws regulating gaming establishments were drawn up in 1276.[95] Fines were levied in accordance with the *fueros;* in case of confiscation, the criminal's outstanding obligations had to be satisfied first.[96]

The crown occasionally pardoned criminals, but the cortes asked that pardons granted to habitual offenders be revoked and that others not be issued so easily in the future. Alfonso XI, on the other hand, acceded to a request that he extend a general pardon for all crimes, except treason and heresy, that had been committed up to the time he reached his majority.[97]

It is apparent that the men of the realm were assured in principle that the king would render justice to all, that due process of law would be observed, and that everyone's house and property would be safe-guarded. The complaints of the cortes make clear, however, that this ideal was seldom achieved. Not only were royal officials remiss in their administration of justice, particularly in the matter of inquests and the taking of pledges, but some of them, most notably the *adelantados* and *merinos*, failed to demonstrate the necessary toughness in dealing with criminals.

This overview of the substance of the *cuadernos* relating to government and administration reveals a great gap between theory and practice. The *Espéculo* and the *Partidas* outlined governmental structures and functions, but the principles and regulations found in the law books were not easily translated into actuality. A tension developed between the crown and the cortes due to the differing perceptions of what was beneficial to the king and the kingdom. While the king and his officials made every effort to enhance and expand royal authority, the estates were equally energetic in defending their privileges and regional customs, and in pointing out abuses, oppressive actions, and injustices attributable to officers of the royal court, territorial administrators, judges, and tax collectors. Several factors contributed to the difficulties of governing the realm justly, including the increased size of the royal bureaucracy (the consequence of the increased business of the crown), the peripatetic character of the court, the malice of some officials, and the ineffectiveness of some monarchs, which surely encouraged weakness and incompetence among their subordinates.

A European Perspective

In other European realms, kings and parliaments were contending with comparable issues. Reacting against the influence of evil councillors, the Aragonese Union in the cortes of Zaragoza 1287 insisted on the right to approve persons appointed to the royal council. In England, too, the parliament of 1341 (repeating an earlier demand of the Ordinances of 1311) urged Edward III to appoint the chancellor and other principal officials in parliament and to require them to swear to uphold the law.[98]

The caliber and honesty of those entrusted with the administration of justice was also a common theme. The Aragonese cortes in 1283, 1287, 1301, 1347, and 1348 concerned itself with the role of the justiciar, the judge responsible for adjudicating litigation involving his fellow nobles. The cortes of Zaragoza 1283 also demanded that judges be natives of Aragón and not susceptible to bribery; the use of the inquest was also condemned. The corts of Barcelona 1283 was equally opposed to outside intrusion, insisting that Catalans be tried only in Catalonia, and then by honest judges.[99]

10

The Cortes, Society,
and the Economy

As with government and administration, the cortes mirrored changes wrought in the social and economic structure of Castile and León. With the expansion of the frontiers from the Tagus to the Guadalquivir came a variety of problems. A great Muslim population was uprooted and Christian settlers moved in from the north, often depopulating the places whence they came. The newcomers were not always as adept as their Muslim counterparts who abandoned their trades and their land. On discovering that the promise of quick riches was not fulfilled, many settlers returned to their former homes. Thus the initial repopulation of Andalusia was incomplete, and the final settlement, notable for the establishment of great estates, was postponed for many years.

These demographic changes resulted in inflation and a shortage of manufactured goods, neither of which was easily alleviated. The documentation of the cortes reveals an ever louder series of complaints of bad times, poverty, deserted villages and country areas, hunger, famine, catastrophic harvests, and destruction wrought by climatic upheavals. Food production declined, with consequent scarcity and price rises— disturbances reflected in the devaluation of the coinage. The shortage of food also led to a struggle for control of pasturage. Towns tried to define their municipal boundaries, quarreling with one another and with monasteries over pasturage rights. The concomitant rise of the sheepherding industry contributed to the decline of small sheepherders and intensified litigation over pasturage between the sheepmen and the towns. The uncertainties attending the minorities of Fernando IV and Alfonso XI resulted in a great increase in banditry. Thus when the Black Death struck in the middle of the fourteenth century, the kingdom was already in difficult straits, both socially and economically.[1]

The Nobility

The nobles, whose wealth and power steadily increased, were becoming self-conscious and aggressive in defense of their interests. Thinking of themselves as the king's natural counselors and as the principal defenders of the realm, they demanded ever larger stipends (*soldadas*) in return for their services. Their distinctive juridical status was recognized by Alfonso X when he confirmed their *fueros* in the cortes of Burgos 1272, by Fernando IV at Palencia in 1311, and by Alfonso XI at Burgos in 1338.

Acceptance of knighthood as a separate order in society reflected the nobility's awareness of its status as a privileged class. Alfonso X, who expounded the theory and practice of chivalry in the *Partidas* (II.21), emphasized the observance of rules and the general behavior of the nobility. Magnates who received land from the king were expected to receive knighthood; peasants and their sons were excluded. To encourage knights to maintain their status (especially those in the towns), the king promised 500 *sueldos* and other privileges to anyone whom he or his heir personally knighted. The king's interest was to enhance the warrior tradition because he needed the aid of the nobility in his wars and recognized that knighthood, with its implications of rank and status, could serve his purposes as well as theirs.[2]

At the same time, measures were enacted in the cortes of Seville 1252 (art. 4–6, 12–13) and several times thereafter which curtailed extravagance in wedding celebrations, food, dress, and decorations.[3] The king hoped to check the presumption of the nobles lest they compete with his own luxurious state, but he also acknowledged that the expenditure of vast sums for such purposes would have a negative effect on the economy.

As the nobles derived substantial income from their lordships, they aggressively attempted to expand their territories. Not only did they gain by the distribution of lands in Andalusia, but they exploited their holdings in the more settled northern regions more profitably by granting short-term leases, reimposing long-forgotten tributes, and ousting tenants whenever it suited them. The competition for land was intense, and at Toledo 1273 the nobles objected to grants made to anyone other than a native of the realm.[4] Those who participated in the *hermandad* at Carrión 1317 repeated this principle, warning the regents not to deprive any noble of his land or stipends without reason (art. 62–69).

The nobles also protested Alfonso XI's efforts to diminish their authority in their lordships by limiting their rights of justice and encouraging vassals to sue in the royal court. Despite objections to the appointment of royal officials in the lordship towns, Alfonso XI was reluctant to remove them or to agree to exclude royal *merinos* from the lordships. To the nobles' further annoyance, Alfonso XI also insisted on reviewing grants of immunity, especially those given during the two minorities (Alcalá 1348, art. 3–5, 12–14, 16).

Tensions among the nobility were nowhere more evident than in the competition for those lordships known as *behetrías*. The inhabitants of those lands, situated mostly in Old Castile, were freemen who commended themselves to the protection of the great lords, but who could sever their ties at any moment without giving up ownership of their land. As the peasants restricted the selection of their lord to a certain family, this relationship tended to become hereditary. The bitter rivalry over these lands was emphasized when the rights of illegitimate sons to a share in the *behetrías*, unless specifically granted by the father, were rejected in the cortes of Burgos 1308 (art. 23) and at Palencia 1311 (art. 5). A complaint that nobles were claiming lands in León as *behetrías*, even though there were none there, also illustrates the rampant greed (León 1345, art. 7). With the intention of dividing the *behetrías* among the nobles as a means of resolving disputes over them, Pedro the Cruel (1350–1369) in 1351 caused a record to be drawn up of the extent of these lordships, and the obligations of the peasants to their lords and the crown.[5]

While the nobles quarreled with one another for control of the *be-hetrías*, the towns protested about certain practices that they considered injurious to the crown or their own interests. Magnates, for example, were forbidden to excuse the men of the *behetrías* from customary payments owed to the king; the cortes believed that by insisting on these payments, royal service could be increased by more than 300 knights equipped with horses and arms.[6] The establishment of markets in the *behetrías* and the appointment of judges and scribes in places where there had been none before also stirred opposition, because the towns were impoverished as a result (Medina del Campo 1305, art. 13 C).

In their own lands, the nobles ordinarily were entitled to hospitality and provisions, but they often abused this right. More than once they were admonished to observe these restrictions and not to take provisions from royal or ecclesiastical lands or from *behetrías* without paying for them.[7] For their part, the nobles demanded that royal *merinos* pay for their provisions when visiting noble estates.[8] At times the nobles did not wait for payment of funds assigned to them by the king from various sources, but helped themselves instead; to avert this problem, those who leased royal saltpits, customs duties in Andalusia, and other customary tributes were required to make disbursements within three months to the nobles who were entitled to them (Valladolid 1258, art. 10–11). Nobles allotted a share in the *tercias reales* were warned not to seize the goods of those who had already paid the tithe, but to wait until they were paid by the appropriate officials.[9]

The stipends given to the nobility were a major element in the royal budget, and, on occasion, the cause of contention among recipients. In return, the nobles were expected to render military service, but laxity prompted Alfonso XI to enact a series of laws on this subject at Burgos 1338 (art. 14–32). Royal vassals were required to serve in person—suitably armed and provided with horses wearing armor. For every 1,100 *maravedís* received, a noble had to bring a mounted soldier to the host; for every horseman, an additional footsoldier had to be provided. Horsemen had to have iron caps, breastplates, and thigh and leg armor, and their horses had to be valued at no less than 800 *maravedís*. Failure to serve was punishable by heavy fines and five years exile. The penalty for abandoning the host was death. Latecomers or soldiers not properly equipped would be fined. While the army was on a war footing, gambling and the sale of horses and arms were forbidden (Ordinance of Alcalá 1348, XXXI.1). Many of the nobles failed to take part in the siege of Algeciras but nonetheless accepted stipends, and Alfonso XI ordered an inquest into the matter.[10] When they pleaded later that they had been hard-pressed in recent years to maintain themselves and their horses and arms, he promised to make provision for them (Alcalá 1348, art. 17); he embarked on the siege of Gibraltar soon after, however, so it is unlikely that he had any intention of alleviating the burden of military service.

The potential for violence among the nobility was great and increased during the early fourteenth century. The nobles often resolved their quarrels by armed combat, but the crown consistently attempted to have them adjudicated in the royal court. Alfonso X pledged to do justice to anyone who dishonored a noble or a member of his family, and enabled any man who received a defiance to bring the suit before the royal court (Seville 1253, art. 32, 8 L). During the royal minorities, the nobles were reputed as malefactors of the worst sort, who had to be admonished to seek redress in court rather than in plundering, burning, and killing.[11] Fernando IV obtained their promise not to harbor criminals or thwart royal officials trying to do justice. They also acknowledged the principle of due process and were assured of the security of their households (Palencia 1311, art. 3, 8–9).[12]

In hope of suppressing feuds among the nobles, Alfonso XI promulgated a general pardon for all assaults and injuries, with a few exceptions; he also persuaded them to place their castles under his protection. They were assured further of the king's justice in cases of murder, bodily injury, and inheritance; any challenges still outstanding would also be settled in his court. Otherwise, no one was permitted to defy another until the king attempted to do justice, or had neglected to do so for a year (Burgos 1338, art. 1–5, 9–12).[13] Nobles might be executed or sent into exile as punishment for crimes, but they could not be tortured or imprisoned for debt (Burgos 1345, art. 14).

The hostility that the nobility vented against the crown and other social classes was prompted by legal, social and economic changes that were perceived as threats. The nobles' quarrel with Alfonso X, the crisis of the succession, and the troubles of the two minorities all contributed to their transformation into an unruly force restrained only with difficulty. The *cuadernos* are replete with references to the nobles' criminal behavior: arson, plunder, murder, burning of crops, and seizure of illegal tributes. Alfonso XI regulated their legal rights and procedures and diverted their energy to the reconquest, but these measures served only to postpone the inevitable confrontation that came in the reign of Pedro the Cruel.

The Clergy

Equally myopic and determined to defend their privileged status, the clergy had less power with which to bend the crown to their will. Although the king occasionally pledged to uphold ecclesiastical liberties, as the self-proclaimed champion of Christendom against the infidels he was always able to deny the clergy the full freedom they craved. Of paramount interest to them were episcopal elections, church property, and ecclesiastical jurisdiction.[14]

The prelates objected that pressure put on cathedral chapters made free episcopal elections impossible, and that their rights in the collation of benefices had also been denied. Alfonso XI reminded them that even though he was entitled to authorize elections, they often neglected to ask him to do so.[15] The cortes of Madrid 1329 (art. 80) complained of papal provisions to foreigners, but protests from whatever source do not seem to have altered either royal or papal policies in this regard. Nor does it appear that Alfonso X's renunciation of the *jus spolii* (the goods of deceased prelates) at Valladolid 1255 was observed by his successors,[16] as the prelates complained later.[17] The absenteeism implied in the appointment of foreigners had already drawn the fire of the cortes of Valladolid 1295 (art. 2), which demanded that prelates and other clerics serving in the royal court should reside in their bishoprics, churches, or monasteries.

The tithe constituted one of the principal mainstays of ecclesiastical income. The prelates were pleased, therefore, when Alfonso X (at Valladolid 1255) stressed the obligation of everyone to pay it; his insistence that the crown was also entitled to a third was less well received.[18] Collection of the tithe and the distribution of shares between royal and ecclesiastical officials were continual sources of friction.[19]

The prelates were also anxious to secure confirmation of their lordships and the exclusion of royal officials therefrom.[20] Questions concerning the continuing growth of ecclesiastical lands were prominent, as well, because the crown was under pressure to recover royal domain acquired by the church. The church, conversely, demanded the restoration of properties wrongfully taken by others; to this end, royal officials were instructed to carry out inquests (Valladolid 1325, art. 7, 16, 22 P). Protests against the acquisition of church lands by nobles, either by purchase or by outright seizure, were made several times.[21] Nobles were castigated for plundering church lands, seizing animals, extorting money from peasants, taking illegal pledges, lodging in hospitals intended for the indigent and infirm, erecting strongholds on church lands without permission, demanding hospitality and provisions, imposing tributes on churches and monasteries, and seizing revenues from church property intended for the crown.[22]

Surely the most contentious issue involving the clergy was ecclesiastical jurisdiction. As the townsmen pointed out repeatedly, it was a threat to royal sovereignty when an entire class of citizens was entitled to be judged in courts wholly removed from royal control.[23] Although the *Partidas* (I.6.56–61) attempted to distinguish between spiritual and temporal cases, considerable ambiguity remained.[24] Because of continuing conflicts over royal and ecclesiastical jurisdiction, the cortes of Alcalá 1348 (art. 38) asked Alfonso XI to declare which pleas should be heard by church courts and which by secular courts. He agreed to this request, but there is no evidence that he carried it out or that the Ordinance of Alcalá resolved the problem. Both prelates and townsmen, meanwhile, reacted to the difficulties created by the existence of two separate forms of jurisdiction.

The clergy protested that they were summoned by laymen before secular judges, and that inquests concerning their activities were carried out by laymen; clerics thus accused of crime were then tried in secular courts.[25] The usual practice was that a cleric, upon being arrested by royal officials, would be turned over to the bishop for trial, which the townsmen objected to (Valladolid 1325, art. 33). Alfonso XI agreed that criminous clerics were entitled to be tried by the church, but he reminded the prelates that they should take seriously their obligation to punish as appropriate (Valladolid 1325, art. 21 P). The complicated nature of this issue was pointed out by the assembly of León 1345 (art. 9). Persons who had not received orders but who called themselves clerics committed crimes for which they were duly apprehended, tried, and convicted in secular courts; the ecclesiastical authorities demanded that they be handed over to the church, and secular judges who refused to comply were excommunicated. According to the townsmen, the church failed to punish the guilty, thereby diminishing the king's jurisdiction.[26]

The negligence of public officials in lending support to the church also drew fire from the prelates. Public officials often ignored ecclesiastical censures directed against individuals, or demanded that they be lifted, instead of requiring the person under the ban to seek absolution or be fined.[27] Royal officials were also instructed to carry out inquests concerning crimes committed against the clergy, especially in the case of nobles who took *yantar* from ecclesiastical vassals (Valladolid 1325, art. 3, 16 P). Nobles and others engaged in litigation with the clergy were advised to take pledges only in accordance with proper legal procedures and not on their own authority.[28]

Laymen, on the other hand, complained of being summoned to church courts. They argued that they ought not to be summoned before an ecclesiastical judge in any matter pertaining to temporal jurisdiction, especially cases concerning property rights and inheritances.[29] The practice of summoning laymen to Rome in temporal suits that should be adjudicated in the royal court was also condemned (Zamora 1301, art. 21). Laymen also protested the use of ecclesiastical censures to compel obedience. Alfonso X enacted an ordinance in his cortes (though it is unknown when he did so) forbidding the clergy to interfere with temporal jurisdiction or to excommunicate anyone to force obedience to royal charters. Bishops claiming to be aggrieved were instructed to seek redress from the king. Should they refuse to lift the sentence of excommunication when he asked them to, he would force them to comply by seizing their goods.[30]

The intrusion of ecclesiastical notaries into temporal matters was also denounced. Cathedral clergy were forbidden to serve as public scribes except in ecclesiastical matters because the "king's jurisdiction and sovereignty is lost thereby" (Burgos 1315, art. 51). Inasmuch as clerics could testify only in church courts, they were forbidden to draw up contracts involving laymen. Alfonso XI stipulated that the crown would appoint scribes in cathedral churches who would be laymen and thus punishable in body and goods if they failed in their responsibilities.[31] Notaries appointed by prelates without royal consent, or claiming to have imperial authorization, were forbidden to function (Madrid 1329, art. 29, 60).

The prelates were generally ineffective in persuading the king to defend their liberties. They might have had better success if they had sought alliance with the nobility or the townsmen, but they seem to have nurtured active hostility toward both groups. Left in an isolated state, they could be put off with promises or ignored. No king worthy of his crown could accede fully to their demands concerning episcopal elections, the tithe, and ecclesiastical jurisdiction because they impinged on his sovereignty. Although irritated, the prelates lacked the resources to compel the king to do their bidding; aside from sporadic challenges, they submitted to the authority of the crown.

The Jews

Unlike the clergy and nobility, the Jews were not summoned to the cortes or given a voice in the election of urban representatives. Laws enacted in the cortes, however, often referred to the Jews (and the Moors), emphasizing their minority status and the desire of the Christians to maintain their separate identities. Much of the restrictive legislation enacted by the first Christian emperors was incorporated into the Visigothic Code and then found its way into the codes of Alfonso X.[32]

Aside from objections to the presence of Jews in the royal household and to their serving as tax farmers or collectors (see Chapter 8),[33] the cortes regulated questions of conversion, cohabitation, dress, litigation, debt, and usury. Jews were forbidden to become Moors and vice versa, but no ordinance was made in the cortes concerning the conversion of Christians to Judaism or Islam.[34] Christian women were prohibited from living with Jews or Moors and from acting as nurses to their children. Jews and Moors were not permitted to use Christian names. So that Christians might recognize them (and presumably keep their distance), Jews and Moors were obliged to wear distinctive garb and forbidden to wear certain colors, namely yellow, green, and red, as well as white or gilded shoes, and other adornments of gold and silver. In addition, Moors had to wear their hair in a certain fashion.[35] Urged by the cortes of Palencia 1313 to require Jews to wear a yellow badge on their breasts and shoulders as in France, Infante Juan demurred, saying only that he would do what seemed best (art. 26 J).

The acquisition of property by Jews or Moors and their efforts to avoid payment of taxes also aroused strong feelings. On the grounds that royal revenue would be diminished, Sancho IV required Jews and Moors who had acquired estates formerly owned by Christians to sell them within the year, or suffer confiscation. They were only permitted to own the houses in which they lived with their families.[36]

The Jewish and Moorish communities (*aljamas*) were obliged to pay an annual tribute to the crown, but from time to time individuals tried to escape payment. Thus, Alfonso X forbade anyone to exempt the Moors (Seville 1252, art. 41). Claiming that the Jewish *aljamas* had paid Alfonso X and Sancho IV 6,000 *maravedís* daily (2,190,000 annually), the cortes of Valladolid 1312 (art. 102) lamented that the sum had now declined to one fifth of that, or 1,200 *maravedís* daily (438,000 annually). More than five thousand of the richest Jews were said to be excused from payment, so that the burden fell on poor Jews who were subject to sales taxes, and foreigners who borrowed money at interest. The cortes urged the king to eliminate exemptions and provide for a more equitable distribution of the tax burden. The cortes of Palencia 1313 (art. 32–33 J) also insisted that no Jew, regardless of his rank or privileged status, should be exempt from tribute. As a further means of restricting exemption, the cortes of Valladolid 1322 (art. 60) declared that the "Jews belong to the king" and required them to dwell in royal towns (rather than on the estates of the nobles), and to continue paying taxes with their respective *aljamas* (León 1345, art. 16).

The area of greatest friction between Christians and Jews was commerce, especially moneylending. No Jew was allowed to act for a Christian in a commercial transaction or vice versa.[37] When a Christian borrowed money from a Jew, only documents prepared by a Christian scribe had any legal validity.[38] Alfonso X fixed the rate of interest at 33⅓% in the cortes of Valladolid 1258, and limited the term of the loan to four years (art. 29–30).[39] Each of his successors confirmed his ordinance, until Alfonso XI went so far as to forbid lending money at interest by Christians, Muslims, and Jews (Ordinance of Alcalá, XXIII.1–2).[40] Sancho IV extended the term in which payment might be made from four to six years, and confirmed his father's ordinance concerning pawnbroking, although the text quoted is not identifiable with any of the enactments of the cortes of Alfonso X.[41]

Fernando IV rejected the proposal of the cortes of Valladolid 1299 (art. 13 L) to reduce the term of liability to four years. In fact, in view of Jewish complaints of difficulties in collecting debts because of the civil war, he extended the term from six to nine years (Valladolid 1300, art. 18). Debts contracted in the future, however, would be payable within six years (Zamora 1301, art. 10).[42] The extension to nine years was terminated on the feast of St. John in 1302 (Medina del Campo 1302, art. 10).

Several times thereafter, the townsmen, alleging their impoverished condition, appealed to Alfonso XI to excuse them from as much as a third to a half of their debts to the Jews, and to postpone the term of payment (without interest accruing) for as much as three years. Pointing out that the Jews were also having difficulties meeting their obligations to him, and therefore needed to collect outstanding debts, he agreed only to a reduction of one quarter of the debt and a postponement of one year.[43]

Inevitably, debt became a cause of litigation between Christians and Jews. The latter wanted to use their own officials to compel the recalcitrant to pay, but the townsmen were adamant in insisting that the ordinary municipal judges should have jurisdiction. Sancho IV declared that Jews, while retaining their own law, would not be permitted to have their own judges, but would be justiciable by royal judges appointed in each town (Palencia 1286, art. 15). This principle was repeated in numerous subsequent meetings of the cortes.[44] Forbidden to have their own scribes, the Jews had to employ the ordinary public scribes of the towns.[45] In all pleas, civil and criminal, the testimony of two Christians of good repute was admissible against Jews or Moors.[46] Jews and Moors could be required to swear oaths whose wording was specified by Alfonso X.[47] Fines would be levied in accordance with local *fueros* and not the privileges of the Jews or Moors.[48] In sum, the weight of the law greatly favored the Christians.

The regulations imposed on the Jews by the king and the cortes were based on the proposition that they not only adhered to distinctive theological tenets and forms of worship but also rightfully observed their own law. As contact with their Christian neighbors was unavoidable, conflicts were sure to arise, posing the problem of whose law should be administered. The Christian majority believed that they ought to prevail, and the legislation reflects their view. Even so, it is worth noting that successive monarchs did not overly trouble themselves about enforcing laws intended to maintain the strict separation of different religions. Yet when royal authority was at stake, as in questions of usury, debt, and litigation, they acted to uphold their own advantage. The crown's pragmatic policy prompted the critic, Álvaro Pelayo, to complain that monarchs entrusted their affairs to the Jews and gave them authority over Christians.[49] While wealthier Jews might have benefited from their apparent access to the king, the circumstances of poorer Jews were not much different from those of Christians. As the latter were beginning to feel hard-pressed economically, they vented their hostility indiscriminately against all the Jews, as is evident from the *cuadernos*.

The Economy

The cortes had much to say about the state of the economy because both the king and the estates tried to direct the course of development to their respective, and sometimes common, advantage. The economy was still fundamentally agricultural and pastoral, but the livestock industry underwent an extraordinary expansion as pasturage opened in the south. The annexation of the major southern cities also contributed to the rapid development of overseas trade, radiating from Seville and the Mediterranean coast where the Genoese had been given a favored position by Fernando III, and from the Bay of Biscay where the towns organized the *hermandad de las marismas* to further their opportunities. The growth of commerce made it possible for the mercantile class to gain in wealth, power, and influence.[50]

As the basic wealth of the realm was derived from the land, Alfonso X enacted several measures in the cortes to protect the environment so that plant and animal life could flourish. No one was permitted to take the eggs of hawks or falcons or to remove the birds from their nests while they were hatching or caring for their young. Hunting partridges, hares, and rabbits was restricted, and all hunting was prohibited from the beginning of Lent until Michaelmas. The king's principal concern here may have been to maintain hunting preserves, but the general good was also served if care was taken not to deplete the supply of food and hides too rapidly. The prohibition against cutting down, burning, or injuring someone else's trees emphasized the importance of woodland as a source of firewood and building material for houses, ships, and the like. Anyone found setting fire to woods would be cast into the flames and have his goods confiscated. Fisheries were also protected by laws forbidding anyone to take salmon eggs or kill fish by poisoning streams.[51]

Salt

The uses of salt—one of the most important elements in the economy and a major source of revenue for the crown—were many and varied. Valuable to the human diet, salt was used to season food, preserve fish and meat, feed livestock, and tan hides. Salt was a product much in demand both within and without the peninsula, and it appears that the supply was insufficient for the needs of the people of Castile and León. Significant deposits were located in the provinces of Álava, Guipúzcoa, Guadalajara, and Cuenca. The salt pits most often mentioned by the cortes were at Atienza (Guadalajara), Añana (Álava), Rosío, and Poza (Burgos).[52]

As monopolies of the crown, the salt pits were usually leased, and portions of the royal revenue derived from them were assigned to the nobility. Alfonso X maintained the royal monopoly by forbidding anyone to establish a private salt depot; he fixed the price at which salt could be sold and prohibited its export (presumably because of the lack of sufficient quantities for domestic use).[53] Any merchant selling contraband salt ran the risk of fines and confiscation, but overzealous inspectors who intruded into private homes in search of salt purchased contrary to regulations were reprimanded (Valladolid 1322, art. 47).

In his effort to raise revenues for the defense of the frontier and the maintenance of his fleet, Alfonso XI enacted an ordinance concerning salt in the assembly of Burgos 1338. The produce of salt pits belonging to persons other than the king, and all imported salt, could be sold only to royal agents, who in turn would sell it at prices fixed by the king.[54] The assembly of Madrid 1339 asked the king to enforce the first ordinance he had made concerning salt (whether this referred to the ordinance of 1338 or to another is uncertain); but he decided to review it and perhaps modify it, to improve procedures for distribution, and to control private efforts to circumvent the regulations (art. 25–26). Complaints about the inconvenience of many salt depots were presented in the assembly of Alcalá 1345. The king explained that he wished to facilitate inspections and to establish depots where there already was an abundance of salt, but he promised to reconsider the matter (art. 13).

The continuing search for contraband salt irritated the cortes of Alcalá 1348, so much so that the king agreed that anyone found with only half a *fanega* (less than a bushel) would not have to pay a fine (art. 25). When they objected that people were often forced to accept and to pay for more than they could consume, the king admitted that they should not be required to do so (art. 49).

Alfonso XI, in effect, tightened control over the use and distribution of this essential product, assigning quantities for purchase by each town and appointing inspectors to catch those who tried to buy or sell it privately. Despite the pleas of the cortes, the financial benefit to the crown was such that Alfonso XI refused to modify the regulations in any significant way.

The Mesta

The crown also profited from the expansion of the sheepherding industry, perhaps the most significant economic development of the period. The reconquest, which had extended the frontier from the Tagus river to the Guadalquivir within a century and a half, opened up the lands of La Mancha, Extremadura, and Andalusia to pasturage. Great flocks of sheep owned by the king, nobles, monasteries, and towns annually traversed the sheepwalks extending from León, Logroño, and Soria to the rich pasturage lands of the south. As more land was made available for pasturage, the number of sheep increased, to the immense profit of the sheepowners.

From the late thirteenth century, tensions steadily mounted between the sheepowners and the towns and military orders through whose lands the flocks passed. In order to protect their interests the sheepmen organized an association known as the Mesta. Alfonso X, perhaps hoping to reduce dependence on foreign imports by developing a Castilian woolen industry, granted several major privileges to the Mesta.[55]

The issues in conflict were the sheepwalks themselves, the use of pasturage en route, the imposition of tolls, and the procedures for resolving disputes. In the cortes of Seville 1252, Alfonso X affirmed the right of sheepmen to use streams and traditional sheepwalks. Because the enclosure of pasturage thwarted the sheepmen, he allowed pastures already enclosed to remain so, but commanded new enclosures to be made only in an orderly manner (art. 31, 33). The townsmen argued that the sheep inevitably damaged vineyards and fields, and they insisted that the animals be confined to the usual sheepwalks—La Leonesa, La Segoviana, and La Mancha de Montearagón.[56] They also deliberately tried to obstruct the sheepwalks by settling villages or planting vineyards and orchards in the way. Alfonso XI condemned this but also required the sheepmen to keep away from settled or planted areas (Madrid 1339, art. 32).

As the flocks made their way, the towns tried to levy a variety of tolls on them. Alfonso X fixed the amount of the pasturage toll (*montazgo*) for cattle, sheep, and pigs, and forbade the imposition of more than one toll in a given municipal district or domain of a military order.[57] Other tolls (*ronda, asadura, castellería*) were due only where customary.[58]

To manage the affairs of the Mesta, the crown appointed an official known as the *entregador de los pastores de la Mesta*. As the townsmen were unwilling to be judged by him alone, Sancho IV allowed municipal judges to sit together with him in disputes between the towns and the Mesta, and to restrain the sheepmen from exceeding their judicial authority (Valladolid 1293, art. 7 LEM). Two years later the Andalusian *hermandad* refused to submit to the jurisdiction of the *entregador* because the office had not existed in the time of Fernando III.[59] Continuing abuses led the cortes of Valladolid 1307 (art. 19) to ask that the office be abolished for good and that local judges be permitted to adjudicate suits involving shepherds. Although this demand was repeated at Palencia 1313 (art. 38 J, 40 M), the crown preferred to maintain the arrangement established by Sancho IV.[60]

The migration of flocks benefited the crown so much that it has been suggested that Alfonso X, aware of the revenue potential, organized the Mesta. The royal *servicio de los ganados* was levied as early as 1269 and roused the nobility to insist on its abolition at Toledo 1273. The king, nevertheless, continued to collect it. The cortes later required that it not be levied on flocks remaining within a municipal district or on livestock taken to markets or fairs.[61] By seizing the local *montazgo* over the protests of the towns, Alfonso XI laid the basis for the later royal tax known as *servicio y montazgo*, thereby shaping royal policy for generations to come (Alcalá 1345, art. 11).

In spite of the hostility of the towns to the Mesta, many urban knights appear to have been among those who profited from the ownership of flocks. Municipal objections rested primarily on the fact that the Mesta transcended local control, but there was also an awareness that the expansion of sheepraising was detrimental to agriculture and other aspects of the economy. These protests were usually overridden, however, by the crown's recognition that the migration of flocks was a major source of revenue and that the Mesta was a useful way of controlling the sheepmen.

Trade

Just as the crown regulated sheepraising, it attempted to control and profit from the growth of internal and external trade. The bulk of internal trade was carried on in local weekly markets, but annual fairs held in some of the more important towns attracted merchants from a broader region. Domestic production tended to be limited to the necessities of a given town and its district—cereals, wine, fish, salt, and cloth. The rise of the Mesta gave impetus to the development of the textile industry, especially in towns along the sheepwalks, but most of the products were consumed locally. Foreign trade along the Bay of Biscay, the Mediterranean, and the land borders with the peninsular states involved the export of raw materials such as wool and iron and the import of luxury goods.[62]

Not surprisingly, mercantile activities were the subject of extensive regulations enacted in the cortes. Both Fernando III and Alfonso X forbade merchants and artisans to conspire to fix prices, ordering them to sell their wares freely on the open market.[63] Considering the economic ills afflicting Castile, Alfonso VIII, in a *curia* held at Toledo in 1207, established prices for different types of cloth, animals, hides, and armor. Alfonso X updated these prices in the cortes of Seville 1252 and the assembly of Jerez 1268.[64] Wages were also set at certain levels and workmen were required to accept them (Jerez 1268, art. 32–34). In the cortes of Seville 1250, Fernando III prohibited the organization of confraternities or other associations of merchants, unless they were of a strictly spiritual or social character. Repeating this, Alfonso X also forbade judges other than those appointed by the crown or chosen according to the municipal *fueros* to adjudicate disputes involving merchants.[65] In all of this, royal policy was dictated not by economic theory but by a desire to maintain the untrammeled authority of the crown and to prevent the development of an autonomous mercantile jurisdiction. If prices and wages were to be fixed, the king would do it, not the merchants. Although it might have been argued that guilds would have a beneficial effect on the economy, the potential challenge that they represented to royal power determined that they should be prohibited. The ban was also a means by which the urban knights restrained the merchants and artisans from gaining power in the towns.[66]

As merchants went about their business, they often encountered threats to their safety and other obstacles. As it was in the interest of the crown to maintain order, the *Partidas* (V.7.4) extended royal protection to merchants and their goods. During the royal minorities, however, merchants often complained of being assaulted and robbed on the way to fairs. Foreign merchants were said to be reluctant to enter the kingdom unless they were guaranteed security and freedom to travel without interference or petty harassment by local authorities and without having to pay customs duties except at the assigned customs posts.[67] Spanish merchants traveling abroad were also sometimes attacked and deprived of their goods by lords in southern France and ships from Bayonne.[68] It was partly on this account that the Vizcayan towns organized the *hermandad de las marismas* in 1296.[69] The protection of merchants was perceived primarily as a function of royal jurisdiction, but there was also a realization that such protection would be beneficial to the economy.

Tolls such as *portazgo* were an impediment to internal trade, though an important source of revenue for the crown and local communities. Alfonso X stipulated that they should be levied only where customary, but numerous exemptions were granted—usually for goods and merchandise carried anywhere in the realm except Toledo, Seville, and Murcia.[70] Alfonso XI revoked all exemptions given since the death of his father (Madrid 1329, art. 64), but later, in response to complaints that new tolls were being levied, he confirmed all exemptions granted by Sancho IV, by Fernando IV during his majority, and by himself after 1329. No general exemption was given.[71]

The exchange of goods was facilitated by Alfonso X's ordinance providing for uniform weights and measures. Anyone using false weights and measures was subject to heavy fines; to guard against this, municipal officials were ordered to check all weights and measures each week. Alfonso XI modified his predecessor's ordinance, but maintained the principle of uniformity.[72]

The need for an acceptable medium of exchange was also fundamental for commerce, but the kings manipulated the coinage to their own advantage. The concession of *moneda*, first recorded in the *curia* of Benavente in 1202, was a device to ensure the maintenance of an intact coinage for at least seven years. Occasionally the cortes obtained guarantees that the coinage would not be modified. Alfonso X promised not to alter the money coined at the beginning of his reign (*dineros alfonsís*) and also established equivalences with other monies in circulation (Jerez 1268, art. 12). At Valladolid in 1282 Infante Sancho pledged not to change the coinage, and once he became king he declared that for the rest of his life he would not change the money then being minted.[73] The diversity of coins in circulation was such that Fernando IV pledged to take greater care in the issuance of new money[74] and to stop the widespread circulation of counterfeit coinage. For this purpose, he promulgated an ordinance in the cortes of Burgos 1302 that provided for the appointment of two inspectors in each town.[75] The problem of false coinage continued, however, so that the Castilians proposed that no new coinage be issued until the rest was exhausted and prices were able to return to a more normal level (Medina del Campo 1305, art. 3 C). This idea, however, does not seem to have been accepted.

Foreign Trade

Castile and León produced only limited quantities of goods for export, but foreign trade was also restricted by royal prohibitions against the export of certain goods (*cosas vedadas*). The list of items was established by Alfonso VIII of Castile in the *curia* of Toledo 1207, and by Alfonso IX of León at an uncertain date, and was repeated in the cortes of Seville 1252. Items included horses, mares, hides, cattle, pigs, goats, sheep, hawks, and falcons. The reasoning behind this regulation was to assure an abundance of livestock in the realm, not only for cavalry, military transport, and hunting, but also to encourage the development of cattle- and sheepraising. A merchant was permitted, however, to take a mule laden with merchandise out of the kingdom.[76] The ban on the export of horses and livestock was made operative for ten years in the cortes of Seville 1261 (art. 15), chiefly because of the projected campaign against the Moors, but it never seems to have been allowed to lapse.

Exports were regulated in much greater detail at Jerez 1268. The lists of prohibited goods drawn up in 1252 and 1258 were repeated with some additions—gold, silver, silk, raw wool, wheat, wine, and foodstuffs (art. 14). Gold and silver were added probably because they represented intrinsic wealth, while the other items were necessary to provide adequate food and clothing. The nobles at Toledo 1273 demanded that the list be restricted to those articles forbidden in the reign of Fernando III, but the ban on certain exports was reiterated in subsequent cortes, and some other items were added, such as coins, rabbit skins, and wax.[77] Pedro III of Aragón complained to Alfonso X in 1279 that the prohibition of the export "of almost all merchandise" was injurious to the merchants of both realms and diminished Castile's potential revenues.[78]

Some relaxation of trade restrictions was approved by Alfonso XI, who agreed that, inasmuch as he allowed the Navarrese and Aragonese to export wheat and livestock from his kingdom, his own subjects should be able to do so as well (Madrid 1339, art. 5). He was adamant, however, in opposing the export of horses, especially by the nobles, who had greater need of them for service against the Moors; anyone who violated the ban would be executed (Burgos 1338, art. 13). Some years later, the Castilians, pointing to a great mortality rate among livestock and the consequent hardship on the people, proposed that the export of wheat and meat be forbidden until conditions improved, but that the export of horses should be allowed so men would be encouraged to raise them. Alfonso XI strongly objected, declaring that he would be especially hard hit if any great need for horses arose (Burgos 1345, art. 1, 6). Three years later, noting that his laws discouraged men from raising the horses he required for his wars, he changed his mind and enacted an ordinance intended to stimulate breeding. While the export of colts under four years and of mares was absolutely forbidden, other horses could be shipped abroad, subject to the royal tenth of their value, payable at the usual customs posts (Alcalá 1348, art. 56, 59).[79] Thus, in order to meet his military requirements, he had to allow the nobles and others to profit from the export of horses.

Alfonso X, in the assembly of Jerez 1268, required that goods for export be brought to certain towns where royal officials would inspect each merchant's manifest to prevent the shipment of any forbidden articles. Merchants were also required to import as much as they exported and to give sureties that they would do so. Customs officials had to inform the masters of foreign ships of these regulations and see that they were observed.[80] On several occasions thereafter, merchants were assured that they would not be troubled on the highways or at markets and fairs by a search for prohibited goods, but that this would be done only at the customs posts.[81] Alfonso X refused to abolish customs duties altogether, as the nobles demanded at Burgos 1272, but he did promise (albeit falsely) to stop collection after six years.[82] Customs duties were obviously an important source of revenue, and he was determined to collect them as efficiently as possible. Yet his attempt to achieve a balance of trade by requiring imports to equal exports probably was never successful.

Those found exporting prohibited goods could be punished by confiscation, fines, and exile.[83] As with so many other sources of revenue, the crown leased the collection of fines to tax farmers, authorizing them to conduct inquests to identify violators. The use of a closed inquest for this purpose was prohibited in the cortes of Valladolid 1298 (art. 11), but that prohibition was not always observed. In later years, those who exported contraband goods were pardoned by the king at the request of the cortes.[84]

The data found in the *cuadernos* reveal a society largely dependent on pasturage and the production of raw materials rather than finished goods. Internal needs consumed much of what was produced, leaving smaller amounts for export. The lists of goods whose export was forbidden (*cosas vedadas*) emphasized the scarcity of goods. The aristocracy, nevertheless, had a desire for finer clothes, weapons, food, and luxury items, and sought to obtain them from abroad. The resulting imbalance of trade suggested by the texts thwarted any attempt by the crown or the cortes to strengthen the economy. Castilian society was poor rather than rich, and its economy was limited in its development. Poverty and starvation were the lot of many in times of poor harvests, or worse yet, when the factions contending for power destroyed crops. The effects of such devastation lingered on for many years.

A European Perspective

In the neighboring kingdoms, similar social and economic issues required the attention of the king and the estates. The acquisition of property by the church was a continuing source of tension in Portugal, prompting King Dinis to take restrictive measures in the cortes of Lisbon 1285. Edward I's Statute of Mortmain 1279 attempted to achieve the same result, just as he tried to limit ecclesiastical jurisdiction by means of *Circumspecte agatis* in 1285. Papal provisions and appeals to Rome were regulated by the Statutes of Provisors and Praemunire enacted by Edward III's parliament in 1351 and 1353, respectively. Taxation of the clergy and ecclesiastical jurisdiction were at the root of Philip IV's quarrel with the papacy, causing him to seek popular support by assembling the Estates of Languedoil in 1302.[85]

In the corts of Barcelona 1283, Pedro III considered a wide range of social and economic problems, including the conversion of Saracens and Jews, Jaime I's constitution on usury, the freedom of merchants, and rejection of a salt tax. The Statute of Acton Burnell 1283 promulgated by Edward I was the first of many measures dealing with the activities of merchants in England. The economic consequences of the Black Death resulted in the enactment of the Statute of Laborers by parliament in 1351—its intent was similar to that of the *Ordenamiento de menestrales* enacted by Pedro the Cruel in the cortes of Valladolid 1351.[86]

11

A Final Assessment

The western parliamentary tradition, as this study of the cortes of Castile-León illustrates, is a rich and varied one. Students of comparative constitutional history will recognize that the cortes shared certain characteristics with the English parliament, the French assemblies of estates, and the German imperial diet, but that like them, it was also endowed with its own unique features.

The cortes enjoyed a distinction of sorts because it emerged sooner than parliaments elsewhere in the peninsula and northern and central Europe. This was not because the people of Castile-León possessed a greater genius than others, but was rather the consequence of two important conjunctions of time and place. First, by the twelfth century the municipalities, unlike many of those in northern Europe, were already self-governing entities, directly dependent on the crown with administrative responsibility for both urban settlements and extensive rural areas. In this respect, they may be compared with the city-states of Lombardy and Tuscany. Besides providing significant military contingents for royal campaigns against the Moors, they also served as a source of essential financial aid for the crown.

Second, Roman law, the subject of intensive study in Italy in the twelfth century, had an early impact on the peninsula. Castile-León belonged to the Mediterranean community and was open to the new juridical ideas and methods originating in Italy. Roman law familiarized the Castilians and Leonese with the idea of a corporation that could be represented by a procurator with full powers, and with the principle *quod omnes tangit, ab omnibus debet approbari*, which encouraged the crown to take counsel with all those who might be affected by any major decision. Thus Roman law provided the theoretical justification for the convocation of the municipalities and the practical instruments to bring that about.

Eventually the same principles would facilitate parliamentary development elsewhere, in accordance with the peculiar situation of each country. In England there emerged a single parliament consisting of two houses, the one constituted by the spiritual and temporal lords, and the other by the knights of the shires and burgesses of the towns. The pattern of development in Castile-León was different, in part because of the greater territorial expanse of the kingdom, and in part because of the patchwork fashion in which it was put together over several centuries. As a consequence, each of its constituent elements retained a strong sense of identity. Whereas in England there was only one parliament, a separate cortes originated in both Castile and León; after the union of 1230, both realms were usually convened together in a single cortes, but occasionally they were summoned separately. In this respect, Castilian development bears a closer resemblance to France. There the authority of the king was gradually extended over the several provinces of the kingdom, but each of them retained a consciousness of its special character. Only occasionally did a French assembly of estates represent the greater part of the king's dominions. Most often the estates of Languedoil and Languedoc met simultaneously but in different places; at other times provincial assemblies of estates were convened. Provincial assemblies or cortes in Castile-León met infrequently, but it is striking that during his majority Alfonso XI preferred to deal with partial or regional assemblies rather than a plenary cortes. The similarities between the parliamentary histories of Castile-León and France are also marked in terms of the threefold division of the estates, as compared with the English bicameral parliament.

In assessing the work of the cortes, it should not be forgotten that the cortes, though a parliamentary assembly, was no more a modern parliament than the medieval English parliament or the French assemblies of estates. Much of the argument about its role and functions has been prompted by the assumption that it was essentially the same as the modern cortes of the nineteenth and twentieth centuries. But the cortes was a medieval assembly born out of the medieval milieu to serve medieval needs.

Two questions persistently arise when the development of the medieval cortes or any other parliamentary assembly is considered: how representative was it, and how democratic was it? In comparison with modern parliaments, the representative nature of the medieval cortes was limited, and it did not meet modern standards for a democratic assembly.

In the period discussed in this book, the cortes ordinarily consisted of the prelates, magnates, and representatives of the towns. Members of the two former estates were traditional counselors of the king and sources of political power and influence, whereas the latter typified the comparatively new force of the municipalities. Bishops and magnates, summoned individually on account of their office or their status as vassals of the crown, acted on their own behalf but also in the name of the estates to which they belonged. In that sense bishops and magnates virtually represented the entire body of the clergy and of the nobility, respectively. As for the third estate, self-governing municipalities directly dependent on the crown were represented, rather than the entire conglomerate of urban dwellers. Not all towns were summoned, for many were held in lordship by secular or ecclesiastical lords. Certain geographical areas where there were few autonomous municipalities were represented in the cortes scarcely or not at all. For example, the towns in the modern province of Ciudad Real were unrepresented in the cortes, except that the masters of Calatrava or Santiago, as lords of most of that region, ordinarily participated in the cortes. The rural population was represented insofar as they were considered part of the municipality or dependents of secular or ecclesiastical lords; otherwise they had no direct representation. By comparison, in England the sheriff had the responsibility of determining which towns and boroughs in his county should send representatives to parliament; some were ignored entirely, while others (the so-called rotten boroughs) continued to send representatives long after they had ceased to flourish or even exist.

The cortes was never democratic in the sense that representation was proportional to population size. As a general rule, each municipality was represented by two procurators. Thus, despite obvious variations in numbers of inhabitants, such cities and towns as Seville, Ávila, Burgos, Laredo, Segovia, and León could each be represented by two procurators. This was because the Roman legal principle *quod omnes tangit ab omnibus debet approbari*, on which representation was based, was a principle of juridical rather than democratic consent, as Gaines Post emphasizes. In addition, as the urban aristocracy consolidated its hold over the towns, municipal representatives were chosen from the aristocracy and reflected its interests. Similar situations prevailed both in England, where London, York, Lincoln, and other towns usually sent two burgesses to parliament, and in France, where cities such as Paris and Orléans each sent two procurators. Although the electoral process in modern-day parliaments is democratic, the fact that the representatives as a rule tend to be wealthy and drawn from the legal profession or the mercantile aristocracy raises the same questions: how representative and how democratic is a modern parliament?

In spite of the inadequacies of the cortes when judged by the standards of a modern democratic parliament, the king obviously believed that, together with the three estates, he could treat "the estate of the realm" and take actions that would be binding on everyone who inhabited his dominions, even though all were not summoned to, or directly represented in, the cortes. The cortes was indisputably a creature of the crown. It was the king's court, summoned by him, when and where he wished to summon it. Only after a time did the participants begin to realize that these were new developments, modifications of earlier traditions, and that it was their assembly as well as the king's. The cortes might serve the purposes of the king, but it could also be used by those summoned to attend it.

Although Maria de Molina and Infante Pedro, regents for Alfonso XI, assured the cortes of Palencia 1313 that they would convoke the cortes every two years, the king always considered himself free to summon the cortes when it suited his purposes. Other monarchs gave similar guarantees. Thus, Pedro III pledged in 1283 to convene the Catalan corts each year, and in response to the demands of the Union, both he and Alfonso III agreed to summon the Aragonese cortes annually. The call for annual parliaments was sounded in England in the Provisions of

Oxford 1258, the Ordinances of 1311, and the Statutes of 1330 and 1362. Even so, pledges of this sort were never implemented with consistent regularity and were honored more in the breach than in the observance.

Nevertheless, the king of Castile-León realized that in certain circumstances it was to his advantage to summon the cortes. He needed to take counsel about projected enterprises both at home and abroad, such as the improvement of the economy, the defense of the realm against the Moors, the enactment of laws, and relations with his neighbors, and he needed to obtain financial help to fulfill his burgeoning responsibilities. From a practical standpoint, the cortes enabled the king to bring together all the principal political elements in the kingdom and seek their support and cooperation for policies that he considered essential. Invariably he described his plans as furthering the service of God, his own well-being, and that of the entire realm. In seeking counsel or consent, the king was well aware that any major policy—such as a military campaign, a new law, or the regulation of the succession—was bound to founder without the active collaboration of the estates of the realm. Unless he wished to play the tyrant, he had to persuade, cajole, and convince, otherwise he could expect little success.

Those who were summoned to the cortes came to realize that it also provided them with opportunities. The prelates, whose influence was essentially moral and spiritual, were accustomed to dealing directly with the king. Seeing their primary responsibility as upholding the liberties of the church, they attempted to check royal efforts to tax the clergy without limit, and to curb encroachments on ecclesiastical jurisdiction. They also appealed to the king to defend them against the nobles and townsmen who abused them. The nobles, whose power was primarily military and who, as vassals of the crown, received annual stipends for their service, naturally assumed the role of royal counselors. They were not in awe of the king and endeavored to guide him to right action, as they saw it, and to defend their own special privileges and customs, as they did in the cortes of Burgos 1272.

The townsmen, though perhaps hesitant when summoned initially to the cortes, gradually acquired a greater ease in the presence of the king and the powerful men of the kingdom. Conscious of the importance of their responsibility for the administration of vast areas, and of the value of their militias in the armies of the reconquest, they began to speak up. For them the cortes was an occasion to limit royal demands for extraordinary taxes or to require an appropriate quid pro quo by reforms and improvements in government, economic life, and social relations. By means of their *hermandades*, brought to vigorous life in 1282 and again in 1295 and 1315, they exercised an effective political clout in the cortes that neither the king nor the regents could ignore.

In effect, each of the estates could utilize the cortes to make its concerns known directly to the king, to take steps to protect its particular interests, and to challenge royal policy if necessary. Each estate might define the needs of the realm as a whole in terms of specific issues or problems that affected it directly, and it would be easy to describe the estates as selfish. Yet in pressing its views, each estate could claim, as the king did, to have the well-being of the realm at heart. Out of these differing perceptions and conflicting views, a consensus might be reached as to what was in the best interests of the kingdom as a whole.

Over the course of many years, the roles of the participants changed. The king, who summoned the cortes, might dominate it if he were an especially strong personality; if he were weak, the balance of power might shift to the assembly. Alfonso X seems to have been reasonably successful in persuading the cortes to follow his lead in the first part of his reign, but the denouement, dating at least from his confrontation with the nobility and then with the prelates and townsmen at the cortes of Burgos 1272, was a time of increasing tension and ultimate failure on his part. Thus, the threat that the cortes might pose to royal power was gradually perceived. Consequently, Sancho IV, who needed the support of the cortes early in his reign, tended to avoid convocation once his position on the throne was secure. Fernando IV appears as a weak king whose relationships with the cortes were always tense. His mother, Maria de Molina, must be given the highest marks for her ability to influence the cortes, and to play off contending interests and factions while preserving the throne for her son and later her grandson, Alfonso XI. Even so, during the two royal minorities, the cortes was frequently hostile to the king and the regents. Acknowledging the capacity of the cortes to create difficulties for the crown, Alfonso XI, upon attaining his majority, allowed many years to elapse between convocations, and in the interim divided the estates by summoning partial assemblies rather than the full cortes.

The issues confronting the kings of Castile-León when they met with the cortes hardly differed from those of their contemporaries in England and France. The dispute over the succession to the throne after the death of Fernando de la Cerda was unusual, however, and allowed the cortes, by rejecting counter-claimants, to assist Sancho IV and Fernando IV in consolidating their rights. Sometimes the cortes was summoned to acknowledge the heir to the throne, but its greatest power came during the troublesome minorities when, courted by the different contenders for office, it had a major role in determining the regency. Otherwise, like the English parliament or the French assemblies of estates, the cortes counseled the king concerning such questions as Alfonso X's imperial quest, the proposed invasion of Africa, and the war against the Moors. In addition, the king, like his fellow monarchs elsewhere, promulgated new laws or ordinances in the cortes and often accepted petitions presented to him by the estates, thereby giving them the force of law. These ordinances, whether initiated by the king and his council or by the cortes, covered an extensive range of topics: the administration of justice and taxation, the regulation of the economy, social relationships, and so forth.

As royal power gathered strength in all countries under the influence of Aristotelian thought and Roman law, the prelates, nobles, and townsmen meeting in cortes, parliament, or assembly of the estates strove to influence and perhaps curb the king's actions. As God's vicar, emperor in his own kingdom, acknowledging no superior in temporal matters, the king developed a capacity for arbitrary rule. In counteraction, the cortes often sought written guarantees of their rights and customs. Alfonso X, faced with protest about the influence of Roman law and men trained in the law, confirmed the *fueros* of the nobility and the towns in the cortes of Burgos 1272 and through his son, Fernando de la Cerda, gave similar pledges to the prelates at Peñafiel three years later. The Aragonese nobles obtained like assurances from Pedro III in the General Privilege of 1283 and from Alfonso III in the Privileges of the Union in 1287. Edward I's Confirmation of the Charters in 1297 and Louis X's Charters to the Normans, Burgundians, and others in 1315 were in response to comparable demands for the restoration of the good old laws.

The crown's attempt to establish the principle that royal jurisdiction was paramount resulted in the subordination of municipal and noble courts, but it also provoked a demand that men be tried by their peers. In the cortes of Burgos 1272, Alfonso X had to agree to appoint noble judges in his court to adjudicate litigation involving the nobility. In a similar fashion, Jaime I, Pedro III, and Alfonso III consented that the justiciar of Aragón should be a noble with the same responsibilities. When the clergy protested royal intrusions on ecclesiastical jurisdiction, Alfonso X (Peñafiel 1275), Fernando IV (Valladolid 1295), and Alfonso XI (Valladolid 1325) assured them that their liberties remained intact, though the need for reiteration suggests that the prelates had reason to be ever watchful. In England, Edward I, by means of the statute, *Circumspecte agatis*, attempted to circumscribe the jurisdiction of church courts; Philip IV of France trampled on ecclesiastical privilege when he insisted on trying the bishop of Pamiers in his court.

The novelty of extraordinary taxation also provoked hostility. The king was expected to maintain himself and his government from his customary sources of income, but times had changed. The vision of what government should do had expanded and the rise in the standard of living made the ordinary tributes inadequate. When kings attempted to tap new resources, they had to confirm their obligation to ask consent before imposing extraordinary taxes. Alfonso X made such a pledge in the cortes of Burgos 1277, as did Sancho IV (Valladolid 1293), Fernando IV (Valladolid 1295), and Alfonso XI, who promised the cortes of Madrid 1329 (art. 68) that he would not "levy any extraordinary tribute, special or general, in the entire realm, without first summoning the cortes." Edward I acknowledged this principle in the Confirmation of the Charters in 1297, and Philip VI tacitly did so in the Estates of Languedoil in 1343. The cortes occasionally limited the purpose of the grant, as at Valladolid in 1300, and sometimes granted funds for short terms. Attempts were also made to regulate the collection and subsequent disbursement of taxes. The cortes of Valladolid 1307, Burgos 1315, the assembly of Carrión 1317, and the cortes of Valladolid 1325 and Madrid 1329 asked for an accounting of royal revenues, though none seems to have been carried out in the latter two cases. The English parliament presented similar petitions in 1340 and 1341.

In order to maintain the strength of the crown and minimize the need for extraordinary taxes, efforts were made to curb the dissipation of its resources. Ordinances were enacted by Alfonso VIII at Nájera 1184, Alfonso IX at Benavente 1228, and Sancho IV at Haro 1288 to recover royal lands acquired by the church. Edward I's statute, *De viris religiosis* 1279, attempted to limit such acquisitions in the future. The problem was exacerbated by the clergy's insistence that they should not be required to pay extraordinary taxes. The repercussions of Philip IV's battle with Pope Boniface VIII over this issue were felt well beyond the confines of the kingdom of France. Fernando IV's declaration in the cortes of Valladolid 1300 that the clergy ought to contribute to the up-keep of town walls, because they, like others, enjoyed the protection of the walls, echoed similar arguments made in France. Archbishop Gonzalo of Toledo and the other bishops, emboldened by the papal stance, challenged the king in this regard at Medina del Campo 1302, though they later compromised.

Whenever a king behaved in a particularly arbitrary manner, the charge was often made that he was being led astray by evil counselors. This was essentially the position taken by the nobility in the cortes of Burgos 1308. During the minorities of Fernando IV and Alfonso XI, the townsmen in the cortes of Valladolid 1295, Cuéllar 1297, and Burgos 1315 also tried to secure a dominant place in the royal council. The English nobility tried to control appointments to the royal council through the Provisions of Oxford 1258 and the Ordinances of 1311, while the Aragonese attempted to wrest the same right from Alfonso III in the Privileges of the Union in 1287.

If all these measures to control the king failed, armed resistance was resorted to. Infante Sancho, with the backing of much of the kingdom of Castile, deprived his father of royal power (though he left him with the royal title). The Aragonese nobles threatened to depose Pedro III and Alfonso III if they did not submit to their demands, while in England Simon de Montfort kept Henry III in leading strings. Henry III's grandson, Edward II, who seemed incapable of learning from experience, had the misfortune to be deposed and then murdered in 1327. As these and other examples demonstrate, the study of the cortes in the thirteenth and early fourteenth centuries sheds light on constitutional development across western Europe.

Despite the variety of issues presented to the cortes, there were significant limitations on its influence and power, as there were on other medieval parliamentary assemblies. For example, although its support was important for one who claimed the throne, the cortes, in the strict sense, never elected a king. Nor was it always called upon to recognize the heir to the throne. Although its counsel might be requested concerning foreign affairs, it did not ratify treaties. Moreover, the crown at times collected taxes without obtaining consent and transformed extraordinary taxes into customary tributes. In the reigns of Alfonso X and Sancho IV, the cortes consented to levies for excessively long periods of time, thereby yielding control over taxation. Demands that collection be placed in the hands of trustworthy townsmen were evidently not met with any consistency, and the cortes was unable to establish any permanent means of controlling expenditures. The cortes failed to gain a firm commitment from the crown that there could be no legislation outside the cortes; furthermore, it did not develop any effective means of enforcing the laws—which is, of course, a problem every legislative body has confronted and one that is often exemplified in our own day. The execution and enforcement of the laws was the king's responsibility, but even though he might be conscientious and well-intentioned, there were inevitable failures and lapses.

In some respects, these technical or mechanical weaknesses might have been corrected in time. Far more serious was the lack of any sense of cohesion or common purpose among the estates. Prelates, nobles, and townsmen surely were conscious of their identity as estates, but the first two groups had a stronger sense of unity. Among the towns, regionalism was a potent factor, to the extent that the towns of Extremadura sometimes refused to meet with those of Castile and vice versa. Social change in the towns, marked by a steadily widening gap between *caballeros* and *peones*, resulted in factionalism, which only served to undermine municipal autonomy and leave the towns open to greater royal control or the possibility of being given in lordship to a prelate or noble.

In addition to these divisions among the townsmen, often the estates were hostile to one another and acted at cross-purposes. Of the clergy, nobles, and townsmen, each group felt a strong antipathy toward members of the other two groups. Occasionally prelates and townsmen joined together, as in the *hermandad* of 1282, and the lower nobility and townsmen in 1314, but these were exceptional circumstances and probably did not involve the majority of the most influential prelates or nobles.

On the whole, the *hermandades* tended to polarize the estates rather than bring them together. In their structure and organization, these extralegal associations of towns rivaled the cortes and sometimes overshadowed it completely. The assembly of Carrión 1317, for example, was primarily a meeting of the Castilian *hermandad*, but the regents treated it as they would have the cortes. While the *hermandades* enabled the towns to wield exceptional force in the cortes, their existence, if perpetuated, would have undermined the cortes as an institution.

In varying degrees each of the estates was guilty of being self-centered and self-seeking, and of failing to recognize that in certain instances, it would have been to the benefit of all to act in concert. The lack of a common sense of purpose and direction ultimately worked to the advantage of the crown.

Although we may fault the cortes for deficiencies in its composition, organization, and functions, it is nonetheless true that during the years from 1188 to 1350 it became a prinicipal element in the government of the kingdom of Castile-León. The tradition established at that time extended well into the modern era. After tentative beginnings, the cortes assumed an identifiable shape, developed methods of operation, and confronted the great issues affecting the estate of the king and the kingdom, namely, the succession to the throne, war and peace, legislation, taxation, the administration of justice, the maintenance of law and order, the exploitation of natural resources, the regulation of industry and commerce, and relations among the people of the three religions. As time passed, the cortes developed a greater assurance as to its place in the structure of government, and the crown acknowledged that consultation with the estates assembled in the cortes was necessary and useful for the well-being of the kingdom.

Abbreviations

AC	Archivo Catedralicio
AEM	*Anuario de Estudios Medievales*
AHDE	*Anuario de Historia del Derecho español*
AHN	Archivo Histórico Nacional, Madrid
AHR	*American Historical Review*
AM	Archivo municipal
BAE	*Biblioteca de Autores españoles*
BEC	*Bibliothèque de l'École des Chartes*
BL	British Library, London
BN	Biblioteca Nacional, Madrid
BRAH	*Boletín de la Real Academia de la Historia*
CAX	*Crónica de Alfonso X*
CAXI	*Crónica de Alfonso XI*

CFIV	*Crónica de Fernando IV*
CHE	*Cuadernos de Historia de España*
CHR	*Catholic Historical Review*
CLC	*Cortes de los antiguos reinos de León y Castilla*
CODOM	*Colección de documentos para la historia del reino de Murcia*
CSIV	*Crónica de Sancho IV*
EHR	*English Historical Review*
ES	*España Sagrada*
GCAXI	*Gran Crónica de Alfonso XI*
HID	*Historia, Instituciones, Documentos*
MFIII	Miguel de Manuel, *Memorias para la vida del santo rey Fernando III*
MFIV	Antonio Benavides, *Memorias de Fernando IV*
MHE	*Memorial Histórico Español*
RABM	*Revista de Archivos, Bibliotecas y Museos*
RAH	Real Academia de la Historia, Madrid

Notes

INTRODUCTION

1. Antonio Marongiu, *Medieval Parliaments: A Comparative Study*, tr. S. J. Woolf (London 1968); Luis González Antón, *Las Cortes de Aragón* (Zaragoza 1978), and *Las Uniones aragonesas y las Cortes del reino, 1283–1301*, 2 vols. (Madrid 1975); José Coroleu and José Pella y Forgas, *Las Cortes catalanas*, 2d ed. (Barcelona 1876); Paulo Merea, *O Poder real e as Cortes* (Coimbra 1923).

2. G. O. Sayles, *The King's Parliament of England* (New York 1974); Thomas Bisson, "The General Assemblies of Philip the Fair: Their Character Reconsidered," *Studia Gratiana* 15 (1972): 537–564.

3. Luis Suárez Fernández, "Evolución histórica de las hermandades castellanas," *CHE* 11 (1951): 5–78.

4. Francisco Martínez Marina, *Teoría de las Cortes o grandes juntas nacionales de los reinos de León y Castilla*, 3 vols. (Madrid 1813; reprinted in *BAE*, CCXIX–CCXX, Madrid 1968). I will cite the *BAE* edition.

5. Manuel Colmeiro, *Introducción a las Cortes de los antiguos reinos de León y Castilla*, 2 vols. (Madrid 1883–1884); Roger B. Merriman, "The Cortes of the Spanish Kingdoms in the Later Middle Ages," *AHR* 16 (1911): 476–495. Now outdated is Juan Sempere, *Histoire des Cortes d'Espagne* (Bordeaux 1815), and *Resumen de las antiguas Cortes de España* (Madrid 1834).

6. Wladimir Piskorski, *Las Cortes de Castilla en el período de tránsito de la

edad media a la moderna, tr. Claudio Sánchez Albornoz (Barcelona 1930; reprint Barcelona: Ediciones Albir 1977).

7. Claudio Sánchez Albornoz, *España, un enigma histórico* (Buenos Aires 1962), II, 90–92, and *La Curia regia portuguesa. Siglos XII y XIII* (Madrid 1920); Nilda Guglielmi, "La curia regia en León y Castilla," *CHE* 23–24 (1955): 116–267; 28 (1958): 43–101. Ismael García Ramila's "Las Cortes de Castilla. Origenes y vicisitudes," *RABM* 46 (1925): 84–99, 262–278, is only a sketch.

8. Julio Valdeón, "Las Cortes medievales castellano-leonesas en la historiografía reciente," in Piskorski (reprint 1977), v–xxxv.

9. José Manuel Pérez Prendes, *Cortes de Castilla* (Barcelona 1974), and "Cortes de Castilla y Cortes de Cádiz," *Revista de Estudios políticos* 126 (1962): 321–431; Julio Valdeón Baruque, "Las Cortes castellanas en el siglo XIV," *AEM* 7 (1970–1971): 633–644.

10. Evelyn S. Procter, *Curia and Cortes in León-Castile, 1072–1295* (Cambridge 1980).

11. *Cortes de los antiguos reinos de León y Castilla,* ed. Real Academia de la Historia, 5 vols. (Madrid 1861–1903). Abbreviated as *CLC.* Due to limitations of space I cannot cite all the manuscripts and editions of *cuadernos* that I have seen, but I hope to publish a separate listing.

12. I usually cite the exemplar in *CLC.* The name of the place where the cortes was held will be given, followed by the date and the number of the article in the printed edition, e.g., Valladolid 1258, art. 1. In order to distinguish among *cuadernos* drawn up in the same cortes but given to different regions, the initial letter of the region will be used: C for Castile, L for León, E for Extremadura, A for Andalusia, and M for Murcia. Thus, the citation Medina del Campo 1305, art. 1 CLEM, would refer to art. 1 in four separate *cuadernos* given to Castile, León, Extremadura, and Murcia, respectively. The general *cuaderno* of the cortes of Valladolid 1299 will be identified by the letter G. The *cuadernos* published separately in the cortes of Palencia 1313 by Infante Juan and his rivals, Maria de Molina and Infante Pedro, will be distinguished by the letters J for Juan and M for Maria, as follows: Palencia 1313, art. 1 J, 3 M. *Cuadernos* given to the prelates will be identified by the letter P, e.g., Valladolid 1295, art. 1 P.

13. Rodrigo Jiménez de Rada, *De rebus Hispaniae,* in *Opera,* ed. Francisco Lorenzana (Madrid 1793; reprint Valencia: Anubar 1968); *Chronique latine des rois de Castille,* ed. Georges Cirot (Bordeaux 1913); *Primera Crónica general,* ed. Ramón Menéndez Pidal, 2 vols. (Madrid 1955).

14. Cayetano Rosell, *Crónicas de los reyes de Castilla,* in *BAE,* LXVI (Madrid 1953); *Gran Crónica de Alfonso XI,* ed. Diego Catalan Menéndez Pidal, 2 vols. (Madrid 1977); *Poema de Alfonso XI,* ed. Yo Ten Cate (Madrid 1955).

15. Jofre de Loaysa, *Crónica de los reyes de Castilla, Fernando III, Alfonso X, Sancho IV y Fernando IV, 1248–1305,* ed. and tr. Antonio García Martínez (Murcia 1961).

16. Juan Gil de Zamora, *De preconiis Hispaniae,* ed. Manuel de Castro y Castro (Madrid 1955); Juan Manuel, *Libro de los estados,* ed. R. B. Tate and I. R. Macpherson (New York 1974); Andrés Giménez Soler, *Don Juan Manuel. Biografía y estudio crítico* (Madrid 1932); Álvaro Pelayo (Alvaro Pais), *Espelho dos Reis,* ed. and tr. Miguel Pinto de Meneses (Lisbon 1955).

CHAPTER 1

1. Joseph F. O'Callaghan, *A History of Medieval Spain* (Ithaca 1975); Jocelyn Hillgarth, *The Spanish Kingdoms, 1250–1516*, 2 vols. (Oxford 1976–1978).
2. Derek W. Lomax, *The Reconquest of Spain* (London 1978); Angus MacKay, *Spain in the Middle Ages: From Frontier to Empire, 1000–1500* (New York 1977).
3. Salvador de Moxó, "La nobleza castellano-leonesa en la edad media," *Hispania* 30 (1970): 5–68; Hilda Grassotti, *Las instituciones feudo-vasallaticas en León y Castilla*, 2 vols. (Spoleto 1969).
4. Sánchez Albornoz, *Despoblación y repoblación del valle del Duero* (Buenos Aires 1965); Salvador de Moxó, *Repoblación y sociedad en la España cristiana medieval* (Madrid 1979).
5. María del Carmen Carlé, *Del concejo medieval castellano-leonés* (Buenos Aires 1968).
6. Carmela Pescador, "La caballería popular en León y Castilla," *CHE* 33–34 (1961): 101–238; 35–36 (1962): 56–501; James F. Powers, "The Origins and Development of Municipal Military Service in the Leonese and Castilian Reconquest, 800–1250," *Traditio* 26 (1970): 91–111, and "Townsmen and Soldiers: The Interaction of Urban and Military Organization in the Militias of Medieval Castile," *Speculum* 46 (1971): 641–655; Elena Lourie, "Medieval Spain: A Society Organized for War," *Past and Present* 33–35 (1966): 55–76.
7. Julio González, "Los sellos concejiles de España en la edad media," *Hispania* 5 (1945): 339–384.
8. Sánchez Albornoz, "El aula regia y las asambleas políticas de los Godos," *Estudios Visigóticos* (Rome 1971), 151–252; E. A. Thompson, *The Goths in Spain* (Oxford 1969), 252–260.
9. Gonzalo Martínez Díez, "Las instituciones del reino astúr a través de los diplomas (718–910)," *AHDE* 35 (1965): 59–167; Luis Vázquez de Parga, "El Fuero de León," *AHDE* 15 (1944): 464–498.
10. Alfonso García Gallo, "El Concilio de Coyanza. Contribución al estudio del derecho canónico español de la alta edad media," *AHDE* 20 (1950): 275–633; Fidel Fita, "El Concilio nacional de Burgos en 1080," *BRAH* 49 (1906): 337–384, and "Concilios nacionales de Carrión en 1103 y de León en 1107," *BRAH* 24 (1894): 311–317.
11. Procter, *Curia*, 52–70, 80–92, and "The Towns of León and Castile as Suitors before the King's Court," *EHR* 74 (1959): 1–22, and "The Judicial Use of *Pesquisa* (Inquisition) in León and Castile, 1157–1369," *EHR* Supplement 2 (London 1966).
12. Procter, *Curia*, chapter I; Agustín Millares Carlo, "La cancillería real en León y Castilla hasta fines del reinado de Fernando III," *AHDE* 3 (1926): 227–306.
13. *Chronica Adefonsi Imperatoris*, ed. Luis Sánchez Belda (Madrid 1950), 54–56; Ildefonso Rodríguez de Lama, *Colección diplomática de la Rioja (923–1225)* (Logroño 1976), II, no. 107, pp. 169–170; Luis Fernández, "Colección diplomática del monasterio de San Pelayo de Cerrato," *Hispania Sacra* 26 (1973), no. 4, pp. 290–292.
14. Carrión 1188, Benavente 1202, Burgos 1220, and Zamora 1221. Rodrigo, *De rebus Hispaniae*, VII, 24, p. 166; González, *Alfonso IX*, II, nos. 167, 415, pp. 236–237, 530–531; Procter, *Curia*, no. 1, pp. 268–269.

15. C. M. Ajo y Sáinz de Zúñiga, *Historia de las universidades hispánicas* (Madrid 1957–1960), I, pp. 195–201, 435–436; *Obras del Maestro Jacobo de las Leyes,* ed. Rafael Ureña (Madrid 1924).

16. González, *Alfonso VIII,* III, nos. 966, 987, 1009, pp. 668–669, 704–705, 736–737, and *Alfonso IX,* II, nos. 12, 85, 495, pp. 86, 120, 597.

17. Gaines Post, "A Romano-Canonical Maxim, *Quod omnes tangit,* in Bracton and Early Parliaments," in his *Studies in Medieval Legal Thought: Public Law and the State, 1100–1322* (Princeton 1964), 162–238; Marongiu, "Il principio della democrazia e del consenso (*Quod omnes tangit ab omnibus approbari debet*) nel seculo XIV," *Studia Gratiana* 8 (1962): 555–575; José Antonio Maravall, "La corriente democrática medieval en España y la formula *quod omnes tangit,*" in his *Estudios de historia del pensamiento español. Edad media. Serie primera* (Madrid 1967), 157–175.

18. Post, "Roman Law and Early Representation in Spain and Italy, 1150–1250," and "*Plena Potestas* and Consent in Medieval Assemblies," in his *Studies,* 61–160; Procter, *Curia,* 64–69, 87–93; Joseph F. O'Callaghan, "The Beginnings of the Cortes of León-Castile," *AHR* 74 (1969): 1509–1512.

19. González, *Alfonso IX,* II, nos. 11–12, 167, 221, 662, pp. 23–27, 236–237, 306–308, 737–738; *CLC,* I, 39–48; O'Callaghan, "Beginnings," 1513–1523; Procter, *Curia,* 57–61.

20. González, *Alfonso IX,* II, no. 415, pp. 530–531; Joseph F. O'Callaghan, "Una nota sobre las llamadas Cortes de Benavente," *Archivos Leoneses* 37 (1983): 97–100.

21. González, *Alfonso VIII,* II, nos. 471, 499, pp. 807–808, 857–863; *Chronique latine,* ch. 11, pp. 39–40; Rodrigo, *De rebus Hispaniae,* VII, 24, p. 166; O'Callaghan, "Beginnings," 1512–1513, 1516; Procter, *Curia,* 74–75, 109.

22. Francisco J. Hernández will publish Alfonso VIII's ordinance of 1207.

23. Rodrigo, *De rebus Hispaniae,* IX, 4–5, 10, pp. 195–196, 200; *Chronique latine,* ch. 33–35, 40, pp. 89–93, 98–100; O'Callaghan, "Beginnings," 1525–1526; Procter, *Curia,* 77–78, 110–111.

24. Rodrigo, *De rebus Hispaniae,* IX, 18, pp. 147–148; González, *Fernando III,* III, no. 809, pp. 387–389; O'Callaghan, "Beginnings," 1527–1531; Procter, *Curia,* no. 4, pp. 271–273.

25. O'Callaghan, "Beginnings," 1533–1534; Procter, *Curia,* 105–117.

26. O'Callaghan, "Beginnings," 1512–1514, 1520–1521, 1525–1527.

27. González, *Alfonso IX,* II, nos. 11–12, 84–85, 221, pp. 23–27, 125–129, 306–309, and *Fernando III,* III, no. 809, pp. 387–389; *Fuero viejo,* 1–2; Francisco J. Hernández will publish the ordinance of 1207.

28. Sánchez Albornoz, "La primitiva organización monetaria de León y Castilla," in his *Estudios sobre las instituciones medievales españolas* (Mexico 1965), 471–477; O'Callaghan, "Beginnings," 1518–1520, 1528–1529.

29. Procter, "The Interpretation of Clause 3 of the Decrees of León (1188)," *EHR* 75 (1970): 45–54; Carlé, "*Boni Homines* y Hombres buenos," *CHE* 39–40 (1964): 133–168.

30. González, *Alfonso IX,* II, no. 167, pp. 236–237; O'Callaghan, "Beginnings," 1517, n. 64; Procter, *Curia,* 34–41, 59–69, 85–93.

CHAPTER 2

1. *Crónica del Rey Don Alfonso X, BAE,* LXVI (Madrid 1953), 3–66; Procter, "Materials for the Reign of Alfonso X of Castile 1252–1284," *Transactions of the Royal Historical Society,* 4th Series, 14 (1931): 39–63; Antonio Ballesteros, *Alfonso X* (Barcelona-Madrid 1963; 2d ed. Miguel Rodríguez Llopis, 1984); O'Callaghan, "The Cortes and Royal Taxation during the Reign of Alfonso X of Castile," *Traditio* 27 (1971): 379–398, and "Alfonso X and the Castilian Church," *Thought* 60 (1985): 418–429, and "Paths to Ruin: The Economic and Financial Policies of Alfonso X," in Robert I. Burns, ed., *The Worlds of Alfonso the Learned and James the Conqueror* (Princeton 1985), 41–67.

2. BN 13094, fol. 143; *MFIII,* 314–318; Ballesteros, *Alfonso X,* 90; Martínez Marina, *Teoría, BAE,* CCXIX, 230–231; Procter, *Curia,* 126–127.

3. Piskorski, no. 1, pp. 196–197; Georges Daumet, *Mémoire sur les relations de la France et de la Castille de 1255 à 1320* (Paris, n.d.), no. 1, pp. 143–146.

4. Burgos 1254: *Anónimo de Sahagún,* 76, in Romualdo Escalona, *Historia del real monasterio de Sahagún* (Madrid 1782), 361–362. Toledo 1259: BN 13094, fol. 116; *MHE,* I, no. 71, p. 154; Ballesteros, "El Itinerario de Alfonso el Sabio," *BRAH* 108 (1936): 17, n. 1; José Manuel Nieto Soria, *Las relaciones monarquía-episcopado castellano como sistema de poder, 1252–1312* (Madrid 1983), II, no. 121, pp. 51–53; Toribio Minguella, *Historia de la diocesis de Sigüenza* (Madrid 1900–1913), I, no. 225, pp. 599–601 (25 June 1264).

5. Matías Rodríguez Díez, *Historia de la ciudad de Astorga,* 2d ed. (Astorga 1909), 715–720; Manuel Segura Moreno, *Estudio del Códice gótico (siglo XIII) de la catedral de Jaén* (Jaén 1976), no. 16, pp. 202–203; Manuel Nieto Cumplido, *Orígenes del regionalismo andaluz (1235–1325),* 2d ed. (Madrid 1979), no. 3, pp. 118–119.

6. AHN Uclés, cajón 153, no. 1; *CLC,* I, 86; Ballesteros, *Alfonso X,* 483.

7. Ballesteros, "Las Cortes de 1252," *Anales de la junta para ampliacion de estudios e investigaciones científicas,* 3 (Madrid 1911): 114–143; Ismael García Ramila, "Ordenamientos de posturas y otros capítulos generales otorgados a la ciudad de Burgos por el rey Alfonso X," *Hispania* 5 (1945): 204–222; Georg Gross, "Las Cortes de 1252. Ordenamiento otorgado al concejo de Burgos en las Cortes celebradas en Sevilla el 12 de octubre de 1252 (según el original)," *BRAH* 182 (1985): 95–114; Vicente Argüello, "Memoria sobre las monedas de Alfonso el Sabio," *Memorias de la Real Academia de la Historia* 8 (1852): 29–34; Rodríguez Díez, *Astorga,* 697–713; Antonio López Ferreiro, *Fueros municipales de Santiago y su tierra* (Santiago 1895), 347–372 (15 February 1253); Procter, *Curia,* no. 4, pp. 273–284; *CLC,* I, 54–63 (18 January 1258).

8. *CLC,* I, 64–85 (15 June 1268).

9. *MHE,* I, nos. 34–35, 37, pp. 70–75, 77–79; José Luis Martín et al., *Documentos de los Archivos catedralicio y diocesano de Salamanca (Siglos XII–XIII)* (Salamanca 1977), nos. 260–262, pp. 348–354; Juan Loperráez, *Descripción histórica del obispado de Osma* (Madrid 1788), III, nos. 57–58, pp. 79–83; Minguella, *Sigüenza,* I, no. 209, pp. 572–574; F. Javier Pereda Llarena, *Documentación de la Catedral de Burgos 1254–1293* (Burgos 1984), nos. 24–26, pp. 35–42; Pedro Fernández del Pulgar, *Historia secular y eclesiástica de Palencia* (Madrid 1679), II, 336–341.

10. *MHE,* I, nos. 43–45, pp. 89–100 (July–August 1256); Aquilino Iglesia

Ferreirós, "Privilegio general concedido a las Extremaduras en 1264 por Alfonso X. Edición del ejemplar enviado a Peñafiel en 15 de abril de 1264," *AHDE* 53 (1983): 456–521; Procter, *Curia*, no. 7, pp. 286–291; Antonio Ubieto Arteta, *Colección diplomática de Cuéllar* (Segovia 1961), no. 21, pp. 60–66; Timoteo Domingo Palacio, *Documentos del Archivo general de la villa de Madrid* (Madrid 1888–1943), I, 95–102.

11. Ballesteros, "Cortes de 1252," 114–143; *CLC*, I, 54–63 (Valladolid 1258), 64–85 (Jerez 1268); Rodríguez Díez, *Astorga*, 715–720; O'Callaghan, "Paths to Ruin," 43–54.

12. Robert A. MacDonald, "Problemas políticos y derecho alfonsino considerados desde tres puntos de vista," *AHDE* 54 (1984): 25–53, and "El Espéculo atribuido a Alfonso X, su edición y problemas que plantea," *España y Europa, un pasado jurídico común. Actas del I Simposio internacional del Instituto de Derecho Común*, ed. Antonio Pérez Marín (Murcia 1986), 611–653; O'Callaghan, "Sobre la promulgación del *Espéculo* y del *Fuero real*," *Estudios en homenaje a Don Claudio Sánchez Albornoz en sus 90 anos*, III (1985): 167–179.

13. Alfonso García Gallo, "El Libro de las Leyes de Alfonso el Sabio: Del Espéculo a las Partidas," *AHDE* 21 (1951): 345–548, and "Nuevas observaciones sobre la obra legislativa de Alfonso X," *AHDE* 46 (1976): 609–670; Aquilino Iglesia Ferreirós, "Alfonso el Sabio y su obra legislativa: Algunas reflexiones," *AHDE* 50 (1980): 531–561, and "Fuero real y Espéculo," *AHDE* 52 (1982): 111–192; Jerry Craddock, "La cronología de las obras legislativas de Alfonso X el Sabio," *AHDE* 51 (1981): 365–418.

14. Piskorski, no. 1, 196–197.

15. *CAX*, 18, p. 13; *Crónica de Jaume I* (Barcelona 1926–1962), ed. J. M. Casacuberta and Enric Bagüe, IX, 7–8.

16. *Anónimo de Sahagún*, ch. 74–75, p. 60; *CAX*, 3, 18, pp. 5, 13; Thomas Rymer, *Foedera, Conventiones, Litterae et cuiuscunque Acta publica inter Reges Angliae et alios quovis Imperatores, Reges, Pontifices, Principes* (London 1704–1735), I, 503–510.

17. *CAX*, 6, 19, pp. 6–7, 13–14; Rodríguez Díez, *Astorga*, 715–720.

18. *MHE*, I, nos. 43–45, pp. 89–100; Iglesia Ferreirós, "Privilegio general," 513–521; *CAX*, 9, p. 10.

19. Loaysa, *Crónica*, 7, p. 68; *CAX*, 17, pp. 12–13; Procter, *Curia*, 232.

20. *MHE*, I, nos. 69, 71, pp. 151, 154–155; Ballesteros, "El Itinerario de Alfonso el Sabio," *BRAH* 108 (1936): 17, n. 1; Mingüella, *Sigüenza*, I, no. 225, pp. 599–601.

21. *CAX*, 24–26, 67–68, 75, pp. 21–23, 53, 59–60 (Burgos 1272, Segovia 1278, Burgos 1281, Seville 1281); AM Toledo, cajón 1, legajo 1, no. 3 (Burgos, 13 April 1274), and Fernández del Pulgar, *Palencia*, II, 344–345; Loaysa, *Crónica*, 19, p. 90 (Burgos 1276); J. M. Escudero de la Peña, "Súplica hecha al Papa Juan XXI para que absolviese al rey de Castilla D. Alfonso X del juramento de no acuñar otra moneda que los dineros prietos," *RABM* 2 (1872): 58–59 (Burgos, 9 May 1277).

22. *CAX*, 47, 50, 53–58, pp. 35, 37, 41–47 (Almagro, Ávila 1273); *CLC*, I, 85–86 (Almagro); Ramón Menéndez Pidal, *Documentos lingüísticos de España: Reino de Castilla* (Madrid 1919), no. 229, pp. 300–302 (Peñafiel 1275); Emiliano González Díez, *Colección diplomática del concejo de Burgos (884–1369)* (Burgos 1984), no. 44, pp. 129–130 (Alcalá and Toledo 1275–1276); Ballesteros, "Burgos y la rebelión del Infante Don Sancho," *BRAH* 119 (1946): 118–119.

23. González Díez, *Burgos*, nos. 96, 98–99, pp. 179, 181–183; *CAX*, 73, p. 57.

24. *CAX*, 75–76, pp. 60–61; Loaysa, *Crónica*, 28, p. 102; *MHE*, II, no. 198, pp. 59–63.

25. *MHE*, II, nos. 202–203, pp. 67–70; *CAX*, 77, pp. 64–65; Luis Fernández Martín, "La participación de los monasterios en la hermandad de los reinos de Castilla, León y Galicia (1282–1284)," *Hispania Sacra* 25 (1972): 5–35.

26. *CAX*, 23–26, pp. 19–26; *El Fuero viejo de Castilla* (Madrid 1777), ed. Ignacio Jordán del Asso and Miguel de Manuel Rodríguez, prologue, pp. 1–3; Palacio, *Madrid*, I, 113–117; Emilio Sáez et al., *Los Fueros de Sepúlveda* (Segovia 1953), no. 13, pp. 196–198; O'Callaghan, "The Cortes and Royal Taxation," 384–388.

27. *CAX*, 40–50, 53–58, pp. 30–37, 41–47; *CLC*, I, 85–86; Pereda Llarena, *Burgos 1253–1294*, no. 105, pp. 150–151.

28. *CAX*, 59, pp. 47–48; Fernández del Pulgar, *Palencia*, II, 344–345; Palacio, *Madrid*, I, 119–122; Ciriaco Miguel Vigil, *Colección histórico-diplomática del ayuntamiento de Oviedo* (Oviedo 1889), no. 36, p. 63; Tomás González, *Colección de cédulas, cartas patentes, provisiones, reales órdenes y documentos concernientes a las provincias vascongadas* (Madrid 1829–1833), V, no. 59, pp. 189–190; Ubieto Arteta, *Cuéllar*, no. 30, pp. 73–74; González Díez, *Burgos*, no. 42, pp. 127–128; *MHE*, I, no. 137, p. 305.

29. Menéndez Pidal, *Documentos*, no. 229, pp. 300–302; Mateo Escagedo Salmón, *Colección diplomática. Privilegios, escrituras y bulas en pergamino de la insigne y real iglesia colegial de Santillana* (Santoña 1927), I, 155–157.

30. *CAX*, 61–67, pp. 48–53.

31. González Díez, *Burgos*, no. 44, pp. 127–130; Loaysa, *Crónica*, 19, p. 90; *CAX*, 66–67, pp. 52–53.

32. *CAX*, 67–68, p. 53; *MHE*, I, no. 145, p. 327; Fidel Fita, "Dos obras inéditas de Gil de Zamora," *BRAH* 5 (1884): 146; Procter, *Curia*, 143.

33. *CAX*, 68, p. 53; Loaysa, *Crónica*, 24, p. 96.

34. *MHE*, I, nos. 140–141, pp. 308–324; Ubieto Arteta, *Cuéllar*, no. 32, pp. 75–76, and *Colección diplomática de Riaza 1258–1457* (Segovia 1959), no. 3, pp. 8–9; Miguel Vigil, *Oviedo*, no. 41, p. 75; María Dolores Guerrero Lafuente, *Historia de la ciudad de Benavente en la edad media* (Benavente 1983), no. 4, p. 425; Fernández del Pulgar, *Palencia*, III, 323; Diego de Colmenares, *Historia de la ciudad de Segovia*, new ed. (Segovia 1969–1975), I, 412–413; Juan Agapito y Revilla, *Los privilegios de Valladolid* (Valladolid 1906), no. 33–xiv, p. 55; Minguella, *Sigüenza*, I, no. 240, pp. 622–624.

35. González Díez, *Burgos*, nos. 81, 83, pp. 164–166.

36. *CAX*, 75, pp. 59–60; González Díez, *Burgos*, nos. 112–113, pp. 199–201; *Las Cantigas de Santa Maria*, ed. Walter Mettmann (Coimbra 1959–1974; reprint Vigo 1981), II, no. 386, pp. 339–341.

37. Loaysa, *Crónica*, 28, p. 102; *CAX*, 75–76, pp. 59–61; Pereda Llarena, *Burgos 1253–1294*, no. 173, pp. 237–241; *MHE*, II, nos. 202–203, pp. 67–70; Francisco Berganza, *Antigüedades de España* (Madrid 1721), I, 175; Escalona, *Sahagún*, nos. 264, 266, pp. 616–622; Marius Ferotin, *Recueil des chartes de l'abbaye de Silos* (Paris 1897), no. 243, pp. 272–273; Augusto Quintana Prieto, *Tumbo viejo de San Pedro de Montes* (León 1971), nos. 374–375, pp. 481–487; M. Mañueco Villalobos and J. Zurita Nieto, *Documentos de la iglesia colegial de*

Santa Maria la Mayor de Valladolid (Valladolid 1917), III, pp. 27–29; Antonio Álvarez de Morales, *Las hermandades. Espresión del movimiento comunitario en España* (Valladolid 1974), no. 1, pp. 267–268.

38. *CAX*, 76–77, pp. 62–65; *MHE*, II, nos. 228–229, pp. 110–134; Georges Daumet, "Les testaments d'Alphonse X, le savant, roi de Castille," *BEC* 67 (1906): 70–99.

39. *Crónica de Sancho IV, BAE*, LXVI (1953), 69–90; Mercedes Gaibrois de Ballesteros, *Historia del reinado de Sancho IV de Castilla*, 3 vols. (Madrid 1922).

40. Loaysa, *Crónica*, 57, p. 146.

41. *CLC*, I, 95–99 (Palencia), 99–106 (Haro), 106–130 (Valladolid).

42. *CSIV*, 1, pp. 69–70; Loaysa, *Crónica*, 35, p. 114; Luis Fernández, "Colección diplomática del monasterio de San Pedro de Cerrato," *Hispania Sacra* 26 (1973): no. 11, pp. 299–301; Gaibrois, *Sancho IV*, III, no. 173, pp. civ–cv; Mañueco Villalobos and Zurita Nieto, *Santa Maria la Mayor de Valladolid*, II, no. 94, pp. 122–124.

43. Procter, *Curia*, 120, 149, 162, 174, 179.

44. *CSIV*, 4, 8, pp. 75–76, 86; Gaibrois, *Sancho IV*, I, clx–clxiii, clxvii, clxx, clxxvii–clxxviii, and III, no. 108, p. lxix; Martín, *Salamanca*, no. 395, pp. 494–496.

45. *CSIV*, 1, pp. 69–70; Loaysa, *Crónica*, 35, p. 114; Fernández, "San Pelayo de Cerrato," no. 11, pp. 299–301.

46. *CSIV*, 2, p. 72; AM León, no. 24; Procter, *Curia*, 120, 149, 162, 174, 179.

47. *CLC*, I, 95–99; Alberto Barrios García et al., *Documentación medieval del Archivo municipal de Alba de Tormes* (Salamanca 1982), no. 15, pp. 53–56; Rodríguez Díez, *Astorga*, 857–860; Miguel Vigil, *Oviedo*, 92–93.

48. Mañueco Villalobos and Zurita Nieto, *Santa Maria la Mayor de Valladolid*, II, no. 94, pp. 122–124; Gaibrois, *Sancho IV*, I, clxxx–clxxxviii, and III, no. 173, pp. civ–cv; Yitzhak Baer, *A History of the Jews in Christian Spain* (Philadelphia 1966), I, 132–133.

49. *CSIV*, 3–5, pp. 74–79; Loaysa, *Crónica*, 39–40, pp. 118–120.

50. *CSIV*, 5, p. 79; *CLC*, I, 99–106; Pereda Llarena, *Burgos 1254–1293*, no. 226, pp. 190–194; Menéndez Pidal, *Documentos*, no. 141, pp. 182–186; González, *Colección*, V, 226–233; Luis Sánchez Belda, *Cartulario de Santo Toribio de Liébana* (Madrid 1948), no. 200, pp. 225–226; Martín, *Salamanca*, no. 412, pp. 519–522; Mañueco Villalobos and Zurita Nieto, *Santa Maria la Mayor de Valladolid*, III, no. 103, pp. 165–172. The cortes of Burgos 1301 (art. 6) and Zamora 1301 (art. 13) both cite the cortes of Haro.

51. *CSIV*, 8–9, p. 86; *CLC*, I, 125; Mercedes Gaibrois, "Tarifa y la política de Sancho IV de Castilla," *BRAH* 74 (1919): 418–436, 521–529; 75 (1919): 349–355; 76 (1920): 53–77, 123–150, 420–448; 77 (1920): 192–215.

52. *CLC*, I, 106–117, 117–130; Valentín Sáinz Díaz, *Notas históricas sobre la villa de San Vicente de la Barquera* (Santander 1973), 545–552; Esteban García Chico, *Los privilegios de Medina de Rioseco* (Valladolid 1933), 220–223; Ángel Govantes, *Diccionario geográfico-histórico de España: La Rioja* (Madrid 1846), no. 30, pp. 313–319; Rodríguez Díez, *Astorga*, 861–868; Ignacio Jordán del Asso and Miguel de Manuel Rodríguez, *Cortes celebradas en los reynados de Don Sancho IV y de Don Fernando IV* (Madrid 1775), 1–13; Palacio, *Madrid*, I, 139–155; Nieto Cumplido, *Regionalismo*, no. 20, pp. 155–166; *CODOM*, IV, no. 153, pp. 135–143.

53. *CSIV,* 12–13, pp. 89–90; Loaysa, *Crónica,* 57, p. 146.

54. *Crónica de Fernando IV, BAE,* LXVI (1953), 93–170; Antonio Benavides, *Memorias de Fernando IV de Castilla* (Madrid 1869), I, 1–243; César González Mínguez, *Fernando IV de Castilla (1295–1312): La guerra civil y el predominio de la nobleza* (Valladolid 1976).

55. *CLC,* I, 130–133 (1295), 133–135 (prelates, 1295), 135–136 (1297), 139–142 (Castile 1299), 142–145 (León 1299), 145–150 (Burgos 1301), 151–161 (Zamora 1301); BN 1270 fol. 4r–7r (1300); González Mínguez, *Fernando IV,* no. 3, pp. 352–353 (1298), and "Otro ordenamiento de las Cortes de Valladolid de 1299," *Hispania* 40 (1980): 415–426; *MFIV,* II, nos. 87, 111, 131, 182, pp. 122–123, 157–158, 181–183, 254–257 (1297, 1298, 1299, 1301); Jordán del Asso and Manuel Rodríguez, *Cortes,* 14–18 (1299); Fernández del Pulgar, *Palencia,* III, 350–353.

56. *MFIV,* II, nos. 3–4, pp. 3–13; Luis G. de Valdeavellano, "Carta de hermandad entre los concejos de la Extremadura castellana y del arzobispado de Toledo en 1295," *Revista portuguesa de historia* 12 (1969): 57–76; Guerrero Lafuente, *Benavente,* no. 7, pp. 437–441.

57. Barrios García, *Alba de Tormes,* no. 18, pp. 59–61; Josefa Sanz Fuentes, "Cartas de hermandad concejíl en Andalucía: El caso de Écija," *HID* 5 (1978): no. 1, pp. 413–418; Agustín Muñoz y Gómez, "Concejos de Córdoba, Sevilla y Jerez de la Frontera. Carta inédita de su hermandad en 1296," *BRAH* 36 (1900): 306–316; Nieto Cumplido, *Regionalismo,* nos. 23–25, pp. 169–191; Carmen Argente del Castillo Ocaña, "Las hermandades medievales en el Reino de Jaén," *Andalucía medieval* 2 (1978): 21–22; Suárez Fernández, "Hermandades," no. 4, pp. 51–55; *CODOM,* III, no. 112, pp. 110–16; *MFIV,* II, no. 29, pp. 46–51.

58. *CFIV,* 1, pp. 93–95; *CLC,* I, 130–133; Ubieto Arteta, *Cuéllar,* no. 44, pp. 100–102; Guerrero Lafuente, *Benavente,* no. 8, pp. 442–445; Miguel Vigil, *Oviedo,* no. 67, pp. 107–108; Rodríguez Díez, *Astorga,* 722–724; Barrios García, *Alba de Tormes,* no. 19, pp. 61–64; Fernández del Pulgar, *Palencia,* III, 349–325; García Chico, *Medina de Rioseco,* 32–35; Mingüella, *Sigüenza,* I, 646–647; *MFIV,* II, no. 177, pp. 263–264; Sáinz Díaz, *San Vicente de la Barquera,* 46–48; Nieto Cumplido, *Regionalismo,* no. 22, pp. 168–169.

59. *MFIV,* II, nos. 3–4, pp. 3–13; Valdeavellano, "Carta de hermandad," 57–76.

60. *CLC,* I, 135–136, art. 1.

61. *CLC,* I, 133–135; *MFIV,* II, nos. 17, 22–23, pp. 33–35, 40–42; Mañueco Villalobos and Zurita Nieto, *Santa María la Mayor de Valladolid,* III, no. 125, pp. 288–291; *CODOM,* V, no. 15, pp. 20–22; Martín, *Salamanca,* no. 435, pp. 546–548; Fernández del Pulgar, *Palencia,* II, no. 22, pp. 369–370; Pereda Llarena, *Documentación de la catedral de Burgos 1294–1316* (Burgos 1984), no. 309, pp. 24–25; Ubieto Arteta, *Cuéllar,* no. 46, pp. 104–106; Loperráez, *Osma,* III, no. 92, pp. 235–236; Martínez Marina, *Teoría, BAE,* CCXIX, 88–89.

62. *CFIV,* 1, pp. 96–106; González Mínguez, *Fernando IV,* no. 2, pp. 348–350.

63. See note 57. Fernando Morales Belda, *La hermandad de las marismas* (Barcelona 1973); *MFIV,* II, no. 57, pp. 81–85; Sáinz Díaz, *San Vicente de la Barquera,* 472–477; Gregorio de Balparda, *Historia crítica de Vizcaya y sus fueros* (Madrid 1924), III, no. 19, pp. 65–69; Álvarez Morales, *Hermandades,* nos. 3–4, pp. 269–271; González Mínguez, *Contribución al estudio de las hermandades*

en el reinado de Fernando IV de Castilla (Vitoria 1974); Martínez Díez, "La hermandad alavesa," *AHDE* 43 (1973): no. 2, pp. 107–110.

64. *CFIV,* 1–2, 4–6, 8–9, pp. 96, 108, 111, 115–116, 119–122; Loaysa, *Crónica,* 60–61, 78–83, pp. 152–154, 180–189; *MFIV,* II, no. 135, pp. 188–189; Miguel Vigil, *Oviedo,* nos. 69–70, pp. 110–111; Martín, *Salamanca,* no. 465, pp. 592–593.

65. *CFIV,* 6–9, pp. 118–119; *CLC,* I, 145–150, art. 23 (Burgos 1301), 151–161 (Zamora 1301).

66. *CFIV,* 8–9, pp. 119–122.

67. *CLC,* I, 161–165 (Medina del Campo 1302), 165–169 (Burgos 1302), 169–172 (Medina del Campo 1305, León), 172–179 (1305, Castile), 179–184 (1305, Extremadura), 184–197 (Valladolid 1307), 197–221 (Valladolid 1312); *MFIV,* II, nos. 332, 335–336, 387, 408, 510, pp. 482–487, 490–497, 567–576, 605–607, 732–738; O'Callaghan, "Las Cortes de Fernando IV: Cuadernos inéditos de Valladolid 1300 y Burgos 1308," *HID* 13 (1986): 315–328; *CFIV,* 16, p. 162; González Díez, *Burgos,* no. 171, pp. 290–291.

68. *CFIV,* 10–11, 15, pp. 125–127, 131, 156–159; Giménez Soler, *Juan Manuel,* nos. 71–72, pp. 184–185; *MFIV,* II, no. 71, pp. 404–405; Palacio, *Madrid,* I, 181–188; Ubieto Arteta, *Cuéllar,* no. 54, pp. 120–125.

69. Prelates: *MFIV,* II, nos. 541, 543–544, 546, pp. 789–791, 793–799, 800–805. Nobles: *CFIV,* 19, pp. 168–169; *MFIV,* II, nos. 510, 560, pp. 736–737, 822–823; *CLC,* I, 207–208.

70. *CFIV,* 8–11, pp. 121–133; *CLC,* I, 161–169; Rodríguez Díez, *Astorga,* 869–873 (Medina del Campo 1302); Barrios García, *Alba de Tormes,* no. 24, pp. 69–74; Ubieto Arteta, *Cuéllar,* no. 50, pp. 111–115; *MFIV,* II, nos. 276–293, pp. 411–434.

71. *CFIV,* 13–14, pp. 137–150; *CLC,* I, 169–184 (1305); 184–197 (1307); *MFIV,* II, nos. 332, 335–336 (1305), 387 (1307), pp. 482–487, 490–497, 567–576; Jordán del Asso and Manuel Rodríguez, *Cortes,* 18–42 (1305, 1307); González Mínguez, *Fernando IV,* nos. 20, 24, pp. 366–371, 375–378 (1305, 1307); Palacio, *Madrid,* II, 189–207 (1307).

72. *CLC,* I, 197–221; Rodríguez Díez, *Astorga,* 884–907; *MFIV,* II, no. 510, pp. 732–738.

73. José Sánchez Herrero, *Concilios provinciales y sínodos toledanos de los siglos XIV y XV* (Seville 1976), no. 1, pp. 165–172; *MFIV,* II, nos. 197, 200, 203, 208, 214, pp. 279–280, 283, 285–291, 307, 316; Fernández del Pulgar, *Palencia,* II, 398–399; Martínez Marina, *Teoría, BAE,* CCXIX, 201.

74. *MFIV,* II, nos. 541, 543–544, 546, 560, pp. 789–791, 793–799, 900–905; Ubieto Arteta, *Cuéllar,* no. 63, pp. 140–145; Pereda Llarena, *Burgos 1294–1316,* nos. 453–454, pp. 288–296.

75. *MFIV,* II, nos. 531, 554, pp. 770–773, 816; *ES,* XVIII, 373–378; Pereda Llarena, *Burgos 1294–1316,* no. 447, p. 281.

76. *CFIV,* 15–16, pp. 156–160; Giménez Soler, *Juan Manuel,* nos. 179, 183, pp. 354–358; O'Callaghan, "Cortes de Fernando IV," 324–328; *MFIV,* II, no. 408, pp. 605–607.

77. *CFIV,* 19, pp. 168–169; *MFIV,* II, nos. 510, 560, pp. 736–737, 822–823; *CLC,* I, 207–208.

78. *CFIV,* 10–11, 13–16, 20, pp. 133, 139–156, 162, 169; Loaysa, *Crónica,* 87, p. 195; *MFIV,* II, nos. 208, 214, 243, 271, 432, 582–583, pp. 307, 316, 365–367, 404–405, 639–641, 861–863; Giménez Soler, *Juan Manuel,* nos.

120, 192–195, pp. 315–316, 364–366; Ubieto Arteta, *Cuéllar*, no. 54, pp. 120–125; Palacio, *Madrid*, I, 181–188. Cortes of Burgos 1308, art. 3–4, 9–11, 18, in O'Callaghan, "Cortes de Fernando IV," 324–328.

79. Giménez Soler, *Juan Manuel*, nos. 192–195, pp. 364–366; *MFIV*, II, nos. 541, 543–544, 546, pp. 789–791, 793–799, 900–905; Valladolid 1312, art. 83.

80. *CFIV*, 17, 20, pp. 163–164, 169–170.

81. *Crónica de Alfonso XI*, *BAE*, LXVI (1953): 173–392; *Gran Crónica de Alfonso XI*, ed. Diego Catalán, 2 vols. (Madrid 1977); *Poema de Alfonso XI*, ed. Yo Ten Cate (Madrid 1956); Esther González Crespo, *Colección documental de Alfonso XI. Diplomas reales conservados en el Archivo Histórico Nacional, Sección de Clero, Pergaminos* (Madrid 1985).

82. *CLC*, I, 221–233 (Juan, Palencia 1313), 233–245 (Maria and Pedro, Palencia 1313), 247–272 (*hermandad*, 1315), 272–292 (Burgos 1315), 293–299 (prelates, Burgos 1315). Giménez Soler, *Juan Manuel*, nos. 282, 286–294, 296–298, 302–303, 307, pp. 438–448, 450–457; Antonio López Ferreiro, *Historia de la santa a.m. iglesia de Santiago de Compostela* (Santiago 1898–1909), V, no. 58, pp. 165–167; *CAXI*, 6, p. 178; *GCAXI*, 7, vol. I, p. 290.

83. Ubieto Arteta, *Cuéllar*, no. 71, pp. 156–158; López Ferreiro, *Historia*, V, no. 61, pp. 175–178; Pereda Llarena, *Burgos 1294–1316*, no. 491, pp. 360–363; *CAXI*, 8, p. 180; *GCAXI*, 10, vol. I, p. 196.

84. *CLC*, I, 330–336 (Medina del Campo 1318), 337–369 (Valladolid 1322), 369–372 (monasteries, 1322); Escalona, *Sahagún*, no. 287, pp. 645–646; *CAXI*, 12, 27, pp. 182, 191–192; *GCAXI*, 16, 34, 37, vol. I, pp. 307, 345–346, 350, vol. II, 471–472; *Poema de Alfonso XI*, 75–78, p. 479; Giménez Soler, *Juan Manuel*, no. 368, pp. 71, 496–498.

85. Juan Ignacio Ruíz de la Peña, "La hermandad leonesa de 1313," *León medieval* (León 1978), 139–164; Giménez Soler, *Juan Manuel*, nos. 258, 262–263, 265–266, pp. 419–420, 422–427; *CAXI*, 1–2, 6, pp. 174–175; 178; *GCAXI*, 2–3, 7, vol. I, pp. 278–281, 290.

86. Prelates: Martínez Marina, *Teoría*, *BAE*, CCXIX, 92; Suárez Fernández, "Hermandades," no. 7, pp. 58–60. Nobles: *CLC*, I, 253, 258 (Burgos 1315, art. 9, 17).

87. *CLC*, I, 247–272, 300 (Burgos 1315, Cuéllar 1316); Martínez Marina, *Teoría*, *BAE*, CCXX, no. 10, pp. 91–103; Miguel Vigil, *Oviedo*, 296. *Hermandades* of 1316: *CAXI*, 9, p. 180; *GCAXI*, 12, vol. I, p. 299; Eliseo Sáinz Ripa, *Colección diplomática de las colegiatas de Albelda y Logroño*, 3 vols. (Logroño 1981), no. 126, pp. 182–190.

88. *CLC*, I, 299–329 (Carrión 1317); AHN Registro de Escrituras de la Orden de Calatrava, V, fol. 182r–188r, 202r–203r; AM Cuenca, 17–1, fol. 74; *CAXI*, 15–18, pp. 184–187; *GCAXI*, 22–25, vol. I, pp. 322–331; Giménez Soler, *Juan Manuel*, nos. 353–355, pp. 484–488.

89. *CAXI*, 3–6, 13–14, pp. 175–178, 182–184; *GCAXI*, 4–7, 17–21, vol. I, pp. 280–285, 290, 308–319; *Poema de Alfonso XI*, 51–52, pp. 477–479; *CLC*, I, 221–233, 233–247; Giménez Soler, *Juan Manuel*, nos. 303, 307, pp. 451–457; *ES*, XXVI, 345; Pereda Llarena, *Burgos 1294–1316*, no. 474, pp. 327–333.

90. *CLC*, I, 272–292 (Burgos 1315); Martínez Marina, *Teoría*, *BAE*, CCXX, no. 11, pp. 104–113; Barrios García, *Alba de Tormes*, no. 25, pp. 74–89; *CAXI*, 15–27, pp. 184–192; *GCAXI*, 23–24, 37–38, vol. I, pp. 325–346, 350–351, vol. II, pp. 471–472; *Poema de Alfonso XI*, 75–79, p. 479.

91. *CLC,* I, 337–372 (Valladolid 1322); *CAXI,* 28–31, 34–37, pp. 192–197; *GCAXI,* 35, 39–43, 45–49, vol. I, pp. 352–353, 355–361, 364–367, 369, vol. II, 473–475; *Poema de Alfonso XI,* 91–100, p. 480.

92. Palencia 1313, art. 37 J, art. 31 M; Carrión 1317, art. 69–74; Medina del Campo 1318, art. 9, 24; *CLC,* I, 247–272 (Burgos 1315).

93. Palencia 1313, art. 4 J, 10 M; Burgos 1315, art. 4; Carrión 1317, art. 10; *CAXI,* 8, 12, 27, 29, 31, pp. 179–182, 191–195; *GCAXI,* 9–10, 13, 15, 34, 40, 42, vol. I, pp. 295–296, 301, 307, 345–346, 353, 359–360, vol. II, pp. 471–472; Ubieto Arteta, *Cuéllar,* no. 71, pp. 156–158; Giménez Soler, *Juan Manuel,* no. 337, p. 472; Barrios García, *Alba de Tormes,* no. 29, pp. 97–99.

94. *CLC,* I, 372–389 (Valladolid 1325), 389–400 (prelates, 1325), 401–443 (Madrid 1329), 492–593 (Ordinance of Alcalá 1348), 593–626 (Alcalá 1348).

95. AC Toledo, 0.8.B.2.8; AC Sevilla, legajo 4, nos. 18–19; AC Zamora, Museo catedralicio, legajo 10-(C3), nos. 5–6; AC León, Museo catedralicio; López Ferreiro, *Historia,* VI, nos. 14–15, pp. 61–72; *ES,* XVI, 253.

96. *CLC,* I, 443–456 (Burgos 1338), 456–476 (Madrid 1339), 477–483 (Alcalá 1345), 483–492 (Burgos 1345), 627–637 (León 1345); *CAXI,* 253–255, pp. 330–331; *GCAXI,* 332–335, vol. II, pp. 443–449 (Llerena 1340).

97. *CAXI,* 99–101, pp. 233–235; *GCAXI,* 120–122, vol. II, pp. 506–514; *Poema de Alfonso XI,* 388–396, p. 489.

98. *CAXI,* 95, 154–155, 177, 260–263, pp. 231, 273–275, 287, 336–338; *GCAXI,* 118, 176–177, vol. I, pp. 500–501, vol. II, pp. 124–127; Rafael Floranes, *Memorias y privilegios de la muy noble y muy leal ciudad de Vitoria* (Madrid 1922), 222–223.

99. Valladolid 1325, art. 40; 1325, art. 10 P; *CAXI,* 38–39, 41–42, pp. 198–200; *GCAXI,* 50–51, 53–54, vol. I, pp. 373–377, 379–381; Giménez Soler, *Juan Manuel,* nos. 385–386, 388–391, 395, 403–406, pp. 506–510, 512–514, 519–523, 673–674.

100. *CLC,* I, 401–437 (Madrid 1329); *CAXI,* 48–75, 78, 80, 82, pp. 202–220, 222–224; *GCAXI,* 72–97, 99, 101, 103, vol. I, pp. 411–459, 462–463, 467–468, 472–473; Giménez Soler, *Juan Manuel,* nos. 413–472, 476, pp. 527–575; Salvador de Moxó, "La promoción política y social de los letrados en la corte de Alfonso XI," *Hispania* 35 (1975): 5–29.

101. González, *Colección,* V, no. 107, pp. 319–320; López Ferreiro, *Historia,* VI, nos. 14–15, pp. 61–72; *ES,* XVI, 253; *CAXI,* 40, 80–82, pp. 199, 222–224; *GCAXI,* 52, 101, 103, vol. I, pp. 378, 467–468, 472–473.

102. *CAXI,* 81–91, 95–97, 111, 128, 154–155, 177, pp. 223–228, 230–231, 245, 259, 273–274, 287; *GCAXI,* 102–112, 116–117, 226–250, vol. I, pp. 470–490, 496–499, vol. II, pp. 16–76.

103. *CLC,* I, 443–456 (Burgos 1338), 456–476 (Madrid 1339); *CAXI,* 196, 243, 253–255, pp. 292–293, 318–319, 330–331; *GCAXI,* 213, 296, 332–335, vol. II, pp. 196–197, 349–352, 443–449.

104. *CAXI,* 260–263, 336, pp. 336–338, 389; *CLC,* I, 477–483 (Alcalá 1345), 483–492 (Burgos 1345), 627–637 (León 1345).

105. *CLC,* I, 492–593 (Ordinance of Alcalá 1348), 593–626 (Alcalá 1348); *CAXI,* 338–339, pp. 390–392; Ignacio Jordán del Asso and Miguel de Manuel Rodríguez, *El Ordenamiento de Leyes* (Madrid 1774).

106. Harold V. Livermore, *A New History of Portugal* (Cambridge 1966),

81–83; Thomas N. Bisson, *The Medieval Crown of Aragon: A Short History* (Oxford 1986), 88, 90–92, 107–109.

107. Joseph R. Strayer, *The Reign of Philip the Fair* (Princeton 1980), 271–272, 286.

108. R. G. Davies and J. H. Denton, eds. *The English Parliament in the Middle Ages* (Philadelphia 1981).

CHAPTER 3

1. Alfonso García Gallo, *Manual de historia del derecho español*, 3rd ed. (Madrid 1967), I, 692, 811–812; Diego García de Campos, *Planeta* (Madrid 1943), ed. Manuel Alonso, 410; Juan Manuel, *Libro de los estados* (Oxford 1974), ed. R. B. Tate and I. R. Macpherson, I, 50, 84, 93, pp. 87–89, 168, 193–197; Sancho IV, *Castigos e documentos* (Bloomington 1952), ed. Agapito Rey, 10–12, pp. 81, 86, 89, 91; Luciana de Stefano, *La sociedad estamental de la baja edad media española a la luz de la literatura de la época* (Caracas 1964); José Antonio Maravall, "La sociedad estamental castellana y la obra de don Juan Manuel," in his *Estudios*, 451–472.

2. Pérez Prendes, *Cortes*, 73–76; Valdeón, "Las cortes," xii–xviii.

3. Piskorski, 13; Lucas of Túy, *Crónica*, 103, p. 450; *Espéculo*, prologue and II.1.5; Medina del Campo 1302 (art. 6 E, 8 L).

4. *El Cantar de mío Cid*, 4th ed. (Madrid 1954), ed. Ramón Menéndez Pidal, III, 1142; *Poema de Fernán González* (Madrid 1966), ed. Alonso Zamora Vicente, 166–168, 220; Giménez Soler, *Juan Manuel*, 673–674.

5. Madrid, BN 13094, fol. 143; *MFIII*, 314–318; Ballesteros, *Alfonso X*, 90; Piskorski, no. 1, pp. 196–197; *Anónimo de Sahagún*, 74–76, pp. 360–362.

6. Julio González, "Repoblación de la Extremadura leonesa," *Hispania* 3 (1945): 195–273, and "La Extremadura castellana al mediar del siglo XIII," *Hispania* 34 (1974): 236–474; Emilio Mitre Fernández, "La actual Extremadura en las cortes castellanas de la baja edad media," *Príncipe de Viana* 47 (1986): 555–564.

7. Ballesteros, "Las Cortes de 1252," 120–121.

8. *CAX*, 76, p. 61; Ballesteros, *Alfonso X*, 995–996; Ruíz de la Peña, "Hermandad leonesa," 139–164; *CAXI*, 1–2, pp. 174–175; *CLC*, I, 299–329; Colmeiro, I, 218; Piskorski, 19.

9. Ballesteros, "Las Cortes de 1252," 122–123; *CLC*, I, 54 (Valladolid 1258), 64 (Jerez 1268).

10. Benavides, *MFIV*, I, 307–320.

11. Giménez Soler, *Don Juan Manuel, Biografía y estudio crítico* (Madrid 1932).

12. *Primera Crónica general*, ch. 1070, vol. II, p. 746; *Anónimo de Sahagún*, 74–75, p. 360; Mingüella, *Sigüenza*, I, no. 225, pp. 599–601; *CLC*, I, 178; Colmeiro, I, 16.

13. *Castigos e documentos*, *BAE*, LI, ch. 40, p. 164.

14. Juan Manuel, *Libro de los estados*, II, prologue, ch. 45–50, pp. 213–216. General citations of prelates: Jerez 1268, Burgos 1272, Peñafiel 1275, Burgos 1276, Valladolid 1282, Haro 1288, Medina del Campo 1291, Valladolid 1293, 1295, Cuéllar 1297, Medina del Campo 1302, 1305, Palencia 1311, Valladolid

1312, Burgos 1315, Medina del Campo 1316, Carrión 1317, Valladolid 1322, 1325, Madrid 1329, 1337, Alcalá 1348.

15. Piskorski, 29–33; Colmeiro, I, 18.

16. Citation of archbishops: Toledo 1254, Valladolid 1258, Toledo 1259, Seville 1261, Valladolid 1325. Bishops: Seville 1252, Toledo 1254, Valladolid 1258, Toledo 1259, Seville 1261, Burgos 1269, Valladolid 1282, Madrid 1309, Medina del Campo 1318, Valladolid 1325.

17. Citation of orders or masters: Seville 1252, 1261, Segovia 1278, Valladolid 1282, 1293, 1295, 1298, Medina del Campo 1305, Valladolid 1325, Madrid 1329.

18. *MHE*, II, nos. 202–203, pp. 67–70.

19. *CAX*, 26, p. 23; Escudero de la Peña, "Súplica," 58–59; Quintana Prieto, *Tumbo viejo de San Pedro de Montes*, no. 374, pp. 481–482; *CLC*, I, 133.

20. *MHE*, I, nos. 34–35, 37, pp. 70–75, 77–79 (Valladolid 1255), and II, nos. 198, 203, pp. 59–63, 68–70 (Valladolid 1282); *CAX*, 26, p. 23 (Burgos 1272); Menéndez Pidal, *Documentos*, no. 229, pp. 300–302 (Peñafiel 1275).

21. *CSIV*, 8, p. 86 (Medina del Campo 1291); *CLC*, I, 133–135 (Valladolid 1295); Sánchez Herrero, *Concilios*, no. 1, pp. 165–172 (Peñafiel 1302); *MFIV*, II, nos. 22 (Valladolid 1295), 197, 203 (Peñafiel 1302), 531 (Salamanca 1310), 541, 543–544, 546 (Palencia 1311), 554 (Zamora 1311), pp. 40, 279–280, 285–291, 770–773, 789–790, 793–799, 800–805, 816; Suárez Fernández, "Hermandades," no. 6, pp. 57–58 (Zamora 1311).

22. *CLC*, I, 293–299 (Burgos 1315), 369–373 (Valladolid 1322), 388–400 (Valladolid 1325); Suárez Fernández, "Hermandades," no. 7, pp. 58–60 (*hermandad* of 1314); Ubieto Arteta, *Cuéllar*, no. 71, pp. 156–158 (Medina del Campo 1316); Pereda Llarena, *Burgos 1294–1316*, no. 491, pp. 360–363; López Ferreiro, *Historia*, V, no. 61, pp. 175–176, and VI, nos. 14–15, pp. 61–72 (Medina del Campo 1326).

23. O'Callaghan, "The Ecclesiastical Estate in the Cortes of León-Castile, 1252–1350," *CHR* 67 (1981): 185–213; Ana Arranz Guzman, "Clero y Cortes castellanas: Participación y diferencias interestamentales," *En la España medieval. Homenaje al Profesor Salvador de Moxó* (Madrid 1986), II, 49–58.

24. Juan Manuel, *Libro de los estados*, I, 89, pp. 181–184.

25. Sánchez Albornoz, *España*, II, 56–74; Pérez Prendes, *Cortes*, 15–42, 73–75.

26. Henrique da Gama Barros, *História da administração pública em Portugal nos séculos XII a XV*, 2d ed. (Lisbon 1945–1954), ed. Torquato de Sousa Soares, I, 575; Colmeiro, I, 17; Pérez Prendes, *Cortes*, 73–74.

27. Juan Manuel, *Libro de los estados*, I, 18, pp. 34–35; Pérez Prendes, *Cortes*, 75.

28. *Partidas*, II.11.1; Juan Manuel, *Libro de los estados*, I, 90, p. 84, and *Libro del caballero e del escudero*, *BAE*, LI (1952): 234–264; *Partidas*, II, 21; Maria Isabel Pérez de Tudela y Velasco, *Infanzones y caballeros. Su proyección en la esfera nobiliaria castellana-leonesa* (Madrid 1979).

29. Citation of *infanzones*: Almagro 1273, Valladolid 1293, Burgos and Zamora 1301, Medina del Campo and Burgos 1302, Medina del Campo 1305, Valladolid 1307, Palencia 1313, Valladolid 1325, Madrid 1329, Burgos 1338. *Caballeros*: Seville 1250, 1261, Burgos 1272, Almagro 1273, Valladolid 1298,

Burgos and Zamora 1301, Medina del Campo and Burgos 1302, Medina del Campo 1305, Valladolid 1307, 1325, Madrid 1329, Burgos 1338. Piskorski, 26; *CAX*, 36, p. 39; *CLC*, I, 261–262, 300.

30. *CAX*, 47, p. 35 (Burgos 1272); *CLC*, I, 85–86 (Almagro 1273).

31. *CFIV*, 17, p. 238; *MFIV*, II, nos. 510, 560, 736–737, 822–823 (Palencia 1311); *CLC*, I, 207–208 (Palencia 1311), 443–456 (Burgos 1338), 543–574 (Alcalá 1348).

32. González, *Alfonso VIII*, II, nos. 471, 499, pp. 807–808, 857–863; O'Callaghan, "Beginnings," 1512–1513.

33. *MFIV*, II, no. 4, pp. 7–13 (León and Galicia); Valdeavellano, "Carta de hermandad," 57–76 (Extremadura and Castile).

34. *CLC*, I, 267–271.

35. Piskorski, 35; Procter, *Curia*, 161.

36. Hilda Grassotti, "Concejos de señorío en las cortes de Castilla," in her *Estudios medievales españoles* (Madrid 1981), 329–346; López Ferreiro, *Fueros*, 597; Mingüella, *Sigüenza*, II, no. 69, p. 488.

37. González, *Fernando III*, III, no. 809, pp. 387–389.

38. Martín, *Salamanca*, no. 395, pp. 494–496.

39. *Espéculo*, IV.8; *Fuero real*, I.7.6; I. 10.12; *Leyes del estilo*, 11–17; *Partidas*, III.2.13; III.5; III.18.98.

40. Procter, "The Towns of León and Castile as Suitors before the King's Court," *EHR* 74 (1959): 1–22; Carlé, "Boni homines y hombres buenos," *CHE* 39–40 (1964): 133–168; Post, "Roman Law," 61–90; Gama Barros, *História*, III, 178–181.

41. *CAX*, 75, p. 59; Ubieto Arteta, *Cuéllar*, no. 22, p. 66; *CODOM*, II, nos. 81, 85, pp. 74–77; Miguel Vigil, *Oviedo*, nos. 64, 92–93, 100, 121, pp. 103, 143–145, 158–159, 202; Gaibrois, *Sancho IV*, III, no. 306, pp. cxciii–cxiv.

42. *CODOM*, III, nos. 111, 113, pp. 109–111, 116–117; *MFIV*, II, nos. 27, 31, 302, 307, 318, pp. 45, 52, 450, 454–455, 464–465; Post, "Plena Potestas," 91–162.

43. González, *Fernando III*, III, no. 809, pp. 387–389; Martín, *Salamanca*, no. 395, pp. 494–496; *MFIV*, II, nos. 3–4, pp. 3–13.

44. *CLC*, I, 64; *CAX*, 75, p. 59; Teofilo Ruíz, "Prosopografía burgalesa: Sarracín y Bonifaz," *Boletín de la Institución Fernán González* 54 (1975): 467–499.

45. Pérez Prendes, *Cortes*, 80–81.

46. González, *Fernando III*, III, no. 809, pp. 387–389; Amando Represa Rodríguez, "Notas para el estudio de la ciudad de Segovia en los siglos XII–XIV," *Estudios Segovianos* 1 (1949): 290–294; *MHE*, I, no. 86, pp. 187–191.

CHAPTER 4

1. *CAX*, 24, 75, pp. 20–21, 59; González Díez, *Burgos*, nos. 112–113, pp. 199–201.

2. *CFIV*, 8–10, 14–15, pp. 121–125, 150, 156–159; *CAXI*, 6–7, p. 178; *GCAXI*, 7–8, vol. I, pp. 291–293; *CLC*, I, 401.

3. *CAX*, 24–25, 50, 59, 67, 75, pp. 21, 37, 47, 53, 59; *CFIV*, 1, 3, 6–7, 10, 12, 14, 16, 19, pp. 94, 111, 117, 119, 123, 137, 150, 162, 169; *CAXI*, 1–3, 7–8, 12, 27, 38, 80, pp. 175, 178, 182, 191, 198, 222; *CLC*, I, 140 (Valladolid 1299),

169 (Medina del Campo 1305), 185 (Valladolid 1307), 372 (1325), 401 (Madrid 1329).

4. *Cantigas*, vol. II, p. 339, stanza 20.

5. Giménez Soler, *Juan Manuel*, no. 368, pp. 496–498; Pedro López de Ayala, *Crónica de Pedro I*, 1351, 2, *BAE*, LXVI, 412; Madrid, AHN Uclés, carpeta 153, no. 1.

6. *Fuero real*, I.4.1; Pérez Prendes, *Cortes*, 68; Hilda Grassotti, "La ira regia en León y Castilla," *CHE* 37–38 (1965): 5–135; Piskorski, 68–70; Colmeiro, I, 17.

7. *CFIV*, 10, pp. 123–125.

8. Sánchez Albornoz, "Señoríos y ciudades: Dos diplomas para el estudio de sus reciprocas relaciones," *AHDE* 6 (1929): 456–459; López Ferreiro, *Historia*, VI, no. 31, pp. 91–93; Julián Sánchez Ruano, *El Fuero de Salamanca* (Salamanca 1870), xxiv; Procter, *Curia*, 139–140.

9. González Díez, *Burgos*, nos. 96, 98–99, pp. 179, 181–183.

10. *CLC*, I, 169; Giménez Soler, *Juan Manuel*, nos. 386, 472, pp. 509–510, 573–574; López Ferreiro, *Fueros*, 597.

11. *CAX*, 28, p. 24; *MHE*, II, no. 198, pp. 59–63; Pereda Llarena, *Burgos 1254–1293*, no. 173, pp. 237–241; *CAXI*, 3, pp. 175–176; *CLC*, I, 221.

12. *CAX*, 24, 75, pp. 21, 59; *Fuero viejo*, prologue, pp. 1–3; Palacios, *Madrid*, I, 113–117; González Díez, *Burgos*, nos. 112–113, pp. 199–201.

13. Martín, *Salamanca*, no. 395, pp. 494–496.

14. *CFIV*, 1, 3–8, 10, 12–16, pp. 94, 114, 117, 119, 123, 136–137, 150, 169.

15. *CAXI*, 3, 6–8, 12, pp. 175–176, 178–179, 182; *GCAXI*, 37, vol. I, p. 350, and 35, vol. II, pp. 473–475.

16. Giménez Soler, *Juan Manuel*, nos. 385–386, pp. 506–510, 512–513; López Ferreiro, *Fueros*, 597.

17. Burgos 1274, 1276, 1277, Valladolid 1282, Burgos 1287, Valladolid 1293, 1299, 1300, Burgos 1301, Medina del Campo 1302, Burgos 1304, Medina del Campo 1305, Valladolid 1307, Burgos 1308, Valladolid 1312, Palencia 1313, Valladolid 1321, 1322, Madrid 1329.

18. St. John's: Segovia 1278, Haro 1288, Valladolid 1295, Zamora 1301, Burgos 1302, 1315. Circumcision/Epiphany: Valladolid 1258, Seville 1261, Jerez 1268, Madrid 1309, Alcalá 1348. Martinmas: Burgos 1254, Seville 1281, Valladolid 1284, Palencia 1286.

19. Pentecost: Burgos 1287, Valladolid 1314, 1318. Michaelmas: Seville 1252, Burgos 1272. Candlemas: Cuéllar 1297, Valladolid 1298. Assumption: Medina del Campo 1318. Christmas: Toledo 1259.

20. Ballesteros, *El Itinerario de Alfonso el Sabio* (Madrid 1935), p. 228, n. 2, and "Burgos y la rebelión del Infante Don Sancho," 114; *MHE*, I, nos. 71, 84–85, pp. 154–155, 181–183; Menéndez Pidal, *Documentos*, no. 353, p. 467; Nilda Guglielmi, "Posada y Yantar," *Hispania* 26 (1966): 5–29.

21. *CAX*, 25, p. 21.

22. *MFIV*, II, no. 4, p. 12; Valdeavellano, "Carta de hermandad," 73.

23. *CAXI*, 3, pp. 175–176; *GCAXI*, 4–5, vol. I, pp. 280–285; Madrid, BN 1270, fol. 8r–15r (ordinance of 1328); Martínez Marina, *Teoría*, *BAE*, CCXIX, 252–253.

24. *Cantigas*, II, 339–340; *CAX*, 25, pp. 21–22; *CFIV*, 1, p. 95; *CAXI*, 40, p. 199; *CLC*, I, 372.

25. *CLC*, I, 55 (Valladolid 1258), 131 (1295), 137 (1298), 140, 142 (1299), 145–146 (Burgos 1301), 151 (Zamora 1301), 166 (Burgos 1302), 169 (Medina del Campo 1305), 184–185 (Valladolid 1307), 222, 234, (Palencia 1313), 300 (Carrión 1317), 370 (Valladolid 1322), 372 (1325), 401 (Madrid 1329); Ballesteros, "Las cortes de 1252," 122; Rodríguez Díez, *Astorga*, 715 (Seville 1261); *CAX*, 25, 75, pp. 22, 59 (Burgos 1272, Seville 1281).

26. *MHE*, I, no. 71, pp. 154–155; *CAX*, 24–25, 75, pp. 22–23, 59; Fernández del Pulgar, *Palencia*, III, 344–345; Rodríguez Díez, *Astorga*, 715; *CLC*, I, 85–86; Escudero de la Pena, "Súplica," 58–59; Menéndez Pidal, *Documentos*, no. 201, p. 257; *CFIV*, 16, 20, pp. 162–169.

27. Piskorski, no. 1, pp. 196–197; Loaysa, *Crónica*, 19–21, pp. 90–91; *CAX*, 67–68, p. 53; *CLC*, I, 64.

28. Ballesteros, "Las cortes de 1252," 122; *CLC*, I, 106, 117, 401.

29. *MFIV*, II, nos. 22, 200, pp. 40, 283; Martínez Marina, *Teoría*, BAE, CCXIX, 88–89.

30. *CAX*, 19, p. 14; Pedro López de Ayala, *Crónica de Enrique II*, 1373, ch. 10, *BAE*, LXVIII, 20.

31. Pedro López de Ayala, *Crónica de Don Pedro I*, 1351, ch. 15–17, *BAE*, LXVI, 419, and n. 1 (charter to Toledo, 9 November 1351); Eloy Benito Ruano, *La prelación ciudadana: Las disputas por la precedencia entre las ciudades de la corona de Castilla* (Toledo 1972).

32. Rodríguez Díez, *Astorga*, 715; *CAXI*, 40, p. 199.

33. *CAX*, 26, 75, pp. 23, 59–60; *Castigas*, II, 339–340.

34. Loaysa, *Crónica*, 20–21, pp. 90–91.

35. Ballesteros, "Las cortes de 1252," 122; *CLC*, I, 54, 64; Rodríguez Díez, *Astorga*, 715.

36. *CLC*, I, 95 (1286), 106, 117 (1293), 184–185 (1307); *CFIV*, 15, pp. 150–151.

37. *CLC*, I, 106–117 (1293, Castile), 117–130 (1293, León), 169–172 (1305, León), 172–179 (1305, Castile), 179–184 (1305, Extremadura); Palacio, *Madrid*, I, 139–150 (1293, Extremadura); *CODOM*, IV, no. 153, pp. 135–143 (1293, Murcia); Nieto Cumplido, *Regionalismo*, no. 20, pp. 155–166 (1293, Andalusia).

38. Ubieto Arteta, *Cuéllar*, no. 21, p. 60; CLC, I, 64, *CAX*, 26, p. 23.

39. *CFIV*, 1–2, 15, pp. 96, 107–108, 151–152; *MFIV*, II, no. 22, p. 40; Loaysa, *Crónica*, 60–61, pp. 153–154.

40. *CFIV*, 1, p. 96; *CLC*, I, 170.

41. *CAX*, 25–26, 39–40, 44, 47, pp. 22–23, 30–32, 34–35; *CLC*, I, 85–86.

42. *CFIV*, 19, pp. 168–169; *MFIV*, II, nos. 510, 560, pp. 736–737, 822–823; *CLC*, I, 207 (1312), 443–456 (1338); *CAXI*, 186, pp. 292–293.

43. *CAX*, 26, p. 23 (1272); Menéndez Pidal, *Documentos*, no. 229, pp. 300–302 (1275); *CLC*, I, 133–135 (1295), 193–199 (1315), 389–400 (1325); *MFIV*, II, nos. 385 (1307), 541, 543, 546 (1311), pp. 565–566, 789–791, 793–805; González Mínguez, *Fernando IV*, no. 23, p. 374 (1307); López Ferreiro, *Historia*, V, no. 61, pp. 175–178 (1316), and VI, nos. 14–15, pp. 61–72 (1326).

44. Roger B. Merriman, "The Cortes of the Spanish Kingdoms in the Later Middle Ages," *AHR* 16 (1911): 484.

45. Rodríguez Díez, *Astorga*, 715–720; *MHE*, I, no. 140, pp. 309–324; *CAX*, 18, 47, 75, pp. 13, 35, 59–60; *Cantigas*, no. 386, vol. II, pp. 339–340; O'Callaghan, "Cortes and Royal Taxation," 386–389.

46. *CFIV,* 1–2, 15, pp. 96, 108, 150–151; Loaysa, *Crónica,* 60–61, pp. 152–154.

47. *CFIV,* 15, pp. 150–151.

48. Burgos 1301, art. 14; Zamora 1301, art. 27; Medina del Campo 1302, art. 14; 1305, art. 13 E, 14 C; Valladolid 1307, art. 35; 1312, art. 103; Palencia 1313, art. 49 M; Burgos 1315, art. 55; Carrión 1317, art. 73; Valladolid 1322, art. 105; 1325, art. 42; Madrid 1329, art. 89; 1339, art. 24; Alcalá 1345; Burgos 1345; León 1345, art. 31; Alcalá 1348, art. 53.

49. *Cantigas,* II, 339–341.

50. Francis Palgrave, *Parliamentary Writs* (London 1827–1834), I, 30; Barcelona, Archivo de la Corona de Aragón, Register 332, fol. 202v.

51. García Gallo, *Manual,* II, nos. 1072, 1095, 1111–1116, pp. 899, 933, 952–955.

CHAPTER 5

1. Juan Manuel, *Libro del caballero et del escudero,* 3, 24, *BAE,* LI, 235, 238.

2. *Forum Iudicum,* Primus titulus, in *Fuero juzgo en latín y castellano,* ed. Real Academia Española (Madrid 1815), I–X; *Espéculo,* II.5.1, II.16.5, V.2.33; *Partidas,* II.15.3–5, II.20.5; Sancho IV, *Castigos e Documentos* (Bloomington 1952), ed. Agapito Rey, 11, 14, pp. 114, 119.

3. Rodrigo, *De rebus Hispaniae,* IX, 1, 5, pp. 192–193, 196–197; *Chronique latine,* 31, 33–35, pp. 82, 89–93; Sánchez Albornoz, "La sucesión al trono en los reinos de León y Castilla," in his *Estudios,* 675–678.

4. Rodrigo, *De rebus Hispaniae,* IX, 14–15, pp. 203–205; *Chronique latine,* 60–61, pp. 132–134; Lucas of Túy, *Crónica,* 92, p. 427; González, *Fernando III,* II, no. 270, pp. 311–314; O'Callaghan, "Beginnings," 1527.

5. Lucas of Túy, *Crónica,* 103, pp. 449–450; *CAX,* 1, p. 3; *Anónimo de Sahagún,* 74–75, p. 360; *Cantigas de escarnho e de mal dezir dos Cancioneiros medievais galego-portugueses,* ed. Manuel Rodríguez Lapa (Coimbra 1970), no. 167, p. 261.

6. *CSIV,* 1, p. 69–70; Loaysa, *Crónica,* 33–34, pp. 110–112.

7. *CFIV,* 1, pp. 93–95.

8. Barrios García, *Alba de Tormes,* no. 18, pp. 59–61; AM León, no. 49; *MFIV,* II, nos. 3–4, pp. 3–13; Luis G. de Valdeavellano, "Carta de hermandad entre los concejos de la Extremadura castellana y del arzobispado de Toledo en 1295," *Revista portuguesa de historia* 12 (1969): 57–76.

9. *CFIV,* 1, p. 95. Martínez was one of the *personeros* of León in the *hermandad* of 3 August.

10. Josefa Sanz Fuentes, "Cartas de hermandad concejíl en Andalucía: El caso de Écija," *HID* 5 (1978): no. 1, pp. 413–418; Agustín Muñoz y Gómez, "Concejos de Córdoba, Sevilla y Jerez de la Frontera. Carta inédita de su hermandad en 1296," *BRAH* 36 (1900): 306–316; Nieto Cumplido, *Regionalismo,* nos. 23–25, pp. 169–176; Suárez Fernández, "Hermandades," no. 4, pp. 52–55; Carmen Argente del Castillo Ocaña, "Las hermandades medievales en el reino de Jaén," *Andalucía medieval* 2 (1978): 21–22; *CODOM,* III, no. 112, pp. 110–116; BL, Add. MSS 9917, no. 47, fol. 160.

11. *CFIV,* 1, pp. 96–100; González Mínguez, *Fernando IV,* no. 2, pp. 348–352.

12. *MFIV,* II, no. 57, pp. 81–85; Sáinz Díaz, *San Vicente de la Barquera,* 472–477; Gregorio de Balparda, *Historia crítica de Vizcaya y sus fueros* (Madrid 1924), III, no. 189, pp. 65–69; Álvarez Morales, *Las hermandades,* nos. 3–4, pp. 269–271; González Mínguez, *Contribución al estudio de las hermandades en el reinado de Fernando IV* (Vitoria 1974); Martínez Díez, "La hermandad alavesa," *AHDE* 43 (1973): no. 2, pp. 107–110.

13. *CFIV,* 2–4, pp. 107–111; *CLC,* I, 135–139; Loaysa, *Crónica,* 76, p. 178; *MFIV,* II, nos. 100, 112, pp. 140–143, 159; Nieto Cumplido, *Regionalismo,* no. 26, pp. 191–199.

14. *CFIV,* 4–9, pp. 111–122; Loaysa, *Crónica,* 78–85, pp. 180–192; *CLC,* I, 139–161.

15. *CFIV,* 10, 13, pp. 123–129, 137; Loaysa, *Crónica,* 87, p. 195; *CLC,* I, 161–165; *MFIV,* II, no. 213, pp. 311–313; Giménez Soler, *Juan Manuel,* nos. 46, 57, pp. 262–264, 273–274.

16. *CFIV,* 20, p. 169; *CAXI,* 1, 99–101, pp. 173, 233–236; *GCAXI,* 120–122, vol. I, pp. 506–514; *Poema de Alfonso XI,* 489; Sánchez Albornoz, "Un ceremonial inédito de la coronación de los reyes de Castilla," in his *Estudios,* 739–763.

17. *Chronique latine,* 40, pp. 98–100; Rodrigo, *De rebus Hispaniae,* IX, 10, 18, pp. 200, 207; *Anónimo de Sahagún,* 76, pp. 361–362; *CAX,* 18, p. 13; *Crónica de Jaume I,* IX, 7–8.

18. González, *Alfonso VIII,* II, nos. 471, 499, pp. 808, 857–863; *Chronique latine,* 11, pp. 39–40; Rodrigo, *De rebus Hispaniae,* VII, 24, p. 166.

19. O'Callaghan, "Beginnings," 1520–1521; Ballesteros, *Alfonso X,* 50–52.

20. Piskorski, no. 1, pp. 196–197; Daumet, *Mémoire,* no. 1, pp. 143–146.

21. Ballesteros, *Alfonso X,* 118–119; Sánchez Albornoz, "Señoríos y ciudades," 456–459; López Ferreiro, *Historia,* V, no. 31, pp. 91–92.

22. *CAX,* 59, pp. 47–48; Fernández del Pulgar, *Palencia,* II, 344–345; Craddock, "La cronología de las obras legislativas de Alfonso X el Sabio," *AHDE* 51 (1981): 401–403.

23. *CAX,* 61–67, pp. 48–53; Ballesteros, *Alfonso X,* 769, 785; Procter, *Curia,* 139, 230.

24. *CAX,* 67–68, p. 53; Loaysa, *Crónica,* 19–21, pp. 90–91; *Anales Toledanos III,* in *ES,* XXIII, 420; Bernat Desclot, *Crónica* (Barcelona 1949–1951), ed. M. Coll i Alentorn, III, 10–13; Ballesteros, *Alfonso X,* 780–791; Procter, *Curia,* 140–142.

25. Loperráez, *Osma,* III, no. 76, p. 212; Ballesteros, *Alfonso X,* 824, 841; *MHE,* I, no. 143, pp. 325–326; Daumet, *Mémoire,* no. 7, pp. 157–158.

26. Francisque Michel, ed., *Histoire de la guerre de Navarre par Guillaume Anelier,* in *Collection de documents inédits sur l'Histoire de France* (Paris 1856), 651–655.

27. Fray Juan Gil de Zamora, *Liber de preconiis civitatis Numantine,* in Fidel Fita, "Dos obras inéditas de Gil de Zamora," *BRAH* 5 (1884): 146; *MHE,* II, no. 228, p. 113; Ferotin, *Recueil* no. 230, p. 262; Procter, *Curia,* 143.

28. *CAX,* 68, 75–76, pp. 53, 59–60; Loaysa, *Crónica,* 14, p. 96; Procter, *Curia,* 146–147.

29. *CAX,* 75–76, pp. 60–61; *MHE,* II, no. 197, pp. 58–59; Ballesteros, *Alfonso X,* 963–964, 994–996; Procter, *Curia,* 146–148.

30. *CAX,* 76, p. 61; Loaysa, *Crónica,* 298, p. 102; Ballesteros, *Alfonso X,* 966, 996.

31. Pereda Llarena, *Burgos 1254–1293*, no. 173, pp. 237–241; *MHE*, II, no. 198, pp. 59–63; Linehan, *Spanish Church*, 220–221.

32. *CAX*, 76, p. 61; González Díez, *Burgos*, nos. 118, 120–122, pp. 205–210; *MHE*, II, no. 209, pp. 78–80; *CODOM*, III, no. 77, pp. 70–71; González, *Colección*, VI, no. 83, pp. 231–233; Villar y Macías, *Salamanca*, I, no. 8, pp. 395–396.

33. *MHE*, II, no. 202, pp. 67–68; Ferotin, *Recueil*, no. 243, pp. 272–273; Escalona, *Sahagún*, no. 264, pp. 616–617; Berganza, *Antigüedades*, I, 175; Luis Fernández, "La participación de los monasterios en la hermandad de los reinos de Castilla León y Galicia (1282–1284)," *Hispania Sacra*, 25 (1972): 5–35.

34. *MHE*, II, no. 203, pp. 68–70; Quintana Prieto, *Tumbo viejo de San Pedro de Montes*, no. 374, pp. 481–482; Mañueco Villalobos and Zurita Nieto, *Santa Maria la Mayor de Valladolid*, III, pp. 27–29.

35. *MHE*, II, nos. 205–206, pp. 73–75; Nieto Cumplido, *Regionalismo*, nos. 9–11, pp. 131–136; *Colección de documentos inéditos para la historia de España*, 112 vols. (Madrid 1842–1845), CXII, 3–6; Manuel González Jiménez, "La hermandad entre Sevilla y Carmona (Siglos XII a XVI)," *Andalucía medieval. Actas del I Congreso de Historia de Andalucía* (Córdoba 1978), II, p. 4, n. 6.

36. Quintana Prieto, *San Pedro de Montes*, no. 375, pp. 482–487; Escalona, *Sahagún*, no. 266, pp. 618–622; Álvarez Morales, *Hermandades*, no. 1, pp. 267–268.

37. Fernandez, "Participación," 25–27; *MHE*, II, no. 213, pp. 86–87; Martín, *Salamanca*, no. 389, pp. 487–488.

38. *CAX*, 76–77, pp. 62–64; *MHE*, II, nos. 228–229, pp. 110–134; Georges Daumet, "Les testaments d'Alphonse le savant, roi de Castille," *BEC* 67 (1906): 70–99; *CODOM*, III, no. 79, pp. 73–74.

39. *MHE*, II, nos. 220, 224, pp. 94–97, 102–103; Martín *Salamanca*, no. 391, pp. 489–490.

40. *CAX*, 77, pp. 64–65; Pereda Llarena, *Burgos 1254–1293*, no. 180, pp. 246–247; Gaibrois, *Sancho IV*, I, cli, clvii, clxxiii, and III, nos. 5, 83, pp. ii–iii, liii–liv.

41. Daumet, "Testaments," 87–89; *MHE*, II, no. 229, pp. 122–134; Procter, *Curia*, 182.

42. *CSIV*, 1–2, 12–13, pp. 69, 72, 89–90; Loaysa, *Crónica*, 33, p. 110; AM León, no. 24; Procter, *Curia*, 120, 149, 174, 179.

43. *CFIV*, 19, pp. 168–169; Giménez Soler, *Juan Manuel*, no. 231, p. 397.

44. *CAXI*, 104–105, p. 239; Ferotin, *Recueil*, nos. 352, 354, pp. 364–365; Palacio, *Madrid*, I, 248–249; Antonio C. Floriano, *Documentación histórica del Archivo Municipal de Cáceres (1229–1471)* (Cáceres 1987), no. 44, pp. 77–78; AM Murcia, Cartulario 1352–1382 Eras, fol. 99r, 106v.

45. *CAXI*, 95, 137, pp. 230, 264; *GCAXI*, 159, vol. II, pp. 15, 934; Ferotin, *Recueil*, nos. 357, 359, pp. 366–367.

46. Martínez Marina, *Teoría*, BAE, CCXIX, 217–228; Piskorski, 109–118; Pérez Prendes, *Cortes*, 115–122.

47. *CAX*, 59, pp. 47–48; Ballesteros, *Alfonso X*, 683–687; Procter, *Curia*, 135–136.

48. *CFIV*, 1, pp. 94–95; *CLC*, I, 130–135; *MFIV*, II, no. 22, p. 40.

49. *CAXI*, 1, p. 173; *GCAXI*, 1–2, vol. I, pp. 276–278; Giménez Soler, *Juan Manuel*, nos. 249–255, 258, 262–263, pp. 413–420; Juan Ignacio de la Peña, "La hermandad leonesa de 1313," *León medieval* (León 1978), 139–164.

50. Giménez Soler, *Juan Manuel*, nos. 265–266, pp. 424–427; *CAXI*, 1–2, pp. 174–175; *GCAXI*, 2–3, vol. I, pp. 278–281; *Bullarium Ordinis Militiae de Calatrava* (Madrid 1761) 498–500; Nieto Cumplido, *Regionalismo*, no. 29, pp. 205–212; Argente del Castillo Ocaña, "Hermandades," II, 32.

51. *CAXI*, 3, pp. 175–176; *GCAXI*, 4, vol. I, pp. 282–283; Giménez Soler, *Juan Manuel*, no. 263, pp. 423–424.

52. *CLC*, I, 221–233 (Juan), 233–247 (Maria and Pedro).

53. *CAXI*, 4–6, pp. 176–178; *GCAXI*, 5–7, vol. I, pp. 285–290; Giménez Soler, *Juan Manuel*, nos. 272–273, 276–278, pp. 431–432, 435–436.

54. Giménez Soler, *Juan Manuel*, nos. 282, 286–294, 296–298, 302–303, pp. 438–448, 450–455; Pereda Llarena, *Burgos 1294–1316*, no. 474, pp. 327–333.

55. Pereda Llarena, *Burgos 1294–1316*, no. 475, pp. 332–333; Loperráez, *Osma*, III, no. 100, pp. 251–252; López Ferreiro, *Historia*, V, nos. 56–57, pp. 159–165; Suárez Fernández, "Hermandades," nos. 7–8, pp. 58–60.

56. *CLC*, I, 247–271 (*hermandad*), 271–292 (cortes); *CAXI*, 7–8, pp. 178–180; *GCAXI*, 8–9, vol. II, pp. 293–295.

57. *CAXI*, 9–10, p. 180; *GCAXI*, 11–13, vol. I, pp. 299–301; *CLC*, I, 299–329.

58. *CAXI*, 12, p. 182; *GCAXI*, 14–16, vol. I, pp. 302–307; *CLC*, I, 330–336 (Medina del Campo); Barrios García, *Alba de Tormes*, no. 29, pp. 97–99.

59. *CAXI*, 13–20, pp. 182–188; *GCAXI*, 17–27, vol. I, pp. 308–334; Giménez Soler, *Juan Manuel*, nos. 347–349, 353–355, pp. 478–479, 484–488; AM Cuenca, 17-1, fol. 74 ff.

60. *CAXI*, 27, pp. 191–192; *GCAXI*, 34, 37–38, vol. I, pp. 345–346, 350–351; Giménez Soler, *Juan Manuel*, no. 368, pp. 71, 496–498; Fidel Fita, "El concilio de Palencia en 1321," *BRAH* 52 (1908): 17–48.

61. *CAXI*, 38, p. 198; *GCAXI*, 50, vol. I, pp. 373–375, and 35, vol. II, pp. 473–475; *CLC*, I, 337–372; Giménez Soler, *Juan Manuel*, nos. 371, 380, 385–387, pp. 499, 504, 506–510; Juan Manuel, *Chronicon*, in *MFIV*, I, 678.

62. Joaquim Ferreira, *História de Portugal* (Porto 1951), 195; *Chronique catalane de Pierre IV d'Aragón*, ed. Amedée Pagès (Toulouse 1941), 77–83.

63. *Chronique de Pierre IV*, 153; William Stubbs, *Constitutional History of England*, 4th ed. (Oxford 1883), II, 378–381.

64. *Colección de documentos inéditos del Archivo general de la Corona de Aragón* (Barcelona 1847–1910), VI, nos. 50–52, pp. 180–189; Edouard Perroy, *The Hundred Years War* (New York 1965), 71–76; *Chronique de Pierre IV*, 240–244.

CHAPTER 6

1. Martínez Marina, *Teoría*, *BAE*, CCXIX, 335–336; Colmeiro, I, 63–64; Piskorski, 188–194; Pérez Prendes, 131–136.

2. González, *Alfonso IX*, II, no. 11, p. 24; Procter, "The Interpretation of Clause 3 of the Decrees of León (1188)," *EHR* 75 (1970): 45–53.

3. González, *Alfonso VIII*, no. 471, p. 808; *Chronique latine*, 11, pp. 39–40; Rodrigo, *De rebus Hispaniae*, VII, 24, pp. 166–167; O'Callaghan, "Beginnings," 1512, 1516.

4. González, *Alfonso IX*, II, no. 11, p. 14.

5. Thomas Rymer, *Foedera, conventiones, litterae et cuiuscunque acta publica*

inter reges Angliae et alios quovis imperatores, reges, pontifices, principes (London 1704–1735), I, 503–510.

6. *Los miraculos romanzados,* in Sebastián de Vergara, *Vida y milagros de Santo Domingo de Silos* (Madrid 1736), 131; Gregorio de Balparda, *Historia crítica de Vizcaya y sus fueros* (Madrid 1924), II, no. 387, p. 537; *CAX,* 3, p. 5; Procter, *Curia,* pp. 127, 284, n. 5.

7. *Crónica de Jaume I,* IX, 7–8; *CAX,* 66–67, pp. 52–53; Loaysa, *Crónica,* 19, p. 90.

8. *CFIV,* 1, 4, 6–9, pp. 94, 111–113, 118–122, 129–131; Loaysa, *Crónica,* 77, p. 180; *MFIV,* II, no. 213, pp. 312–313.

9. Loaysa, *Crónica,* 7, p. 68; *CAX,* 17, pp. 12–13; Ballesteros, *Alfonso X,* 177–189.

10. Bruce Gelsinger, "A Thirteenth-Century Norwegian-Castilian Alliance," *Mediaevalia et Humanistica,* New Series, 10 (1981): 55–80; *CLC,* I, 54–63.

11. AM Toledo, cajón 10, legajo 1, no. 1, excerpted in Ballesteros, *Alfonso X,* 225–228; O'Callaghan, "The Cortes and Royal Taxation," 382–383.

12. *MHE,* I, no. 71, pp. 154–155; Minguella, *Sigüenza,* I, no. 225, pp. 599–601; Ballesteros, "Itinerario," *BRAH* 108 (1936): 17, n. 1.

13. Besides the Moorish kings, royal vassals included Duke Hugh of Burgundy, Count Guy of Flanders, Duke Henry of Lorraine, Alfonso, Luis and Juan, sons of John of Brienne, former emperor of Constantinople, Viscount Gaston of Béarn, and Viscount Guy of Limoges. *MHE,* I, no. 70, pp. 152–154 (2 October 1259).

14. Robert L. Wolff, "Mortgage and Redemption of an Emperor's Son: Castile and the Latin Empire of Constantinople," *Speculum* 29 (1954): 45–84.

15. *Setenario,* ch. 9–10, ed. Kenneth Vanderford (Buenos Aires 1945), pp. 15–19; *MHE,* I, no. 69, p. 151; Ballesteros, *Alfonso X,* 214–243; Cayetano Socarras, *Alfonso X of Castile: a Study on Imperialistic Frustration* (Barcelona 1976).

16. Fernández del Pulgar, *Palencia,* II, 344–345.

17. *CAX,* 18, p. 13.

18. *CAX,* 47, p. 35; *MHE,* I, no. 37, p. 305; O'Callaghan, "The Cortes and Royal Taxation," 386–388.

19. *CAX,* 48–58, pp. 36–47.

20. Fernández del Pulgar, *Palencia,* II, 344–345; *CAX,* 59, p. 47.

21. *CAX,* 59, p. 47–48; Palacio, *Madrid,* I, 119–122; Miguel Vigil, *Oviedo,* no. 36, p. 63; González, *Colección,* V, no. 59, pp. 189–190; Ubieto Arteta, *Cuéllar,* no. 30, pp. 73–74; AM León, no. 14; González Díez, *Burgos,* no. 42, pp. 127–128.

22. Ballesteros, *Alfonso X,* 712–732; Socarras, *Alfonso X,* 209–244.

23. *CAX,* 75, p. 59; Ballesteros, *Alfonso X,* 934–935.

24. *Chronique latine,* 19, 21, 43, pp. 57–58, 62, 102; Rodrigo, *De rebus Hispaniae,* VII, 36, p. 126, and VIII, 3, p. 127.

25. *Primera Crónica general,* II, ch. 1070, p. 746; *CAX,* 3, p. 5; *El Anónimo de Sahagún,* 74–75, p. 360.

26. *MHE,* I, no. 15, pp. 26–29; Rymer, *Foedera,* I, pt. I, p. 510.

27. Procter, *Curia,* 128; see above, Chapter 2, note 10.

28. Miguel Vigil, *Oviedo,* no. 22, p. 46.

29. *MHE,* I, nos. 72–75, pp. 155–160, 164–166; *CAX,* 19, pp. 13–14;

Colección de documentos inéditos del Archivo General de la Corona de Aragón, ed. Prosper de Bofarull (Barcelona 1847–1910), VI, nos. 34, 36, pp. 149–154.

30. Rodríguez Díez, *Astorga*, 715–720.

31. *CAX*, 6, pp. 6–7; *MHE*, I, no. 140, pp. 309–324.

32. Iglesia Ferreirós, "Privilegio general," 513–521; *CAX*, 9, p. 10.

33. *Les Registres de Clément IV*, ed. E. Jordan (Paris 1900–1945), nos. 15–17, 126, pp. 890, 896.

34. *MHE*, I, no. 101, pp. 221–223; Nieto Cumplido, *Regionalismo*, no. 5, pp. 122–125.

35. *CLC*, I, 64–85.

36. *CAX*, 43–58, pp. 32–47.

37. *CAX*, 61–65, pp. 48–52; González Díez, *Burgos*, no. 44, pp. 129–130.

38. Menéndez Pidal, *Documentos*, no. 201, p. 257; Ballesteros, *Alfonso X*, 791–793.

39. Ubieto Arteta, *Cuéllar*, no. 32, pp. 75–76; Escudero de la Peña, "Súplica," 58–59; Ballesteros, *Alfonso X*, 835–837.

40. *CAX*, 69–72, pp. 54–56; O'Callaghan, "The Cortes and Royal Taxation," 392–393.

41. González Díez, *Burgos*, nos. 87–89, 92–94, 105, pp. 169–173, 175–177, 190–191; Ballesteros, *Alfonso X*, 908–909.

42. *CAX*, 75, pp. 59–60; Procter, *Curia*, 146–147.

43. *CAX*, 76–77, pp. 62–63.

44. Fernández "San Pelayo de Cerrato," no. 11, pp. 299–301; Ubieto Arteta, *Cuéllar*, no. 38, pp. 82–87.

45. *CSIV*, 2, 8–9, pp. 71, 86; *CLC*, I, 106–117, 117–130.

46. *CFIV*, 2, 4, pp. 107–108, 111.

47. *CFIV*, 10, p. 125; Loaysa, *Crónica*, 87, p. 195.

48. *CFIV*, 16–17, pp. 161–164; *MFIV*, II, nos. 416–419, pp. 621–626; Giménez Soler, *Juan Manuel*, nos. 192–195, pp. 364–366.

49. *CFIV*, 17, 19–20, pp. 163–164, 168–170; *CLC*, I, 197–221.

50. *CAXI*, 12–14, pp. 182–184; *GCAXI*, 14–21, vol. I, pp. 302–319; *CLC*, I, 330–336; Barrios García, *Alba de Tormes*, no. 29, pp. 97–99.

51. *CAXI*, 40, 80, 82, pp. 199, 222–224; *GCAXI*, 52, 101, 103, vol. I, pp. 378, 467–468, 472–473; *CLC*, I, 443–456 (1338).

52. *CAXI*, 196, 243, pp. 298, 318–319; *GCAXI*, 296, vol. II, pp. 349–352.

53. *CAXI*, 253–255, pp. 330–331; *GCAXI*, 332–335, vol. II, pp. 443–449.

54. *CAXI*, 259–263, pp. 335–338; *CLC*, I, 477–483 (Alcalá, art. 8, 12, 15), 483–492 (Burgos, art. 8, 11–12), 627–637 (León, art. 26–29).

55. Procter, *Curia*, 185.

56. Giménez Soler, *Juan Manuel*, nos. 192–195, pp. 364–366.

57. José Coroleu e Inglada and José Pella y Forgas, *Las cortes catalanas*, 2d ed. (Barcelona 1876), 185–190; *Recueil général des anciennes lois françaises* (Paris 1822–1833), IV, 734; *Rotuli parliamentorum* (London 1776–1777), II, 165.

CHAPTER 7

1. Martínez Marina, *Teoría*, BAE, CCIX, 323–325; Colmeiro, I, 66–71; Piskorski, 125; Pérez Prendes, *Cortes*, 111–114, 136–151; Procter, *Curia*, 204.

2. González, *Alfonso IX*, II, nos. 11–12, 84–85, 192, pp. 23, 26, 125, 129, 267.

3. See the *Espéculo* and *Fuero real* in *Opúsculos legales del Rey Don Alfonso el Sabio*, 2 vols., ed. Real Academia de la Historia (Madrid 1836), and *Las Siete Partidas del Rey Don Alfonso el Sabio*, 3 vols., ed. Real Academia de la Historia (Madrid 1807; reprint 1972); Gaibrois, *Sancho IV*, III, nos. 287, 295, pp. clxxv, clxxxiv–clxxxv.

4. Procter, *Curia*, 203–204; *Primera Partida según el Manuscrito ADD. 20787 del British Museum*, ed. Juan Antonio Arias Bonet (Valladolid 1975), I.1.13.

5. Post, "A Romano-Canonical Maxim, *Quod omnes tangit*, in Bracton and Early Parliaments," 163–240; Maravall, "La corriente democrática medieval en España y la fórmula *Quod omnes tangit*," 157–175.

6. García Gallo, "Nuevas observaciones sobre la obra legislativa de Alfonso X," *AHDE* 46 (1976): 609–670, and "El Libro de las Leyes de Alfonso el Sabio: Del *Espéculo* a las *Partidas*," *AHDE* 21 (1951): 345–528; Aquilino Iglesia Ferreirós, "Alfonso X el Sabio y su obra legislativa: Algunas reflexiones," *AHDE* 50 (1980): 531–561; Robert A. MacDonald, "Problemas políticos y derecho alfonsino considerados desde tres puntos de vista, *AHDE* 54 (1984): 25–53; O'Callaghan, "Sobre la promulgación del *Espéculo* y del *Fuero real*," *Estudios en homenaje a Don Claudio Sánchez Albornoz en sus 90 años*, III (1985): 167–179.

7. Robert A. MacDonald, "El *Espéculo* atribuído a Alfonso X, su edición y problemas que plantea," *España y Europa, un pasado jurídico común. Actas del I Simposio internacional del Instituto de Derecho Común*, ed. Antonio Pérez Martin (Murcia 1986), 611–653; Craddock, "La cronología de las obras legislativas de Alfonso X el Sabio," *AHDE* 51 (1981): 364–418.

8. *CLC*, I, 87–94; Craddock, "Cronología," 367; Martínez Marina, *Ensayo histórico-crítico sobre la antigua legislación y principales cuerpos legales de los reynos de León y Castilla* (Madrid 1808), 349–350.

9. MacDonald, "El Espéculo," 642–644.

10. Charters to Aguilar de Campóo (14 March 1255), Sahagún (25 April), Oña (23 November); *MHE*, I, no. 27, pp. 57–62; Muñoz, *Fueros*, 313–320; Alamo, *Oña*, II, no. 537, pp. 656–657.

11. The text in *Opúsculos legales*, II, 1–169, was finished at Valladolid on 30 August 1255. The editors (I, vi) indicated that most of the codices were dated 25 August in Valladolid; Craddock, "Cronología," 376–379; MacDonald, "Progress and Problems in Editing Alfonsine Juridical Texts," *La Corónica* 6 (1978): 74–81, identified at least thirty-six medieval codices.

12. *CLC*, I, 94; *CAX*, 9, p. 8; *El Fuero viejo de Castilla*, prologue, pp. 2–3; Juan Sanz García, *El Fuero de Verviesca y el Fuero real* (Burgos 1927), 71, 398–399.

13. *MHE*, I, nos. 43–45, pp. 89–100; Ballesteros, "El Fuero de Atienza," *BRAH* 68 (1916): 264–270; Francisco Layna Serrano, *Historia de la villa de Atienza* (Madrid 1945), 503–504; Loperráez, *Osma*, III, nos. 60–61, pp. 86–185; Juan Martín Carramolino, *Historia de Ávila, su provincia y obispado* (Madrid 1872), II, no. 8, pp. 491–493. Other charters dated 1257 to 1265 are in *MHE*, I, nos. 59, 83, 91, 102, pp. 124–127, 175–180, 202–203, 224–228; AM Agreda, no. 8; AM Béjar, no. 4; Palacio, *Madrid*, I, 85–91; Ballesteros, "Itinerario," *BRAH* 107 (1935): 59, n. 1. The general confirmation to Extremadura is in Ubieto Arteta, *Cuéllar*, no. 21, pp. 60–65.

14. O'Callaghan, "Promulgación," 177–179.

15. García Gallo, "El Libro de las Leyes," 391–402; Craddock, "Cronología," 386–398; Aquilino Iglesia Ferreirós, "Fuero real y Espéculo," *AHDE* 52 (1982): 111–191.

16. *CAX*, 22–24, pp. 18–21; Ballesteros, *Alfonso X*, 568–577; Procter, *Curia*, 133.

17. *CAX*, 25–26, pp. 21–23.

18. *El Fuero viejo*, prologue, pp. 1–3.

19. Ballesteros, *Alfonso X*, 581; Procter, *Curia*, 180, 191, 198.

20. *CAX*, 27–39, pp. 24–30.

21. Palacio, *Madrid*, I, 113–117; AM Béjar, carpeta 1, doc. 5; Emilio Sáez et al., *Los Fueros de Sepúlveda* (Segovia 1953), no. 13, pp. 196–198; *Privilegios reales y viejos documentos*, X, Cuenca, no. 6; Aquilino Iglesia Ferreirós, "El Privilegio general concedido a las Extremaduras en 1264 por Alfonso X," *AHDE* 53 (1983): 487–488.

22. García Gallo, "El Libro de las Leyes," 406–407, and "Nuevas Observaciones," 649–650; MacDonald, "Problemas políticos," 38–41, 51–52, and "El Espéculo," 645–646.

23. *CLC*, I, 87–94; Aquilino Iglesia Ferreirós, "Las Cortes de Zamora de 1274 y los Casos de Corte," *AHDE* 41 (1971): 945–971; Procter, *Curia*, 137–138.

24. *CLC*, I, 87–94; *MHE*, I, no. 148, pp. 333–335; Gaibrois, *Sancho IV*, I, clxxx–clxxxviii.

25. Cortes of Madrid 1329, art. 1, *CLC*, I, 401–437; Rafael Gibert, "El Ordenamiento de Villarreal 1346," *AHDE* 25 (1955): 703–729; Galo Sánchez, "El Ordenamiento de Segovia de 1347," *Boletín de la Biblioteca Menéndez Pelayo* 4 (1922): 301–320; *CAXI*, 93, pp. 228–229.

26. *CLC*, I, 165–169 (to Illescas, 10 March 1303), 197–215 (1312); *MFIV*, II, no. 229, pp. 344–346; Colmeiro, I, 201–202; González Mínguez, *Fernando IV*, 141–142.

27. *CLC*, I, 492–593; Ignacio Jordán del Asso y del Río and Miguel de Manuel y Rodríguez, *El Ordenamiento de Leyes que D. Alfonso XI hizo en las Cortes de Alcalá de Henares el año de 1348* (Madrid 1774; reprint Valladolid 1975).

28. Ballesteros, "Cortes de 1252," 122; López Ferreiro, *Fueros*, 364; *CLC*, I, 116, 129 (Valladolid 1293, art. 24 L, 27 C).

29. *CLC*, I, 54–63; Rodríguez Díez, *Astorga*, 715–720.

30. Excommunication (Zamora 1301, art. 11; Valladolid 1307, art. 24); chancery (Palencia 1286 art. 9); notaries (Valladolid 1293, art. 5 L; Zamora 1301, art. 5; Valladolid 1325, art. 12, from *Fuero real*, I.8.1); exports (Palencia 1313, art. 17 J; Burgos 1315, art. 17; Valladolid 1322, art. 43; Madrid 1339, art. 15); Jewish usury, debts, pawnbroking (Valladolid 1293, art. 21, 24 L, 23–24, 27 C; Zamora 1301, art. 10; Valladolid 1307, art. 18, 28; Palencia 1313, art. 30 J; Burgos 1315, art. 26; Valladolid 1312, art. 100; Carrión 1317, art. 31; Valladolid 1322, art. 56, 58; 1325, art. 15).

31. *CLC*, I, 95–99 (Palencia 1286), 99–106 (Haro 1288), 106–117 (Valladolid 1293, Castile), 117–130 (1293, León); Palacio, *Madrid*, I, 139–150 (1293, Extremadura); *CODOM*, IV, no. 153, pp. 135–143 (1293, Murcia); Nieto Cumplido, *Regionalismo*, no. 20, pp. 155–166 (1293, Andalusia).

32. Haro 1288 (Valladolid 1293, art. 17 C); Palencia 1286 (Valladolid 1293, art. 20 L, 22 C, 25 C). Chancery (Medina del Campo 1302, art. 15; Madrid

1329, art. 31); Jews (Valladolid 1307, art. 18, 28; 1312, art. 100; Palencia 1313, art. 30 J); exports (Palencia 1313, art. 17 J; Burgos 1315, art. 17; Valladolid 1322, art. 43).

33. *CLC*, I, 130–133 (Valladolid 1295), 133–135 (1295, prelates), 135–136 (Cuéllar 1297), 136–139 (Valladolid 1298), 139–142 (Valladolid 1299, Castile), 142–145 (1299, León), 145–150 (Burgos 1301), 151–161 (Zamora 1301).

34. *CLC*, I, 161–165 (Medina del Campo 1302), 165–169 (Burgos 1302), 169–172 (Medina del Campo 1305, León), 172–179 (1305, Castile), 179–184 (1305, Extremadura), 184–197 (Valladolid 1307), 197–221 (Valladolid 1312).

35. *CLC*, I, 221–233, 233–247 (Palencia 1313), 147–272 (Burgos 1315, *hermandad*), 272–292 (Burgos 1315), 292–299 (1315, prelates), 299–329 (Carrión 1317), 330–336 (Medina del Campo 1318), 337–369 (Valladolid 1322), 369–372 (1322, abbots).

36. *CLC*, I, 372–389 (Valladolid 1325), 389–400 (1325, prelates), 401–437 (Madrid 1329), 456–476 (1339), 477–483 (Alcalá 1345), 483–492 (Burgos 1345), 593–626 (Alcalá 1348), 627–637 (León 1345); López Ferreiro, *Historia*, VI, no. 14, pp. 61–71 (Medina del Campo 1326, prelates).

37. Ubieto Arteta, *Cuéllar*, no. 21, pp. 60–66 (Seville 1264); *CLC*, I, 64–85 (Jerez 1268); Menéndez Pidal, *Documentos*, no. 229, pp. 300–302 (Peñafiel 1275); *MFIV*, II, nos. 510, 541, pp. 736–737, 789–790 (Palencia 1311); *CLC*, I, 443–456 (Burgos 1338).

38. Also Seville 1250; Valladolid 1282; Valladolid 1293 (art. 1 CLEM); Valladolid 1295 (art. 1); Cuéllar 1297 (art. 1); Valladolid 1298 (art. 5, 8); 1299 (art. 2 L, 14 C); Medina del Campo 1302 (art. 1–2); 1305 (art. 1 L, 11 CEL); Valladolid 1307, (art. 31); 1312 (art. 44, 84); Palencia 1313 (art. 13 M, 45 J); Burgos 1315 (art. 3, 55); Medina del Campo 1318 (art. 9, 24); Valladolid 1322 (art. 104); 1325 (art. 9, 24); Madrid 1329 (art. 1); 1339 (art. 1); Alcalá 1345 (art. 1); 1348 (art. 1).

39. Rodríguez Díez, *Astorga*, 720.

40. Confirmation is usually in an unnumbered paragraph at the end of the text. See Seville 1252, Valladolid 1258, Seville 1261, Palencia 1286, Haro 1288, Valladolid 1293, 1295, 1298, 1299, Burgos 1301, Zamora 1301, Medina del Campo 1302, 1305 (art. 14–15 LEM, 19 C), Valladolid 1307, 1312, Palencia 1313, Burgos 1315, Medina del Campo 1318, Valladolid 1322, 1325, Madrid 1329, Alcalá 1348.

41. Jerez 1268 (to Seville); Palencia 1286 (León); Cuéllar 1297 (Logroño).

42. *Posturas* (Seville 1252, Valladolid 1258, Jerez 1268); *privilegio* (Valladolid 1295, towns); *carta* (Valladolid 1295, prelates 1298, 1299; Burgos 1301, 1302; Valladolid 1322, 1325, bishops); *ordenamiento* (Zamora 1301, Burgos 1301, Medina del Campo 1302, Valladolid 1307, 1312; Medina del Campo 1318, Alcalá 1348); *cuaderno* (Medina del Campo 1305, Valladolid 1312, Palencia 1313, Burgos 1315, Carrión 1317, Medina del Campo 1318, Valladolid 1322; 1325, towns; Madrid 1329, Burgos 1338, Madrid 1339, Alcalá 1345, Burgos 1345, León 1345).

43. *CSIV*, 1, pp. 69–70; Loaysa, *Crónica*, 35, p. 114.

44. *Portugaliae Monumenta Historica, Leges* (Lisbon 1856), I, 183; *Cortes de los antiguos reinos de Aragón y de Valencia y Principado de Cataluña* (Madrid 1896–1919), I, pt. 1, p. 145; *Statutes of the Realm* (London 1810–1828), I, 189.

45. *Los Fueros de Aragón*, ed. Gunnar Tilander (Lund 1937), II, 7–8; García Gallo, *Manual*, II, nos. 1072, 1095, pp. 895–901, 933–936.

46. García Gallo, *Manual*, II, no. 151, pp. 95–96; *Cortes de . . . Cataluña*, I, 170; *Statutes of the Realm*, I, 297; *Rotuli Parliamentorum*, II, 126–131, 135–139.

CHAPTER 8

1. Miguel Ángel Ladero Quesada, "Las transformaciones de la fiscalidad regia castellano-leonesa en la segunda mital del siglo XIII (1252–1312)," *Historia de la Hacienda española (Homenaje al Profesor García de Valdeavellano* (Madrid 1982), 323–324; "Les Cortes de Castille et la politique financière de la Monarchie 1252–1369," *Parliaments, Estates and Representation* 4 (1984): 107–116; O'Callaghan, "The Cortes and Royal Taxation during the Reign of Alfonso X of Castile," *Traditio* 27 (1971): 379–398.
2. Juan Gil de Zamora, *Liber de preconiis Hispaniae*, III, 2–4, pp. 27–41; Álvaro Pelayo, *Speculum regum*, 240, 250.
3. Pereda Llarena, *Burgos 1254–1293*, no. 26, pp. 41–42; Ubieto Arteta, *Cuéllar*, no. 32, pp. 75–76; González Díez, *Burgos*, no. 125, p. 212.
4. *MFIV,* II, nos. 3–4, 541, 543–544, 546, pp. 7–13, 789–791, 793–799, 800–805; Ubieto Arteta, *Cuéllar*, no. 63, pp. 140–145; Pereda Llarena, *Burgos 1294–1316*, nos. 453–454, pp. 288–296.
5. González Díez, *Burgos*, no. 44, pp. 129–130; Ubieto Arteta, *Cuéllar*, no. 32, pp. 75–76; *CAX*, 75, pp. 59–60.
6. *CLC*, I, 99–106; *CSIV,* 8, p. 86.
7. Martín, *Salamanca*, no. 465, pp. 592–593; *CFIV,* 8–9, pp. 119–121.
8. *CAXI*, 12, 40, 80, pp. 182, 199, 222; Barrios García, *Alba de Tormes*, no. 29, pp. 97–99.
9. González Díez, *Burgos*, no. 44, pp. 129–130.
10. Post, "*Plena Postestas* and Consent in Medieval Assemblies," *Studies*, 91–162.
11. González, *Alfonso VIII*, II, no. 344, pp. 522–524; Rodrigo, *De rebus Hispaniae*, VIII, 3, pp. 177–178.
12. *Les Registres de Grégoire IX*, ed. Lucien Auvray (Paris 1896–1910), II, nos. 3315–3316, cols. 473–474; *Les Registres de Innocent IV*, ed. Elie Berger (Paris 1884–1921), I, no. 2538, p. 377.
13. Ballesteros, "Cortes de 1252," 114–143, art. 44; Martín, *Salamanca*, nos. 255, 262, pp. 341–342, 352–354; *MHE*, I, nos. 34–35, pp. 70–75; O'Callaghan, "Ecclesiastical Estate," 191–192.
14. *Les Registres de Clément IV*, ed. E. Jordan (Paris 1893–1945), nos. 890, 896, pp. 350–352; *Les Registres de Nicolas III*, ed. J. Gay (Paris 1898–1938), nos. 739–741, 743, pp. 338–340, 342–344.
15. José Goñi Gaztambide, *Historia de la bula de la cruzada en España* (Vitoria 1958), 299–300, 323–329.
16. Pereda Llarena, *Burgos 1254–1293*, no. 26, pp. 41–42; Fernández del Pulgar, *Palencia*, II, 340–341; Menéndez Pidal, *Documentos*, no. 201, p. 257; *CSIV,* 8, p. 96; Gaibrois, *Sancho IV*, II, 294–297; Ubieto Arteta, *Cuéllar*, no. 71, pp. 156–158; *MFIV,* II, no. 213, p. 316; *CAXI*, 40, 177, pp. 199, 287; Suárez Fernández, "Hermandades," no. 7, pp. 58–60.
17. *CLC*, I, 85–86; *CAX*, 25, p. 22; Serrano, *Covarrubias*, no. 124, pp. 158–159; *CAXI*, 154, p. 273.
18. Hilda Grassotti, "Un emprestíto para la conquista de Sevilla," *CHE*

45–46 (1967): 191–247; *MHE,* I, no. 33, p. 68; *MFIV,* II, nos. 3–4, pp. 6, 11; *CAXI,* 111, 128, 154, 183, pp. 245, 259, 273, 291.

19. González, *Alfonso IX,* II, no. 167, p. 237; Martín, *Salamanca,* no. 260, pp. 347–350; Mingüella, *Sigüenza,* I, no. 261, pp. 576–578; Fernández del Pulgar, *Palencia,* II, 338–339; Loperráez, *Osma,* III, no. 58, pp. 81–83; AM Toledo, cajón 10, legajo 1, no. 1; *MHE,* I, nos. 4, 132, pp. 5–8, 292–295, and II, no. 177, p. 27; O'Callaghan, "Beginnings," 1518–1520; "Ecclesiastical Estate," 192–193.

20. Ballesteros, *Alfonso X,* 225–228; *CAX,* 40, pp. 30–31; González Díez, *Burgos,* nos. 118, 120–122, 125, pp. 205–210, 212; *MHE,* II, no. 209, pp. 79–80.

21. Royal letter to Seville, 12 February era 1322 (recte 1326) or 1288, AM Sevilla, Tumbo, no. 29, fol. 30r–30v; Gaibrois, *Sancho IV,* I, clii–cliii, clvii–clviii, clxxiv–clxxv.

22. *CFIV,* 1, 20, pp. 96, 169; Loaysa, *Crónica,* 60, pp. 152–154; *CAXI,* 12, 40, 80, 82, 155, 282, pp. 182, 199, 222–224, 273, 354.

23. *MFIV,* II, no. 3, p. 4; *Fuero viejo,* I.1.1; *Partidas* (III.18.10).

24. Fernández del Pulgar, *Palencia,* II, 340–341; Pereda Llarena, *Burgos 1254–1293,* no. 26, pp. 41–42.

25. *CLC,* I, 85–86; *CAX,* 21, 23–25, pp. 17, 21–22; González Díez, *Burgos,* no. 40, pp. 124–125; Ubieto Arteta, *Cuéllar,* no. 23, p. 67.

26. *CAX,* 18, 47, pp. 13, 35; González Díez, *Burgos,* no. 42, pp. 127–128; AC Toledo, A3A17; AM León, no. 14; *MHE,* I, no. 137, p. 305; Palacio, *Madrid,* I, 119–122; Miguel Vigil, *Oviedo,* no. 36, p. 63; Ubieto Arteta, *Cuéllar,* no. 30, pp. 73–74; González, *Colección,* V, no. 59, pp. 189–190.

27. González Díez, *Burgos,* no. 44, pp. 129–130; AC Toledo, Z8D41; Menéndez Pidal, *Documentos,* no. 201, p. 257; Ballesteros, *Alfonso X,* 787, 793, 838; Procter, *Curia,* 191–192.

28. *MHE,* I, no. 140, pp. 308–324; Yitzhak Baer, *A History of the Jews in Christian Spain* (Philadelphia 1966), II, 126–128.

29. AM León, nos. 15–17; *MHE,* I, nos. 140–141, pp. 308–324; Ubieto Arteta, *Cuéllar,* nos. 32, 34, pp. 75–76, 78–79; *Colección diplomática de Riaza (1258–1457)* (Segovia 1959), no. 3, pp. 8–9; Miguel Vigil, *Oviedo,* no. 41, p. 75; Fernández del Pulgar, *Palencia,* III, 323; Berganza, *Antigüedades,* II, no. 183, p. 492; Juan Agapito y Revilla, *Los Privilegios de Valladolid* (Valladolid 1906), no. 33–XIV, p. 55; Colmenares, *Segovia,* I, 412–413; Mingüella, *Sigüenza,* I, no. 240, pp. 622–624; Fidel Fita, "La Guardia, villa del Partido de Lillo, Provincia de Toledo, datos históricos," *BRAH* 11 (1887): 413–414; Floriano, *Cáceres,* no. 8, p. 20; Dionisio Nogales Delicado, *Historia de la muy noble y leal ciudad de Ciudad Rodrigo* (Ciudad Rodrigo 1882), 65; Barrios García, *Alba de Tormes,* no. 13, p. 51.

30. Escudero de la Peña, "Súplica hecha al Papa Juan XXI para que absolviese al rey de Castilla, Don Alfonso X, del juramento de no acuñar otra moneda que los dineros prietos," *RABM* 2 (1872): 58–59.

31. *CAX,* 68–69, pp. 53–54; Ballesteros, *Alfonso X,* 785.

32. *MHE,* I, no. 153, pp. 339–341; González Díez, *Burgos,* nos. 77, 87–89, 92, 94, pp. 158–160, 169–172, 175, 177.

33. *CAX,* 75, pp. 59–60.

34. González Díez, *Burgos,* nos. 118, 120–122, 125, pp. 205–210, 212; *MHE,* II, no. 209, pp. 78–80; González, *Colección,* VI, no. 83, pp. 231–233; *CODOM,* III, no. 77, pp. 70–71.

35. González Díez, *Burgos*, no. 125, p. 212; Gaibrois, *Sancho IV*, I, cl–cli, clvii, clxxiii, and III, nos. 5, 83, pp. ii–iii, liii–liv.

36. Loaysa, *Crónica*, 57, p. 146; Gaibrois, *Sancho IV*, III, nos. 1, 15, pp. i, xi; González Díez, *Burgos*, no. 135, p. 220.

37. Ubieto Arteta, *Cuéllar*, no. 38, pp. 82–87; Baer, *Jews*, I, 131–132.

38. Gaibrois, *Sancho IV*, I, clx–clxiii, clxvii–clxviii, clxx, clxxviii, and III, no. 108, p. lxix.

39. *CLC*, I, 99–106; López Ferreiro, *Historia*, V, 45, pp. 123–124; Procter, *Curia*, 194; Gaibrois, *Sancho IV*, I, xxx, xxxvii, li, lv, lxiii, lxvi, lxix, lxxi, lxxxvii–lxxxviii.

40. *CSIV*, 8–9, p. 86; *CLC*, I, 125; Eliseo Vidal Beltrán, "Privilegios y franquicias de Tarifa," *Hispania* 17 (1957): 3–78.

41. Gaibrois, *Sancho IV*, I, pp. xxx–xxxi, xxxvi–xxxix, xlviii, li, lv, lxiii, lxxx, xci.

42. Barrios García, *Alba de Tormes*, no. 16, pp. 57–58; Gaibrois, *Sancho IV*, III, nos. 500, 506, 592, pp. cccliii–ccliv, cccxlvi–cccxlvii, cdiv–cdvii.

43. *CSIV*, 10–11, pp. 87–89; Gaibrois, *Sancho IV*, II, 294–297, and III, nos. 524–529, 535–540, 544–546, 548, 562, 570–571, pp. ccclx–ccclxv, ccclxviii–ccclxxiv, cclxxxi–ccclxxxii, ccclxxxvi–ccclxxxviii; "Tarifa y la política de Sancho IV de Castilla," *BRAH* 76 (1920): 430–433, 437–439, and *BRAH* 77 (1920): 212–215.

44. *MFIV*, II, nos. 1, 3–4, pp. 1–13; Valdeavellano, "Carta de Hermandad," 70–74; *CFIV*, 1, pp. 93, 96; Loaysa, *Crónica*, 60–61, pp. 152–154; *CLC*, I, 134.

45. *CFIV*, 2, 4–6, 8–9, pp. 108, 111, 115–116, 119–122; *MFIV*, II, no. 135, pp. 188–189; Miguel Vigil, *Oviedo*, nos. 69–70, pp. 110–111; Martín, *Salamanca*, no. 465, pp. 592–593; AC Toledo Z8D43.

46. Loaysa, *Crónica*, 87, p. 195; *CFIV*, 10–11, pp. 125–127, 133.

47. José Sánchez Herrero, *Concilios provinciales y sínodos toledanos de los siglos XIV y XV* (Seville 1976), no. 1, pp. 165–172; Martínez Marina, *Teoría*, *BAE*, CCXIX, 201; *MFIV*, II, nos. 208, 214, 223–224, pp. 307, 316, 335–338; López Ferreiro, *Fueros*, 313–314.

48. *CFIV*, 11, p. 133; *MFIV*, II, no. 271, pp. 404–405; Ubieto Arteta, *Cuéllar*, no. 54, pp. 210–215; Palacio, *Madrid*, I, 181–188.

49. *CFIV*, 13–14, pp. 139–140, 144, 146; Giménez Soler, *Juan Manuel*, no. 120, pp. 315–316; *MFIV*, II, no. 349, p. 516.

50. *CFIV*, 15, p. 151; *CLC*, I, 184–197; AC Toledo, Z8D48, Z8D49; Francisco Hernández, *Los Cartularios de Toledo: Catálogo documental* (Madrid 1985), no. 513, p. 453; Villar y Macías, *Salamanca*, IV, 93; González Mínguez, *Fernando IV*, no. 23, p. 374; *MFIV*, II, no. 385, pp. 565–566; Pereda Llarena, *Burgos 1294–1316*, no. 420, pp. 244–245.

51. Colmeiro, I, 209; Piskorski, 150; González Mínguez, *Fernando IV*, 242.

52. *CFIV*, 16, p. 160; AM Cuenca, legajo 2, no. 5; *MFIV*, II, no. 408, pp. 605–607; O'Callaghan, "Cortes de Fernando IV," 324–328.

53. *CFIV*, 16, p. 162; Giménez Soler, *Juan Manuel*, nos. 192–195, pp. 364–365.

54. *CFIV*, 20, p. 169; AC Toledo, Z8D410; Hernández, *Toledo*, no. 515, p. 454; *MFIV*, II, nos. 243, 582–583, pp. 365–367, 861–863.

55. Juan Ignacio Ruíz de la Peña, "La hermandad leonesa de 1313," *León medieval* (León 1978), 139–164; *CLC*, I, 223, 236.

56. Suárez Fernández, "Hermandades," no. 7, pp. 58–60; José Antonio García Luján, *Privilegios reales de la Catedral de Toledo (1086–1462). Formación del patrimonio de la S.I.C.P. a través de las donaciones reales* (Toledo 1982), II, no. 99, pp. 233–235; Serrano, *Covarrubias*, no. 124, pp. 158–159; Pereda Llarena, *Burgos 1294–1316*, no. 469, pp. 319–320.

57. *CAXI*, 8, p. 179, and *GCAXI*, ch. 9, vol. I, p. 295; Miguel Vigil, *Oviedo*, no. 104, p. 169; *CLC*, I, 316 (Carrión 1317, art. 45).

58. Ubieto Arteta, *Cuéllar*, no. 71, pp. 156–158; López Ferreiro, *Historia*, V, no. 61, pp. 175–178: Pereda Llarena, *Burgos 1294–1316*, no. 491, pp. 360–363; *CAXI* 8–9, p. 180; *GCAXI*, ch. 10, 12, vol. I, pp. 296, 299.

59. *CAXI*, 10, 12, pp. 180–182; *GCAXI*, ch. 13, 16, vol. I, pp. 301, 307; Giménez Soler, *Juan Manuel*, no. 337, p. 472; Barrios García, *Alba de Tormes*, no. 29, pp. 97–99.

60. *CAXI*, 19–27, 29, 31, pp. 187–193, 195; *GCAXI*, ch. 24–34, 40, 42, vol. I, pp. 327–346, 353, 359 and ch. 34, vol. II, pp. 471–472; Giménez Soler, *Juan Manuel*, no. 380, p. 504.

61. *CAXI*, 40, p. 199; *GCAXI*, ch. 52, vol. I, p. 378; González, *Colección*, V, no. 107, pp. 319–320.

62. López Ferreiro, *Historia*, VI, nos. 14–15, pp. 61–72; *ES*, XVI, 253; *CAXI*, 80, pp. 222–224; *GCAXI*, ch. 101, 103, vol. I, pp. 467–468, 472–473.

63. *CAXI*, 154–155, 177, 196, 253–255, pp. 273–274, 287, 298, 330–331; *GCAXI*, ch. 176–177, 332–335, vol. II, pp. 125–127, 443–449.

64. Ladero Quesada, "Transformaciones," 332–333; Asunción López Dapena, *Cuentas y gastos (1292–1294) del Rey D. Sancho IV el Bravo (1284–1295)* (Córdoba 1984).

65. González, *Alfonso IX*, II, no. 167, p. 237; *CLC*, I, 85–86; *CAX*, 18, p. 13; *MHE*, I, nos. 137, 140–141, pp. 305, 308–324; *MFIV*, II, no. 271, pp. 404–405.

66. Hilda Grassotti, "Un empréstito para la conquista de Sevilla" *CHE* 45–46 (1967): 191–247; González Díez, *Burgos*, nos. 44, 77, pp. 129–130, 158–160; *CAXI*, 27, pp. 191–192.

67. *MHE*, I, no. 140, pp. 309–310; *CAX*, 40, p. 31; González, *Colección*, VI, no. 258, pp. 117–118; Klein, *The Mesta*, 257; Procter, *Curia*, 195–196.

68. Zamora 1301 (art. 33–34); Medina del Campo 1302 (art. 7 L); Valladolid 1318 (art. 16); Madrid 1339 (art. 4, 28); Alcalá 1345 (art. 7), 1348 (art. 43).

69. *CAX*, 26, 39, pp. 22, 30; *CLC*, I, 85–86; Quintana Prieto, *San Pedro de los Montes*, no. 375, p. 483.

70. *CAX*, 18, p. 13; González Díez, *Burgos*, nos. 38, 85, pp. 121, 168; Gaibrois, *Sancho IV*, III, no. 592, pp. cdiv–cdvii; *CFIV*, 1, p. 93; *MFIV*, II, nos. 1, 4, pp. 1–2, 8.

71. *CAXI*, 128, p. 259; *GCAXI*, ch. 150, vol. II, pp. 75–76; AM Murcia, Cartulario 1332–1382 Eras, fol. 110v–111v; Salvador de Moxó, *La Alcabala. Sus orígenes, concepto y naturaleza* (Madrid 1963).

72. *CAXI*, 259–263, pp. 335–338.

73. Miguel Ángel Ladero Quesada and Manuel González, "La población en la Frontera de Gibraltar y el Repartimiento de Vejer (Siglos XIII y XIV)," *HID* 4 (1977), no. 21, pp. 244–245.

74. Pedro I, 18 January 1351, *CODOM*, VII, no. 19, pp. 23–28.

75. *CAX*, 18, p. 13; *MHE*, I, nos. 137, 140–141, pp. 305, 308–324; O'Callaghan, "The Cortes and Royal Taxation," 387–391.

76. *CFIV,* 2, 4–6, 8–11, 13–16, 20, pp. 108, 111, 115–116, 119–122, 125–127, 133, 139–140, 144, 146, 151, 162, 169.

77. *CAXI,* 8, 10, 12, 40, 80, pp. 179–182, 199, 222–224; García Luján, *Toledo,* II, no. 99, pp. 233–235; Serrano, *Covarrubias,* no. 124, pp. 158–159; Pereda Llarena, *Burgos 1294–1316,* no. 469, pp. 319–320; Miguel Vigil, *Oviedo,* no. 104, p. 169; Barrios García, *Alba de Tormes,* no. 29, pp. 97–99; González, *Colección,* V, no. 1207, pp. 319–320; López Ferreiro, *Historia,* VI, nos. 14–15, pp. 61–72.

78. *CFIV,* 15–16, pp. 159–160; AM Cuenca, legajo 2, no. 5; O'Callaghan, "Cortes de Fernando IV," 324–328; *MFIV,* II, no. 408, pp. 605–607.

79. *CAXI,* 8–10, pp. 179–181.

80. *CAXI,* 80, 82, pp. 223–224; Sánchez Belda, *Galicia,* no. 1041, p. 441 (12 December 1329).

81. *MHE,* I, no. 140, pp. 309–324; O'Callaghan, "Cortes and Royal Taxation," 390–391; Baer, *Jews,* I, 126–128.

82. Gaibrois, *Sancho IV,* I, clxxx–clxxxviii; *CSIV,* 4, pp. 75–76; Baer, *Jews,* I, 132–133; Procter, *Curia,* 200.

83. Haro 1288 (art. 20–21); Valladolid 1293 (art. 9 CE); 1295 (art. 5); 1299 (art. 13); 1300 (art. 3, 7); Burgos 1301 (art. 16, 19); Zamora 1301 (art. 14); Medina del Campo 1302 (art. 5–6, 8, 19); 1305 (art. 9–10 C, 8 E, 9 L); Valladolid 1307 (art. 16); Palencia 1313 (art. 7, 31 J, 20 M); Burgos 1315 (art. 6); Carrión 1317 (art. 8, 20, 50); Valladolid 1322 (art. 18–19, 82); 1325 (art. 24–25); Madrid 1339 (art. 20).

84. Carrión 1317 (art. 45); Alcalá 1348 (art. 21, 50); Ubieto Arteta, *Cuéllar,* no. 54, p. 122; *MFIV,* II, no. 491, p. 706; Serrano, *Covarrubias,* no. 118, pp. 153–154.

85. Seville 1252 (art. 36); 1261 (art. 18); Palencia 1286 (art. 13); Burgos 1301 (art. 3); Zamora 1301 (art. 20); Burgos 1308 (art. 12); Madrid 1339 (art. 19).

86. Seville 1252 (art. 34); Jerez 1268 (art. 42–43); Haro 1288 (art. 23); Valladolid 1300 (art. 8, 16); Burgos 1301 (art. 4); Medina del Campo 1302 (art. 16); Burgos 1308 (art. 25); Palencia 1313 (art. 7 J, 20 M); Burgos 1315 (art. 6); Carrión 1317 (art. 50); Valladolid 1322 (art. 18).

87. Madrid 1339 (art. 2, 27); León 1345 (art. 3, 20); Alcalá 1348 (art. 28); Valladolid 1293 (art. 10, 18 C).

88. Valladolid 1293 (art. 9 C); Carrión 1317 (art. 13).

89. Valladolid 1300 (art. 16); Burgos 1301 (art. 4); Zamora 1301 (art. 20); Carrión 1317 (art. 17); Valladolid 1322 (art. 26).

90. *MHE,* II, no. 177, p. 27; Valladolid 1293 (art. 14a, 14b); Zamora 1301 (art. 35); Medina del Campo 1305 (art. 11 L); Valladolid 1307 (art. 35 to Vitoria); Palencia 1313 (art. 26, 30, 36, 39 M); Burgos 1315 (art. 40–42, 44); Medina del Campo 1318 (art. 11); Valladolid 1322 (art. 68–70, 74); Salvador de Moxó, "Exenciones tributarias en Castilla a fines de la edad media," *Hispania* 21 (1961): 163–188.

91. Haro 1288 (art. 4–27); Valladolid 1293 (art. 9 C, 14 M, 15 LE); 1312 (art. 105); Carrión 1317 (art. 10–12, 45); Valladolid 1325 (art. 34–35, 39); Madrid 1339 (art. 3).

92. *Portugaliae Monumenta Historica, Leges,* I, 183, 196–197, 210; José Coroleu and José Pella y Forgas, *Las Cortes catalanas,* 2d ed. (Barcelona 1876), 114–115.

93. John Bell Henneman, *Royal Taxation in Fourteenth Century France: The*

Development of War Financing 1322–1356 (Princeton 1971), 167–177, 227–238, 264–301.

94. *Statutes of the Realm*, I, 289–290; *Rotuli Parliamentorum*, II, 126–131.

CHAPTER 9

1. Valladolid 1295, art. 3; Palencia 1313, art. 6 J, 3 M.

2. *Espéculo*, II.12–13; *Partidas*, II.9.5, 26.

3. Valladolid 1258, art. 7, 16–17; Seville 1261, art. 2–3; Valladolid 1307, art. 12; Burgos 1308, art. 16; Valladolid 1312, art. 38, 88.

4. Valladolid 1307, art. 12; Madrid 1329, art. 23.

5. Valladolid 1298, art. 4; Medina del Campo 1302, art. 15; also Valladolid 1300, art. 11; Burgos 1304, art. 4; Nilda Guglielmi, "Posada y Yantar: Contribución al estudio del léxico de las instituciones medievales," *Hispania* 26 (1966): 5–40, 165–219.

6. Valladolid 1307 (art. 10), probably due to a copyist's error, specified ten years, but Valladolid 1312 (art. 91) gave six.

7. Palencia 1313, art. 24 J, 29 M; Burgos 1315, art. 23; Carrión 1317, art. 27; Valladolid 1322, art. 99.

8. Valladolid 1325, art. 27; Alcalá 1348, art. 49; Valladolid 1325, art. 12 P.

9. Valladolid 1295, art. 10; 1307, art. 9; Palencia 1313, art. 12 J, 37 M; Burgos 1315, art. 12; Valladolid 1322, art. 36; 1325, art. 27.

10. Valladolid 1307, art. 11–12; 1312, art. 98; Madrid 1339, art. 30; Alcalá 1345, art. 14; 1348, art. 37.

11. Valladolid 1325, art. 30; Alcalá 1345, art. 14; 1348, art. 27.

12. Valladolid 1312, art. 35, 37; *Partidas*, II.9.15.

13. *Espéculo*, II.14.2–3; *Fuero real*, II.3.8; *Partidas*, II.16.1–4; Valladolid 1300, art. 13, 22; Medina del Campo 1305, art. 5; Burgos 1308, art. 20; Valladolid 1322, art. 101; Madrid 1329, art. 10.

14. Burgos 1308, art. 19–20, 22; Valladolid 1312, art. 76, 93.

15. Valladolid 1299, art. 7 L; Burgos 1308, art. 15; Valladolid 1312, art. 1–26.

16. *Espéculo*, II.12.2; *Partidas*, II.9.4; Agustín Millares Carlo, "La cancillería real en León y Castilla hasta fines del reinado de Fernando III," *AHDE* 3 (1926): 227–306; Procter, "The Castilian Chancery during the Reign of Alfonso X, 1252–1284," *Oxford Essays in Medieval History presented to Herbert E. Salter* (Oxford 1934), 104–121; Luis Sánchez Belda, "La cancillería castellana durante el reinado de Sancho IV (1284–1295)," *AHDE* 21–22 (1951–1952): 171–223.

17. Valladolid 1295, art. 8; 1299, art. 2; Palencia 1313, art. 10 J, 19 M; Burgos 1315, art. 9–10.

18. Valladolid 1293, art. 5 L; 1299, art. 2; *Espéculo* IV.12.14; *Partidas*, II.9.7.

19. Valladolid 1295, art. 8–9; 1299, art. 5–6 L; 1307, art. 4; Filemón Arribas Arranz, "Los registros de cancillería de Castilla," *BRAH* 162 (1968): 171–200.

20. Burgos 1301, art. 1; Medina del Campo 1305, art. 2 CL.

21. Valladolid 1312, art. 9–18, 24–26, 29–30; *Espéculo*, II.12.6; IV.12.1–2, 5–7; *Partidas*, II.9.8, III.19.5.

22. Valladolid 1293, art. 15 M, 16 CLE; Palencia 1313, art. 10 J, 18 M; also Valladolid 1312, art. 39; Madrid 1329, art. 30.

23. Valladolid 1293, art. 16 L, 17 C; 1299, art. 5 G; 1300, art. 4; Burgos 1301, art. 22; Zamora 1301, art. 8; Medina del Campo 1302, art. 3–4; 1305, art. 2, 8, 11 C, 7 LE; Valladolid 1307, art. 3, 22, 32; 1312, art. 33–34, 80; Palencia 1313, art. 19 M; Carrión 1317, art. 54; Valladolid 1325, art. 34 P; Madrid 1329, art. 77; León 1345, art. 2. Benjamín González Alonso, "La fórmula 'Obedézcase pero no se cumpla' en el derecho castellano de la baja edad media," *AHDE* 50 (1980): 469–487; José Luis Bermejo Cabrera, "La idea medieval de contrafuero en León y Castilla," *Revista de estudios políticos* 187 (1973): 299–306.

24. Valladolid 1295, art. 9; 1312, art. 42; Palencia 1313, art. 11 J; Burgos 1315, art. 11; Valladolid 1322, art. 35; 1325, art. 3; Madrid 1329, art. 33; 1339, art. 1.

25. Palencia 1286, art. 9; Medina del Campo 1302, art. 15 LE; Valladolid 1307, art. 5; 1322, art. 8; 1325, art. 5; Madrid 1329, art. 31; also Valladolid 1298, art. 6; 1299, art. 2 G; Medina del Campo 1305, art. 7 C; Palencia 1313, art. 19 M; Madrid 1329, art. 87.

26. Medina del Campo 1302, art. 14 L; 1318, art. 12, 15; Miguel Ángel Pérez de la Canal, "La justicia de la corte de Castilla durante los siglos XIII al XV," *HID* 2 (1975): 383–481.

27. *Espéculo*, IV.2.12; *Partidas*, III.3.5; Ordinance of Zamora 1274, art. 46; Aquilino Iglesia Ferreirós, "Las cortes de Zamora de 1274 y los casos de corte," *AHDE* 41 (1971): 945–972.

28. Seville 1264, art. 10; Valladolid 1293, art. 13 M, 14 LE; Burgos 1301, art. 7; Zamora 1301, art. 12. See also the Ordinance of Zamora, art. 27; Medina del Campo 1305, art. 22; 1318, art. 17–18; Madrid 1339, art. 6; Burgos 1345, art. 7.

29. Valladolid 1258, art. 8; Seville 1261, art. 13; Zamora 1274, art. 42–44.

30. Medina del Campo 1305, art. 15–16 C; Valladolid 1307, art. 1; 1312, art. 1, 46; Madrid 1329, art. 1, 76; 1339, art. 22; León 1345, art. 21; Alcalá 1348, art. 23.

31. *Espéculo*, IV.2.1–3; *Partidas*, II.9.18, III.4; Valladolid 1293, art. 4 C; 1307, art. 2; Palencia 1313, art. 8 M, 19 J; Burgos 1315, art. 19; Carrión 1317, art. 5; Valladolid 1322, art. 9; 1325, art. 2; Madrid 1329, art. 2.

32. Zamora 1274, art. 17; Valladolid 1293, art. 20 C; Zamora 1301, art. 1; Valladolid 1307, art. 1–2; Madrid 1329, art. 4.

33. Valladolid 1312, art. 3, 5, 46; Medina del Campo 1318, art. 21.

34. Valladolid 1258, art. 18; Seville 1261, art. 14; Zamora 1274, art. 24, 33–34; Valladolid 1312, art. 4; Palencia 1313, art. 19 J; Burgos 1315, art. 19; Valladolid 1322, art. 2; 1325, art. 2; Madrid 1329, art. 2; Ordinance of Villarreal 1346, art. 1–2; Ordinance of Alcalá 1348, XX.1.2.

35. Valladolid 1298, art. 7; 1299, art. 2 G, 8 L; 1300, art. 6.

36. Valladolid 1293, art. 9 LE, 14 C; 1300, art. 6; Palencia 1313, art. 8 M, 19 J; Burgos 1315, art. 19; Valladolid 1318, art. 21; 1325, art. 2.

37. *CAX*, 23–25, 40, pp. 19–24, 30–31.

38. *Espéculo*, IV.2.11; *Partidas*, II.9.19, III.23.17–20; Valladolid 1312, art. 29, 78; Ordinance of Alcalá 1348, XIII and XIV.

39. Seville 1252, art. 35; 1253, art. 1 L; Valladolid 1295, art. 13; 1299, art. 14 L.

40. Valladolid 1258, art. 9; Seville 1264, art. 17; Zamora 1274, art. 16–17, 22–34, 47; Valladolid 1312, art. 45; Alcalá 1348, art. 40; *Espéculo*, IV.2.7; *Partidas*, III.4.7–8, 12.

41. Zamora 1274, art. 18, 36–39, 41; Valladolid 1299, art. 8 L; 1307, art. 3; 1312, art. 5–6, 8, 11, 40; Carrión 1317, art. 23–24; Valladolid 1322, art. 12–13; Ordinance of Alcalá 1348, XV.

42. Seville 1252, art. 16; Zamora 1301, art. 29.

43. Seville 1252, art. 37; 1253, art. 60 L; Valladolid 1258, art. 38; Seville 1261, art. 26; Zamora 1274, art. 1–16; Valladolid 1312, art. 23, 27–28; Madrid 1329, art. 32; *Espéculo*, IV.9; *Fuero real*, I.9.2; *Partidas*, III.6; Ordinance of Alcalá 1348, III.

44. Valladolid 1312, art. 48, 51–58; also *Espéculo*, II.13.5; *Partidas*, II.9.20; Zamora 1274, art. 30; Palencia 1313, art. 18 J; Burgos 1315, art. 34; Carrión 1317, art. 25; Valladolid 1322, art. 66; Madrid 1329, art. 5–10; Alcalá 1348, art. 28; Ordinance of Alcalá 1348, XX.3.6.

45. *Espéculo*, II.13.4–5, IV.3.1–7, 11–13, 18; *Leyes para los Adelantados mayores*, in *Opúsculos legales*, II, 173–177; *CAX*, 25, p. 21; Palencia 1311, art. 2; Ordinance of Alcalá 1348, XX.7.9; Rogelio Pérez Bustamante, *El gobierno y la administración territorial de Castilla (1230–1474)* (Madrid 1976), I, 48–57, 63–71, 200–202, 299–301.

46. Burgos 1301, art. 5; 1308, art. 14; Valladolid 1312, art. 60; Palencia 1313, art. 5, 21 J; Burgos 1315, art. 20; Carrión 1317, art. 28; Valladolid 1322, art. 49; Madrid 1329, art. 11, 19, 21; 1339, art. 16; León 1345, art. 4.

47. Seville 1253, art. 19 L; González, *Alfonso IX*, II, nos. 11–12, 84–85, pp. 23–28, 125–129.

48. Valladolid 1312, art. 68, 79–80; 1322, art. 50; 1325, art. 16; Madrid 1329, art. 78–79; also Carrión 1317, art. 28.

49. Seville 1253, art. 14, 20 L; Palencia 1286, art. 8; Valladolid 1293, art. 6 C; Medina del Campo 1305, art. 8; Valladolid 1307, art. 36 (Vitoria); 1312, art. 65, 79; 1325, art. 16; 1325, art. 13 P; Madrid 1329, art. 14; Alcalá 1348, art. 15; also Valladolid 1299, art. 12; 1300, art. 15; Palencia 1311, art. 6 (nobles); Burgos 1315, art. 37.

50. Seville 1253, art. 10, 15 L; Valladolid 1298, art. 10; 1312, art. 63, 67; Madrid 1329, art. 12, 15–17; 1339, art. 7, 9; León 1345, art. 4.

51. Seville 1253, art. 15–17 L; Palencia 1286, art. 8; Valladolid 1312, art. 59, 61–62, 64, 66, 69, 71–72, 75; Palencia 1313, art. 5, 21, 41 J; Burgos 1315, art. 20, 35; Carrión 1317, art. 48–49; Valladolid 1322, art. 17, 49; Madrid 1329, art. 11, 18–20.

52. Valladolid 1298, art. 12; Medina del Campo 1305, art. 1, 17 C, 3 E; Valladolid 1307, art. 31 (Vitoria); 1312, art. 92; 1325, art. 36.

53. Cuéllar 1297, art. 3–7; Valladolid 1298, art. 1–2; 1300, art. 1–2, 24, 27; Burgos 1301, art. 15, 21; Zamora 1301, art. 2, 7, 24.

54. León 1188, González, *Alfonso IX*, II, no. 11, p. 25; Seville 1253, art. 2 L; Valladolid 1307, art. 27; Palencia 1313, art. 23 J; Burgos 1315, art. 22; Valladolid 1322, art. 52; 1325, art. 21; Madrid 1329, art. 75.

55. Valladolid 1299, art. 11; Burgos 1301, art. 9; Zamora 1301, art. 3; Medina del Campo 1302, art. 15; 1305, art. 10 L; Valladolid 1307, art. 8; Burgos 1308, art. 7–8; Palencia 1311, art. 4 (nobles); Valladolid 1312, art. 89; Palencia 1313, art. 42 J, 32, 46 M; Burgos 1315, art. 50; Carrión 1317, art. 34; Medina

del Campo 1318, art. 22–23; Valladolid 1322, art. 39, 78–80, 89; 1325, art. 17; Madrid 1329, art. 70, 74.

56. Valladolid 1312, art. 79–80; Carrión 1317, art. 28; Madrid 1339, art. 16; León 1345, art. 4; Salustiano Moreta, *Malhechores feudales: Violencia, antagonismos y alianzas de clases en Castilla, Siglos XIII–XIV* (Madrid 1978), 58–59.

57. Seville 1250; Palencia 1286, art. 11–12; Valladolid 1293, art. 3 E; 1295, art. 6; Zamora 1301, art. 17, 26; Medina del Campo 1302, art. 21 L; 1305, art. 21 (Salinas de Añana); Valladolid 1307, art. 14; Burgos 1308, art. 4–5, 47; Palencia 1313, art. 9 J, 14 M; Burgos 1315, art. 8; Valladolid 1322, art. 31–32, 34; 1325, art. 7; Madrid 1329, art. 46–48; 1339, art. 24, 29.

58. Medina del Campo 1305, art. 4, 10 E, 13 C; Valladolid 1307, art. 15; Burgos 1308, art. 4; Madrid 1329, art. 9.

59. Palencia 1286, art. 2; Valladolid 1293, art. 2–3 LEM; Palencia 1313, art. 14 J, 41M; Burgos 1315, art. 14, 49; Valladolid 1322, art. 77; 1325, art. 18; Madrid 1329, art. 69.

60. Valladolid 1307, art. 29; Palencia 1313, art. 38 M; Burgos 1315, art. 45; *CAX*, 23–24, pp. 19–21.

61. Palencia 1286, art. 2; Valladolid 1307, art. 25.

62. Valladolid 1298, art. 8; Medina del Campo 1305, art. 1 E, 3 L, 4 C; Valladolid 1307, art. 7; 1312, art. 82; Palencia 1313, art. 8 J, 29 M; Burgos 1315, art. 7; Medina del Campo 1318, art. 20; Valladolid 1322, art. 27, 87; Madrid 1329, art. 79; Alcalá 1348, art. 11.

63. Palencia 1286, art. 4; Valladolid 1293, art. 4 LEM; Zamora 1301, art. 6; Medina del Campo 1302, art. 18; 1305, art. 5 L; Valladolid 1307, art. 13; 1312, art. 81, 97; Palencia 1313, art. 8, 22 J, 23 M; Burgos 1315, art. 21; Carrión 1317, art. 28–29; Valladolid 1322, art. 51; 1325, art. 11; Madrid 1329, art. 66.

64. Agustín Bermúdez Aznar, *El corregidor en Castilla durante la baja edad media, 1348–1474* (Madrid 1974).

65. Seville 1252, art. 35; 1253, art. 17; Medina del Campo 1305, art. 9 L; Valladolid 1312, art. 48.

66. Valladolid 1293, art. 13 M, 14 LE; Burgos 1301, art. 7; Zamora 1301, art. 12; Medina del Campo 1318, art. 18; also Palencia 1313, art. 43 J; Burgos 1315, art. 36; Carrión 1317, art. 26, 37; Valladolid 1322, art. 28.

67. Valladolid 1293, art. 6 LEM, 13, 22 C; 1299, art. 10–12 G; Palencia 1313, art. 47 M; Burgos 1315, art. 48; Medina del Campo 1318, art. 20.

68. Valladolid 1293, art. 5 LEM, 19 C; Zamora 1301, art. 5; Medina del Campo 1302, art. 18 L; 1305, art. 4 L, 5 E, 6 C; Valladolid 1307, art. 20; 1312, art. 49; Palencia 1313, art. 15 J; Burgos 1315, art. 15; Valladolid 1322, art. 42; 1325, art. 12. Also *Fuero real*, I.8.1–7; *Espéculo*, IV.12.3, 8–10.

69. Valladolid 1293, art. 5 E; 1299, art. 6 G; Medina del Campo 1302, art. 17–18 E; 1305, art. 4 L, 5 E, 6 C; Burgos 1308, art. 27; Madrid 1329, art. 43.

70. *Espéculo*, IV.12.54–60; *Fuero real*, I.8.1; Valladolid 1293, art. 5 LEM, 19 C; Zamora 1301, art. 5; Valladolid 1325, art. 12.

71. Medina del Campo 1305, art. 4 L; Valladolid 1307, art. 20.

72. Burgos 1301, art. 17; Zamora 1301, art. 2, 17; Burgos 1315, art. 51; Valladolid 1322, art. 93.

73. *MHE*, I, nos. 43–45, pp. 89–100; Ureña, *Fuero de Cuenca*, 861–862; Loperráez, *Osma*, III, nos. 60–61, pp. 86–185; Layna Serrano, *Atienza*, 503–504.

74. Ubieto Arteta, *Cuéllar*, no. 21, pp. 60–66; Iglesia Ferreirós, "Privilegio

general concedido a las Extremaduras," 460–477; Palacio, *Madrid*, I, 85–92; *MHE*, I, nos. 91, 202, pp. 202–203, 224–226; Valladolid 1293, art. 10 E.

75. Palencia 1286, art. 5; Carrión 1317, art. 9; Ubieto Arteta, *Cuéllar*, no. 54, pp. 121–122.

76. Valladolid 1293, art. 11, 12 LE; Carrión 1317, art. 25; Medina del Campo 1318, art. 13; Valladolid 1322, art. 83; Madrid 1329, art. 49; Ubieto Arteta, *Cuéllar*, no. 54, pp. 121–122; AM Cuenca, legajo 2, no. 12.

77. Valladolid 1293, art. 3 G; 1300, art. 12; Burgos 1301, preamble; Zamora 1301, art. 30; Medina del Campo 1302, art. 16 L; Valladolid 1307, art. 34 (Vitoria); Carrión 1317, art. 9; Valladolid 1322, art. 84; Madrid 1329, art. 49; 1339, art. 33; Alcalá 1348, art. 46.

78. Valladolid 1293, art. 3 C; 1295, art. 11; Burgos 1301, art. 9; Valladolid 1307, art. 21; Palencia 1313, art. 13 J, 15, 17, 22, 33 M; Burgos 1315, art. 13; Carrión 1317, art. 32; Valladolid 1322, art. 37–38; 1325, art. 6; Madrid 1329, art. 39; 1339, art. 10; *Espéculo*, II.7.

79. González, *Fernando II*, no. 41, pp. 305–307; *Alfonso IX*, II, no. 662, pp. 737–738; "Sobre la fecha de las cortes de Nájera," *CHE* 61–62 (1977): 357–361; O'Callaghan, "Una nota sobre las llamadas cortes de Benavente," *Archivos Leoneses* 37 (1983): 97–100.

80. Haro 1288, art. 13; Valladolid 1299, art. 7; Zamora 1301, art. 13; Valladolid 1307, art. 23; *Espéculo*, II.5.1, V.11.33; *Partidas*, II.15.5; *Castigos e Documentos*, 11, 14, pp. 114, 119.

81. Gaibrois, *Sancho IV*, III, no. 173, pp. civ–cv; Mañueco Villalobos and Zurita Nieto, *Santa María la mayor de Valladolid*, II, no. 94, pp. 122–124; Valladolid 1293, art. 17 C; 1300, art. 21; Zamora 1301, art. 4.

82. Valladolid 1295, art. 7; Cuéllar, 1297, art. 3; Valladolid 1298, art. 9; 1299, art. 7; 1300, art. 21; Burgos 1301, art. 6; Medina del Campo 1305, art. 12 C; Valladolid 1307, art. 8.

83. Palencia 1313, art. 3 J, 9, 50 M; Burgos 1315, art. 2, 54; Valladolid 1322, art. 2, 81.

84. Ubieto Arteta, *Cuéllar*, nos. 71–72, pp. 156–159 (1316); López Ferreiro, *Historia*, VI, nos. 14–15, pp. 61–72 (1326); Serrano, *Covarrubias*, nos. 157–158, pp. 185–186 (1339); Valladolid 1325, art. 10, 20; Madrid 1329, art. 38; Burgos 1345, art. 9.

85. Zamora 1301, art. 4; Palencia 1313, art. 43 M; Burgos 1315, art. 46; Valladolid 1322, art. 29–30, 31, 33, 96–99, 102.

86. González, *Alfonso IX*, II, no. 11, pp. 23–24; Palencia 1286, art. 7; Haro 1288, art. 22; Valladolid 1299, art. 1 G, 3 L; 1300, art. 26; Burgos 1301, art. 4; Zamora 1301, art. 8, 19; Valladolid 1307, art. 30; Palencia 1313, art. 14, 41, 43 J; Burgos 1315, art. 35–36; Carrión 1317, art. 68; Valladolid 1325, art. 3, 8, 16, 26; Burgos 1345, art. 13.

87. *Espéculo*, III.11; *Fuero real*, II.8.3; *Partidas*, III.17; Procter, *The Judicial Use of Pesquisa in León and Castile 1157–1369. English Historical Review*, Supplement 2 (London 1966).

88. Palencia 1286, art. 7, 11; Valladolid 1298, art. 11; 1299, art. 4 GL; Burgos 1304, art. 1; Valladolid 1307, art. 34; 1312, art. 66, 72, 74, 85–86; Palencia 1313, art. 24 M; Burgos 1315, art. 39; Valladolid 1322, art. 67; 1325, art. 31; Madrid 1329, art. 62, 88.

89. Seville 1252, art. 34, 36; 1253, art. 6, 18, 21, 58, 60; 1261, art. 18; Haro 1288, art. 23; Valladolid 1298, art. 2; 1299, art. 10; Burgos 1301, art. 3–4; Me-

dina del Campo 1302, art. 16 E, 19 L; 1305, art. 5 E, 13 L; Valladolid 1307, art. 26; 1312, art. 70; Burgos 1315, art. 48; Carrión 1317, art. 48–49; Valladolid 1322, art. 76; *Fuero real*, III.19.2, 5.

90. González, *Alfonso IX*, II, no. 12, pp. 25–28; Valladolid 1293, art. 10 LEM.

91. León 1188, art. 5; Seville 1253, art. 2 L; Valladolid 1298, art. 12; Zamora 1301, art. 16, 31; Medina del Campo 1305, 1, 17 C, 3 E; Valladolid 1307, art. 29; 1312, art. 93; Palencia 1313, art. 23 J; Burgos 1315, art. 22; Medina del Campo 1318, art. 20, 22–23; Valladolid 1322, art. 52; 1325, art. 21, 36; Madrid 1329, art. 75.

92. León 1194, González, *Alfonso IX*, II, no. 84, p. 128; Valladolid 1298, art. 3; 1312, art. 47, 72; 1322, art. 100; *Libro de los fueros de Castilla*, ed. Galo Sánchez (Barcelona 1981), 118; *Fuero real*, II.8.3.

93. González, *Alfonso IX*, II, no. 11, p. 25; Seville 1253, art. 4 L; Burgos 1308, art. 6.

94. Seville 1253, art. 4–5, 7, 9, 11–13, 23–24 L; Seville 1264, art. 5; Jerez 1268, art. 38; Zamora 1301, art. 16; Burgos 1308, art. 21.

95. Jerez 1268, art. 35–36; *Ordenamiento de Tafurerías*, in *Opúsculos legales*, II, 213–231.

96. Seville 1253, art. 19 L; Valladolid 1293, art. 14 C, 16–18 M, 17–19 LE; Valladolid 1325, art. 35.

97. Zamora 1301, art. 28; Burgos 1308, art. 24; Valladolid 1312, art. 26, 31, 77; Palencia 1313, art. 8 M; Madrid 1329, art. 71–72; Burgos 1345, art. 20; María Inmaculada Rodríguez Flórez, *El perdón real en Castilla: Siglos XIII–XVIII* (Salamanca 1971).

98. Luis González Antón, *Las uniones aragonesas y las cortes del reino, 1283–1301* (Madrid 1975), I, 76–86, 163–172, 305–344; *Rotuli parliamentorum*, II, 126–131; *Statutes of the Realm*, I, 157.

99. García Gallo, *Manual*, II, no. 1072, 895–901; *Colección de documentos inéditos de la Corona de Aragón*, XXXVIII, 17–74; *Chronique de Pierre IV*, ch. IV, pp. 252–263, 276–278; *Cortes de . . . Cataluña*, I, 141–142.

CHAPTER 10

1. Julio Valdeón Baruque, *Los conflictos sociales en el reino de Castilla en los siglos XIV y XV* (Madrid 1975); Teófilo Ruíz, "Expansion et changement: La conquête de Seville et la société castillane (1248–1350)," *Annales: Economies, Sociétés, Civilisations* 34 (1979): 548–565.

2. Seville 1253, art. 22 L; Valladolid 1258, art. 23–25; Seville 1261, art. 7–9; Seville 1264, art. 11–13, 15.

3. Valladolid 1258, art. 13–15, 44–46; Seville 1261, art. 9–12, 22, 27; Jerez 1268, art. 6, 13, 37, 40; Burgos 1338, art. 33–43; Madrid 1339, art. 18; Alcalá 1348, art. 30, 86–131.

4. *CAX*, 40, pp. 30–31; Salvador de Moxó, "Los señoríos: En torno a una problemática para el estudio del regimen señorial," *Hispania* 24 (1964): 185–236, 399–430; "La nobleza castellana en el siglo XIV," *AEM* 7 (1970–1971): 494–510; "De la nobleza vieja a la nobleza nueva: La transformación nobiliaria en la baja edad media," *Cuadernos de Historia* 3 (1969): 1–210.

5. Sánchez Albornoz, "Las Behetrías," *Estudios*, 9–316; Martínez Díez,

Libro Becerro de las Behetrías de Castilla, 3 vols. (Madrid 1981); Bartolomé Clavero, "Behetrías, 1255–1356: Crísis de la institución de señorío y de la formación de un derecho regional de Castilla," *AHDE* 44 (1974): 201–342.

6. Valladolid 1258, art. 21; Seville 1261, art. 6.

7. Seville 1253, art. 14, 20 L; Valladolid 1258, art. 19–20; Seville 1261, art. 4–6; Valladolid 1293, art. 21 C; 1299, art. 10–12 G; 1307, art. 27; Burgos 1308, art. 26; Palencia 1311, art. 1, 7; 1313, art. 8 J, 29 M; Burgos 1315, art. 7; Valladolid 1322, art. 27; Ordinance of Alcalá, XXXII.3; *Fuero viejo,* I.8.9.

8. Palencia 1311, art. 6; Alcalá 1348, art. 6.

9. Valladolid 1298, art. 8; also 1293, art. 8; 1325, art. 8 P; *CAX,* 40, pp. 30–31.

10. Alcalá 1345, art. 5; León 1345, art. 19.

11. Zamora 1301, art. 31; Valladolid 1307, art. 36; Ordinance of Alcalá, XXXII.1–2.

12. Burgos 1315, art. 14; Carrión 1317, art. 70; Valladolid 1322, art. 4.

13. Ordinance of Alcalá, XXIX, XXXII; *Fuero viejo,* I.5.1–18.

14. O'Callaghan, "The Ecclesiastical Estate in the Cortes of León-Castile, 1252–1350," *CHR* 67 (1981): 185–213, and "Alfonso X and the Castilian Church," *Thought* 60 (1985): 417–429.

15. Valladolid 1295, art. 3 P; Ordinance of Alcalá 1348, XXXII.58; *Partidas,* I.5.18; Gaibrois, *Sancho IV,* III, no. 208, pp. cxxv–cxxvii.

16. Mingüella, *Sigüenza,* I, no. 209, pp. 572–574; Martín, *Salamanca,* no. 261, pp. 350–352; Loperráez, *Osma,* III, no. 58, pp. 81–83; also González, *Alfonso VIII,* II, no. 344, pp. 583–584; *Alfonso IX,* II, nos. 84–85, 221, pp. 125–129, 306–308; *Fernando III,* III, no. 372, pp. 428–429; *Fuero real,* I.5.2.

17. Valladolid 1295, art. 1–2 P; 1325, art. 32 P.

18. Martín, *Salamanca,* nos. 255, 262, pp. 341–342, 352–354; *MHE,* I, nos. 34–35, pp. 70–75; Menéndez Pidal, *Documentos,* no. 228, pp. 299–300.

19. Seville 1252, art. 44; Seville 1264, art. 1–2; Valladolid 1298, art. 8; 1325, art. 8 P; Madrid 1339, art. 3; Alcalá 1345, art. 10; 1348, art. 20–21, 24.

20. Burgos 1315, art. 8–9 P; Valladolid 1325, art. 2, 23, 37–38 P.

21. Peñafiel 1275, art. 4; Palencia 1313, art. 44 M; Burgos 1315, art. 14 P; Valladolid 1325, art. 15, 27, 31 P.

22. Burgos 1315, art. 2, 4, 10–13 P; Valladolid 1322, art. 2; 1325, art. 3–6, 10–11, 14, 18–19, 24, 30 P.

23. Zamora 1301, art. 11; Valladolid 1307, art. 34; Burgos 1315, art. 52; Medina del Campo 1318, art. 2; Valladolid 1322, art. 94; 1325, art. 20, 33; León 1345, art. 10.

24. León 1188, art. 5; González, *Alfonso IX,* II, no. 11, p. 24. *Espéculo,* I.14.11, stated that spiritual and temporal pleas were distinguished in Book VI, but it is not extant.

25. Peñafiel 1275, art. 1, 5; Valladolid 1295, art. 4 P; Burgos 1315, art. 7–8 P; 1325, art. 21, 33 P; Gaibrois, *Sancho IV,* III, nos. 20, 330–340, pp. xiii–xiv, ccx–ccxvi.

26. Muñoz, *Fueros,* 371–372; Demetrio Mansilla, *Iglesia castellano-leonesa y curia romana en los tiempos del Rey San Fernando* (Madrid 1945), no. 26, p. 303; *MHE,* I, no. 129, pp. 288–289; Sánchez, *Libro de los Fueros de Castiella,* no. 224, p. 118.

27. Peñafiel 1275, art. 2; Valladolid 1325, art. 9, 35 P; Madrid 1329, art. 61; Alcalá 1348, art. 26.

28. Burgos 1315, art. 3 P; Valladolid 1325, art. 10, 17, 25–26 P.

29. Valladolid 1299, art. 8 C; 1307, art. 34; Burgos 1315, art. 52; Medina del Campo 1318, art. 3; Valladolid 1322, art. 92; Madrid 1329, art. 58; Burgos 1345, art. 18; Alcalá 1348, art. 39.

30. Zamora 1301, art. 11; also Valladolid 1299, art. 9 L; 1307, art. 24.

31. Burgos 1315, art. 51, 53; Valladolid 1322, art. 93, 95; 1325, art. 23, 28; Madrid 1329, art. 59.

32. *Fuero Juzgo*, XII.2–3; *Fuero real*, IV. 2; *Partidas*, VII.24.

33. Medina del Campo 1305, art. 8 E, 9 CL; Palencia 1313, art. 31 J, 25 M; Medina del Campo 1318, art. 4; Madrid 1329, art. 37.

34. Seville 1252, art. 19; 1253, art. 68 L; *Fuero real*, IV.1.

35. Seville 1252, art. 40–41; 1253, art. 63–64 L; Valladolid 1258, art. 26–27, 38; Seville 1261, art. 25, 29–30; Jerez 1268, art. 7–8, 29–31, 38; Palencia 1313, art. 27, 29, 34–35 J, 42 M; Burgos 1315, art. 24; Valladolid 1322, art. 54.

36. Valladolid 1293, art. 22 M, 23 LE, 26 C; Cuéllar 1297, art. 6; Valladolid 1300, art. 20; Madrid 1329, art. 57.

37. Jerez 1268, art. 29; Burgos 1315, art. 25; Valladolid 1322, art. 55.

38. Palencia 1313, art. 28 M; Valladolid 1322, art. 61; Madrid 1329, art. 53.

39. Seville 1261, art. 16; Jerez 1268, art. 29, 44; José Amador de los Ríos, *Historia de los Judíos en España* (Madrid 1960), 913; *Leyes nuevas*, in *Opúsculos legales*, 181; *Fuero real*, IV.2.5–6.

40. Valladolid 1293, art. 21 LEM, 23 C; Zamora 1301, art. 10; Valladolid 1307, art. 28; 1312, art. 100; Palencia 1313, art. 25, 30 J; Burgos 1315, art. 26, 29; Valladolid 1322, art. 56, 58; 1325, art. 14–15; Madrid 1329, art. 55; León 1345, art. 11; also Alcalá 1348, art. 2, 54.

41. Valladolid 1293, art. 20, 22 M, 21, 23 LE, 23–24, 26 C.

42. Medina del Campo 1305, art. 12; Burgos 1315, art. 4; Carrión 1317, art. 31; Medina del Campo 1318, art. 5; Madrid 1329, art. 55; Alcalá 1345, art. 4, 9; 1348, art. 22; Ordinance of Alcalá, IX.2.

43. Burgos 1315, art. 27–28; Carrión 1317, art. 30; Valladolid 1322, art. 57; 1325, art. 14; 1325, art. 29 P; Madrid 1339, art. 13; Alcalá 1345, art. 4; Burgos 1345, art. 5; León 1345, art. 22; Alcalá 1348, art. 18, 55; Ordinance of Alcalá, XXIII.

44. Valladolid 1293, art. 12, 25 C, 21 M, 22 LE; 1299, art. 11–12 L; 1300, art. 10; Burgos 1301, art. 18; Zamora 1301, art. 9; Valladolid 1307, art. 18, 28; Burgos 1308, art. 28; Palencia 1313, art. 22, 30 J; Burgos 1315, art. 30; Valladolid 1322, art. 59; Madrid 1329, art. 44, 56; 1339, art. 8; *Fuero real*, III.20.1; Gaibrois, *Sancho IV*, III, nos. 343–344, pp. ccxviii–ccxix.

45. Valladolid 1300, art. 14; Burgos 1301, art. 17.

46. Palencia 1313, art. 28 J, 27 M; Burgos 1315, art. 23 A; Valladolid 1322, art. 43; Madrid 1329, art. 54; 1339, art. 21.

47. Valladolid 1258, art. 22–27; Jerez 1268, art. 45–47; *Espéculo*, V.11.15–17; also Seville 1252, art. 59; 1253, art. 61.

48. Palencia 1313, art. 27 M; Burgos 1315, art. 23 A; Valladolid 1322, art. 53.

49. Álvaro Pelayo, *Speculum regum*, 128.

50. Charles Dufourcq and Jean Gautier-Dalché, *Historia económica y social de la España cristiana en la edad media* (Barcelona 1983).

51. Seville 1252, art. 21–22, 29–31, 39; 1253, art. 45–46, 54–55, 64 L; Valladolid 1258, art. 34–35, 41–43; Seville 1261, art. 19–21; Jerez 1268, art. 17, 20, 39; *Fuero real*, IV.5.11.

52. Miguel Gual Camarena, "Para un mapa de la sal hispana en la edad media," *Homenaje a Jaime Vicens Vives* (Barcelona 1965–1967), I, 483–497.

53. Haro 1288, art. 16; Medina del Campo 1302, art. 13 E; Palencia 1313, art. 16, 44 J; Burgos 1315, art. 16, 38; Medina del Campo 1318, art. 19; Valladolid 1322, art. 31, 45–46.

54. González Crespo, *Alfonso XI*, no. 257, pp. 434–439.

55. Julius Klein, "Los privilegios de la Mesta de 1273 y 1278," *BRAH* 64 (1914): 202–219, and *The Mesta: A Study in Spanish Economic History, 1273–1836* (Cambridge 1920): Charles J. Bishko, "The Castilian as Plainsman: The Medieval Ranching Frontier in La Mancha and Extremadura," "The Andalusian Municipal Mestas in the 14th–16th Centuries: Administrative and Social Aspects," and "The Peninsular Background of Latin American Cattle Ranching," in his *Studies in Medieval Spanish Frontier History* (London 1980).

56. Valladolid 1258, art. 40; Medina del Campo 1302, art. 7 L; Palencia 1313, art. 45 M; Burgos 1315, art. 32; Medina del Campo 1318, art. 14; Valladolid 1322, art. 62; *Fuero real*, IV.6.4–5.

57. Seville 1252, art. 32, 43; 1253, art. 56, 66 L; Valladolid 1258, art. 31; Zamora 1301, art. 34; *CAX*, 40, pp. 30–31.

58. Valladolid 1258, art. 32; 1293, art. 10 LEM; 1299, art. 9 E, 10 L; Palencia 1313, art. 35 M; Burgos 1315, art. 43; Madrid 1329, art. 63.

59. Nieto Cumplido, *Regionalismo*, no. 23, pp. 169–176.

60. Medina del Campo 1302, art. 7 L; Palencia 1313, art. 38 J, 40 M; Burgos 1315, art. 33; Madrid 1339, art. 32; Alcalá 1348, art. 42.

61. *MHE*, I, no. 140, p. 314; *CAX*, 40, pp. 30–31; Valladolid 1293, art. 8 LEM; Zamora 1301, art. 33; Medina del Campo 1302, art. 7 L; Valladolid 1307, art. 19; Medina del Campo 1318, art. 16; Valladolid 1322, art. 64; Madrid 1339, art. 4, 38; Alcalá 1345, art. 7; 1348, art. 43; Nieto Cumplido, *Regionalismo*, no. 23, pp. 169–176; Ubieto Arteta, *Cuéllar*, no. 84, pp. 122–123.

62. Carlé, "Mercaderes en Castilla, 1252–1512," *CHE* 21–22 (1954): 146–328; Luis G. de Valdeavellano, *El mercado: Apuntes para su estudio en León y Castilla durante la edad media*, 2d ed. (Seville 1975).

63. Seville 1250, Gonzalez, *Fernando III*, III, no. 909, pp. 387–389; Seville 1252, art. 11; 1253, art. 35 L; Valladolid 1258, art. 28, 37; Seville 1261, art. 24; Jerez 1268, art. 27; *Partidas*, V.7.2.

64. Francisco Hernández plans to publish the text of 1207; *CAX*, 5, p. 6; Seville 1252, art. 1–3, 7–10, 17–18, 23–28; Jerez 1268, art. 2–5, 9–13, 15–16, 18–20; Carlé "El precio de la vida en Castilla del Rey Sabio al Emplazado," *CHE* 15 (1951): 132–156.

65. Seville 1250, González, *Fernando III*, III, no. 909, pp. 287–389; 1252, art. 14; 1253, art. 38 L; Valladolid 1258, art. 28, 36; Seville 1261, art. 23; Jerez 1268, art. 41.

66. O'Callaghan, "Paths to Ruin: The Economic and Financial Policies of Alfonso the Learned," in Robert I. Burns, ed., *The Worlds of Alfonso the Learned and James the Conqueror* (Princeton 1985), 41–67.

67. Valladolid 1293, art. 4 C, 10 LEM; 1300, art. 9, 28; Medina del Campo 1305, art. 18 C; Valladolid 1307, art. 32 (Vitoria); 1322, art. 86; *Fuero real*, IV.6.1–3.

68. Burgos 1345, art. 10, 15; León 1345, art. 6; Alcalá 1348, art. 51.

69. *MFIV*, II, no. 57, pp. 81–85; Francisco Morales Belda, *La hermandad de las marismas* (Barcelona 1973).

70. Seville 1252, art. 37; 1253, art. 61 L; Valladolid 1258, art. 33; Seville 1261, art. 21; Zamora 1301, art. 32; Burgos 1315, art. 42; Valladolid 1322, art. 42; *Partidas*, V.7.5.

71. Burgos 1345, art. 17; León 1345, art. 23, 25.

72. Seville 1261, art. 31; Jerez 1268, art. 26; *Fuero real*, III.10.1; Ordinance of Alcalá, XXIV.55; AM León, no. 6; Ureña, *Fuero de Cuenca*, 867–868.

73. Palencia 1286, art. 3; Haro 1288, art. 19; *CSIV*, 3, p. 73.

74. Cuéllar 1297, art. 2; Zamora 1301, art. 22–23.

75. *CLC*, I, 165–169; Medina del Campo 1302, art. 22 L; Alois Heiss, *Descripción general de las monedas hispano-cristianas*, 3 vols. (Zaragoza, n.d.); Octavio Gil Farrés, *Historia de la moneda española* (Granada 1968).

76. Francisco Hernández plans to publish the text of 1207; Seville 1252, art. 19–21; 1253, art. 43–44 L; Valladolid 1258, art. 12, 41; Seville 1261, art. 15; *Espéculo*, IV.12.57; *Leyes del Estilo*, 204 in *Opúsculos legales*, II, 320; Sánchez, *Libro de los Fueros de Castilla*, no. 138, p. 72.

77. *CAX*, 25, 40, 47, pp. 21–22, 30–31, 35; Haro 1288, art. 19, 24; Valladolid 1300, art. 10, 23; Burgos 1302, art. 1; Valladolid 1307, art. 24; Palencia 1313, art. 17 J, 34 M; Burgos 1315, art. 17; Carrión 1317, art. 47; Valladolid 1322, art. 43.

78. *MHE*, II, no. 163, pp. 7–8. Wendy R. Childs, *Anglo-Castilian Trade in the Later Middle Ages* (Manchester 1978); Teófilo Ruíz, "Castilian Merchants in England, 1248–1350," in William Jordan, Bruce McNab, and Teófilo Ruíz, eds., *Order and Innovation: Essays in Honor of Joseph R. Strayer* (Princeton 1976), 173–186.

79. Yves Renouard, "Un sujet de recherches: l'exportation des chevaux de la péninsule ibérique en France et en Angleterre au moyen âge," *Homenaje a Jaime Vicens Vives*, I, 571–577.

80. Jerez 1268, art. 21–25; also Burgos 1301, art. 14.

81. Valladolid 1300, art. 23, 28; Burgos 1301, art. 11; Medina del Campo 1305, art. 18 C; Valladolid 1312, art. 94; Palencia 1313, art. 4 J, 34 M; Carrión 1317, art. 22; Valladolid 1322, art. 43; Madrid 1339, art. 4; Alcalá 1348, art. 72.

82. *CAX*, 25, 40, 47, pp. 21–22, 30–31, 35; *CLC*, I, 85–86; *MHE*, I, no. 140, p. 321; also Burgos 1301, art. 20; León 1345, art. 18.

83. Jerez 1268, art. 24; Burgos 1301, art. 12; Alcalá 1348, art. 59.

84. Valladolid 1312, art. 74, 86, 104–105; 1322, art. 44; Madrid 1329, art. 65; Alcalá 1345, art. 6.

85. Livermore, *A New History of Portugal*, 84; William Stubbs, *Select Charters and Other Illustrations of English Constitutional History*, 9th ed. (Oxford 1913), 451–452; *Statutes of the Realm*, I, 53–54, 317–318, 329; Strayer, *Philip IV*, 237–277.

86. *Cortes de . . . Cataluña*, I, 140–145; *Statutes of the Realm*, I, 53–54, 311; *CLC*, II, 75–124.

Bibliography

MANUSCRIPT SOURCES

Cuadernos and other pertinent documents are found in the following archives:

Madrid, Archivo Histórico Nacional
  Secciones: Clero, Ordenes Militares, Códices
Madrid, Biblioteca Nacional
  MS 23, Ordenamientos de Cortes (15th century)
  MS 1270, Ordenamientos y Cortes (18th century)
  MSS 430, 612, 716, 838, 9910, 9378, 13030
Madrid, Real Academia de la Historia
  Colecciones: Abella, Fernández Guerra y Orbe, Gayoso, Martínez Marina, Mateos Murillo, Sáez, Salazar, Sobreira
Escorial, Biblioteca de El Escorial
  L.II.21, Ordenamientos reales (15th century)
  O.I.16, Ordenamientos de Cortes (15th century)
  Z.I.8, Z.I.9, Z.I.10, Z.II.4, Z.II.5, Z.II.6, Ordenamientos reales (15th century)
Seville, Biblioteca Colombina.
  Manuscritos de legislación, I.
Simancas, Archivo General
  Sección I, Patronato real, legajos 69–91. Cortes de Castilla, 1295–1655.

London, British Library
   Additional MSS 9915–9935, Colección de Cortes, 21 vols. (18th century)
   Additional MS 21448, Cortes de España (18th century)
New York, Hispanic Society
   HC 380/685, Colección de Cortes 1255–1395, 5 vols. (18th century)
Municipal Archives: Agreda, Alba de Tormes, Astorga, Ávila, Avilés, Béjar, Benavente, Briones, Burgos, Cáceres, Córdoba, Cuéllar, Cuenca, Écija, Ledesma, León, Logroño, Madrid, Medina de Rioseco, Miranda de Ebro, Mula, Murcia, Niebla, Oviedo, Plasencia, Salinas de Añana, Segovia, Seville, Talavera, Toledo, Valladolid, Vitoria, Zamora; Nantes, France
Cathedral Archives: Astorga, Ávila, Burgos, Calahorra, Cartagena, Cuenca, León, Lugo, Orense, Osma, Oviedo, Palencia, Salamanca, Santiago de Compostela, Seville, Toledo, Zamora

PRINTED SOURCES

NARRATIVE AND LITERARY SOURCES

Alfonso X. *Las Cantigas de Santa María.* 4 vols. Ed. Walter Mettmann. Coimbra 1959–1974. Reprint, 2 vols., Vigo 1981.
Álvaro Pelayo. *Speculum regum (Espelho dos Reis).* Ed. tr. Miguel Pinto de Meneses. Lisbon 1955.
Anónimo de Sahagún. Ed. Romualdo Escalona, *Historia del real monasterio de Sahagún.* Madrid 1782.
Chronique latine des rois de Castille. Ed. Georges Cirot. Bordeaux 1913.
Crónica del Rey Don Alfonso X. BAE, LXVI (1953): 3–66.
Crónica del Rey Don Alfonso XI. BAE, LXVI (1953): 173–392.
Crónica del Rey Don Fernando IV. BAE, LXVI (1953): 91–172.
Crónica del Rey Don Sancho IV. BAE, LXVI (1953): 69–90.
Gran Crónica de Alfonso XI. 2 vols. Ed. Diego Catalán. Madrid 1977.
Jofre de Loaysa. *Crónica de los reyes de Castilla, Fernando III, Alfonso X, Sancho IV y Fernando IV, 1248–1305.* Ed. tr. Antonio García Martínez. Murcia 1961. Reprint 1982.
Juan Gil de Zamora. *Liber de preconiis Hispaniae.* Ed. Manuel de Castro y Castro. Madrid 1955.
Juan Manuel. *Libro de los estados.* Ed. R. B. Tate and I. R. Macpherson. New York 1974.
Lucas of Túy. *Crónica de España.* Ed. Julio Puyol. Madrid. 1926.
Poema de Alfonso XI. Ed. Yo Ten Cate. Madrid 1955.
Rodrigo Jiménez de Rada. *De rebus Hispaniae,* in *Opera.* Ed. Francisco Lorenzana. Madrid 1793. Reprint, Valencia 1968.
Sancho IV. *Castigos e documentos.* Ed. Agapito Rey. Bloomington 1952.

DOCUMENTARY SOURCES

Agapito y Revilla, Juan. *Los privilegios de Valladolid.* Valladolid 1906.
Alfonso X. *Espéculo de las leyes,* in *Opúsculos legales del Rey Don Alfonso el Sabio,* I.
———. *Fuero real,* in *Opúsculos legales,* II, 1–169.
———. *Opúsculos legales del Rey Don Alfonso el Sabio.* 2 vols. Ed. Real Academia de la Historia. Madrid 1836.

————. *Las Siete Partidas del Rey Don Alfonso el Sabio*. 3 vols. Ed. Real Academia de la Historia. Madrid 1801.

Alfonso XI. *El Ordenamiento de leyes que Don Alfonso XI hizo en las Cortes de Alcalá de Henares*. Ed. Ignacio Jordán del Asso and Miguel de Manuel Rodríguez. Madrid 1774.

Ballesteros, Antonio. "Las Cortes de 1252," *Anales de la junta para ampliación de estudios e investigaciones científicas*, 3 (1911): 114–143.

Barrios García, Ángel, Alberto Martín Exposito, and Gregorio del Ser Quijano. *Documentación medieval del Archivo municipal de Alba de Tormes*. Salamanca 1982.

Benavides, Antonio. *Memorias de Fernando IV.* 2 vols. Madrid 1860.

Carriazo, Juan de Mata. *Colección diplomática de Quesada*. Jaén 1975.

Colección de documentos para la historia del reino de Murcia. Ed. Juan Torres Fontes. 5 vols. to date. Murcia 1963–.

Cortes de los antiguos reinos de León y Castilla. 5 vols. Ed. Real Academia de la Historia. Madrid 1861–1903.

Daumet, Georges. "Les testaments d'Alphonse le Savant, roi de Castille," *BEC* 67 (1906): 70–99.

Escagedo Salmón, Mateo. *Colección diplomática: Privilegios, escrituras y bulas en pergamino de la insigne y real iglesia colegial de Santillana*. 2 vols. Santoña 1927.

Escudero de la Peña, J. M. "Súplica hecha al Papa Juan XXI para que absolviese al Rey de Castilla D. Alfonso X del juramento de no acuñar otra moneda que los dineros prietos," *RABM* 2 (1872): 58–59.

España Sagrada. 52 vols. Ed. Enrique Flórez et al. Madrid 1754–1779.

Ferotin, Marius. *Recueil des chartes de l'Abbaye de Silos*. Paris 1897.

Fita, Fidel. "El Concilio nacional de Palencia en 1321," *BRAH* 52 (1908): 17–48.

Floriano, Antonio. *Documentación histórica del Archivo municipal de Cáceres (1229–1471)*. Cáceres 1987.

Fuero Juzgo en Latín y Castellano. Ed. Real Academia de la Historia. Madrid 1815.

Fuero viejo de Castilla. Ed. Ignacio Jordán del Asso and Miguel de Manuel Rodríguez. Madrid 1777.

García Chico, Esteban. *Los privilegios de Medina de Rioseco*. Valladolid 1933.

García Luján, José Antonio. *Privilegios reales de la Catedral de Toledo (1086–1462): Formación del patrimonio de la S.I.C.P. a través de las donaciones reales*. 2 vols. Toledo 1982.

García Ramila, Ismael. "Ordenamientos de posturas y otros capítulos generales otorgados a la ciudad de Burgos por el Rey Alfonso X," *Hispania* 5 (1945): 179–235, 385–439.

Gibert, Rafael. "El Ordenamiento de Villa Real 1346," *AHDE* 25 (1955): 703–729.

González, Tomás. *Colección de cédulas, cartas patentes, provisiones, reales ordenes y documentos concernientes a las provincias vascongadas, copiadas . . . de los registros en el Real Archivo de Simancas*. 6 vols. Madrid 1829–1833.

González Crespo, Esther. *Colección documental de Alfonso XI: Diplomas reales conservados en el Archivo Histórico Nacional. Sección de Clero. Pergaminos*. Madrid 1985.

González Díez, Emiliano. *Colección diplomática del concejo de Burgos (884–1369)*. Burgos 1984.

González Mínguez, César. "Otro Ordenamiento de las cortes de Valladolid de 1298," *Hispania* 40 (1980): 415–426.

Gross, Georg. "Las Cortes de 1252: Ordenamiento otorgado al concejo de Burgos en las cortes celebradas en Sevilla el 12 de octubre de 1252 (según el original)," *BRAH* 182 (1985): 95–114.

Hernández Díez, José, Antonio Sancho Corbacho, and Francisco Collantes de Terrer. *Colección diplomática de Carmona.* Seville 1941.

Higueras Maldonado, Juan. *Documentos latinos del siglo XII al XVII en los Archivos de Baeza.* Jaén 1974.

———. *Documentos latinos de Úbeda.* Jaén 1975.

Iglesia Ferreirós, Aquilino. "El Privilegio general concedido a las Extremaduras en 1264 por Alfonso X: Edición del ejemplar enviado a Peñafiel en 15 de abril de 1264," *AHDE* 53 (1983): 456–521.

Jordán del Asso, Ignacio, and Miguel de Manuel Rodríguez. *Cortes celebradas en los reynados de Don Sancho IV y de Don Fernando IV.* Madrid 1775.

López Ferreiro, Antonio. *Fueros municipales de Santiago y de su tierra.* Santiago de Compostela 1895.

Mañueco Villalobos, M., and J. Zurita Nieto. *Documentos de la iglesia colegial de Santa María la Mayor de Valladolid.* Valladolid 1917.

Manuel, Miguel de. *Memorias para la vida del Santo Rey Fernando III.* Madrid 1800. Reprint, Barcelona 1975.

Martín, José Luis, Luis Miguel Villargarcía, Florencio Marcos Rodríguez, and Marciano Sánchez Rodríguez. *Documentos de los Archivos catedralicio y diocesano de Salamanca (Siglos XII–XIII).* Salamanca 1977.

Martín Lázaro, Antonio. "Colección diplomática municipal de la ciudad de Béjar," *Revista de ciencias jurídicas y sociales* 4 (1921): 287–304, 449–464.

Menéndez Pidal, Ramón. *Documentos lingüísticos de España: Reino de Castilla.* Madrid 1919.

Miguel Vigil, Ciriaco. *Colección histórico-diplomática del ayuntamiento de Oviedo.* Oviedo 1889.

Muñoz, Tomás. *Colección de fueros municipales y carta pueblas de los reinos de Castilla, León, Corona de Aragon y Navarra.* Madrid 1847.

Palacio, Timoteo Domingo. *Documentos del Archivo general de la Villa de Madrid.* 6 vols. Madrid 1888–1943.

Pereda Llarena, F. Javier. *Documentación de la Catedral de Burgos (1254–1293).* Burgos 1984.

———. *Documentación de la Catedral de Burgos (1294–1316).* Burgos 1984.

Quintana Prieto, Augusto. *Tumbo viejo de San Pedro de Montes.* León 1971.

Ruíz de la Peña, Juan Ignacio. "La hermandad leonesa de 1313," *León medieval* (1978): 139–164.

Rymer, Thomas. *Foedera, conventiones, litterae et cuiuscunque acta publica inter reges Angliae et alios quovis imperatores, reges, pontifices, principes.* 20 vols. London 1704–1735.

Sáez, Emilio, Rafael Gibert, Manuel Alvar, and Atilano G. Ruíz-Zorrilla. *Los Fueros de Sepúlveda.* Segovia 1953.

Sáinz Ripa, Eliseo. *Colección diplomática de las colegiatas de Albelda y Logroño.* 3 vols. Logroño 1981.

Sánchez, Galo. *Libro de los fueros de Castilla.* Barcelona 1924. Reprint 1981.

———. "Ordenamiento de Segovia 1347," *Boletín de la Biblioteca Menéndez Pelayo* 4 (1922): 301–320.

Sánchez Belda, Luis. *Cartulario de Santo Toribio de Liébana, 790–1625*. Madrid 1948.
———. *Documentos reales de la edad media referentes a Galicia*. Madrid 1953.
Sánchez Herrero, José. *Concilios provinciales y sínodos toledanos de los siglos XIV y XV*. Seville 1976.
Segura Moreno, Manuel. *Estudio del Códice gótico (siglo XIII) de la Catedral de Jaén*. Jaén 1976.
Serrano, Luciano. *Cartulario del Infantado de Covarrubias*. Madrid 1907.
Ubieto Arteta, Antonio. *Colección diplomática de Cuéllar*. Segovia 1961.
Ureña, Rafael. *El Fuero de Cuenca*. Madrid 1935.
Valdeavellano, Luis G. de. "Carta de hermandad entre los concejos de la Extremadura castellana y del arzobispado de Toledo en 1295," *Revista portuguesa de Historia* 12 (1969): 57–76.
Vaquerizo, Gíl, and Rogelio Pérez Bustamante. *Colección diplomática del Archivo municipal de Santander: Documentos reales (Siglos XIII–XVI)*. Santander 1977.

SECONDARY WORKS

Álvarez de Morales, Antonio. *Las hermandades: Expresión del movimiento comunitario en España*. Valladolid 1974.
Andalucía medieval: Nuevos estudios. 2 vols. Ed. Cristóbal Torres Delgado. Córdoba 1979.
Argente del Castillo Ocaña, Carmen. "Las hermandades medievales en el reino de Jaén," *Andalucía medieval* 2 (1978): 21–32.
Baer, Yitzhak. *A History of the Jews in Christian Spain*. 2 vols. Tr. Louis Schoffman. Philadelphia 1966.
Ballesteros, Antonio. *Alfonso X*. Barcelona-Madrid 1963. Reprint, Barcelona 1984.
———. *Sevilla en el siglo XIII*. Madrid 1913.
———. "Burgos y la rebelión del Infante Don Sancho," *BRAH* 119 (1946): 93–194.
———. "El Itinerario de Alfonso el Sabio," *BRAH* 104 (1934): 49–88, 455–516; 105 (1934): 123–180; 106 (1935): 83–150; 107 (1935): 21–76, 381–418; 108 (1936): 15–42; 109 (1936): 377–460.
Benito Ruano, Eloy. *Hermandades en Asturias en la edad media*. Oviedo 1972.
———. *La prelación ciudadana: Las disputas por la precedencia entre las ciudades de la Corona de Castilla*. Toledo 1972.
Bishko, Charles J. *Studies in Medieval Spanish Frontier History*. London 1980.
Burns, Robert I., ed. *The Worlds of Alfonso the Learned and James the Conqueror. Intellect and Force in the Middle Ages*. Princeton 1985.
Carlé, María del Carmen. *Del concejo medieval castellano-leonés*. Buenos Aires 1968.
———. "Boni homines y hombres buenos," *CHE* 39–40 (1964): 133–168.
———. "Mercaderes en Castilla (1252–1512)," *CHE* 21–22 (1954): 146–328.
———. "El precio de la vida en Castilla del Rey Sabio al Emplazado," *CHE* 15 (1951): 132–156.
Colmeiro, Manuel de. *Introducción a las Cortes de los antiguos reinos de León y Castilla*. 2 vols. Madrid 1883–1903.

Colmenares, Diego. *Historia de la ciudad de Segovia*. New ed. 3 vols. Segovia 1969–1975.

Craddock, Jerry. "La cronología de las obras legislativas de Alfonso X el Sabio," *AHDE* 51 (1981): 365–418.

Daumet, Georges. *Étude sur l'alliance de la France et de la Castille du XIVe au XVe siècle*. Geneva 1898.

———. *Mémoire sur les relations de la France et de la Castille de 1255 a 1320*. Paris 1913.

Fernández Martín, Luis. "La participación de los monasterios en la hermandad de los reinos de Castilla, León y Galicia (1282–1284)," *Hispania Sacra* 25 (1972): 5–35.

Gaibrois de Ballesteros, Mercedes. *Historia del reinado de Sancho IV de Castilla*. 3 vols. Madrid 1922.

———. "Tarifa y la política de Sancho IV de Castilla," *BRAH* 74 (1919): 418–436, 521–529; 75 (1919): 340–355; 76 (1920): 53–77, 123–160, 420–448; 77 (1920): 192–215.

Gama Barros, Henrique de. *História da Administração pública em Portugal nos séculos XII a XV.* 2d ed. 11 vols. Ed. Torquato de Sousa Soares. Lisbon 1945–1954.

García Gallo, Alfonso. *Manual de historia del derecho español*. 2 vols. Madrid 1967.

———. "El Libro de las leyes de Alfonso el Sabio: Del Espéculo a las Partidas," *AHDE* 21 (1951): 345–548.

———. "Nuevas observaciones sobre la obra legislativa de Alfonso X," *AHDE* 46 (1976): 609–670.

Gibert, Rafael. *El concejo de Madrid*. Madrid 1949.

Giménez Soler, Andres. *Don Juan Manuel: Biografía y estudio crítico*. Madrid 1932.

González, Julio. *Alfonso IX*. 2 vols. Madrid 1944.

———. *Regesta de Fernando II*. Madrid 1943.

———. *Reinado y diplomas de Fernando III*. 3 vols. Córdoba 1980–1986.

———. *El reino de Castilla en la época de Alfonso VIII*. 3 vols. Madrid 1960.

———. "La Extremadura castellana al mediar del siglo XIII," *Hispania* 34 (1974): 265–464.

———. "Sobre la fecha de las cortes de Nájera," *CHE* 61–62 (1977): 357–361.

González Jiménez, Manuel. "La hermandad entre Sevilla y Carmona (Siglos XII a XVI)," *Andalucía medieval* 2 (1978): 4–32.

González Mínguez, César. *Contribución al estudio de las hermandades en el reinado de Fernando IV de Castilla*. Vitoria 1974.

———. *Fernando IV de Castilla 1295–1312: La guerra civil y el predominio de la nobleza*. Valladolid 1976.

Grassotti, Hilda. *Estudios medievales españolas*. Madrid 1981.

Guglielmi, Nilda. "La curia regia en León y Castilla," *CHE* 22–23 (1955): 116–267; 28 (1958): 43–101.

———. "Posada y yantar: Contribución al estudio del léxico de las instituciones medievales," *Hispania* 26 (1966): 5–40, 165–219.

Hillgarth, Jocelyn. *The Spanish Kingdoms 1250–1516*. 2 vols. Oxford 1976–1978.

Iglesia Ferreirós, Aquilino. "Alfonso X el Sabio y su obra legislativa: Algunas reflexiones," *AHDE* 50 (1980): 531–561.

———. "Las cortes de Zamora de 1274 y los casos de corte," *AHDE* 41 (1971): 845–872.

———. "Fuero real y Espéculo," *AHDE* 52 (1982): 111–191.

Klein, Julius. *The Mesta: A Study in Spanish Economic History 1273–1836.* Cambridge 1920.

Ladero Quesada, Miguel Ángel. "Les cortes de Castille et la politique financière de la monarchie 1252–1369," *Parliaments, Estates and Representation* 4 (1984): 107–124.

———. "Las transformaciones de la fiscalidad regia castellano-leonesa en la segunda mitad del siglo XIII (1252–1312)," *Historia de la hacienda española: Homenaje al Profesor García de Valdeavellano.* Madrid 1982, 319–406.

Linehan, Peter. *The Spanish Church and the Papacy in the Thirteenth Century.* Cambridge 1971.

Loperráez, Juan. *Descripción histórica del obispado de Osma.* 3 vols. Madrid 1788.

López Ferreiro, Antonio. *Historia de la santa a. m. iglesia de Santiago de Compostela.* 11 vols. Santiago 1898–1909.

MacDonald, Robert. "El Espéculo atribuído a Alfonso X, su edición y problemas que plantea," *España y Europa: Un pasado jurídico común. Actas del I simposio internacional del Instituto de Derecho común.* Ed. Antonio Pérez Martín. Murcia 1986, 611–653.

———. "Law and Politics: Alfonso's Program of Political Reform," in Burns, *The Worlds of Alfonso the Learned and James the Conqueror,* 150–202.

———. "Problemas políticos y derecho alfonsino considerados desde tres puntos de vista," *AHDE* 54 (1984): 25–53.

Maravall, José Antonio. *Estudios de historia del pensamiento español. Edad media. Serie primera.* Madrid 1967.

Marongiu, Antonio. *Medieval Parliaments: A Comparative Study.* Tr. S. J. Woolf. London 1968.

———. "Il principio della democrazia e del consenso (*quod omnes tangit ab omnibus approbari debet*) nel XIV secolo," *Studia Gratiana* 8 (1962): 555–575.

Martínez Díez, Gonzalo. "La hermandad alavesa," *AHDE* 43 (1973): 5–111.

Martínez Marina, Francisco. *Teoría de las cortes o grandes juntas nacionales de León y Castilla.* 3 vols. Madrid 1813. Reprinted in *BAE,* CCXIX–CCXX, Madrid 1968.

Merriman, Roger B. "The Cortes of the Spanish Kingdoms in the Later Middle Ages," *AHR* 16 (1911): 476–495.

Mingüella, Toribio. *Historia de la diocesis de Sigüenza.* 3 vols. Madrid 1900–1913.

Morales Belda, Fernando. *La hermandad de las marismas.* Barcelona 1973.

Moreta, Salustiano. *Malhechores-feudales: Violencia, antagonismos y alianzas de clases en Castilla: Siglos XII–XV.* Madrid 1978.

Moxó, Salvador de. *La Alcabala: Sus origenes, concepto y naturaleza.* Madrid 1963.

———. "La promoción política y social de los letrados en la corte de Alfonso XI," *Hispania* 35 (1975): 5–30.

———. "La sociedad política castellana en la época de Alfonso XI," *Cuadernos de Historia* 6 (1975): 186–326.

Nieto Cumplido, Manuel. *Origenes del regionalismo andaluz 1235–1325.* Madrid 1979.

Nieto Soria, José Manuel. *Las relaciones monarquía-episcopado castellano como sistema de poder (1252–1312).* Madrid 1983.

O'Callaghan, Joseph F. *A History of Medieval Spain*. Ithaca 1975.
————. "Alfonso X and the Castilian Church," *Thought* 60 (1985): 417–429.
————. "The Beginnings of the Cortes of León-Castile," *AHR* 74 (1969): 1503–1537.
————. "The Cortes and Royal Taxation during the Reign of Alfonso X of Castile," *Traditio* 27 (1971): 379–398.
————. "Las cortes de Fernando IV: Cuadernos inéditos de Valladolid 1300 y Burgos 1308," *HID* 13 (1987): 315–328.
————. "The Ecclesiastical Estate in the Cortes of León-Castile 1252–1350," *CHR* 67 (1981): 185–213.
————. "Una nota sobre las llamadas cortes de Benavente," *Archivos Leoneses* 37 (1983): 97–100.
————. "Paths to Ruin: The Economic and Financial Policies of Alfonso the Learned and their Contribution to his Downfall," in Burns, *The Worlds of Alfonso the Learned and James the Conqueror*, 41–67.
————. "Sobre la promulgación del Espéculo y del Fuero real," *Estudios en homenaje a don Claudio Sánchez Albornoz en sus noventa años*. 3 vols. to date. Buenos Aires 1983–1985, vol. 3: 167–179.
Pérez Bustamante, Rogelio. *El gobierno y la administración de los reinos de la Corona de Castilla (1230–1474)*. 2 vols. Madrid 1976.
Pérez de Tudela y Velasco, Maria Isabel. *Infanzones y caballeros: Su projección en la esfera nobiliaria castellano-leonesa: Siglos IX–XIII*. Madrid 1979.
Pérez de la Canal, Miguel Ángel. "La justicia de la corte de Castilla durante los siglos XII al XV," *HID* 2 (1975): 383–481.
Pérez Prendes, José Manuel. *Cortes de Castilla*. Barcelona 1974.
Piskorski, Wladimir. *Las cortes de Castilla en el período de tránsito de la edad media a la moderna 1188–1520*. Tr. Claudio Sánchez Albornoz. Barcelona 1930. Reprint 1977.
Post, Gaines. *Studies in Medieval Legal Thought: Public Law and the State 1100–1322*. Princeton 1964.
Powers, James F. *A Society Organized for War: The Iberian Municipal Militias in the Central Middle Ages, 1000–1284*. Berkeley 1988.
Procter, Evelyn. *Curia and Cortes in León and Castile 1072–1295*. Cambridge 1980.
————. *The Judicial Use of Pesquisa (Inquisition) in León and Castile 1157–1369*. *English Historical Review*, Supplement 2, London 1966.
————. "The Castilian Chancery during the Reign of Alfonso X, 1252–1284," in *Oxford Essays in Medieval History presented to Herbert E. Salter*. Oxford 1934, 104–121.
————. "The Interpretation of Clause 3 in the Decrees of León," *EHR* 85 (1970): 45–54.
————. "Materials for the Reign of Alfonso X of Castile, 1252–1284," *Transactions of the Royal Historical Society*, 4th Series, vol. 14 (1931): 39–63.
————. "The Towns of León and Castile as Suitors before the King's Court," *EHR* 74 (1959): 1–22.
Rodríguez Díez, Matías. *Historia de la ciudad de Astorga*. 2d ed. Astorga 1909.
Ruiz, Teofilo. "Oligarchy and Royal Power: The Castilian Cortes and the Castilian Crisis 1258–1350," *Parliaments, Estates and Representation* 2 (1982): 95–101.

————. "The Transformation of the Castilian Municipalities: The Case of Burgos 1248–1350," *Past and Present* 77 (1977): 3–32.

Sáinz Díaz, Valentín. *Notas históricas sobre la villa de San Vicente de la Barquera.* Santander 1973.

Sánchez, Galo. "Sobre el Ordenamiento de Alcalá 1348 y sus fuentes," *Revista de derecho privado* 3 (1922): 353–368.

Sánchez Albornoz, Claudio. *España, un enigma histórico.* 2 vols. Buenos Aires 1962.

————. *Estudios sobre las instituciones medievales españolas.* Mexico City 1965.

Sánchez Belda, Luis. "La cancillería castellana durante el reinado de Sancho IV (1284–1295)," *AHDE* 21–22 (1951–1952): 171–223.

Sanz Fuentes, María Josefa. "Cartas de hermandad concejíl en Andalucía: El Caso de Écija," *HID* 5 (1978): 403–429.

Suárez Fernández, Luis. "Evolución histórica de las hermandades castellanas," *CHE* 16 (1951): 6–78.

Valdeavellano, Luis G. de. *Curso de historia de las instituciones españolas de los orígenes al final de la edad media.* Madrid 1968.

Valdeón, Julio. *Los conflictos sociales en el reino de Castilla en los siglos XIV y XV.* Madrid 1975.

————. "Aspectos de la crísis castellana en la primera mitad del siglo XIV," *Hispania* 29 (1969): 6–24.

————. "Las cortes castellanas en el siglo XIV," *AEM* 7 (1970–1971): 633–644.

————. "Las cortes medievales castellano-leonesas en la historiografía reciente," in Piskorski, *Las cortes de Castilla,* v–xxxv.

Index

University of Pennsylvania Press
MIDDLE AGES SERIES
Edward Peters, General Editor

Edward Peters, ed. *Christian Society and the Crusades, 1198–1229.* Sources in Translation, including The Capture of Damietta by Oliver of Paderborn. 1971

Edward Peters, ed. *The First Crusade: The Chronicle of Fulcher of Chartres and Other Source Materials.* 1971

Katherine Fischer Drew, trans. *The Burgundian Code: The Book of Constitutions or Law of Gundobad and Additional Enactments.* 1972

G. G. Coulton. *From St. Francis to Dante: Translations from the Chronicle of the Franciscan Salimbene (1221–1288).* 1972

Alan C. Kors and Edward Peters, eds. *Witchcraft in Europe, 1110–1700: A Documentary History.* 1972

Richard C. Dales. *The Scientific Achievement of the Middle Ages.* 1973

Katherine Fischer Drew, trans. *The Lombard Laws.* 1973

Henry Charles Lea. *The Ordeal.* Part III of Superstition and Force. 1973

Henry Charles Lea. *Torture.* Part IV of Superstition and Force. 1973

Henry Charles Lea (Edward Peters, ed.). *The Duel and the Oath.* Parts I and II of Superstition and Force. 1974

Edward Peters, ed. *Monks, Bishops, and Pagans: Christian Culture in Gaul and Italy, 500–700.* 1975

Jeanne Krochalis and Edward Peters, ed. and trans. *The World of Piers Plowman.* 1975

Julius Goebel, Jr. *Felony and Misdemeanor: A Study in the History of Criminal Law.* 1976

Susan Mosher Stuard, ed. *Women in Medieval Society.* 1976

James Muldoon, ed. *The Expansion of Europe: The First Phase.* 1977

Clifford Peterson. *Saint Erkenwald.* 1977

Robert Somerville and Kenneth Pennington, eds. *Law, Church, and Society: Essays in Honor of Stephan Kuttner.* 1977

Donald E. Queller. *The Fourth Crusade: The Conquest of Constantinople, 1201–1204.* 1977

Pierre Riché (Jo Ann McNamara, trans.). *Daily Life in the World of Charlemagne.* 1978

Charles R. Young. *The Royal Forests of Medieval England.* 1979

Edward Peters, ed. *Heresy and Authority in Medieval Europe.* 1980

Suzanne Fonay Wemple. *Women in Frankish Society: Marriage and the Cloister, 500–900.* 1981

R. G. Davies and J. H. Denton, eds. *The English Parliament in the Middle Ages.* 1981

Edward Peters. *The Magician, the Witch, and the Law.* 1982

Barbara H. Rosenwein. *Rhinoceros Bound: Cluny in the Tenth Century.* 1982

Steven D. Sargent, ed. and trans. *On the Threshold of Exact Science: Selected Writings of Anneliese Maier on Late Medieval Natural Philosophy.* 1982

Benedicta Ward. *Miracles and the Medieval Mind: Theory, Record, and Event, 1000–1215.* 1982

Harry Turtledove, trans. *The Chronicle of Theophanes: An English Translation of anni mundi 6095–6305 (A.D. 602–813).* 1982

Leonard Cantor, ed. *The English Medieval Landscape.* 1982

Charles T. Davis. *Dante's Italy and Other Essays.* 1984

George T. Dennis, trans. *Maurice's Strategikon: Handbook of Byzantine Military Strategy.* 1984

Thomas F. X. Noble. *The Republic of St. Peter: The Birth of the Papal State, 680–825.* 1984

Kenneth Pennington. *Pope and Bishops: The Papal Monarchy in the Twelfth and Thirteenth Centuries.* 1984

Patrick J. Geary. *Aristocracy in Provence: The Rhône Basin at the Dawn of the Carolingian Age.* 1985

C. Stephen Jaeger. *The Origins of Courtliness: Civilizing Trends and the Formation of Courtly Ideals, 939–1210.* 1985

J. N. Hillgarth, ed. *Christianity and Paganism, 350–750: The Conversion of Western Europe.* 1986

William Chester Jordan. *From Servitude to Freedom: Manumission in the Sénonais in the Thirteenth Century.* 1986

James William Brodman. *Ransoming Captives in Crusader Spain: The Order of Merced on the Christian-Islamic Frontier.* 1986

Frank Tobin. *Meister Eckhart: Thought and Language.* 1986

Daniel Bornstein, trans. *Dino Compagni's Chronicle of Florence.* 1986

James M. Powell. *Anatomy of a Crusade, 1213–1221.* 1986

Jonathan Riley-Smith. *The First Crusade and the Idea of Crusading.* 1986

Susan Mosher Stuard, ed. *Women in Medieval History and Historiography.* 1987

Avril Henry, ed. *The Mirour of Mans Saluacioune.* 1987

María Rosa Menocal. *The Arabic Role in Medieval Literary History.* 1987

Margaret J. Ehrhart. *The Judgment of the Trojan Prince Paris in Medieval Literature.* 1987

Betsy Bowden. *Chaucer Aloud: The Varieties of Textual Interpretation.* 1987

Felipe Fernández-Armesto. *Before Columbus: Exploration and Colonization from the Mediterranean to the Atlantic, 1229–1492.* 1987

Michael Resler, trans. *EREC by Hartmann von Aue.* 1987

A. J. Minnis. *Medieval Theory of Authorship.* 1987

Uta-Renate Blumenthal. *The Investiture Controversy.* 1988

Robert Hollander. *Boccaccio's Last Fiction:* Il Corbaccio. 1988

Ralph Turner. *Men Raised from the Dust: Administrative Service and Upward Mobility in Angevin England.* 1988

David Anderson. *Before the Knight's Tale: Imitation of Classical Epic in Boccaccio's Teseida.* 1988

Charlotte A. Newman. *The Anglo-Norman Nobility in the Reign of Henry I.* 1988

Joseph F. O'Callaghan. *The Cortes of Castile-León, 1188–1350.* 1989